ARABIC IN CONTEXT

Cambridge Semitic Languages and Cultures

General Editor: Geoffrey Khan

This is the first Open Access book series in the field; it combines the high peer-review and editorial standards with the fair Open Access model offered by OBP. The series includes philological and linguistic studies of Semitic languages, editions of Semitic texts, and studies of Semitic cultures. Titles cover all periods, traditions and methodological approaches to the field. The editorial board comprises Geoffrey Khan, Aaron Hornkohl, Esther-Miriam Wagner, Anne Burberry, and Benjamin Kantor.

You can access the full series catalogue here: https://www.openbookpublishers.com/series/2632-6914

If you would like to join our community and interact with authors of the books, sign up to be contacted about events relating to the series and receive publication updates and news here: https://forms.gle/RWymsw3hdsUjZTXv5

Arabic in Context

Essays on Language, Dialects, and Culture in Honour of Martin R. Zammit

Edited by
Anthony Frendo and Kurstin Gatt

UNIVERSITY OF CAMBRIDGE
Faculty of Asian and Middle Eastern Studies

OpenBook Publishers

https://www.openbookpublishers.com

All external links were active at the time of publication unless otherwise stated and have been archived via the Internet Archive Wayback Machine at https://archive.org/web

Any digital material and resources associated with this volume will be available at https://doi.org/10.11647/OBP.0445#resources

Semitic Languages and Cultures 31

ISSN (print): 2632-6906
ISSN (digital): 2632-6914

ISBN Paperback: 978-1-80511-492-5
ISBN Hardback: 978-1-80511-493-2
ISBN Digital (PDF): 978-1-80511-494-9

DOI: 10.11647/OBP.0445

Cover image: Text in Algerian written in Arabic script from Soualah Mohammed, *Cours moyen d'arabe parlé* (1924), https://commons.wikimedia.org/wiki/File:Algerian_arabic_%D9%84%D9%87%D8%AC%D8%A9_%D8%AC%D8%B2%D8%A7%D8%A6%D8%B1%D9%8A%D8%A9.png
Cover design: Jeevanjot Kaur Nagpal

The fonts used in this volume are Charis SIL, Scheherezade New, SBL Hebrew and SBL Greek.

CONTENTS

Acknowledgements vii

Anthony J. Frendo and Kurstin Gatt
Honouring a Gentleman, A Scholar, a Teacher, and a Pastor: The Legacy of Martin R. Zammit 1

Guram Chikovani
The Current Situation in Arabic-Speaking Kishlaks of Central Asia 13

Andrei A. Avram
Contextual Neutralisation of Voicing in Maltese Obstruents: A Historical Perspective 33

Michael Cooperson
Al-Shidyāq's Account of the Maltese Language: An Annotated Translation 75

Aharon Geva-Kleinberger
On the Arabic Dialect of the Jews of Qāmišli (North-East Syria) 109

Catherine Taine-Cheikh
Interpreting the Traces: On the Grammaticalisation of *ʔaṯar* 135

Sumikazu Yoda
Variations in the Writing System and Style of the Modern Judaeo-Arabic of Libya 175

Mario Cassar
Some Arab and Muslim Names Discernible in Maltese Toponymy....201

Bruno Herin
Koineisation and Language Contact in Syrian Ṭuroyo....261

George Grigore
Locatives in the Spoken Arabic of Mardin (Turkey)....299

Kurstin Gatt
Perceptions of Malta in Arabic Proverbs and Idioms....315

David Wilmsen
Recognisably Arabian: A Levantine/South-Arabian Morphosyntactic Bundle in Maltese....339

Ioana Feodorov
Soul Inspiration from Wadi el Natrun: Ostrich Eggs as Reminders of Vigilance in Praying....381

Index....415

ACKNOWLEDGEMENTS

We would like to thank all the contributors to this *Festschrift* in honour of the Reverend Professor Martin R. Zammit. It is obvious that without their input this volume would have never seen the light of day.

Special thanks are due to Professor Geoffrey Khan, Regius Professor of Hebrew at the University of Cambridge and editor of the *Cambridge Semitic Languages and Cultures* series published by the Cambridge-based Open Book Publishers, for having agreed to consider this set of studies for publication in this prestigious series.

Last, but definitely not least, we would like to thank Dr Anne Burberry, copyeditor of the aforementioned series. She did a marvellous job for which we are both very thankful indeed. We particularly appreciated her acuteness.

Anthony J. Frendo
Kurstin Gatt
University of Malta, Tal-Qroqq, Msida, Malta
September 2024

ACKNOWLEDGEMENTS

HONOURING A GENTLEMAN, A SCHOLAR, A TEACHER, AND A PASTOR: THE LEGACY OF MARTIN R. ZAMMIT

Anthony J. Frendo and Kurstin Gatt

It is difficult to honour properly someone who is self-effacing, intelligent, practical, and always ready to help. We are referring to Martin Zammit, whose contributions to the field of Semitic Studies need no introduction. However, it is worthwhile to write something about Martin's background (both personal and academic), in order to better appreciate his contributions to the fields of Arabic, Arabic dialectology, Syriac, and, not least, comparative Semitic lexicography.

Martin was born in 1958 in Valletta, the son of a barber and of a mother who was always a dedicated housewife, seeing to the upbringing of Martin and his six siblings. This scenario provided a very positive, lively, and dynamic environment that contributed to who Martin is and why he always acted in the way that he did. It also accounts for Martin's excellent relationship with his colleagues both at home and abroad.

During his early years, Martin was involved in the *Circolo Gioventù Cattolica* in Valletta, where he received a Roman Catholic Catechism education. However, what significantly influenced

 https://doi.org/10.11647/OBP.0445.01

his academic journey was the books he found in his brother's library. The latter was a secondary school teacher who had a collection of books related to the Maltese language. Among them, two books stood out: Ġużè Aquilina's *Papers in Maltese Linguistics*, published in 1961 by the University of Malta, and Arthur Sammut's *Mill-pinna ta' Saydon: Ġabra ta' Proża tal-Monsinjur Professur P. P. Saydon*, published in 1972 by Klabb Kotba Maltin. These books, especially Sammut's work, deeply inspired Martin and he vividly remembers being captivated by the Arabic dialectal specimens that featured in Sammut's book. This experience sparked Martin's insatiable curiosity about the Maltese language and its connection to Arabic.

Hence, it comes as no surprise that in 1973, during his third year of secondary education, Martin embarked on a self-driven journey to learn Arabic. At that time, Arabic was not part of the curriculum in Maltese state schools, and it was not officially taught. Despite these challenges, Martin's passion for the Arabic language and its links to Maltese persisted, setting the course for his academic pursuits in later life.

The aforementioned passion that Martin had for the study of the Arabic language was further enriched by his work experiences. In 1976, Martin began his career at the Libyan Cultural Centre in Valletta, where he had the opportunity to immerse himself in Arabic culture and language. The following year, he was transferred to the Libyan Embassy in Sliema; this allowed him to continue his Arabic language journey. This early work experience played a pivotal role in enhancing Martin's understanding of and proficiency in Arabic. In 1978, Martin was given a role at the

Ministry of Foreign Affairs, specifically working at the Arabic desk. After a few months, he was reassigned to the secretariat of the Office of the Prime Minister, where his primary task was to translate documents into Arabic. This was an exciting time for Malta, as it was opening up to the Arab World, with a special focus on Libya.

The story of Martin's connection with the Arabic language and culture continued in a remarkable way, since his Arabic language skills drew the attention of the then Prime Minister, Dom Mintoff. The latter asked Martin to serve as his private secretary, a position that Martin held from 1978 until December 1984. During this period, he had the privilege of accompanying the Prime Minister on various official visits to Arab countries, where he acted as his interpreter and translator. These visits included destinations such as Morocco, Algeria, Tunisia, Libya, Egypt, Syria, Iraq, Kuwait, the UAE, Saudi Arabia, and Yemen.

Whilst performing the tasks just mentioned, Martin found time to visit the University of Malta Library to explore books related to the Arabic language and linguistics. He found himself increasingly captivated by this field of study, particularly the intricacies of Arabic dialectology. However, at that time, he had not made the decision to formally enrol in Arabic studies at the University of Malta, as his work commitments precluded that.

However, Martin would soon establish links with the University of Malta and eventually become a member of its academic staff. This transition was marked by a series of significant developments. In December 1984, Prime Minister Dom Mintoff resigned from his post. During the following period, from 1985 to

1986, Martin served as his personal assistant. However, with the change in administration in 1987, he found himself in a unique situation as a civil servant without any assigned duties. In 1988, a turning point in his career came about through the personal initiative of the then University Rector, Revd Prof. Peter Serracino Inglott. Martin was seconded to the University of Malta, and was placed at the Institute of Linguistics. This move was instrumental in redirecting his career towards academia. During the same year, at the age of 30, Martin embarked on an evening bachelor's degree course, where he studied Classics (Greek and Latin) and Arabic.

The aforementioned study opened the way for Martin to acquire various academic degrees from the University of Malta. In 1992, he completed his B.A. General in Arabic and Classics; a year later, he furthered his studies, obtaining a B.A. Honours in Arabic. His academic studies culminated in 1998, when he successfully obtained a Ph.D. in Arabic and Semitic Studies. Following the completion of his doctorate, Martin transitioned into a full-time academic role at the University of Malta, specifically in the Department of Arabic.

Once Martin started lecturing in the Department of Arabic, he embarked on an interesting academic career at the University of Malta. However, his various roles at the Univesity before starting his lecturing duties should also be noted. From 1988 to 1996, Martin served as a Research Assistant at the Institute of Linguistics; between 1996 and 1999, he held the position of Assistant Executive Director at the Mediterranean Institute. Additionally, he served as the Academic Coordinator for the History of Mediterranean Civilisation programme within the Faculty of Arts. In 1999, Martin was appointed as a Lecturer in the Department of Arabic (later the Department of Arabic and Near Eastern Studies, then the Department of Oriental Studies, and now the Department of Middle Eastern and Asian Languages and Cultures), where he also assumed the role of coordinating the Arabic language programme within the department. In 2005, Martin was promoted to the grade of Senior Lecturer. From 2010 until 2012, he assumed the role of Director at the Institute of Linguistics and concurrently became the Head of the then Department of Oriental Studies within the Faculty of Arts, a position he held until 2017. In 2011, Martin was promoted to the rank of Associate Professor, then finally, in 2022, Martin's academic journey reached a significant milestone when he was promoted to the grade of Full Professor.

The transition from Martin's early career experiences to an accomplished academic path was marked by his continuous pursuit of knowledge and dedication to the field of Arabic and Semitic Studies. It was shaped by a combination of personal initiative, supportive mentors, and opportunities that allowed him to contribute to academia and the University of Malta. Martin believes that the prime mover had always been his passion for whatever he embarked upon. He always considered his academic life to be the cultivation of the interests he cherished most, be it Arabic, Semitic languages, or Maltese. He owes much of this balance to a degree of organisational skills that helped him move on from one stage to another in his career. Even when the going was tough, having to cope with his family obligations, he religiously observed a particular timetable, which allowed him to reconcile some difficult family commitments with teaching, research, and administrative duties. Moreover, he affirms that a sense of sacrifice is at the basis of all worthwhile endeavours—obviously including his own.

The aforementioned organisational skills helped Martin to maintain a balance between work and play. Indeed, beyond his strictly academic pursuits, Martin also cultivated several hobbies and interests that have significantly enriched his life and contributed to his personal growth and well-being. One of his foremost hobbies was Amateur Radio. Engaging in this hobby has been a source of immense satisfaction and learning for Martin. It has not only provided him with a deep appreciation for communication technologies but also complemented his passion for foreign language learning. Amateur Radio allowed him to connect with people from diverse cultural and linguistic backgrounds around the world, fostering intercultural understanding whilst improving Martin's own language skills. This hobby has not only expanded his knowledge but has also connected him to a global community of enthusiasts who share his interests.

Another activity that Martin enjoys is taking leisurely walks in the countryside. These outings provide him with a serene escape from academic rigours and allow him to immerse himself in the beauty of nature. These moments of tranquillity help him to rejuvenate and maintain a balanced lifestyle, promoting his overall well-being.

One of Martin's deep interests is the exploration of World Music, particularly the traditional music of different countries, with a specific affinity for Middle Eastern music. The melodies, rhythms, and stories within this genre of music resonate with him on a personal level. Listening to World Music not only broadens Martin's cultural horizons but also serves as a means of relaxation and escape from the demands of academia. This appreciation for music from diverse cultures adds a layer of cultural richness to his life and has a positive impact on his emotional and mental well-being.

Martin's above-mentioned academic pursuits have had their own memorable moments or milestones. He singles out his research visits to various Arab countries, which brought him into direct contact with remarkable scholars who have been invaluable in shaping his academic journey. These encounters often helped Martin in identifying research projects that he would not otherwise have undertaken. Martin also thinks that much of what we experience and uncover in our research subsequently permeates into our teaching. These real-world insights and experiences have enhanced his ability to impart knowledge to his students.

The points mentioned thus far leave no doubt as to why Martin's research interests are so variegated. Indeed, they include Qur'ānic, Classical, and Dialectal Arabic, Arabic translation, Syriac, and Maltese studies. Martin has never been content with focusing solely on one research interest. His academic journey has seen a remarkable evolution in his research focus. Beginning with his Ph.D. research, which delved into Qur'ānic lexicology, he subsequently ventured into other forms of Arabic, including classical and dialectal Arabic. He has also worked on Arabic–Maltese translation, including the translation of the Qur'ān into Maltese. Aramaic, particularly Syriac, was another significant area of research, culminating in the publication of his *Syriac Chrestomathy* by Gorgias Press in 2006. In the later years of his academic career, Martin dedicated most of his research to exploring the Arabic element in the Maltese language.

Martin is grateful to his mentors, of which he mentioned four. He started by mentioning one of us (Anthony J. Frendo), saying that he taught him Biblical Hebrew and research skills that were solidly founded on the principle of academic rigour and that, more importantly, he instilled in him a passion for philology. The late Professor Abdul Mawla al-Baghdadi (Al-Fateh University, Tripoli) opened doors for Martin to the Libyan world in its various facets, be it language, culture, or society. Martin will always cherish his true friendship. He has also benefitted from the mentorship of Prof. Abdul Hamid Fehri (Sfax University, Tunisia). His friendship was an indispensable catalyst for Martin's dialectal research on Tunisian Arabic, mainly concerning the Kerkennah islands. Finally, he is also grateful to Prof. Sebastian Brock (University of Oxford), who was of great encouragement and help in the preparation of Martin's latest book, namely his aforementioned *Syriac Chrestomathy*.

Martin's academic journey was not without its challenges, of which the most significant one was that of balancing the three key duties expected of academics at the University of Malta: teaching, research, and administration. The teaching load was often demanding, and administrative tasks proved time-consuming.

Thus, for example, the downside of his time as Head of Department was that it directly affected his research output, as administrative tasks, including regular meetings, consumed a substantial portion of his time. In such circumstances, little time was left for research, which Martin often chose to conduct during holidays and academic breaks. He advises aspiring academics facing similar challenges to prioritise time management, seek support and collaboration with colleagues, and maintain a strong commitment to their research goals. In fact, even the time that he spent as Head of Department proved to be very positive for Martin; his excellent relationships with all his colleagues ensured the smooth running of the Department.

Martin retired from the University of Malta at the end of September 2023. This did not mean that he had no academic plans ready for his retirement. Thus, for example, he intends to work on, and publish in Maltese, a comparative grammar of the Maltese language. The story, however, does not end here, since on 21 December 2014 the Apostolic Exarch for Greece had ordained Martin as sub-deacon for the Greek Catholic Church of our Lady of Damascus in Valletta. A year later, on 20 December 2015, His Excellency Dimitrios Salachas ordained Martin as a deacon to continue serving the aforementioned church under the former's guidance. Martin's spiritual journey culminated on 11 June 2017, when he was ordained to the priesthood within the Greek-Catholic Church of Our Lady of Damascus, Valletta, by the Apostolic Exarch for Greece, His Excellency Bishop Manel Nin. Then, on a momentous occasion on 18 July 2021, he was installed as the parish priest, officially taking on the role of Papàs.

Martin's aforementioned spiritual journey and apostolic work overlapped with his final years at the University of Malta. Notwithstanding this, his journey did not detract from his full commitment to his university duties. Martin's path to eventually becoming the Papàs of the local Greek Catholic Church had deep-seated roots and it also saw him achieving more academic qualifications. Martin had a lifelong fascination with the Eastern Christian tradition. From his early childhood, he had been captivated by this rich and vibrant religious heritage. What further cemented this interest was the close proximity of the Greek Catholic Church to his family home in Valletta. Moreover, he had enjoyed a long and meaningful friendship with the parish priest, Papàs Vito Borgia, who had played a pivotal role in nurturing Martin's spiritual journey.

Martin became actively involved in the Greek Catholic Church and considered it to be his spiritual home. Within these sacred walls, he celebrated significant life events, such as his Byzantine rite marriage and the baptism of his two children. In 2009, when Papàs Vito Borgia retired and returned to his native Sicily, he was succeeded by Archimandrite George Mifsud, who took on this significant role at the remarkable age of 83.

Archimandrite George Mifsud, recognising Martin's dedication to and passion for the Greek Catholic Church, suggested that he embark on a path that would eventually lead him to the priesthood. After careful consideration, Martin decided to comply with the Archimandrite's suggestion, and so he started his theological studies. This educational journey culminated in the attainment of the following degrees: in 2015, Martin obtained a Bachelor of

Divinity from Heythrop College, University of London, and then in 2019, he furthered his theological studies by obtaining a Master of Theology in Orthodox Studies from the University of Winchester.

The foregoing points illustrate clearly how Martin stuck to his academic routine and research even when called to take on apostolic duties. We wish him many long, happy, and fruitful years both in his academic and in his pastoral work. We also look forward to Martin publishing his planned comparative grammar of the Maltese language and other projects that he has in mind to undertake.

The papers on various topics in Semitic studies published in this volume are meant as a small token of appreciation to Martin, who has always taught those around him so much: by his unassuming presence, and by his vast knowledge of Semitic languages (amongst other tongues, such as Greek), as well as by the pastoral care he gave to his students and now gives to his parishioners. *Ad multos annos.*

THE CURRENT SITUATION IN ARABIC-SPEAKING KISHLAKS[1] OF CENTRAL ASIA

Guram Chikovani

1.0. Introduction

Central Asian Bukhara (BAD) and Qashqa-Darya (QAD) Arabic dialects belong to peripheral Arabic. Like Maltese, these dialects developed independently of the Arab world for a long time, without contact with literary Arabic. The Arabs living in the Arabic-speaking villages (kishlaks) of Uzbekistan cannot read or write Arabic. For them, Arabic is the spoken language they use at home. Education in schools and universities is carried out in Uzbek. The official language of the country is Uzbek. Arabic, as the native language of the locals, is not included in the school curriculum of Arabic-speaking kishlaks. In recent times, Uzbek has come to be used by Arabic speakers for communication outside the house, including in their native kishlaks. Thus, we have an interesting linguistic picture. According to my observations, Arabs use Arabic outside the house when they do not want others to understand the contents of their conversation.

[1] Kishlak, in Turkic languages of Central Asia, means village or rural settlement of nomadic Turkic peoples. Etymologically, this word is related to Turkic *qış* 'winter'.

 https://doi.org/10.11647/OBP.0445.02

Arabic-speaking kishlaks of the Bukhara and Qashqa-Darya regions of Uzbekistan were discovered in the 30s of the last century by the St Petersburg ethnographic expedition (Burykina and Izmaylova 1930). In 1935, academician Ignaty Krachkovsky's pupil, Georgian Arabist George Tsereteli, arrived in the region and conducted linguistic fieldwork. As a result of a thorough study of the Arabic-speaking kishlaks in the Gijduvan area of the Bukhara region and the Qarshi area of the Qashqa-Darya region, the scientist singled out two Arabic dialects—Bukhara and Qashqa-Darya. The Bukhara dialect bears the signs of the *qeltu* Arabic dialects, while the Qashqa-Darya dialect shows more similarities with the *gelet* Arabic dialects (Tsereteli 1941; 1954).[2]

In the 1930s, George Tsereteli singled out the following Arabic-speaking kishlaks in the Bukhara and Qashqa-Darya regions (Tsereteli 1941, 134):

1. Bukhara region:
   Gijduvan district—kishlaks *ǧōgarī, čaġdarī, šohan-beg.*
   Vabkend district—kishlak *ʿarab ḫōne* (same as *ʿarabīn.* According to some, the name of this kishlak is *mir-suleymōn,* or *rosbadanī*).
2. Qashqa-Darya region:
   Beshkend district—kishlaks *qamašī* and *ǧeynau.*

A great contribution to the study of Central Asian Arabic was made by I. Vinnikov, who devoted significant works to the

[2] In the 1970s, at the Arabic Dialectology lectures of Tbilisi State University's Semitology Department, Prof. George Tsereteli referred to these dialects as *qāl* and *gāl* dialects.

Central Asian Arabic dialect (Vinnikov 1962; 1969). The works by N. Yushmanov (1931), W. Fischer (1961), V. Akhvlediani (1985), O. Jastrow (1995; 1997; 1998; 2005; 2014), and K. Versteegh (1984–1986) are also noteworthy.

In 2018, I conducted a scientific expedition with Arabist Zviad Tskhvediani to the Arabic-speaking villages of Uzbekistan's Bukhara and Qashqa-Darya regions to get acquainted and study the linguistic situation. We ascertained that, at present, the area of Arabic language dissemination in these regions had reduced sharply. In particular, in the Bukhara region, Arabic is preserved only in the village of Jogari, whereas in the Qashqa-Darya region, Arabic is still remembered by the elderly residents of the village of Jeynau. I have visited Central Asia several times for scientific purposes since 1980 and, as a result, published a number of works (Chikovani 2002; 2007; 2008; 2009; 2022). During fieldwork in 1980, 1986, and 2000, I had never noticed such a sharp decrease in the level of Arabic language knowledge as is confirmed now. I tried to investigate the situation. My observation revealed the following circumstances: in 1980, during my first expedition, the Arab informants recorded by George Tsereteli and Isaac Vinnikov in the 1930s were extremely old but still communicative. At that time (i.e., in the 1980s), their children were already elderly. They more or less spoke Arabic but not like their parents. In the 1980s, their age ranged from 50 to 60 years. Today, the vast majority of the next generation after those children does not know Arabic. As mentioned above, individuals only use it at home to talk with family members, and barely that. Their speech is characterised by frequent code-switching and merging, an excess of Uzbek and Tajik words and expressions, foreign syntactic constructions unnatural for Arabic and caused by language contact, a frequency of word production compared to form production, and other lexical and linguistic phenomena, which I will discuss later.

Below are presented some linguistic features and characteristics that have developed in Central Asian Arabic.

2.0. The Verbal Composites

In QAD, the following groups of verbal composites are distinguished:

1. The composites where the meaning is defined by the first verb: *ʿayyanāt-tammaw*[3] 'they saw', 'they looked at', e.g., *ademiāt ʿayyanāt-tammaw, zōka i̯ bēta daẖal*[4] 'The people saw that he entered the house'; *ništera-noġsa* 'we buy', e.g., *naḥnat i̯ bozōr motgōwa ništera-noġsa* 'We buy a cow in the bazaar (market)'.
2. The composites where the meaning is defined by the second verb: *iṣōr-iaġade* 'he goes', e.g., *pōšō i̯ bozōr iṣōr-iaġade*

[3] This composite consists of two Arabic words, *ʿayyanāt (ʿayyn < ʿāyyana* عاين 'to see', 'to view') and *tammaw* (*tammaw < tamma* تم 'to become complete', 'to be finished, done'; 'to come into being').

[4] The words, expressions, and sentences cited as examples were recorded by me in Arabic-speaking villages of Central Asia. Arabs sometimes pronounce the same words differently. They do not particularly respect the length and shortness of the vowels. The words and expressions were recorded by me the way the informant was pronouncing them.

'Pasha went to the bazaar (market)'; *raššaw-maddaw* 'they went', e.g., *ademiāt i‿buḫōro raššaw-maddaw* 'The people went to Bukhara'.

3. The composites with words of synonymous meaning: *ġada-mad* 'he went', 'he was walking', 'he set out', e.g., *walad bōy i‿darb ṭalaʿ, zōka i‿ğaddu ġada-mad* 'The Bey's son set out on the road and went to his grandfather'. The composites of this type are applied mainly to express the Intensive.
4. There are composites which have acquired a new meaning. A composite of this type does not convey the meaning of any of its members: *ʿabar-ğāʿ* 'he leaped', 'he jumped out', e.g., *fad way sahriya*[5] *zōk sabi beiga tam, ademiāt ʿayyanāt-tammaw, šāfū mim bōy ḥoyṭa ʿabar-ğāʿ* 'One morning the boy was late (*beiga tam* < *bāqī tam* بقي تمّ). The people saw (*ʿayyanāt-tammaw*—this composite carries the meaning of its first member) [how] he jumped out of the Bey's house'. In this case, the composite *ʿabar-ğāʿ* acquires a meaning different from the meaning of the members forming the composite. According to the context, the meaning of it is 'leaped', 'jumped out', 'dashed'.
5. The next group consists of the composites the first member of which is an Arabic verbal form and the second a foreign word, for example, an Uzbek or Tajik one. In some cases, the second member is a verbal form of Russian

[5] *fad way sahriya* means 'one morning'. *fad* (< *fard* فرد) means 'one', 'a single one', 'a single person'. This Arabic word has the meaning of an indefinite pronoun in Central Asian dialects.

origin: *anā ib-rūhi ademiāt ʿamal asi-afarmid* 'I give work to people (i.e., engage them)'. *afarmid* is from the Russian *oformlyayu* (оформляю) 'to arrange', 'to administrate'. It is encased in the Arabic morphological form and shaped according to the Arabic verbal paradigm. Namely, in the form *afarmid,* the informant identified the vowel *a* as being the first-person prefix in Arabic: *aʿmal, afarmid... ʿamalān asi* 'I work' is also noteworthy. It is a complex verbal form and conveys the Present Indefinite, being produced by adding the Imperfective form of the Arabic verb *sawa* (*sawiyya* سَوِى 'to be equivalent', 'to be equal'; in QAD 'to do something') in a corresponding person to the masdar of the first stem.[6] In QAD, *sawa* ('made') carries out the function of an auxiliary verb: *ʿamalān isi* 'he works (usually)', *rakabān asi* 'I break in horses (on the whole, usually)'. In QAD, the *masdar* is formed by the suffix *ān* added to the stem of the verb: *ʿamal-ān* 'working', *rakab-ān* 'saddling'.

6. In QAD, those composites form a separate group whose first member is of foreign origin and the second an Arabic verb: *omadan-ğīt* 'I came'.
7. Rarely, a composite consists of members both of foreign origin: *iltimōs-lutfan* 'I'm sorry', 'if I may'. The member words of this composite are of Uzbek origin.

---

[6] *asi* 'I am doing' is the first person of the Arabic verb *sawiyya* in the Imperfective form.

8. Cases are noted in the dialect when the context defines the meaning of a composite. A composite within a sentence sometimes has the meaning of the first and sometimes of the second member: *nāmat-tammat* 'she fell asleep', *šāfa-laga* 'he met'. At the same time, there is an abundance of composites with fixed meanings: *mad-ġada* 'he went away'.
9. There are few noteworthy cases when one of the members of a composite independently has the second member's meaning, e.g., *äfändi ṭalaʿ* 'an Effendi went'. Arabic *ṭalaʿ* is in QAD mainly used with the meaning 'ascended', 'appeared'. Here the informant should have applied the composite *ṭalaʿ-mad* 'went', 'set out'. The disappeared second member of the composite *(mad)* defines the composite's meaning.

3.0. The Code-Switching

Code-switching in QAD and BAD is language alternation. It happens in the speech of Arabs during communication. As they speak Arabic, the Arabs use Uzbek and Tajik sentences, sentence fragments, and words, as well as different morphemes of foreign origin. I consider such borrowing of words or morphemes from another language to be code-switching.

Recently, in the Qashqa-Darya region, we have noted cases of code-switching. Examples:

(1) *i͜ giddāmo* ***bōġ i sovḫōz hast.***[7]
'There **is a farm garden** in front of it.'

(2) *mōratna i͜ ḫ****onai kalōn*** *kānaw.*
'Our women (wives) were **in the big room.**'

Numerous instances of using two-component syntagmas of the Uzbek language have been revealed:

(3) *waladān i͜ zġīr i͜ darb ṭalaʿ, i͜ hama medrese ġada-mad, zōka* ***dil-murōdning kitōbi*** *ḫaza-mad.*
'The younger son set off, he went to that madrasah, he took **Dilmurod's book** (lit.: **Dilmurod—his book**) [with] him.'

(4) *pošō i͜* ***gappāt*** *i͜ bōi* ***ğudō ḫairōn*** *sōr,* ***usmaning otasi*** *sayaḥ. ugūb zōka ihamzōk sayal:* ***usmaning otasi*** *agar inta, li mā gulta?*
'The Pasha was **very surprised** by the Bey's **words,** [he] called for **Usman's father** (lit.: **Usman—his father**). Then he asked him, "**If you are Usman's father**, why didn't you say (this) [before]?"'

(5) *ileynā i͜ ğeynāu* **болалар боġčasi** ***hast.***
'**There is (we have) a kindergarten** here in Jeynau (lit.: **children—their garden**).'

The informants often use the Uzbek and Tajik forms in parallel with the Arabic interrogative pronouns and particles. These are: *kim* 'who?' (Uzbek), e.g., *i͜ ḫonai kim?* 'Who is at home?'; *nima* 'what?' (Uzbek), e.g., *nima eš ʿamal (hast)?* 'What's the matter?'; *či* 'is it not?', 'really?', 'is it possible?', 'surely not' (Uzbek), e.g.,

---

[7] In the examples, the foreign words used in code-switching are emboldened.

sobḫōz-či hamāna? '(Is) there (really) a farm here?'; *kī* 'who?' (Tajik); *čī* 'what?' (Tajik), e.g., *äfändi i̯bawōra min-ki min-či (ma) dāri* 'The Effendi does not know who (and) what (i.e., local news) in Bavora'.[8] *mī* is a Tajik interrogative particle. It is used as a suffix and gives the sentence interrogative content. It is also represented in the Uzbek language. Constructions with the particle *mī* are widespread in Central Asian Arabic:

(6) *bōzōr ibʿīr* ***hast-mi?***
'**Is [here]** a camel bazaar?'

(7) *zīka* ***ḫušrūya hast-mi***?
'**Is** she **beautiful**?'

Layers may be distinguished within lexical units. In one word, for example, there can simultaneously be Arabic, Persian, and Uzbek constituents. Consider, for instance, *apaksah* 'I clean it'. The following are distinguished here: 1. *a*—the first-person prefix of the imperfective of the Arabic verb; 2. Tajik *pokusa* 'pure', 'holy'; 3. *ah/h*—the third-person Arabic pronominal suffix. Here occurs the same phenomenon as in Persian, where often, in three-word or four-word sentences, all the words are of Arabic origin, but the construction is Persian. For instance: *moʿallim, ḫisobdār waladu i̯medrese daḫalu* 'The teacher (and) the accountant's son entered the school'. There are layers in the words here that one has to read, disassemble, uncover, and explain their composition.

---

[8] Bavora is a district in the village of Jeynau.

4.0. Changes Resulting from Language Contact and Internal Development Processes

Both dialects have frequent cases of replacing form production with word production. For example, the third-form perfective *kātab* of the three-consonantal verb was lost. It was replaced by the Tajikised form *mukōtiba sawa.* At present, this form has also been lost, and in its place has appeared the Tajik–Arabic form *navištan sawa,* with the meaning ‘to send a letter’, ‘to inform (somebody)’.

The form *bieġa* < Arabic بقى ‘remain’, ‘stay’ is no longer used and heard in speech. In its place, there mainly occurs Tajik *mondan: i̯ ḥōiṭ mondan* ‘remained at home’.

There are cases when the Arabic dialect replaces the lost Arabic word not with the Tajik–Uzbek equivalent, but with another Arabic word or expression: *anā bint ōḫuz* ‘I will marry’ (‘I’ll take her’). Here, the word *zawwağ* was lost and replaced by the Arabic word *ḫaza,* meaning ‘to take’. At present, it also means ‘buying’ in both dialects: *anā way saḥrīya i̯ bozor amid, iḥmōr ōḫuz* ‘I will go to the bazaar tomorrow morning, I will buy a donkey’. Thus, *šira/štarā* was replaced by *ḫaza.* However, not infrequently, here and there, *štarā* still occurs together with *ḫaza* and, as a result, there appeared the composite *ḫazeyt-štareyt: anā i̯ buḫōro ġadeyt, iḥmōr ḫazeyt-štareyt* ‘I went to Bukhara, bought a donkey’.

Arabic *ltagā* ‘met’ was in QAD replaced by the bilingual Arabic composite *royğā* < *ra’ā-ğāya* ‘looked’-‘came’, ‘arrived’: *wal-adīn izġīr i̯ darb kokōyāta royğā* ‘The younger boy met his [elder] brothers on the road’.

The dual is sometimes conveyed by the Arabic numeral *isnēna/isnēnta: dilmurod way bint isnēnta rakab* 'Dilmurod and the daughter (both) mounted the horse'.

As mentioned above, the dialect is actively replacing Arabic lexemes with Tajik and Uzbek words. In this regard, the Arabic–foreign composites are worth noting, as they represent a kind of transitional step on the way to replacing the Arabic term with a foreign one: *zōka qimmat-buho kānaw* 'this was a precious stone'. The second member in this composite, *-buho* 'precious', is a Tajik word.

Here we should mention the Arabic *zēn šāfā* 'fell in love', widespread in both dialects. It has long since replaced the classical Arabic *ḥabba*. In recent times, I have recorded *ošiq šudan* (ошик шудан) with this meaning, which is of Tajik origin.

The occurrence of the double plural has increased in the dialect. This is due to the fact that the suffix *īn* indicating the regular plural has lost its function. For example, in the word *farasīnāt* 'horses', to the suffix *īn* is added *āt: farasīnāt beyzā kānawāt* 'the horses were white'. The singular form of the word *farasīnāt* is *faras. farasīn* is a transitive form used recently as plural and rarely as singular. The plural number of *faras* is expressed mainly with double plural markers: *faras-īn-āt.*

Some personal pronouns have been combined with the pronominal suffix. Such a case is recorded in the second person singular: *intak (int-ak): intak ʾeš saweyt?* 'What did you do?'

In the first-person plural, we have *naḥn-āt.* This is due to the fact that the pronoun has lost the ability to express the plural, and this function has been taken over by the suffix *āt.*

5.0. The Vocabulary

At present, the vocabulary is heavily influenced by the Tajik and Uzbek languages. Examples of this were given above. Despite this, the language tries to preserve its Arabic vocabulary. There are cases of using old vocabulary. For example, *ġazal* is recorded with the meaning of 'sing': *čumčuġa zēna ġazal kēyyin itgūl* 'the bird was singing sweetly' (lit.: 'was saying a sweet song'). In classical Arabic, a *ġazal* is a lyrical, amorous poem. The presence of the term in Central Asian Arabic with the meaning of 'singing' proves that, in the distant past, the Arabic ghazal was recited and sung, and this remained in the memory of our Arabs.

There are several forms recorded in the dialect that are noteworthy from the viewpoint of the history of the Arabic language and the tendency of internal language development. Let me quote some of them:

avbar < Arabic *ʿabar.* The occurrence of labiodental *v* in the dialectal form can be explained by the loss of *ʿayn.* The substitution of labiodental *v* for *ʿayn* is phonetically acceptable. Thus, the dialect manages to keep three consonants in the root, which is important from the point of view of the history of the formation of the root and its development in the common Arabic language.

suhūr 'son-in-law'. Forms of the broken plural existing in the dialect mostly express a singular, for example, *qubūr* 'grave'; *ʿiyāl* 'son', e.g., *dük salāsat ʿiyāl-ke kēin ʿandun* 'He had three sons'. *ke* is a shortened form of Arabic *kēin.* The shortened form *ke* in a sentence is followed by a full form *kēin.* Repeating the word emphasises the fact that the man had three sons.[9]

In parallel with the form *qubūr* just mentioned, the form *qabr* is also used in BAD: *ilay salās yumāt qabri qaraúlya sū!* 'Three days guard my grave!' The use of broken plural forms with the meaning of the singular in Central Asian Arabic is an important linguistic phenomenon. From the point of view of research on the history of the formation and development of the broken plural forms in the Arabic language, it is remarkable.

ǧazīra in BAD means 'desert'. This is especially important given that the Arabian Peninsula, most of which is desert, is called in Arabic *ǧazīratu-l-ʿarab.*

ḫidme 'military service'. Cf. Arabic *ḫidmatun: al-ḫidma al ʿaskariyya* 'military service' (Baranov 1996). *ḫidme* with the meaning of military service is also found in the modern Arabic dialects. In Lane's Lexicon (1968, 711), one of the meanings of *ḫidma* is 'pay for service'. In modern Persian, the compulsory military service for a conscripted young man is called *ḫedmat-e wazīfe* (Miller 1953). This meaning of *ḫidme* is interesting for us because of those tax privileges mentioned by al-Fāriqī that were established for Arabs by King David IV. According to al-Fāriqī, the Georgian king established *ḫidma* (tax). The *ḫidma* of Georgians, Jews, and Arabs was respectively five, four, and three dinars per annum (Tsereteli 1975, 71). We can assume that here the matter in view is an annual military tax. *ḫidma* can also mean an annual tax paid

[9] I do not exclude the possibility that *-ke* in *ʿiyāl-ke* may be an Iranian suffix *-kī//kin.* In some cases in QAD, it expresses a diminutive: *zēnkin* 'small and beautiful'.

by the population to the king for different kinds of services (security, maintenance of order, etc.) rendered by the government to the population of the town.

rōden—cf. Arabic *ʾarḍun* pl. *ʾarāḍin, ʾarḍūna, ʾaraḍāt*—'ground', 'soil', 'country', 'land'. The parallel forms of the word *rōd//rōwd* < *rōḍ//rōwḍ* that exist in BAD are interesting. The dialect tries to restore three consonants in the root *(r, w, ḍ)*, which is curious from the point of view of research on Semitic root structure. Finding such a phenomenon in Central Asian Arabic provides a basis for assuming reliable existence of three consonants at the initial stage of development of the Arabic language root structure.

It is typical in some Semitic languages to move the verb to the end of the sentence. Wolf Leslau (1948, 232), in his review of Henri Fleisch's famous work, notes that, in Akkadian and Amharic, the insertion of a verb in the final position of the sentence is found, which may be the influence of a non-Semitic language. Leslau explains this phenomenon in Amharic as resulting from the influence of a Cushitic language. Moving the verb to the end of the sentence is also characteristic of QAD: *zōka-i̯ dilmurād, eš ṣorana adri, gāl* 'I know what is wrong with (what happened to) Dilmurod, he said'.

There are cases when the form of a word is preserved, but the meaning is lost, e.g., *staḫarrağ*, which derives from the tenth form: *istaḫrağ*. Thus, as a result of combining the second and tenth forms, we get a new one, the meaning of which does not match that of either the second or the tenth form: 'come out', 'lead out', 'bring out'.

6.0. Conclusion

In conclusion, I would like to remark that several significant linguistic phenomena are still recorded in Central Asian Arabic dialects. Thus, I think the research on the Arabic dialects in the Arabic-speaking kishlaks of Uzbekistan's Bukhara and Qashqa-Darya regions should continue, even if in future only a few people speak Arabic there. Arabic dialectologists should travel there and record the material. In 1986, while in the regions of Bukhara and Qashqa-Darya, I was informed that in the Qashqa-Darya region, in kishlak Qamashi of the Qarshi area, the only Arab left who knew Arabic was 89-year-old Abdel Mu'min Waladin Mirzo. I set off to him. We talked for a long time. He related to me the adventures of the Arabs in Qamashi. He told me that the inhabitants of this kishlak were Arabs from the Quraysh and Hashim tribes, whose ancestors settled in Qashqa-Darya in the seventh century. The material provided by Abdel Mu'min Waladin Mirzo contains invaluable information on the history of the Arabs in Central Asia. The recordings present noteworthy materials for the history of the Arabic language, old lexical units—words no longer used in literary Arabic today—and phonetically significant peculiarities of the consonants' articulation. This example illustrates that the uniqueness of a language is not determined by the number of speakers but by linguistic features.

References

Akhvlediani, Vladimir G. 1985. *Bukhara Arabic Dialect.* Tbilisi: Science. [Russian].

Baranov, Kharlampy Karpovich. 1996. *Arabic–Russian Dictionary*. Moscow: Russian Language. [Russian].

Burykina, Natalya Nikolaevna, and Maria Markovna Izmaylova. 1930. 'Some Data on the Language of the Arabs of the Kishlak Jugara of the Bukhara District and the Kishlak Jeynau of the Qashqa-Darya District of the Uzbek SSR'. In *Notes of the Collegium of Orientalists at the Asian Museum of the USSR Academy of Sciences*, vol. 5, 527–49. Leningrad: Publishing House of USSR Academy of Sciences. [Russian].

Chikovani, Guram. 2002. *Central Asian Arabic Dialects: Qashqa-Darya Dialect (Phonology, Grammar, Vocabulary)*. Tbilisi: Publishing House 'Language and Culture'. [Georgian].

———. 2007. *Central Asian Arabic Dialects: Qashqa-Darya Dialect (Text, Translation, Comment)*. Tbilisi: Publishing House 'Khironi'. [Georgian].

———. 2008. *Qashqa-Darya Arabic Dialect of Central Asia*. Tbilisi: Mtserali. [Russian].

———. 2009. *Bukhara Dialect of Arabic Language*. Tbilisi: Mtserali. [Georgian and Russian].

———. 2022. *The Arabic Dialects in Central Asia: Qashqa-Darya and Bukhara Dialects*. Tbilisi: Free and Agricultural Universities Press.

Fischer, Wolfdietrich. 1961. 'Die Sprache der arabischen Sprachinsel in Uzbekistan'. *Der Islam* 36: 232–63.

Jastrow, Otto. 1995. 'Towards a Reassessment of Uzbekistan Arabic'. In *Proceedings of the 2nd International Conference of l'Association Internationale pour la Dialectologie Arabe (AIDA), Held at Trinity Hall in the University of Cambridge,*

10–14 September 1995, edited by Joe Cremona, Clive Holes, and Geoffrey Khan, 95–104. Cambridge: University Publications Centre.

———. 1997. 'Wie arabisch ist Uzbekistan-Arabisch?' In *Built on Solid Rock: Studies in Honour of Professor Ebbe Egede Knudsen on his 65th Birthday April 11th 1997,* edited by Elie Wardini, 141–53. Oslo: Novus.

———. 1998. 'Zur Position des Uzbekistan-Arabischen'. In *Annäherung an das Fremde: XXVI. Deutscher Orientalistentag vom 25. bis 29.9.1995 in Leipzig,* edited by Holger Preissler and Heidi Stein, 173–84. Zeitschrift der Deutschen Morgenländischen Gesellschaft supplement 11. Stuttgart: Steiner.

———. 2005. 'Uzbekistan Arabic: A Language Created by Semitic–Iranian–Turkic Linguistic Convergence'. In *Linguistic Convergence and Areal Diffusion: Case Studies from Iranian, Semitic and Turkic,* edited by Éva Ágnes Csató, Bo Isaksson, and Carina Jahani, 133–39. Abingdon: RoutledgeCurzon.

———. 2014. 'Dialect Differences in Uzbekistan Arabic and Their Historical Implications'. *Alf Lahga wa Lahga: Proceedings of the 9th AIDA Conference held in Pescara in 2011,* edited by Olivier Durand, Angela Daiana Langone, and Giuliano Mion, 205–12. Neue Beihefte zur Wiener Zeitschrift für die Kunde des Morgenlandes 8. Vienna: Lit Verlag.

Lane, Edward William. 1968. *Arabic–English Lexicon.* Beirut: Librairie Du Liban.

Leslau, Wolf. 1948. Review of *Introduction à l'ètude des langues sémitiques: Eléments de bibliographie* by Henri Fleisch. *Word* 4 (3): 230–33.

Miller, Boris Vsevolodovich. 1953. *Persian–Russian Dictionary*. Moscow: State Publishing House of Foreign and National Dictionaries. [Russian].

Tsereteli, George. 1941. 'To the Characteristics of the Language of Central Asian Arabs (Preliminary Report)'. In *Proceedings of the Second Session of the Association of Arabists: October 19–23, 1937*, edited by I. Y. Krachkovsky, 133–48. Moscow-Leningrad: Publishing House of USSR Academy of Sciences. [Russian].

———. 1954. 'The Arabic Dialects in Central Asia'. In *Papers Presented by the Soviet Delegation at the XXIII International Congress of Orientalists: Semitic Studies*, 7–36. Moscow: Publishing House of USSR Academy of Sciences. [Russian and English].

———. 1975. 'Al-Fārikī Ibn al-Azraq: Min Ta'riḫ al-Mayyafariqin'. In *Arabic Reader*, edited by S. Jikia, 68–75. Tbilisi: Publishing House of Tbilisi University.

Versteegh, Kees. 1984–1986. 'Word Order in Uzbekistan Arabic and Universal Grammar'. *Orientalia Suecana* 33–35: 444–53.

Vinnikov, Isaak Natanovich. 1962. 'A Dictionary of the Bukhara Arabs' Dialect'. *Palestinian Collection* 10 (73): 3–246. [Russian].

———. 1969. *The Language and Folklore of Bukhara Arabs*. Moscow: Publishing House 'Science'. [Russian].

Yushmanov, Nikolay Vladimirovich. 1931. 'Arabic Speech of the Soviet East'. *Culture and Writing of the East* 10: 76–84. [Russian].

CONTEXTUAL NEUTRALISATION OF VOICING IN MALTESE OBSTRUENTS: A HISTORICAL PERSPECTIVE

Andrei A. Avram

1.0. Introduction

Comparison with Arabic (Ar.), its putative ancestor, shows that Modern Maltese (Mod. M) exhibits several instances of spontaneous voicing (Cohen 1966; 1967) and devoicing in its Semitic component. The following examples illustrate voicing:

(1) a. **t* > *d*
Ar. ***t**isʿīn* > Mod. M. ***d**isgħin* 'nine'
b. **k* > *g*
Ar. ***k**aḏab* > Mod. M. ***g**ideb* '[he] lied'
c. **ṣ* > *z*
Ar. ***ṣ**abaʿ* > Mod. M. ***z**aba'* '[he] painted'

As for devoicing, it is found in cases such as:

(2) a. **d* > *t*
Ar. ***d**araǧa* > Mod. M. ***t**arġa* 'stair'
b. **ǧ* > *č*
Ar. ***ǧ**aḥad* > Mod. M. ***ċ**aħad* '[he] denied'

 https://doi.org/10.11647/OBP.0445.03

In addition, Modern Maltese exhibits regressive voicing assimilation (Borg 1975, 15; 1997, 250), i.e., the underlying contrast between voiced and voiceless obstruents is neutralised before another obstruent, with the preceding obstruent agreeing in voicing with the following one. Regressive voicing assimilation triggers therefore either obstruent devoicing or obstruent voicing, as illustrated in the examples (from Borg 1975) under (3) and (4), respectively:

(3) a. [ʔa**t**fa] 'rowing' vs [ʔa**d**ef] 'he rowed'
b. [**s**fi:n] 'dancing' vs [**z**ifen] 'he danced'

(4) a. [**v**dejtna] 'you redeemed us' vs [**f**eda] 'he redeemed'
b. [**z**di:ri] 'waistcoats' vs [**s**idrijja] 'waistcoat'

Regressive voicing assimilation can be captured by the rule below (Avram 2022a, 232):

(5) $[+\text{obstr}] \rightarrow [+\text{obstr}, \alpha\ \text{voice}] / \_\ [+\text{obstr}, \alpha\ \text{voice}]$

Generally, mixed obstruent clusters do not occur in Modern Maltese, i.e., voiced obstruents do not occur before voiceless ones and voiceless obstruents do not occur before voiced ones.

Modern Maltese also exhibits word-final obstruent devoicing (see e.g. Cohen 1966, 13; Borg 1975, 19; Borg 1997, 223; Borg and Azzopardi-Alexander 1997, 307). The relevant rule can be formulated as follows (Avram 2020, 28):

(6) $[+\text{obstr}] \rightarrow [-\text{voice}]\ /\ \_\#$

Parawahera (1994–1995, 174) shows that word-final obstruent devoicing precedes regressive voicing assimilation. Consider the derivation of [ħops] 'bread':

(7)	a. /ħobz/	UR
	ħobs	word-final devoicing
	ħops	regressive voicing assimilation
	[ħops]	SR

The reverse ordering would yield an incorrect surface form:

(7)	b. /ħobz/	UR
	ħobz	regressive voicing assimilation
	ħobs	word-final devoicing
	*[ħobs]	SR

As shown by Parawahera (1994–1995, 174), regressive voicing assimilation spreads over to the neighbouring consonants in a cluster:

(8)	/niktbu/	UR
	nikdbu	regressive voicing assimilation of *t*
	nigdbu	regressive voicing assimilation of *k*
	[nigdbu]	SR

The facts briefly outlined above need to be treated differently. Spontaneous voicing and devoicing are not systematic processes and appear to go back to the earliest stages of Maltese. Voicing of */t/, for instance, is attested in Megiser's 1588 wordlist (Megiser 1606):

(9) *dischin* 'ninety'

Similarly, devoicing of */d/, for instance, is attested in Caxaro's *Cantilena* (second half of the fifteenth century), the first extant text in Maltese:

(10) *tirag* 'stairs'

As for regressive voicing assimilation and word-final obstruent devoicing, they are context-dependent and apply systematically, as phonological rules. Moreover, Maltese did not initially have either of these two phonological rules (Avram 2017b; 2020; 2021; 2022a). The present paper is an attempt at reconstructing the parallel diachrony of these two phonological processes in Maltese.

The paper is structured as follows. §2.0 presents the corpus and the methodology. §3.0 is concerned with regressive voicing assimilation and word-final obstruent devoicing in earlier stages of Maltese. §4.0 discusses the findings.

2.0. Corpus and Methodology

The corpus of Maltese covers a period ranging from the second half of the fifteenth century to the end of the eighteenth century. It consists of (i) texts: Caxaro's *Cantilena* (Wettinger and Fsadni 1968), Buonamico's *Sonnet* (Cachia 2000), *Salve Regina* (Said 2017), the sermons of Ignazio Saverio Mifsud ('Ġabra tal-Malti Qadim' n.d.; Zammit Ciantar 1985), de Soldanis' (1750) grammar, the translation of *Dottrina Cristiana* (Wzzino 1752), de Soldanis' (1758) *Sonetto punico-maltese* (Cremona 1953), de Soldanis' dialogues ('Id-Djalogi ta' de Soldanis' n.d.; see also Pullicino 1947), end of eighteenth-century sermons (Bonelli 1897; Fenech 2016), Navarro's quatrains (Guignard 1791), the translation of *La Via Sagra* (Cannolo 1796); (ii) samples of Maltese in archival records of the Roman Inquisition in Malta (Cassar 2005; Cassar 2011); (iii) lexicographical works: Megiser's 1588 wordlist (Megiser 1610), Thezan's dictionary (Cassola 1992), *Il 'Mezzo*

Vocabolario' Maltese-Italiano del '700 (Cassola 1996), Skippon's 1664 wordlist (Skippon 1732), Maius' (1718) wordlist, de Sentmenat's vocabulary (Queraltó Bartrés 2003), de Soldanis' dictionary (after 1760); (iv) place names, personal names, and nicknames: Abela (1647), Wettinger (1980; 1983), Camenzuli (2002), Avram (2012; 2016).

The timeline of these changes is inferred from the orthography used in the sources. Further evidence is adduced from metalinguistic comments by eighteenth-century authors (de Soldanis 1750; Vassalli 1791; 1796).

The number of examples has been kept to a reasonable minimum. All examples appear in the orthography or transcription system used in the sources. The original glosses in Catalan, German, Italian, or Latin in the sources have all been translated into English.

3.0. Regressive Voicing Assimilation and Word-final Obstruent Devoicing in Early Maltese

3.1. The Fifteenth Century

Maltese is very poorly attested in the fifteenth century. The only text discovered so far, dated c. 1450, is Caxaro's *Cantilena* (Wettinger and Fsadni 1968). Other attestations, including personal names and place names, are found in notarial documents.

Caxaro's *Cantilena* provides evidence for the non-occurrence of regressive voicing assimilation:

(11) *sib[t] tafal* '[I] found clay'

According to Cohen and Vanhove (1991, 190), “le suffixe –ṯ... a été omis à la fin de sib par le copiste à cause de la liaison avec le mot suivant,” which was “un phénomène très fréquent au Moyen Âge.” Therefore, Caxaro’s <sib> should read <sibt>, i.e., the voiced /b/ does not undergo regressive voicing assimilation and is not devoiced.

Also, as already noted by Cohen and Vanhove (1991, 181), in Caxaro’s *Cantilena* “la neutralisation sourde/sonore en finale au profit de la sourde... n’est pas attestée.” All relevant forms exhibit word-final voiced obstruents, as in the two examples below:

(12) a. *cal**b*** ‘heart’
b. *tre**d*** ‘you.SG want’

As shown in Avram (2012; 2016; 2017b), while personal names and place names recorded in notarial documents contain many instances of word-final voiced obstruents, as in (13), there is only one doubtful case of a devoiced one (14):

(13) a. *muhamu**d***
b. *mita Jlchade**d*** ‘of the iron’

(14) *Muhamet*

3.2. The Sixteenth Century

Sixteenth-century Maltese is also rather poorly documented. The extant records consist of a wordlist, samples of Maltese in the archival records of the Roman Inquisition, and personal names and place names attested in notarial documents.

Megiser’s (1606) wordlist contains the first instances of regressive voicing assimilation of obstruents, in an onset cluster (15a) and in a coda cluster (15b), respectively:

(15) a. ***gu**ir*[1] 'big.M'
b. *cho**ps*** 'bread'

The wordlist also contains three forms with word-final voiced obstruents (16) vs eight with devoiced ones (17):

(16) a. *vehe**b*** 'gold'
b. *kel**b*** 'dog'
c. *chtie**b*** 'book'

(17) a. *ecne**p*** 'grapes'
b. *nissito**p***[2] '[I] drink'
c. *taje**p*** 'good.M'
d. *bel**t*** 'town'
e. *quacha**t*** 'one.M'
f. *guar**t*** 'rose'
g. *embi**t*** 'wine'

The archival records of the Roman Inquisition in Malta (Cassar 2005; Cassar 2011) show that word-final voiced obstruents continue to occur:

(18) a. *tai**b*** 'good.M'
b. *ixibe**b*** 'virgins'

However, a few instances of word-final devoiced obstruents are also found:

(19) a. *chasa**p*** 'rod, cane'
b. *iddue**p*** 'the mares'

---

[1] Where <u> is an error of transcription or a misprint and should read <b>.

[2] An error of transcription; cf. Mod M. *nixrob*.

Consider, finally, place names. These also attest to the continuing occurrence of word-final voiced obstruents. Two such examples are reproduced below:

(20) a. *ta misge**d*** 'of the synagogue'
b. *il mueye**d*** 'the table lands'

As for word-final devoiced obstruents, there is a single instance; however, the same place name is also transcribed with a voiced obstruent:

(21) *gebel labia**th*** ~ *gebel labio**d*** 'the white rock'

3.3. The Seventeenth Century

Beginning with the seventeenth century, Maltese is better documented. The same holds for regressive voicing assimilation and word-final obstruent devoicing. However, as shown below, forms exhibiting regressive voicing assimilation sometimes compete with forms that do not agree in voicing, and devoiced obstruents continue to occur in word-final position.

First, consider evidence from the archival records of the Roman Inquisition in Malta in the seventeenth century (Cassar 2005; Cassar 2011). There is an instance of regressive voicing assimilation:

(22) *hie**pch**a* '[he] remains]'

In word-final position, both voiced and devoiced obstruents are found, as seen in (23) and (24), respectively:

(23) a. *chihe**d*** '[he] sat'
b. *ihaia**d*** '[he] says'

(24) *rmi**t*** 'ashes'

In Thezan's dictionary (Cassola 1992), written by 1647, most relevant forms exhibit obstruent clusters which do not agree in voicing. Consider the following examples:[3]

(25) a. *arko**bt**ein* 'kneeling'
b. *e***ذ ح***er* 'appear!'
c. ق*a*ع ***dt*** '[I] sat'
d. *ke**b**ش* 'ram'
e. *me*ش*e**b**ه* 'likened.M'

However, some forms illustrate regressive voicing assimilation of all types of obstruents—i.e., stops, fricatives, and affricates—in onset (26), word-medial (27), and coda clusters (28):

(26) a. ***pt**ala* 'holiday'
b. ***pk**eit* '[I] cried'
c. ***t**خ**alt* '[I] entered'
d. ***p**ش**ein* 'for nothing'
e. ***p**ح**al* 'like'
f. ***p**چ**ei*چ*a* 'small piece'

(27) a. ش*e**pk**a* 'net'
b. *me**p**خ**ara* 'see!'
c. *e**tf**en* 'bury!'
d. *e**sf**en* 'dance!'
e. *e*ث ح*a*ق[4] 'laugh!'

(28) a. *se**pt*** 'Saturday'
b. *se**p**ه* 'dawn'
c. خ*ame*ش**t** '[I] soiled'

[3] Thezan uses several Arabic letters; see Cassola (1993), Avram (2023).

[4] In earlier Maltese, [θ] is a reflex of */dˤ/ (see Avram 2014; 2021).

Particularly strong evidence is provided by examples of regressive voicing assimilation in paradigms and families of words (Avram 2023), such as in the forms on the left below:

(29) a. ش*e**p**ka* 'net' vs ش*e**b**iek* 'nets'
 b. *e**s**fen* 'dance!' vs ***z**efen* '[he] danced'
 c. *ne**p***ه 'barking' vs *ne**b**a*ح 'to bark'

Finally, there is also evidence of variation in the phonetic realisation of obstruents in pre-obstruent position:

(30) *li**p**sa* vs *li**b**sa* 'garment'

The overwhelming majority of word-final obstruents occurring in the entries are voiced. This is true of over 400 forms listed in Thezan's dictionary (Avram 2020, 49). Selected examples are given below:

(31) a. *bie**b*** 'door'
 b. *bar**d*** 'cold'
 c. *geu**z*** 'nut'
 d. خ*are**g*** '[he] went out'

However, some 50 forms (Avram 2020, 49) exhibit devoiced obstruents in word-final position. As can be seen in the examples under (32), all types of obstruents are represented, and word-final obstruent devoicing also applies to Romance loanwords, as in (32d):

(32) a. غ*ar**p*** 'sunset'
 b. *ermie**t*** 'ash'
 c. ڨ*abe**s*** '[he] jumped'
 d. *preie**s*** '[PL of *preza*] prey'

e. ح*au*ث[5] 'trough'
f. *a*ع*a*چ 'ivory'

Again, examples in paradigms and families of words, as in the forms on the left below, constitute strong evidence for the occurrence of word-final devoicing (Avram 2023):

(33) a. *gera**t*** 'cricket' vs *gera**d**iet* 'crickets'
b. *mensu*چ 'woven.M.SG' vs *mensu**g**in* 'woven-PL'
c. *preie**s***.PL vs *pre**z**a* 'prey'

However, there is also evidence of variation, i.e., different forms in the paradigm of several words derived from the same root exhibit either devoiced or voiced obstruents in word-final position. Consider the following example:

(34) *a*ع*zi**z*** 'dear.M.SG' vs *a*ع*zie**s*** 'dear.PL'

The occcurrence of both word-final voiced (35) and devoiced (36) obstruents is also attested in the place names recorded by Abela (1647):

(35) a. *Aayn Clie**b*** 'fountain of the dogs'
b. *Aayn Hadi**d*** 'the iron fountain'

(36) a. *Mitahle**p*** 'where cows are milked'
b. *Kibur elihu**t*** 'the Jews' graves'

In Skippon's 1664 wordlist (Skippon 1732, 624–26) there are 39 forms with word-final voiced obstruents vs nine forms with devoiced ones. Examples of each type are provided below:

---

[5] Where [θ] is a reflex of */dˤ/.

(37) a. *dehe**b*** 'gold'
     b. *bar**d*** 'cold'

(38) a. *tachse**p*** '[you.SG] think'
     b. *raa**t*** 'thunder'

Obstruent clusters do not agree in voicing, as illustrated by the following examples:

(39) a. ***kb**ir* 'big.M'
     b. *reko**bt*** 'knee'

The last seventeenth-century source examined, Buonamico's 1672 *Sonnet* (Cachia 2000, 18), contains three forms with word-final voiced obstruents (40) and two with devoiced ones (41):

(40) a. *cqal**b*** 'heart'
     b. *scha**b*** 'clouds'
     c. *uar**d*** 'rose'

(41) a. *ar**t*** 'earth'
     b. *bar**t*** 'cold'

All the three relevant forms with obstruent clusters exhibit regressive voicing assimilation:

(42) a. ***ph**al* '[like]'
     b. *ne**pt**et* '[it.F] sprouted'
     c. *te**pk**i* '[she] cries'

3.4. The Eighteenth Century

Maltese is considerably better documented in the eighteenth century. The number of extant texts is significantly bigger and, moreover, these cover a wide range of genres: sermons, dialogues, poems, translations, a grammar, and several lexicographical works.

The first text examined is the Maltese version of the Marian hymn *Salve Regina* (Camilleri 2016; Said 2017). Its dating is not definitely established: both Camilleri (2016, 8) and Said (2017, 53) estimate that it was written in the seventeenth or eighteenth century. The text contains three instances of word-final obstruents, all of which are devoiced (43), and one obstruent cluster which agrees in voicing (44):

(43) a. *alhu**t*** 'the river'
b. *lar**t*** 'the earth'
c. *ule**t*** 'birth'

(44) *ne**pc**u* '[we] cry'

In Maius' (1718) wordlist, there is an equal number of forms with voiced and devoiced obstruents in word-final position, as shown in (45) and (46), respectively:

(45) a. *bie**b*** 'door'
b. *dee**b*** 'gold'
c. *taie**b*** 'good.M'

(46) a. *i**t*** 'hand'
b. *kueke**bh***[6] 'star'
c. *guar**t*** 'rose'

---

[6] But it is not clear what <bh> stands for.

There is also one instance of an obstruent cluster agreeing in voicing:

(47) *ho**ps*** 'bread'

The sermons of Ignazio Saverio Mifsud (Zammit Ciantar 1985; 'Ġabra tal-Malti Qadim' n.d.), considered by some to be the first prose work in Maltese and covering the period 1739–1746, include forms with obstruent clusters which do not agree in voicing, such as:

(48) a. ***b't**ant* 'with so much'
b. ***b's**ebhu* 'with his finger'

However, this is the first Maltese text in which obstruent clusters that agree in voicing outnumber those that do not. Given below are some representative examples of regressive voicing assimilation in various positions; these include a Romance loanword in (49e):

(49) a. ***p'c**aua* 'with force'
b. ***psc**aiac* 'with your feet'
c. ***th**alt* '[I] entered'
d. *dar**pt**ein* 'twice'
e. *prie**tk**i* 'sermons'
f. *hsi**pt*** '[I] thought'
g. *ho**ps*** 'bread'

Variation is also attested, i.e., obstruent clusters occurring in the same word or in similar phrases may agree in voicing or not:

(50) a. ***bsc**i* ~ ***psc**i* 'with some'
b. ***bc**ertu* 'with a certain-M' ~ ***pc**erta* 'with a certain-F'
c. *ti**bc**a* ~ *ti**pc**a* '[you] remain'

There are very few words which exhibit word-final voiced obstruents, such as:

(51) a. *mahbu*__*b*__ 'loved.M'
b. *inhogo*__*b*__ '[he] was liked'
c. *haggie*__*g*__[7] '[he] kindled'

Forms illustrating word-final devoicing, such as those under (52), constitute the clear majority and many of these are consistently spelled with a devoiced obstruent; this is also the case with Romance loanwords, such as the one in (52e).

(52) a. *rae*__*p*__ 'monk'
b. *taie*__*p*__ 'good.M'
c. *ihi*__*t*__ '[he] says'
d. *uihe*__*t*__ 'one.M'
e. *scon*__*t*__ 'according to'

Variation between voiced and devoiced word-final obstruents, as in (53), is only rarely attested:

(53) *clu*__*b*__ ~ *clu*__*p*__ 'hearts'

Consider next the Catalan–Maltese vocabulary attributed to the Marquis de Sentmenat and believed to have been written at the beginning of the second half of the eighteenth century (Queraltó Bartrés 2003, 7). The entries and the texts include both forms with obstruent clusters that do not agree in voicing and others that do. However, forms that exhibit regressive voicing assimilation outnumber by a ratio of two to one those that do not. The

[7] Where the word-final <g> stands for [ʤ].

first set of examples under (54) illustrates the occurrence of mixed obstruent clusters:

(54) a. *dar**bt**ein* ‘twice’
b. ***kb**ira* ‘big-F’
c. [*ma*] *titlo**bx***[8] ‘do not ask!’

Regressive voicing assimilation is attested in onset, word-medial, and coda clusters, as illustrated by the examples below:

(55) a. ***pk**aila* ‘spinach’
b. ***ph**al* ‘like’
c. *i**pk**i* ‘[he] cries’
d. *e**thhh**ol* ‘enter!’
e. *to**gb**a* ‘hole’
f. *hho**ps*** ‘bread’

The vocabulary contains an almost equal number of forms with word-final voiced and devoiced obstruents: 25 vs 22. Examples of each type are given in (56) and (57), respectively:

(56) a. *midru**b*** ‘wounded.M’
b. *rahe**b*** ‘monk’
c. *ar**d*** ‘earth’
d. *ilhhhei**d***[9] ‘Easter’

(57) a. *sali**p*** ‘cross’
b. *marri**t*** ‘sick’

---

[8] Where <x> represents [ʃ], in accordance with the spelling conventions of Catalan.

[9] Where <hhh> represents [ʕ] (Queraltó Bartrés 2003, 13).

c. *txer**ph***[10] 'deer'
d. *zeuhue**tx*** 'pair'

As shown by example (57c), Romance loanwords also display word-final obstruent devoicing.[11]

In Wzzino's (1752) translation of *Dottrina Christiana*, the first book printed in Maltese, forms with mixed clusters are still attested:

(58) a. ***sd**irna* 'our chest'
b. *ji**fd**i* '[he] redeems'
c. *ħho**bs*** 'bread'

However, forms that display regressive voicing assimilation outnumber those that do not by a ratio of two to one. Given below are several such examples, which include a Romance loanword (59c):

(59) a. ***pt**aiel* 'holidays'
b. ***p-ch**ul* 'with every'
c. ***pc**eieċ* 'small pieces'
d. ***żg**har* 'small.PL'

As for obstruents in word-final position, voiced ones, such as those under (60), outnumber devoiced ones, such as those under (61):

(60) a. *dnu**b*** 'sin'
b. *Lhu**d*** 'Jews'
c. *żeu**ġ*** 'two'

---

[10] Where <tx> represents [tʃ], in accordance with the spelling conventions of Catalan, and <ph> presumably stands for [f].

[11] The Maltese word for 'deer' is derived from Sicilian *cervu*.

(61) a. *mislu**p*** ‘crucified.M’
b. *uie**t*** ‘valley’
c. *aġhzes* ‘beloved.M’

Finally, there are a number of forms that appear to reflect variation in the phonetic realisation of word-final obstruents:

(62) a. *tinsa**b*** ~ *tinsa**p*** ‘[it.F] is found’
b. *lar**d*** ~ *l’ar**t*** ‘the earth’
c. *jinhhtie**ġ*** ~ *jinhhtie**ċ*** ‘[it.M] is needed’

The examples under (64)–(82) are all from various works by de Soldanis. Consider first his grammar and dictionary (de Soldanis 1750), which contains obstruent clusters that do not agree in voicing as well as others that exhibit regressive voicing assimilation. Examples of the former type include:

(63) a. ***qb**ir* ‘big.M’
b. *ge**bt*** ‘[I] brought’
c. *hha**sb**a* ‘thought’
d. *ne**bhh*** ‘barking’

In forms such as the following, obstruent clusters agree in voicing:

(64) a. ***phh**alu* ‘like him’
b. ***sf**in* ‘dance’
c. *e Se**pt*** ‘Saturday’
d. *hha**ps*** ‘prison’

Significantly, variation in the phonetic realisation of obstruent clusters is also illustrated or sometimes even explicitly mentioned by de Soldanis (1750, 187 and 193, respectively):

(65) a. *reqba, rogba* 'riding'
　　b. *hhobs* or *chops* 'bread'

In de Soldanis' (1750) grammar and dictionary, voiced obstruents continue to be found in word-final position in forms such as:

(66) a. *sciorob* '[he] drank'
　　b. *maqghad* 'seat'

However, these are outnumbered by forms displaying word-final obstruent devoicing, which include a Romance loanword (67d):

(67) a. *ghenep* 'grapes'
　　b. *qelp* 'dog'
　　c. *eżiet* 'more'
　　d. *supperf* 'haughty'

Variation is also attested in the pronunciation of various words (68), and is sometimes explicitly mentioned by de Soldanis. It is also attested in the paradigm of some words (69):

(68) a. *bieb* or *biep* 'door'
　　b. *qarab* or *qarap* 'close'
　　c. *tajeb* or *tajep* 'good.M'
　　d. *rmièt* or *ramed* 'ashes'

(69) *ghàd* '[he] said' ~ *ighit* '[he] says'

De Soldanis' *Dialogues*, written after 1760 ('Id-Djalogi ta' de Soldanis' n.d.; see also Pullicino 1947), present a similar picture. On the one hand, there are a few instances of obstruent clusters which do not agree in voicing, two of which are reproduced below:

(70) a. *gebt* '[I] brought'
　　b. *ma en hhobsc* '[I] don't love'

On the other hand, forms exhibiting regressive voicing assimilation are well represented in all positions—onset clusters, as in (71), word-medially, as in (72), and coda clusters, as in (73):

(71) a. *__pk__aina* '[we] remained'
b. *__db__eddel* '[it] changed'
c. *__ph__haga* 'with a thing'

(72) a. *ie__pk__a* '[he] remains'
b. *ie__tch__ol* '[he] enters'

(73) a. *hhse__pt__* '[I] thought'
b. *ghage__st__* '[I] have grown old'
c. *ma żeue__sctc__* 'I did not get married'

De Soldanis' *Dialogues* also reflect variation occurring in the same word (74a), the paradigm of a word (74b), or a word family (74c):

(74) a. *te__bk__a* ~ *te__pk__a* '[she] remains'
b. *sehhe__bt__ek* 'your partner' ~ *sehhe__pt__i* 'my partner'
c. *n-el__bs__u* '[we] get dressed' ~ *le__ps__in* 'dressed-PL'

As for word-final obstruents, forms with voiced ones are outnumbered by those with devoiced ones (Avram 2020, 43). The following are examples of voiced (75) and devoiced (76) obstruents occurring in word-final position:

(75) a. *t-escro__b__* '[you] drink'
b. *gdi__d__* 'new.M'
c. *żuie__g__* 'wedding'

(76) a. *klie__p__* 'dogs'
b. *mara__t__* '[he] got sick'
c. *t-akbe__s__* '[you] jump'
d. *hhueie__c__* 'goods'

Also attested is variation in the same word (77) or the paradigm of a word (78):

(77) a. *embagha**d*** ~ *embagha**t*** 'then'
b. *engha**d*** ~ *engha**t*** 'was said'
c. *tri**d*** ~ *tri**t*** '[you] want'

(78) a. *e si**b*** '[he] finds' ~ *sa**p*** '[he] found'
b. *t ahhse**b*** '[you] think' ~ *n-ahhse**p*** '[I] think'

The last of de Soldanis' texts considered here is the *Sonetto punico-maltese* (Cremona 1953). Obstruent clusters are represented by a single instance (79):

(79) ***thh**altlu* '[you] inserted it for him'

The text contains an almost equal number of word-final voiced and devoiced obstruents, illustrated in (80) and (81), respectively:

(80) a. *kite**b*** '[he] wrote'
b. *ghi**d*** 'feast day'
c. *zeu**g*** 'two'

(81) a. *ezie**t*** 'more'
b. *gi**t*** 'good'

Consider next evidence from *Il Mezzo Vocabolario Maltese–Italiano del '700* (Cassola 1996), the second dictionary of Maltese, in chronological order. The dictionary is only partially preserved: its first 68 pages are missing from the original manuscript and it starts with the letter *Ghe* (Cassola 1996, 13; Cachia 2000, 48) Both its author and its dating are controversial. Cassola (1996, 17) only writes that the "provenience of the compiler is undoubtedly Maltese." Cachia (2000, 49–50), however, suggests that the author might be Pelagio Mifsud, a Catholic priest. According to

Cassola (1996, 16), the dictionary was compiled in the period 1765–1775, whereas Cachia (2000, 50) dates its compilation earlier, around 1750. Most obstruent clusters do not agree in voicing. Illustrative examples include the following:

(82) a. *__qb__ir* 'big.M'
b. *rco__bt__ein* 'knees'
c. *lie__bs__a* 'dressed-F'
d. *giarra__bt__* '[I] tried'
e. *re__bh__* 'victory, win'

However, regressive voicing assimilation is attested in all types of clusters, i.e, onset (83), word-medial (84), and coda clusters (85):

(83) a. *__pt__àla* 'holiday'
b. *__pk__ia* 'rest'
c. *__px__ein* 'for nothing'

(84) a. *ha__pk__a* 'basil'
b. *te__sf__en* '[you] dance'
c. *zeue__xt__u* '[you.pl] married'

(85) *chere__xt__* '[I] got out'

The majority of word-final obstruents are voiced. Consider the following examples:

(86) a. *hessie__b__* 'thought'
b. *kêtie__b__* 'book'
c. *mar__d__* 'illness'
d. *saje__d__* 'fisherman'
e. *machmu__tg__*[12] 'dirty.M'

---

[12] Where <tg> represents [ʤ].

Nonetheless, even though fewer in number, all types of obstruents, i.e., stops, fricatives, and affricates, undergo devoicing in examples such the ones below:

(87) a. *hau**t*** ‘trough’
b. *Milie**t*** ‘Christmas’
c. *tak**b**i**s*** ‘jumping’
d. *sar**tc***[13] ‘saddle’

Three sermons include forms relevant to the occurrence of regressive voicing assimilation. In a 1783 sermon (Bonelli 1897), there are two instances of obstruent clusters that do not agree in voicing (88) and two that do (89):

(88) a. ***sb**ih* ‘beautiful.M’
b. ***sd**egnat* ‘despised.M’

(89) a. ***p-sc**i* ‘in some’
b. ***ph**ala* ‘like its.F’

In a 1788 sermon (Fenech 2016), both mixed obstruent clusters (90) and instances of regressive voicing assimilation (91) are found:

(90) a. ***b’s**ehmu* ‘in his portion’
b. *har**bt**u* ‘[they] destroyed’

(91) a. ***ph**al* ‘like’
b. *ti**th**ol* ‘[you] enter’

Also attested is variation in the same word:

(92) *li**bs**a* ~ *li**ps**a* ‘dress’

---

[13] Where <tc> represents [ʧ].

The 1774 and 1783 sermons in Bonelli (1897) contain instances of word-final voiced obstruents:

(93) a. *insi**b*** ‘[I] find’
 b. *jackle**b*** ‘[it.M] spills’
 c. *ghage**b*** ‘wonder’
 d. *izje**d*** ‘more’

In addition, the 1783 sermon in Bonelli (1897) also attests to variation between word-final voiced and devoiced obstruents, in the paradigm of the same word:

(94) *inghi**d*** ‘[I] say’ ~ *gha**t*** ‘[he] said]’

As for the 1788 sermon in Fenech (2016), both voiced (95) and devoiced (96) obstruents occur in word-final position:

(95) a. *chuieche**b*** ‘stars’
 b. *mo**d*** ‘manner’
 c. ع*aslu**g***[14] ‘twig’

(96) a. *igi**p*** ‘[he] brings’
 b. *ar**t*** ‘earth’
 c. *hueie**c***[15] ‘things’

Variation is found in a few words (97a, b), as well as in the paradigm of some words, as in (97c):

(97) a. *gil**d*** ~ *gil**t*** ‘skin’
 b. *hali**b*** ~ *hali**p*** ‘milk’
 c. *mitlu**b*** ‘demanded.M’ ~ *jitlo**p*** ‘[he] demands’

---

[14] Where <g> represents ʤ].

[15] Where <c> represents [ʧ].

The samples of Maltese in the archival records of the Roman Inquisition in Malta, dating from 1783 to 1792, include only forms displaying regressive voicing assimilation, as in (98), and word-final obstruent devoicing, as in (100):

(98) a. ***ph**al* 'like'
b. *ho**ps*** 'bread'

(99) a. *issi**p*** '[he] finds'
b. *sali**p*** 'cross'

The poem known as 'Navarro's quatrain' (Guignard 1791, 119) contains two forms with obstruent clusters, one of which (100) does not agree in voicing, while the other (101) displays regressive voicing assimilation:

(100) *mas-si*ح***bj**e*ش '[you] don't find'

(101) ***ph**alek* 'like you'

Similarly, both voiced (102) and devoiced obstruents (103) occur in word-final position:

(102) *na*ح*se**b*** '[I] think'

(103) *ti*ش*ro**p*** '[you] drink'

Obstruents that do not agree in voicing are still found in Cannolo's (1796) translation of *Via Sagra*:

(104) a. ***chb**ir* 'big.M'
b. *l'i**bs**a* 'garment'

In the same text, however, other forms display regressive voicing assimilation:

(105) a. ***ps**abar* 'with patience'
b. *ulie**tch**om* 'your birth'

On the other hand, variation between forms with and without regressive voicing assimilation is attested within the paradigm of a word:

(106) *la **tibchusc*** 'don't cry!' ~ ***ipchu*** 'cry!'

As for obstruents in word-final position, forms with voiced and devoiced ones are equally well attested, as in (107) and (108), respectively:

(107) a. *Sali**b*** 'cross'
b. *ghazi**z*** 'dear.M'

(108) a. *ghan**t*** 'at'
b. *gdi**t** / gidi**t*** 'new.M'

The last source examined, an inventory of late eighteenth-century defamatory nicknames and insults (Camenzuli 2002), contains no forms relevant to the occurrence or not of regressive voicing assimilation. As for word-final obstruents, they are all devoiced:

(109) a. *ta' Liswe**t*** 'of black complexion, dark-skinned'
b. *ta' Supper**f*** 'proud, arrogant'
c. *tal-Bron**s*** 'hard-hearted' [lit. 'of bronze']

On the strength of the evidence surveyed in this section, it can be concluded that, towards the end of the eighteenth century, both regressive assimilation and word-final obstruent devoicing appear to have essentially become systematic phonological processes of Maltese.

Additional circumstantial evidence in support of this conclusion can be found in metalinguistic comments made towards the end of the eighteenth century by Vassalli in his first grammar of Maltese (Vassalli 1791) as well as in his dictionary of Maltese (Vassalli 1796).[16]

First, consider Vassalli's comments on regressive voicing assimilation in obstruent clusters. Vassalli (1791, 80) states with regard to the letter *Be Bb* that *ante T K Q S & Š... sonat P* 'before T K Q S & Š... it sounds like P'. Similarly, Vassalli (1791, 90) notes the case of *Zajn Zz*, which *ante Q, T... sonat S* 'before Q, T... sounds like S'. Also, Vassalli (1796, 140) says of the letter *D* that *ante litteras F X K & Q legitur T* 'before the letters F X K & Q it is read T'.

Several passages in Vassalli (1791) refer to the devoicing of obstruents in word-final position: the letter *Be in fine dictionum sonat P* 'at the end of words sounds like P' (Vassalli 1791, 80); the letter *Dal in fine dictionis T profertur* 'at the end of words is pronounced T' (Vassalli 1791, 81); the letter *Gim in fine sonat Č* 'at the end sounds like Č' (Vassalli 1791, 82); the letter *Zajn in fine dictionis sonat S* 'at the end of the word sounds like S' (Vassalli 1791, 90). The following statement may in fact be regarded as being the first formulation of the rule of word-final obstruent devoicing in Maltese: that *litterae B D Ğ... Z in fine dictionum sonos proprios amittunt & pronunciantur ac si essent P T Č... & S* 'the letters B D Ğ... Z at the end of words lose their own sounds and are pronounced as if they were P T Č... & S' (Vassalli 1791, 95). Finally, a similar claim is made in Vassalli (1796, XXXII) with respect to the letters <B> and <D>, about which he specifies

[16] For typographical reasons, the letters specially designed by Vassali (1791; 1796) to render [q], [ʃ], [x], [ʧ], and [ʤ] are replaced with their standard equivalents used in Arabic transliteration.

that *in fine della parola... la prima pronunziasi P, e T la seconda* 'at the end of the word... the first one is pronounced P, and T the second'.

4.0. Discussion and Conclusion

Before discussing the findings, it is necessary to briefly address the issue of the reliability of the sources and therefore of the empirical data.

As seen in §3.0, four of the sources are works by non-Maltese authors: Megiser's wordlist, Thezan's dictionary, Skippon's wordlist, and de Sentmenat's vocabulary. Two of these authors, Hieronymus Megiser and Philip Skippon, were speakers of languages which do not exhibit regressive voicing assimilation in obstruent clusters: German does have obstruent devoicing, but it is syllable-final (Lombardi 1999, 268; Wetzels and Mascaró 2001, 208); in English, there is voicing assimilation of obstruents, but it is progressive, rather than regressive. As for word-final obstruent devoicing, this is a well-known characteristic of German, which English does not have. This might raise doubts about the accuracy of Megiser's transcriptions of Maltese forms with word-final devoiced obstruents. However, the fact that Megiser uses both <p> and <b> for the transcription of bilabial stops in word-final position is strongly indicative of the occurrence of devoicing in the words at issue, as opposed to others which still exhibit a voiced word-final stop. Thezan was a native speaker of

Provençal,[17] which has regressive voicing assimilation of obstruents, but does not exhibit word-final obstruent devoicing. As shown in §3.3, the entries in Thezan's dictionary relevant to the occurrence of regressive voicing assimilation in obstruent clusters and word-final obstruent devoicing, respectively, show that the author was very much aware of the existence of alternants. Finally, de Sentmenat was a native speaker of Catalan, which displays both regressive voicing assimilation of obstruents and word-final obstruent devoicing (Lombardi 1999, 269). There are no significant differences, however, between de Sentmenat's transcriptions and those by other contemporary authors who were native speakers of Maltese. For instance, as mentioned in §3.4, those of de Sentmenat's forms that exhibit regressive voicing assimilation outnumber those that do not by a ratio of two to one. Wzzino, a native speaker of Maltese writing in approximately the same period, has a ratio of more than two to one. It may be concluded, therefore, that de Sentmenat's transcriptions are plausible and tally rather well with those found in other contemporary sources.

Both regressive voicing assimilation and word-final obstruent devoicing are late developments in Maltese. As seen in §3.0, both phonological processes are first attested at the end of the sixteenth century, gather momentum in the seventeenth century and are essentially generalised at the end of the eighteenth century. This late emergence contrasts with the situation in other (European) peripheral dialects of Arabic, with which Maltese is

---

[17] Joseph Brincat, personal communication, September 2023.

frequently compared (Avram 2023). Regressive voicing assimilation is attested much earlier in Andalusi Arabic (Zammit 2009–2010, 31; Institute of Islamic Studies of the University of Zaragoza 2013, 9, 25, 27). Zammit (2009–2010, 31) notes that "Andalusi and Maltese Arabic display cases of contiguous assimilation." One of his examples illustrates regressive voicing assimilation, found in both varieties: Andalusi Ar. *na**t**ḫol*, Mod. M. *nidħol* [ni**t**ħol] '[I] enter'. Similarly, word-final obstruent devoicing is attested much earlier in Sicilian Arabic (Isserlin 1977, 24; Lentin 2006–2007, 78; Avram 2017a, 29–33; 2017b, 24–26; La Rosa 2019, 112, 118, 120). The fact that both regressive voicing assimilation and word-final obstruent devoicing are relatively late developments weakens considerably the case for a Sicilian Arabic ancestry of Maltese. Neither regressive voicing assimilation nor word-final obstruent devoicing can have been inherited from Sicilian Arabic: if they had, they should have been attested in the earliest records of Maltese (Isserlin 1977; Avram 2016b; 2017b).

The occurrence in Maltese of regressive voicing assimilation and word-final obstruent devoicing can also be discussed within the context of modern peripheral dialects of Arabic, several of which exhibit the operation of both phonological rules. For instance, regressive voicing assimilation in obstruent clusters occurs in various Anatolian Arabic dialects (Akkuş 2018, 458–59; Grigore 2007, 53; Lahdo 2009, 46; Akkuš 2020, 143): ***g**bīr* 'big', ***haps*** 'prison', *tzawwəš**t*** '[you.M.SG] got married'. Word-final obstruent devoicing is also attested (Jastrow 2006, 90; Grigore 2007, 44–45; Lahdo 2009, 45; Akkuş 2018, 458; 2020, 143): *ġari**p*** 'stranger', *aḫaṯ* '[he] took', *zaw**č*** 'husband'. Consider also

Nigerian Arabic, in which "a voiced non-sonorant consonant is devoiced before a voiceless consonant or pause" (Owens 1993, 21): *tač* '[you.M.SG] come', ***ǧapha*** 'forehead'. In these modern peripheral dialects of Arabic, however, the two phonological rules at issue are reported not to apply across the board. With respect to regressive voicing assimilation, Owens (1993, 22) notes that in Nigerian Arabic it was recorded "in a few cases" and that it "is not so common as the devoicing rule." As for word-final obstruent devoicing in Anatolian Arabic, "this phonological phenomenon is... not fully spread" (Lahdo 2009, 45) and it appears that "the language is undergoing a transition in this regard" (Akkuş 2020, 143). Maltese, then, differs from such dialects in that these phonological rules have been generalised (but see below).

The diachrony of both rules illustrates the phenomenon of lexical diffusion in Maltese. As is well known, the main tenet of lexical diffusion theory is that sound change is phonetically abrupt, but lexically gradual (McMahon 1994, 50; Blevins 2004, 268; Bybee 2016, 39). On this view, not all words are affected by a sound change at the same time. Rather, the sound change first occurs only in a small subset of the potential targets. In the case of other words, there will be both intra- and inter-speaker variation for a certain period of time, characterised by the coexistence of two competing phonetic realisations—the initial one and the new one resulting from the sound change. At a still later stage, the sound change spreads to other words and to other speakers. The sound change may potentially extend to all relevant lexical items. This appears to be the situation of regressive voicing assimilation and word-final devoicing in Maltese. It should be emphasised that several reasons make it impossible to track in detail the diffusion of regressive voicing assimilation and word-final obstruent devoicing in Maltese. Firstly, data for some of the periods surveyed are rather scarce. Secondly, the available records are certainly representative of several different dialectal varieties of Maltese. For instance, Hull (1994, 394) argues that Thezan's dictionary is based on the seventeenth-century "general vernacular of the island," while Vella (2013) demonstrates that de Soldanis uses the dialect of Gozo. In other cases, however, the varieties at issue cannot be identified. As noted by Cardona (1997, 22), for example, "we do not know whether Megiser or Skippon took those words from the city or from the countryside." Thirdly, the sources may well reflect the orthographic preferences of their authors. Finally, the task is certainly not facilitated by the fact that transcriptions are occasionally marred by inconsistencies. In spite of such objective difficulties, it may be concluded that the spread of regressive voicing assimilation and word-final obstruent devoicing bears the typical hallmarks of lexical diffusion.

Both word-final position obstruent devoicing and regressive voicing assimilation are examples of rule addition, which does not trigger a change in underlying representations. As seen in §1.0, both mixed clusters and word-final voiced obstruents occur underlyingly.

Both regressive voicing assimilation and word-final obstruent devoicing have been persistent rules (in the sense of Cser 2015; Dresher 2015) of Maltese ever since the late eighteenth century. As seen in §3.0, the two phonological rules at issue apply not only to the Semitic component of Maltese, but also to Romance loanwords. Generally, as shown in §1.0, both are operative as synchronic rules, even though some exceptions are found. With respect to regressive voicing assimilation, for instance, Galea (2016, 27) and Galea and Ussishkin (2018, 66–67) write that the "rule is not strictly respected in clusters" in the Semitic component of Maltese. As for word-final obstruent devoicing, it may fail to apply to phonologically non-integrated borrowings from English.[18]

Consider, finally, the typological consequences of regressive voicing assimilation and word-final obstruent devoicing. Lombardi (1994, 53–54; 1999, 268–69), Wetzels and Mascaró (2001, 208–9), and Kenstowicz et al. (2003, 260) have identified several types of languages attested in terms of the criteria of obstruent voicing assimilation and word-final neutralisation of voicing. Arabic—the putative ancestor of Maltese—belongs to the type called "voice unrestricted" by Lombardi (1999, 268), in which there is "contrast of voiced and voiceless obstruents initially, medially, finally and in clusters" (Kenstowicz et al. 2003, 260). However, Modern Maltese belongs to the type characterised by "voicing assimilation in obstruent clusters with word-final neutralization" (Lombardi 1999, 269). It follows, then, that the combined effect of obstruent regressive voicing assimilation and word-final obstruent devoicing has triggered a typological shift.

---

[18] Ray Fabri, personal communication, June 2017.

References

Abela, Giovanni Francesco. 1647. *Della descrittione di Malta isola nel mare siciliano: Con le sue antichita, ed altre notitie*. Malta: Paolo Bonacota.

Agius, Dionisius A. 1996. *Siculo Arabic*. London: Kegan Paul International.

Akkuş, Faruk. 2018. 'Peripheral Arabic Dialects'. In *The Routledge Handbook of Arabic Linguistics*, edited by Elabbas Benmamoun and Reem Bassiouney, 454–71. Abingdon: Routledge.

Akkuş, Faruk. 2020. 'Anatolian Arabic'. In *Arabic and Contact-Induced Change*, edited by Christopher Lucas and Stefano Manfredi, 135–58. Berlin: Language Science Press.

Avram, Andrei A. 2012. 'Some Phonological Changes in Maltese Reflected in Onomastics'. *Bucharest Working Papers in Linguistics* 14 (2): 99–119.

———. 2014. 'The Fate of the Interdental Fricatives in Maltese'. *Romano-Arabica* 14: 19–32.

———. 2016. 'Phonological Changes in Maltese: Evidence from Onomastics'. In *Shifts and Patterns in Maltese*, edited by Gilbert Puech and Benjamin Saade, 49–89. Berlin: De Gruyter Mouton.

———. 2017a. 'On the Phonology of Sicilian Arabic and of Early Maltese'. In *Advances in Maltese Linguistics*, edited by Mauro Tosco and Benjamin Saade, 3–37. Berlin: De Gruyter Mouton.

———. 2017b. 'Word-Final Obstruent Devoicing in Maltese: Inherited, Internal Development or Contact-Induced?'. *Academic Journal of Modern Philology* 6: 23–37.

———. 2020. 'The Diachrony of Word-Final Obstruent Devoicing in Maltese'. In *Maltese Linguistics on the Danube*, edited by Slavomir Čéplö and Jaroslav Drobný, 27–57. Berlin: De Gruyter Mouton.

———. 2021. 'Fortition in the Historical Phonology of Maltese: Two Case Studies'. In *Deconstructing Language Structure and Meaning: Studies on Syntax, Semantics, Language Acquisition, and Phonology*, edited by Mihaela Tănase-Dogaru, Alina Mihaela Tigău, and Mihaela Zamfirescu, 198–219. Newcastle upon Tyne: Cambridge Scholars Publishing.

———. 2022a. 'Regressive Voicing Assimilation in Maltese: Diachrony and Typology'. In *Maltese: Contemporary Changes and Historical Innovations*, edited by Przemysław Turek and Julia Nintemann, 231–61. Berlin: De Gruyter Mouton.

———. 2022b. 'From Interdental Fricatives to Stops in Maltese: A Case of Lexical Diffusion'. In *Studies on Arabic Dialectology and Sociolinguistics: Proceedings of the 13th AIDA International Conference*, edited by Guram Chikovani and Zviad Tskhvediani, 21–33. Kutaisi: Akaki Tsereteli State University.

———. 2023. 'Thezan's *Le regole per la lingua maltese* and the Historical Phonology of Maltese'. Paper presented at the 8th International Conference on Maltese Linguistics, 18–20 September 2023, Universität Bremen.

Blevins, Juliette. 2004. *Evolutionary Phonology: The Emergence of Sound Patterns*. Cambridge: Cambridge University Press.

Bonelli, Luigi. 1897. 'Il dialetto maltese'. *Archivio Glottologico Italiano* 6: 37–70.

Borg, Albert, and Marie Azzopardi-Alexander. 1997. *Maltese*. London: Routledge.

Borg, Alexander. 1975. 'Maltese Morphophonemics'. *Journal of Maltese Studies* 10: 11–28.

———. 1997. 'Maltese Phonology'. In *Phonologies of Asia and Africa*, vol. 1, edited by Allan S. Kaye, 245–85. Winona Lake: Eisenbrauns.

Bybee, Joan. 2016. *Language Change*. Cambridge: Cambridge University Press.

Cachia, Lawrenz. 2000. *Ħabbew l-ilsien Malti*. Zabbar: Veritas Press.

Camenzuli, Anthony. 2002. 'Defamatory Nicknames and Insults in Late Eighteenth Century Malta: 1771–1798'. *Melita Historica* 13 (3): 319–27.

Camilleri, Charlò. 2016. '"Slema ħelic Soltana": Talba f'Instruzione de' Capellani e specialmente de' żeroslimitani—Volum manuskritt fl-Arkivju tal Karmelitani fl-Imdina'. *L-Arkivju* 7: 3–10.

Cannolo, Giuseppe Martino. 1796. *La Via Sagra*. Malta.

Cardona, Tony. 1997. *Introduzzjoni għal lingwistika Maltija*. L-Imsida: Mireva Publications.

Cassar, Mario. 2005. '*Nella lingua nostra nativa*: l-użu tal-Malti fil-processi ta' l-Inkwiżizzjoni Rumana'. *Symposia Melitensia* 2: 57–84.

Cassar, Carmel. 2011. 'Il-Malti fi żmien il-Kavallieri ta' San Ġwan'. *Il-Malti* 82: 12–25.

Cassola, Arnold. 1987–1988. 'Una edizione diversa della lista di voci maltesi del seicento di Hieronymus Megiser'. *Journal of Maltese Studies* 17–18: 72–86.

———. 1992. *The* Biblioteca Vallicelliana: Regole per la lingua Maltese: *The Earliest Extant Grammar and Dictionary of the Maltese Language*. Valletta: Said International.

———. 1993. 'A Mixed Orthography of the Maltese Language: The Latin–Arabic Alphabet'. In *Collected Papers Published on the Occasion of the Collegium Melitense Quatercentenary Celebrations (1592–1992)*, 203–19. Msida: University of Malta.

———. 1996. *Il 'Mezzo Vocabolario' Maltese–Italiano del '700*. Valletta: Said International.

Cohen, David. 1966. 'Le système phonologique du maltais: Aspects synchroniques et diachroniques'. *Journal of Maltese Studies* 3: 1–26.

———. 1967. 'Contribution à la phonologie diachronique du maltais'. In *Verhandlungen des zweiten internationalen Dialektologenkongresses*, vol. 1, edited by Ludwig Erich Schmitt, 164–71. Wiesbaden: Franz Steiner.

Cohen, David, and Martine Vanhove. 1986. 'La Cantilène maltaise du 15ème siècle: remarques linguistiques'. *Comptes-rendus du Groupe linguistique d'études chamito-sémitiques* 29–30: 177–200.

Cowan, William. 1964. 'An Early Maltese Wordlist'. *Journal of Maltese Studies* 2: 217–25.

Cremona, A. 1953. 'Sunett bil-Malti ta' de Soldanis'. *Il-Malti* 2: 59–61.

Cser, András. 2015. 'Basic Types of Phonological Change'. In *The Oxford Handbook of Historical Phonology*, edited by Patrick Honeybone and Joseph C. Salmons, 193–204. Oxford: Oxford University Press.

Dresher, Elan. 2015. 'Rule-Based Generative Historical Phonology'. In *The Oxford Handbook of Historical Phonology*, edited by Patrick Honeybone and Joseph Salmons, 501–21. Oxford: Oxford University Press.

Fenech, Reno. 2016. 'Prietka tal-1788 dwar iċ-Ċintura: Kumment'. *Leħen il-Malti* 85 (35): 183–89.

Grigore, George. 2007. *L'arabe parlé à Mardin: Monographie d'un parler arabe peripherique*. Bucharest: Editura Universităţii din Bucureşti.

Guignard, François-Emmanuel. 1791. *Malte par un voyageur François*. Valletta.

'Ġabra tal-Malti Qadim'. n.d. http://mlrs.research.um.edu.mt/resources/gabrastorika, accessed 23 July 2024.

Hull, Geoffrey. 1994. Review of Arnold Cassola, *The* Biblioteca Vallicelliana: Regole per la lingua maltese: *The Earliest Extant Grammar and Dictionary of the Maltese Language*. *Journal of Semitic Studies* 39 (2): 391–395.

'Id-Djalogi ta' de Soldanis'. n.d. http://malti.skola.edu.mt/kotba/djalogi_desoldanis.pdf, accessed 5 January 2017.

Institute of Islamic Studies of the University of Zaragoza. 2013. *A Descriptive and Comparative Grammar of Andalusi Arabic*. Leiden: Brill.

Isserlin, B. S. J. 1977. 'Sicilian Arabic and Maltese: Some Remarks on Their Phonetic Interrelations'. *Journal of Maltese Studies* 11: 19–25.

Jastrow, Otto. 2006. 'Anatolian Arabic'. In *Encyclopedia of Arabic Language and Linguistics*, edited by Kees Versteegh, Mushira Eid, Alaa Elgibali, Manfred Woidich, and Andrzej Zaborski, vol. 1, *A–Ed*, 87–96. Leiden: Brill.

Kenstowicz, Michael, Mahasen Abu-Mansour and Miklós Törkenczy. 2003. 'Two Notes on Laryngeal Licensing'. In *Living on the Edge: 28 Papers in Honour of Jonathan Kaye*, edited by Stefan Ploch, 260–82. Berlin: Mouton de Gruyter.

Lahdo, Ablahad. 2009. 'The Arabic Dialect of Tillo in the Region of Siirt (South-Eastern Turkey)'. PhD dissertation, Uppsala University.

La Rosa, Cristina. 2019. *L'arabo di Sicilia nel contersto maghrebino: Nuove prospettive di ricerca*. Rome: Istituto per l'Oriente C. A. Nallino.

Lentin, Jérôme. 2006–2007. 'L'arabe parlé en Sicile était-il un arabe périphérique?'. *Romano-Arabica* 6–7: 71–84.

Lombardi, Linda. 1994. *Laryngeal Features and Laryngeal Neutralization*. London: Routledge.

———. 1999. 'Positional Faithfulness and Voicing Assimilation in Optimality Theory'. *Natural Language and Linguistic Theory* 17: 267–302.

Maius, Iohannes Henricus. 1718. *Specimen linguae punicae in hodierna Melitensiun superstitis*. Marburg: Muller.

McMahon, April M. S. 1994. *Understanding Language Change*. Cambridge: Cambridge University Press.

Megiser, Hieronymus. 1606. *Propugnaculum Europe. Wahrhafte/ Eigentliche und Ausführliche Beschreibung/der viel und weitberühmten Afrikanischen Insul Malta.* Leipzig: Henning Großn.

Owens, Jonathan. 1993. *A Grammar of Nigerian Arabic.* Wiesbaden: Harrassowitz Verlag.

Parawahera, N. P. 1994–1995. 'Lexical Strata in Maltese'. *Journal of Maltese Studies* 25–25: 166–78.

Pullicino, G. Cassar. 1947. 'Id-Djalogi ta' De Soldanis'. *Il-Malti* 3: 99–125. https://www.um.edu.mt/library/oar/handle/123456789/53532, accessed 6 August 2024.

Queraltó Bartrés, Alexandre. 2003. *Un vocabulari català–maltès manuscript del segle XVIII: Edició, transcripció i estudi.* Barcelona: PPU.

Said, I. 2017. 'Il-kanonku Ġann Piet Franġisk Agius de Soldanis, lessikografu u traduttur'. *L-aċċent* 16: 46–56.

Skippon, Philip. 1732. *An Account of a Journey Made thro' Part of the Low-Countries, Germany, Italy, and France.* London.

de Soldanis, Giovanni Pietro Francesco Agius. 1750. *Nuova scuola di grammatica per agevolmente apprendere la lingua punica maltese, aperta agli studenti maltesi, e forestieri abitanti in Malta.* Roma: Salomoni.

Vassalli, Mikiel Anton. 1791. *Mylsen Phoenico–Punicum sive Grammatica Melitensis.* Rome: Antonio Fulgoni

———. 1796. *Ktŷb yl Klŷm Mâlti: Mfysser byl-Latin u byt-Taljan… Lexicon Melitense–Latin–Italum… Vocabolario maltese: Recato nelle lingue latina e italiana.* Rome: Antonio Fulgoni.

Vella, Olvin. 2013. 'A Gozitan Dialect for Standard Maltese'. Paper presented at the 4th International Conference on Maltese Linguistics, 17–19 June 2013, Lumière University, Lyon.

Wettinger, Godfrey. 1980. 'The Place-Names and Personal Nomenclature of Gozo, 1372–1600'. In *Oriental Studies Presented to Benedikt S. J. Isserlin by Friends and Colleagues on the Occasion of his Sixtieth Birthday 25 February 1976*, edited by Rifaat Y. Ebied and Michael J. L. Young, 173–98. Leiden: Brill.

Wettinger, Godfrey. 1983. 'Some Grammatical Characteristics of the Place-Names of Malta and Gozo in Early Modern Times'. *Journal of Maltese Studies* 15: 31–68.

Wettinger, Godfrey and Mikiel Fsadni. 1968. *Peter Caxaro's Cantilena: A Poem in Medieval Maltese*. Malta.

Wetzels, W. Leo, and Joan Mascaró. 2001. 'The Typology of Voicing and Devoicing'. *Language* 77: 207–44.

Wzzino, Francesco. 1752. *Taġhlim nisrani: Migiub fil Ġharbi bl'ordini ta sant. mem. ta Paulu V—Min gdid stampat fit-Talian mis Sacra Congregazioni tal Propaganda Fidi, u' migiub issa fil Malti*. Rome: Arcangelo Casaletti.

Zammit, Martin R. 2009–2010. 'Andalusi Arabic and Maltese'. *Folia Orientalia* 45–46: 21–60.

Zammit Ciantar, Joe. 1985. 'Malti tas-seklu tmintax'. *Hyphen* 4 (5): 179–207.

AL-SHIDYĀQ'S ACCOUNT OF THE MALTESE LANGUAGE: AN ANNOTATED TRANSLATION

Michael Cooperson

Among readers of Arabic, Aḥmad Fāris al-Shidyāq (c. 1804–1887) is well known for his contributions to literary modernity in Egypt and the Levant.[1] Employed as a tutor, translator, and editor by foreign missionary societies, he lived in Malta from 1828 to 1829 and from 1835 to 1848.[2] Those fourteen years provided the material for his peevish but informative description of the islands, *al-Wāsiṭah fī maʿrifat aḥwāl Māliṭah* 'The Middle

[1] I avoid the conventional term *nahḍah* ('revival' or 'renaissance') because it implies assent to the proposition that the Arabic writing of the Mamluk and Ottoman periods—a span of some 600 years—is decadent and without merit. For a critique of conventional periodisation, see Cooperson (2017). On al-Shidyāq's notion of *nahḍah*, see Bou Ali (2012).

[2] The most extensive account of his time in Malta is Roper (1988, 204–30). For additional details, see Agius (1989–1990), Cassar (2011), and Mercieca (forthcoming).

 https://doi.org/10.11647/OBP.0445.04

Jewel', 'The Intermediary', or 'The Mid-Length Book, on Knowledge of Conditions in Malta'.[3] The *Wāsiṭah* was published (along with an account of England and France) in Tunis in 1863 and reprinted in Istanbul in 1881.[4] Of particular interest is the chapter on Maltese, which offers a welcome glimpse of the language as it existed in the first half of the nineteenth century. It also sheds light on al-Shidyāq's understanding of what counts as good language—a matter which, given his influence as an editor, publisher, novelist, and critic, should be of interest to scholars of Arabic literature.

Al-Shidyāq's account of Maltese does not appear among the selections from *al-Wāsiṭah* translated into English by Pierre Cachia (Cachia 1962–1963). It does appear in Francis X. Cassar's rendering of the whole book into Maltese (al-Shidyāq 1985, 83–95), which I gratefully used as a source for the correct forms of Maltese words. As not all those interested in al-Shidyāq can read

---

[3] The word *wāsiṭah* can mean 'the middle jewel of a necklace' (i.e., the best one), 'intermediary' (in this case, between the subject and the reader), and possibly 'intermediate', i.e., neither a short epistle nor a lengthy treatise. As a skilled user of paranomasia (*tawriyah*), al-Shidyāq may have had all three meanings in mind. For 'Malta', the form *Māliṭah* is required by the rhyme, rhyming prose titles being the norm in this period. The usual modern forms, Mālṭah and Mālṭā, contain a prosodically impossible long vowel before a consonant cluster.

[4] Although modern references to the Istanbul edition imply that it contains revised and expanded versions of both travelogues, the author's reference to additions and corrections appears at the end of the *Kashf al-mukhabbaʾ* (the part dealing with England and France) and seems to apply only to that work, not to the *Wāsiṭah* (*Kashf*, 361).

Maltese, I offer here a complete and annotated English translation. The notes have a twofold purpose: to illuminate for non-Arabist readers the literary and linguistic references al-Shidyāq assumed his audience would understand, and to explain for non-Maltese readers the passages that require knowledge of that language. I do not for a moment imagine that my polyglot colleague Martin Zammit will find anything new to him here. He may nevertheless be amused by this attempt to put al-Shidyāq's ornery prose into fitting English. In any event, I hope he will accept this modest contribution as a token of my respect for his scholarship and my gratitude for his kindness.

As al-Shidyāq's chapter is both disorganised and digressive, it may be helpful to lay out a through line as a guide to the reader. If we step back from the mass of detail and focus on the author's expressions of opinion, we see a remarkable reversal take place before our eyes. His introductory remarks are obnoxious: he dismisses Maltese as a corrupt offshoot of Arabic. Then he sets out to refute the claim of Phoenician descent. He begins by affirming the Arabic roots of Maltese, showing that its phonology is the result of shifts that can be discerned in other varieties. Its semantic innovations, too, are natural developments from the root meaning of Arabic words. He admits that it contains borrowings from other languages, but points out that other Arabic dialects do as well. Not only that: many of the words supposedly unique to Maltese are actually classical Arabic. In some cases, he says, it is only the Maltese who use these words in their original sense. Even their wretched attempts to write verse have counterparts in classical Arabic poetry. By the end of the chapter, the author has not simply refuted the Phoenician thesis: he is holding Maltese up proudly as evidence for the resilience of Arabic. "Has Malta not witnessed," he asks, "a succession of rulers who sought to force its inhabitants to speak other languages? None has succeeded: generation after generation, the Maltese have clung to what Arabic they know" (al-Shidyāq 1881, 66).

Having thus welcomed Maltese back into the Arabic fold, al-Shidyāq might be expected to call upon its speakers to adopt classical Arabic as their language of learning. But he was too astute an observer to propose anything so unlikely.[5] Maltese speakers, he says, perceive their language to be distinct from Arabic, which they dislike so much they refuse to study it. Nor, indeed, can one expect a people who have long been cut off from contact with Arabic and Islamic learning to see their language as an heir of that tradition. And why, after all, should a 'corrupt' language not become a full-fledged one? Isn't Italian, for example, a corruption of Latin? Although he resists following this line of reasoning to its end, he does seem to realise that he cannot reasonably expect an entire population to assent to his notions of purity.

Stubbornly, the author then tries to condemn Maltese on other grounds: namely, that its speakers refuse to employ it as a

---

[5] Mercieca (forthcoming, 16–17) states that al-Shidyāq "sincerely wished" that the Maltese would "revert to Classical Arabic as their spoken language" but "knew that it was a lost cause." I have not found a passage where al-Shidyāq explicitly calls on the Maltese to speak in Arabic, though I admit it is a reasonable inference from his complaints about their language. In any case I agree with Prof. Merceica that al-Shidyāq did not seriously expect anything to change.

medium of literature and scholarship. The language, he says, "is not used for any scholarly purpose, nor has anything of note been written in it" (al-Shidyāq 1881, 55). With this he paints himself into a corner. If Maltese is in fact unsuited to be a language of learning, he can hardly blame its speakers for not writing in it. If, on the other hand, they do write in it, they will have met his standard for having a proper language. In fact, as he well knew, local intellectuals had already produced books in Maltese, or about it. Although he says some very ungenerous things about those books, he must have understood that his bluff had been called.

What is most remarkable about these positions is not that al-Shidyāq held them—he was, after all, a lifelong contrarian—but that they may have helped form his view of Arabic. By way of background, we should note that, although he held strong views regarding usage, his career unfolded in a world where the notion of a strict diglossia between standard and spoken Arabic had not yet taken hold. In his most famous work, *Leg Over Leg* (1885), he mocks the Maronite priests who taught him as a child. Among the things he ridicules is their bad Arabic. "Your brains have been fed with incorrect and lame language from the days when you went to the *kuttāb*" (al-Shidyāq 1885, 1:1:19). This passage makes him seem like a nitpicking prescriptivist. But a bit further on in the same work he expresses his *frustration* with nitpicking prescriptivists: "Wherever you go," he tells the reader, "...you will find people who will criticize you for your way of speaking. Thus, if you use *wāw*, for example, they will say that *fā*ʾ is the more correct, and if you use *aw*, they will say that *am* is preferable, while in some countries, if you put dots below the letter *yāʾ* in the words *qāʾil* or *bāʾiʿ*, you will lose all respect in people's eyes" (al-Shidyāq 1885, 1.11.7).[6] Instead of worrying about matters of form and producing useless exercises in rhetoric, he suggests that the priests use Arabic to spread useful knowledge. If they really cared about the welfare of their congregations, "they would bestir themselves to establish a printing press… to print useful books, whether written originally in Arabic or translated into it…" (al-Shidyāq 1885, 1.1.15). In other words, he is telling speakers of Arabic to do the very same things he would urge the Maltese to do in the *Wāsiṭah*.

From these passages it is clear that al-Shidyāq, despite his nitpickiness about language, did not seek to enshrine correctness as an independent value. Rather, he demanded language be employed in a manner beneficial to its speakers. If writers use Arabic to convey useful information, its speakers will come to respect their language; and at that point, they can have a meaningful discussion of what is correct and what is not. His position, in a word, was that languages thrive not because they meet an abstract standard of correctness, but rather because of how they are used and whether speakers assign value to them. This view is

[6] *Wa-* is the word for 'and' in a merely additive sense, while *fa-* is used to express sequence, consequence, or change of subject. *Aw* means 'or' in the sense of 'and possibly also', while *am* implies that only one of the alternatives can be the case. The words *qāʾil* 'speaker' and *bāʾiʿ* 'vendor' are normatively pronounced with a glottal stop, but they are commonly pronounced and sometimes also written with the letter *yāʾ* instead, especially in older texts.

evidently the one that lies behind his promotion of a standard Arabic capable of addressing the conditions of modern life. Arguably, too, it was a position that he had come to adopt during his sojourn in Malta. For this reason, I would argue, his discussion of Maltese is of equal if not greater significance for the study of Arabic.

The present translation is based on the Istanbul edition of 1881 with the original page numbers given in brackets. Glosses supplied by the author are given in quotation marks, while those given by me appear in square brackets. I have identified the Arabic grammarians he cites but have not tracked down the original passages. Full bibliographical information on almost all of the works he cites may be found in the *Encyclopaedia of Islam*. The author gives his Maltese examples in Arabic script, with occasional mistakes. I have transcribed these into modern Maltese characters, retaining the mistakes. All dates are given according to the Gregorian calendar. Finally, I have tried to reproduce the author's style, including such features as rhyme.

Translation

[56] On the language of the people of Malta

May God guard you, dear reader, from error, and guide you aright in word and deed!

Now then: the Maltese language is a branch of the great tree of Arabic, or a spoiled fruit fallen from its cluster of dates. It is spoken on the islands of Malta and Gozo[7] by notable and commoner alike. The notables also learn Italian and English. The Italian they need for commercial and legal purposes, and the English they vie to acquire because it is spoken by their rulers. Maltese itself is not used for any scholarly purpose, nor has anything of note been written in it. Consisting of common expressions used to meet the needs of an abject life, it is inadequate to the composition of sermons or the production of ecphrastic and erotic verse. For such purposes, the Maltese have recourse to Italian. Their failure to retain any but the most debased elements of their language attests to their ignoble character.

When they take a word they need from Italian, they 'maltify' it by fitting it into the patterns of their language. For example, they say *ma jirnexxix* 'he did not succeed', and *konoxxejtu* 'I became aware of it'.[8] In the first example, *ji-* is the prefix of the imperfect and [57] *-x* is a negative suffix, derived from *shayʾ* '(not) anything', used also in the present-day spoken language of Egypt and Syria. In the second example, we have the first-person subject and third-person object markers.

The Maltese also say things like *għandi pjaċir* 'Pleased to meet you', literally 'I have pleasure', using the prepositional phrase as a fronted predicate and the indefinite noun as a postponed subject, just as in Arabic. Here are some verses of mine in response:

---

[7] Spelled *gh-w-d-sh*, suggesting that al-Shidyāq was hearing it pronounced with *ghayn*, as seems to be confirmed by his observation that "the Gozitans pronounce the gutturals properly" (see p. 93).

[8] I owe *konoxxejtu* to Cassar's translation (al-Shidyāq 1985, 83).

What a tongue: you can't read or write,
Like sails without the galleon!
Try to speak it: you might as well
Mount a bucking stallion.
Its head is Arabic, and so's the tail,
But the middle's all Italian!

'Head' and 'tail' here are figures of speech for the prefixes and suffixes, including the imperfect prefixes; the definite article; and the verbal suffix *-ūn*, all of which survive in a corrupt form. That is, the imperfect prefix and the definite article are always pronounced with the vowel *-i* while the verbal suffix *-ūn* is pronounced *-ū*.

A similar corruption is evident in the fact that, despite the survival of Arabic words, phrases, and structures, especially with regard to everyday topics, as noted above, the Maltese have lost the word *ab* (father). Instead they say *messier*, with *imālah* of the *alif*.[9] This is apparently a corruption of the French *monsieur*, which should be pronounced *monsyūr* [*sic*]. Similarly, they have lost the morning and evening greetings, saying instead *buongiorno għalik*. This phrase may have originated after the conquest of the island, when *al-salāmu ʿalaykum*, as in our part of the world, came to be used only by Muslims among themselves and so stopped being used by the locals. Such an occurrence would be no more surprising than the fact that the half-Arabs who assimilated themselves to the Arabs used different greetings than the true Arabs

---

[9] Since *monsieur* does not contain the sound /a/, much less an etymological *alif*, the author must mean the fronting and closing of /ø/ towards /i/.

did. The expression *ṣabāḥ al-khayr* (good morning), for example, is obviously a mongrel phrase.[10]

Oddly enough, some Maltese notables mimic the Franks in their dress and manner, such that when they speak their own language, it loses its particular charm and becomes difficult to understand. For every sentence they utter in their own language, they throw in a sentence of Italian. Acquired in childhood, this habit now dominates their speech. A certain Maltese scholar told me that while he was living in Italy, he would adjust his thoughts and ideas to the local language. After he returned, he reverted to his own language. To him applies the verse:

> Anyone's manner can be feigned for a time,
> But a man's true nature must show in the end.[11]

Even odder is the Maltese aversion to learning Arabic on account of its similarity to their own language—[58] even though that very similarity would help them acquire Arabic without effort. Many of Malta's trading partners speak Arabic and the islands are home to many speakers of the language. Yet no Maltese shows any interest in learning to read or write Arabic. The

---

[10] Half-Arabs (*muwalladūn*) are children born to Arab fathers and non-Arab mothers in the first generations after the Islamic conquests. The phrase touted today as the authentically Arab equivalent of 'Good morning' is *ʿimta ṣabāḥan* 'may you thrive in the morning!'.

[11] Al-Shidyāq's thinking seems muddled here: first he blames Maltese for retreating before Italian, but then he cites a verse implying that it is bound to reassert itself.

situation is quite different in Europe, where in every nation there are persons who study it seriously.[12]

As Maltese includes words from different languages, there is disagreement, as there always is among people whenever the facts are uncertain and the manner of inquiry erratic, regarding its classification. Some say it is Phoenician because it contains two Phoenician words: *bir* (well) and *sajd* (fishing), as noted at the beginning of this book. Others call it Ethiopic because it contains one word, namely *manbar,*[13] which supposedly means, as it does in Ethiopic, the chair on which a woman sits when giving birth. But this, as it turns out, is false, as I determined by asking speakers of that tongue.

In any event, it should be noted that many of the Arabic words that survive in Maltese derive their meanings by figurative extension, including substitution of cause for effect, of genus for species, or of species for genus. For example, from *waḥiltu* 'I got stuck in the mud', they derive *weħilt* 'I got into trouble'; and from *ṭalab* 'to seek', they derive the intensive participle *tallâb*, meaning 'beggar'. Similarly, *magħlub*, the passive participle of *ghalib* 'to overcome', means 'emaciated', because one who is emaciated is usually overcome by something; and from *fatt* 'to crumble' comes *ftit* 'a little'. There are many other examples, but there is no need to pile on evidence for the obvious.

---

12 Elsewhere, however, al-Shidyāq speaks with exasperation of the many solecisms committed by European scholars of Arabic: al-Shidyāq (1885, 5.3.1-5.5.25).

13 *Manbar* or *mambar*: Maltese for 'birthing chair' (cf. CA *minbar*, 'platform; pulpit').

Manbar, then, would be an example of a term used figuratively, that is, in a manner divergent from its original sense. The same sort of divergence occurs in pure Arabic as well. The base form *nabr* means 'to rise' and the derived form *minbar* means 'instrument or occasion of rising'. This latter term was then used by certain speakers to refer to a specific object, namely a pulpit, and by others to refer to another specific object, namely a birthing chair. The reason, by the way, for my saying 'instrument or occasion of rising' is that in his commentary on al-Ḥarīrī's *Durrat al-ghawwāṣ*, the Imam al-Khafājī writes:[14]

> This is an admirable instance of the difference between nouns referring to tools or instruments operated by hand, which, with a few exceptions, take *i* as the first vowel, as opposed to nouns which designate the instrument by which, as well as the place in which, the action occurs. In nouns of this second type, the first vowel is often *a*, e.g., *marqāh* [set of steps], and *manārah* [lighthouse or minaret]. This is a subtle distinction noticed, and taught, by very few scholars.

To sum up, then, there is no doubt about Maltese being Arabic. Even so, I cannot say whether it is a branch of the Levantine or of the Maghrebi family, as it contains expressions from both, with rather more from the latter. And yet the religious vocabulary comes from the Levant: for example, *quddies* [Mass], *qaddis* [saint], [59] *tqarben* [to take Communion], *isqof* [bishop], and so on, all unknown to the people of the Maghreb.

---

[14] The *Durrat al-ghawwāṣ* is a collection of solecisms compiled by al-Ḥarīrī (d. 1122) and commented on by Shihāb al-Dīn al-Khafājī (d. 1659).

There are Maltese who acknowledge that their language is neither Phoenician nor Ethiopic. Such, however, is their spite, that they will scarce confess that it comes from Arabic. It is well known that every language in the world admits words from foreign languages, either because it must borrow a word it lacks, or because its speakers lived near speakers of the other tongues and mingled with them. This is true of the Arabs and the Persians as well as the Greeks and Romans before them. Even Arabic, despite its vast range of vocabulary and its morphological profusion, contains borrowings from Persian, Greek, Amharic, Sanskrit, Syriac, and Hebrew. Yet no one claims that Arabic is derived from any of these! How, then, can the learned men of Malta declare that Maltese is Phoenician because it contains two words from that language?

Worse yet, the Maltese imagine that the corruption their language has suffered as it diverged from its Arabic source is nothing to be ashamed of. They draw a comparison with Italian, which broke away from Latin and developed its own forms, which are independent of their origins. But this argument fails because Arabic, unlike Latin, is still a living language. Maltese, with the paltry stock it has at its disposal, thus has no excuse for striking out on its own. Maltese, moreover, has never been the vehicle for scholarly or literary composition, nor is it widely spoken. The difference, then, is obvious. Yet the Maltese do not regard their language as corrupt nor do they perceive its ugliness. Indeed, how could they, having never surveyed the beauties of the parent from which it was torn?

Admittedly, the people of the Levant, Egypt, the Hijaz, and other places cannot speak Arabic properly either. The difference is that they admit it: all of them acknowledge the great difference between good and bad language, and all of them aspire to mastery of proper Arabic.

One day I was walking with a group of Maltese. One member of the company, speaking of his language, declared that its drawing in of elements from foreign tongues is one of its *virtues*, as if it had rummaged among all the alluring expressions in the world and chosen[15] the most splendid, like an old woman who catches her husband cheating on her.[16]

So bigoted are the Maltese against speakers of Arabic, and so eager to vilify them, that the most offensive epithet among them is 'Arab', as if the English, and European Christians generally, were more likely to learn Arabic than they are, despite the fact that knowing Maltese means knowing a good deal of Arabic already. This attitude is evident from what happens when a Maltese hears the Arabic word *kharaj* (to go out), which he has been pronouncing since infancy as *ħareġ*:[17] he insists that there is little

---

[15] The text seems to say *intafat*, which makes no sense; I am emending to *intaqat*.

[16] The (proverbial?) old woman is proud of her husband's infidelity because it proves his attractiveness and good taste, which, ironically, reflect well on her. Similarly, the author's interlocutor is proud that his language is so promiscuous. This seems to be the—somewhat strained—point of comparison.

[17] This means 'to go out' in Maltese as well, but is likely to be perceived as *ḥaraj* 'to embarrass' by speakers of Arabic.

difference between the two words, and obstinately refuses to see that the diacritical dot determines whether the word is rightly or wrongly understood. Someone who had learned to pronounce the word properly in the first place would not do this.

Overhearing me converse in Arabic, the Maltese would say, "There isn't much of a difference between our two languages except the accent" [60], by which they meant *my* accent. It never occurs to them that a language must be committed to writing and disciplined by grammar before it can satisfy the needs of its speakers.

At one point one of their authors[18] set himself the task of composing a grammar for the language. Having written an introduction, he drew up a Maltese *alfabeto*,[19] putting first *alif* and then *ʿayn*—an odd choice, as every other language whose alphabet begins with *alif* follows it immediately with *bāʾ*. When I saw this I wrote to him as follows:

> You with your *alfabeto*
> That puts *ʿayn* in second place:
> Small lies will lead to big ones,
> And your grammar's a disgrace.

It is said that all tongues, ancient and modern, begin with *alif*, except for Ethiopic, where it is the seventeenth letter. To judge

---

[18] Mikiel Anton Vassalli, 1764–1829, as is evident from the description of his alphabet. I thank Olvin Vella and Simon Mercieca for discussing this point with me.

[19] Al-Shidyāq uses the Italian term here, because Vassalli does (*alfabeto fonografico*: Vassalli 1827, 2), and because he will use it again in the verse below.

from the order of the letters in Arabic, Syriac, and Hebrew, the Arabic alphabet has nothing to do with the other two.

The Maltese pronounce the *ghayn*, but as *ʿayn*. The *khāʾ* comes out as *ḥāʾ*. The peasants pronounce *qāf* as a glottal stop. They also pronounce the *alif* in words like *qāl* and *bāʿ* with a colouring of *u*, which is striking, as the rabble of Greater Syria do the same. For *ḍād*, the Maltese say *dāl*; and for *ṭāʾ*, *tāʾ*. When an *ʿayn* falls at the beginning or the end of a word, they do not pronounce it at all, saying, for example, *tela'* instead of *ṭalaʿ*, and *sema'* for *samiʿ*. In former times, they reportedly gave *thāʾ* its proper pronunciation.

Hilariously, when the peasants go to work for the people of Valletta, they change their manner of speaking: they pronounce the *ghayn* as *ʿayn* and the *khāʾ* as a *ḥāʾ*, on the assumption that the speech of Valletta is more proper (*hiya l-fuṣḥā*). The people of Gozo pronounce the *alif* in words like *fīhā* and *minhā* as *ē*. All Maltese pronounce the *jīm* in the Levantine manner[20] except in the word *gidi* [baby goat], in which they give it the Egyptian sound.[21] It would seem that the correct pronunciation is close to *sh*, as in the Levantine dialects. Al-Suyūṭī's *Muzhir*, quoting Bahāʾ al-Dīn's *ʿArūs al-afrāḥ* on correct pronunciation,[22] reads as follows (Section 9, item 5):

---

[20] That is, [ʒ], though the actual (present-day) pronunciation is [d͡ʒ].

[21] That is, [g]. Another exception is *gżira* 'island', pl. *gżejjer*.

[22] The *ʿArūs al-afrāḥ*, by Bahāʾ al-Dīn al-Subkī (d. 1371-72), is a commentary on al-Qazwīnī's *Talkhīṣ al-miftāḥ*, an epitome of al-Sakkākī's foundational work on rhetoric. The *Muzhir fī ʿulūm al-lughah* by al-Suyūṭī (d. 1505) is a compilation of opinions on linguistic issues.

> It is said that an awkward cluster occurs when the sounds of a word are articulated too far *or* too close to one another, such that saying the word is like cavorting with fetters on one's legs. Al-Khafājī's *Sirr al-faṣāḥah* quotes al-Khalīl ibn Aḥmad[23] to this effect, but then adds that there are words made up of similar sounds that cause no awkwardness, like *shajar* [tree], *jaysh* [army], and *fam* [mouth], along with words made up of dissimilar sounds that do not cause it either, like *ʿilm* [knowledge] and *buʿd* [distance]. Al-Khafājī concludes that dissimiliarity, no matter how extreme, does not cause awkwardness; rather, it is a condition of euphony.

In his discussion of environmentally conditioned sound changes (*ibdāl*), al-Ashmūnī[24] notes:

> The *shīn* may replace *kāf*, *jīm*, or *sīn*. The word *akramtik* [I honored you], for example, may be pronounced *akramtish*; this is called the *kashkashah* of the Tamīm tribe, as explained above. The word *mudmij* may come out as *mudmish*, as in the saying *ḥablu l-wiṣāl mudmish* [the rope of good fellowship is firmly twined]. Ibn ʿAṣfūr says that this is the only known example. The cause [61] is that *jīm* and *shīn* have proximate points of articulation.

I would note, however, that the *jīm* frequently takes the place of *qāf* and *kāf*, which makes the Egyptian pronunciation more likely. Examples with *qāf* include *qaffa* / *jaffa* [to dry up], said of grass; *miqdhāf* / *mijdāf* [oar]; *qalamuh* / *jamaluh* [he

---

[23] Al-Khalīl was a seventh-century founder of the Arabic grammatical tradition.

[24] Unidentified.

trimmed it]; *qashama / jashama* [?];[25] *shaqqa / shajja* [to split]; *qirqis / jirjis* [gnat]; *qaṣṣa / jazza* [to shear]; *talaqqafa / talajjafa* [to enlarge] (of a cistern); *sharq / sharj* [fissure]; and many others. Examples with *kāf* include *kadda / jadda* [to be assiduous]; *kuhd / juhd* [exertion]; *akinn / ajinn* [?];[26] *karaʿa / jaraʿa* [to swallow]; *kalabah / jalabah* [vicissitude](of fate); *mukālaḥah / mujālaḥah* [to vie in strength with]; *ʿakara / ʿajara (bihi)* [to turn something?]; *riks / rijs* [filth]; and the like. On this view, the Egyptian pronunciation of *jīm* is acceptable.

Supporting this contention is the *Muzhir*, which reports (Section 14) that "unused forms are of two kinds, of which the first contains sounds that cannot be combined in Arabic under any circumstances, like *jīm* and *kāf*, including putting a *kāf* before a *jīm*, or *ʿayn* and *ghayn*, or *ḥāʾ* and *hāʾ*." When adopting foreign words, Arabs sometimes use *jīm* and sometimes *qāf*.[27] For example, you have *dīzaj* [black][28] and *nīranj* [conjuration], but also *rustāq* [district] and *farazdaq* [piece of bread]. Some words have several variants produced by changing two sounds at once, e.g.

---

[25] The verbs *qashama* and *jashama* are attested in various senses but have no obvious meaning in common. *Jashama* may simply be a variant pronunciation of *qashama*, which means (among other things) to pick out the best bits of something, e.g., food. Cassar (al-Shidyāq 1985, 89) leaves the pair untranslated.

[26] So vocalised as nouns, these forms are not attested; but the verbs *akanna* and *ajanna* both mean 'to hide'. Cassar (al-Shidyāq 1985, 89) has *niġġennen* 'I go mad', which presumes the vowelling *ukann* and *ujann*.

[27] Specifically, when adopting Middle Persian words ending in č and g.

[28] So according to Dehkhodā's *Lughatnāmeh*, but not attested in Ibn Manẓūr's *Lisān al-ʿArab* or al-Jawālīqī's *Muʿarrab*.

sahjah, sahkah, and *saḥqah* [a pounding; a blowing away]. In my view, these are dialectal variations. At any rate, Upper Egyptians, North Africans, and Ḥijāzīs all pronounce the *jīm* in the Levantine manner.

The Gozitans pronounce the gutturals properly. Yet they give a coloring of *i* to the long vowel *ū*, saying *miksiwr* [broken] and *miftiwḥ* [open]. They furthermore give a coloring of *u* to the *alif*, saying, for example, *qawʿid* [= *qiegħed* 'placed' or 'present']. They also say *minnkim* [from you] and *ʿalaykim* [for you] with *-kim* for *-kum*, in the manner of the tribe of Rabīʿah and some members of Kalb, as explained in *al-Muzhir*, section 11; this is called *wakm*. And they say *minnhim* [from them] and *bejnhim* [among them], which is also characteristic of Kalb.

Some of the Maltese are foolish enough to claim that they write poetry in this corrupted language of theirs. They call it *taqbil*, and here is an example of it:

Jien, ħanini,[29] sejjer insiefer,
Sejjer insiefer ma nieħdokx miegħi;[30]
Mur u ejja[31] bis-sliema
Alla jżommok fl-imħabba tiegħi.[32]

These shudder-inducing forms call for some explanation.

Jien means *ana* 'I'.

---

[29] Spelled *ḥanīnī*. Cassar (al-Shidyāq 1985, 90) has *ħanina*.

[30] Spelled *maʿī* here but MYʿY (that is, *miegħi*) in the gloss that follows.

[31] Spelled W-HYĀ.

[32] 'My dear, I am soon to depart / Soon to depart, and leave without you. // Go and return safely, and may God keep you in my affection.'

Ħanini means 'beloved', in the vocative without a vocative particle. One oddity of this language is that when one addresses a great figure, one takes the vocative particle from Italian, saying, for example, *o muley* 'O Lord'; but when one addresses some humble object, one uses the Arabic particle, as in *ja tuffieħ* [hey apple] or *ja għeneb* [hey grapes].

Sejjer insiefer is like the Egyptian and Levantine colloquial *rāyiḥ asāfir* 'I'm about to go away'. (In his commentary on the *Lāmiyat al-ʿArab*, al-Zamakhsharī[33] elegantly defines the future tense as referring to an event "non-existent in the present but on its way to becoming real.") [62] The *n-* prefix in *insiefer* indicates the first-person singular, not the plural, which would be *insiefru*, as in North African Arabic.

The *shīn* suffix in *nieħdokx* [not take you] is obligatory in negative and interrogative sentences, as in North African Arabic. Some speakers of Levantine Arabic feel it is needed as well, even at the end of a sentence, and so say things like *mā huwa ktīr-sh* [there isn't much] with the *shīn* cropping up as if it were absolutely necessary.

Miegħi comes from *maʿī* [with me].

Mur is the imperative of *mar* 'to go', which is a proper Arabic word.[34]

Ejja is a verbal noun meaning 'Come over here'. The Arabic equivalent *hay[y]ā* appears many times in the *Qāmūs*,[35] which

---

[33] Jār Allāh al-Zamakhsharī, d. 1144; the commentary is *Aʿjab al-ʿajab*.

[34] The relatively uncommon Arabic verb *mār* is more precisely 'to move from side to side'.

[35] *Al-Qāmūs al-muḥīṭ*, by al-Fīrūzābādī (d. 1415).

explains it as a warning or rebuke. It is an odd word which may derive from *ḥayya* [come!]. This reminds me of the comical story of the desert Arab who heard one man say to another, in Persian, "*Zud!*" and asked his companions what it meant. They said, "It means 'Hurry!'" He replied, "Why doesn't he say *ḥayyun halak*?" producing a clever riddle.[36]

In *jżommok* [keep you], the verb *żamm* comes from *zamm* [to tighten] or *ḍamm* [to hold close]. One beautiful vestige of Arabic to have survived in this place is that the vowel of the object suffix is *u*.[37]

The *-ba* in the word *imħabba* 'affection' is actually pronounced *ba*, as it is in all words bearing the feminine suffix *-a*, e.g., *tajba* and *kbira*. This pronunciation is also a vestige, and it is more beautiful than *e*.[38]

---

[36] This seems to be a riddle of the *uḥjiyyah* type, meaning that each word of the original expression is replaced with a synonym and the result is re-chunked and re-vocalised to produce a new expression. In this case, a possible solution is to replace *ḥayya* ('come') and *halak* ('has perished') with *hayyā* and *māt*, then re-chunk and re-vocalise as *huyyāmun āt*, 'a madman is coming'. Cassar (al-Shidyāq 1985, 90) reads Persian *zūd* as Arabic *zawwid* and translates the rest literally without explaining the riddle.

[37] Al-Shidyāq mistakes the *-u* for a survival of the imperfect indicative suffix. In reality, it is the result of vowel harmony (*e* > *u* conditioned by the *u* of the verb).

[38] That is, than the *imālah* characteristic of some Levantine dialects, in which, for example, *ṭayba* is pronounced *ṭaybe*.

As for *tiegħi*, even their most discerning speakers make a hash of it: they insert, between the two parts of a possessive construction, the sound *tā*, saying, for example, *id-dar tat-tabib* [the doctor's house]. Some of them claim this comes from Italian, where the possessed and the possessor are separated by the particle *di* [of]. Others say it comes from Syriac, which has the same feature. When *tā* takes a pronoun suffix, the *ʿayn* reappears, as in *tagħna*. For this reason,[39] they fail to perceive that the word is a distortion of *matāʿ* 'property'. The same word appears frequently in possessive constructions in North African Arabic, whose speakers drop the initial vowel in keeping with their habit of using word-initial consonant clusters and of abbreviating words. Some even say *ntāʿ*. As for the *ʿayn*, it is hardly pronounced in word-final position, giving, for example, *tela'* [rise] and *qala'* [pull out] instead of *talaʿ* and *qalaʿ*, as noted above. They also drop the *ʿayn* when a pronoun suffix is attached, as in *tlajt* [I rose] and *qlajt* [I pulled out], just as they drop it without the suffix. Pronouncing *ʿayn* as *ā* or as a glottal stop is something Arabs do too, as in *tafaṣṣā* / *tafaṣṣaʿ* [to be pulled free of its skin], *aqnā* / *aqnaʿa* [to enrich; to satisfy]; *al-shamā* / *al-shamaʿ* [wax]; *takaʾkaʾ* / *takaʿkaʿ* [to shrink back]; *zakāʾ* / *zuqāʿ* [to crow] (of a rooster); *zaʾzaʾ* / *zaʿzaʿ* meaning 'to move'; *badaʾ* / *badaʿ* [to initiate], *khabʾah* and *khabʿah*, meaning 'a woman who sometimes conceals herself and sometimes reveals herself'; *khibāʾ* / *khibāʿ* [hiding place]; *khabʾ* / *khabʿ* [something hidden], and many other cases. They even replace medial *ʿayn*, as in *taʾarraḍa* / *taʿarraḍa* [to turn one's side

[39] That is, the disappearance of the *ʿayn* in many cases.

to] and *daʾama* [to prop up] (a wall) / *daʿm*. As for the softening of the glottal stop into the vowel *ā*, it happens too often to require proof. [63] *Mitāʿ* is also mangled by the people of Egypt, who change it to *bitāʿ*. As noted in *Durrat al-ghawāṣṣ*, this variant exists among the Arabs too: they say *bā smuk* instead of *mā smuk* [What is your name?]. Note, also, that the analytic possessive construction is good style because it disambiguates constructs where the adjective might refer to possessor as well as possessed, e.g., *ʿadhābu l-Lāhi l-ʿaẓīm* [God's great torment[40]], which would be clearer if there a particle instead of a construct were used, though when in doubt the default should be to the thing possessed, as stated in the *Mughnī*.[41]

Another example of Maltese versification is the following example, in which the idea is clever even though the prosody is wrong,[42] the diction foul, and the structure flawed:

Il-maħbub ta' qalbi siefer
Lejli u nhari nibkih
Ġegħeltlu bi-dmugħi l-baħar
U bit-tnehidat ta' qalbi r-riħ.[43]

This resembles the verse of Lisān al-Dīn al-Khaṭīb [d. 1375]:

---

[40] Either the one He inflicts on sinners or the one He himself suffers.

[41] *Mughnī al-labīb*, a treatise on syntax by Ibn Hishām (d. 1360).

[42] Reading *maksūr* for *MKSW*.

[43] 'My heart's beloved has departed / I weep for him all day and night. // With my tears I make for him a sea // and with the sighs of my heart, the wind.'

The flanks of the sea throb for you;
The wind draws in its breath and expels a sigh.

And this line, by al-Qāḍī al-Fāḍil [d. 1200]:

As if my flanks, and sighs, and tears
Were hillsides thrashed by winds and floods.

Or this one, by Ibrāhīm ibn Sahl of Seville [d. 1251]:

Greeting riders from where she dwelt,
The flame of her longing lights the fire,
And her tears supply the proffered draught.

Or ʿAlī ibn Ẓāfir's [d. 1216 or 1226] line from *Badāʾiʿ al-badāʾih*: "Her sail is my heart and her sea, my tears."

But let us finish correcting those corrupt expressions.

Ta', as explained above, comes between the two parts of a nominal construct.

In *nibkih*, the *hāʾ* is pronounced *ḥāʾ*. Using the one for the other is an Arabic dialect feature as well, as in *malīh / malīḥ* [salty]; *hāḍūm / ḥāḍūm* [digestible]*; madh / madḥ* [praise]*; tāha / tāḥa* [to lose one's way]; and *shaqqah / shaqqaḥ* [to redden, said of the dates] (of a palm tree).[44]

Al-baħar: with a second *fatḥah*, in accordance with the principle that nouns derived from triliteral roots with a pharyngeal consonant in the second position may take an additional *fatḥah*,

[44] These Arabic examples involve root letters, while the Maltese word in this case is a pronoun suffix.

as in *shaʿr / shaʿar* [hair] and *nahr / nahar* [river]. In his commentary on *Durrat al-ghawwāṣ*, al-Khafājī cites Ibn Jinnī's *Muḥtasib*[45] as follows:

> Suhayl ibn Shuʿayb al-Sahmī read *jaharah* [loud voice] and *zaharah* [flower] with *fatḥahs* throughout. The members of our school prefer a *sukūn* after the combination *fatḥah* plus consonant, admitting, however, that the other pronunciation is an attested variant, as in *nahr / nahar* [river] and *shaʿr / shaʿar* [hair]. This seems to be the correct view.

The following verses were once recited for me at a gathering:

Jiena xtaqt niġi fuq soddtok
Niġi xbieha ta' għasfur
Nitfi l-misbieħ bi-ġwinħajja
Fa[46]-nagħtik bewsa u nerġa' mmur

[64] I told the poet that it would be better to say 'take a kiss', since in that context it is better to take than to give. Puzzled, he asked me to explain the point again, but neither he nor anyone else understood me the second time either. The art of elaborating and topping poetic conceits is in a sorry state indeed.[47]

By *sodda* the Maltese mean 'bed'. In proper Arabic it means 'door of a house'. To me this suggests that the ancestors of the

---

[45] An obscure work by Ibn Jinnī (d. 1002), a grammarian.

[46] Apparently an error for *u* 'and'. The Arabic conjunction *fa-* does not exist in (present-day) Maltese.

[47] Al-Shidyāq seems to be urging the poet to adopt the Arabic device of *murāʿāt al-naẓir*, allowing the choice of words in one place to dictate the collocation needed to extend the figure or conceit.

Maltese were louts who slept in doorways and so applied the name ‘door’ to any sleeping place. Similarly, they call any kind of broom a *mselħa*, a word that originally referred to a tool used for skinning,[48] which is what it originally meant in Maltese but then was applied to anything used to clean a place. There are many similar examples. Nevertheless, in Tripoli, Lebanon, *sodda* is also used for ‘bed’.

I once mentioned to a Maltese who seemed to have a feel for literary matters that Arabic has a great capacity for formal embellishment, including puns. He replied that the same was true of Maltese, citing this sentence: *Għandek ittina tal-laħam. Ittina,* he said, could be the imperfect of *tajtu,* that is, of *ātaytuhu* (I brought him) or *aʿṭaytu* (I gave him). *Tal-laḥam* could mean ‘relating to meat’, referring, for example, to its price. *Għandek* here would be hortatory.[49] In the second meaning, *it-tina* means ‘date’ (the fruit) and is in construct with *tal-laħam,* so the sentence means ‘You have a date of flesh’, an indirect reference to the buttocks.

Their use of *għand* to express necessity, especially with verbs, has no analogue [in other forms of Arabic].

Another one of their vapid puns is *għallieh min għajr ilma* [he boiled it without water], because *għallieh* also means ‘he raised its price’.

---

[48] Here the Arabic text has *salḥ* ‘defecation’, apparently an error for *salkh* ‘skinning’. The two roots have merged in Maltese but are distinct in Arabic.

[49] The meaning of the whole expression would thus be something like ‘You need to give me the [price] of the meat’.

Another survival of proper Arabic is *dar neidja* [a damp house]. The correct form is *nadiyyah*, but the Maltese is still preferable to the *nāṭyah* used in Egypt and the Levant.[50]

Other survivals are *qabla* [*qābilah*], meaning 'midwife'; *ħ*t*r* [?][51] and *mħatra* [*mukhāṭarah*] 'wager'; *għorfa* [*ghurfah*] 'upper room'; *għammru u tammru* [*ʿammarū wa-thammarū*] 'may they live together and be fruitful', as a wish;[52] *bdieli* [*badā lī*] 'it occurred to me';[53] *ittawwal* [*taṭāwal*] 'look out'; *jixref* [*yushrif*] 'look out, look down'; *sadid* [*ṣadid*] 'rust; blight; mildew'; *bitħa* [*baṭḥāʾ*] 'courtyard'; *iġġieldu* [*tajāladū*] 'they fought', which is more correct than *taʿārakū*; *żifen [zafana]*, meaning 'to dance'; *buqal* [*būqāl*] 'drinking pot, jug', which is more correct than the Levantine *sh*rbah* or *nāʿ[ʿ]ārah*; *imieri* [*yumārī*] 'to contradict'; *xeraq*

---

[50] *Niedi* appears in Aquilina (1987, 908) and *nadiyy* in the standard Arabic dictionaries. Hinds and Badawi's Egyptian Arabic dictionary has *nādya* but not *nāṭya* (Badawi and Hinds 1987, 856). All the attested forms mean 'moist'. I have not found any instances in collocation with *dar* 'house', but I assume in that case the term would mean 'damp'.

[51] It is unclear which Arabic and Maltese words al-Shidyāq has in mind. Maltese *ħater* means 'to wager' but *khaṭar* in Arabic does not. Arabic *khiṭra* 'a stake in a horse race', corresponds in form and meaning with the Maltese word *ħatra* 'wager', but al-Shidyāq's word has no feminine ending.

[52] Aquilina (1987, 960) translates it as a perfect ('they lived together…' etc.) and calls it a phrase "occurring in some M[altese] folktales." Arabic *ʿammar* means 'furnish' or 'cause to thrive', and *taʿammar*, though unattested in dictionaries, would be its passive. In standard Arabic, the perfect and optative forms coincide.

[53] The Maltese and the Arabic actually mean 'I changed my mind'.

[*shariq*] 'to choke'; *staqsa* [*istaqṣā*] 'to ask'; *FRṢĀD*[54] [*firṣād*] 'mulberries'; *seffud* [*saffūd*] 'skewer', which the Levantines call *sīkh* or *shīsh*, and which appears in a line by al-Nābighah: "...a skewer forgotten by drinkers in the fire-pit;" *tqażżeż* [*taqazzaz*] 'to shun filth';[55] *għasluġ* [*ghaṣlūj*] 'a stick'; and *ġellewż* [*jillawz*] 'hazelnuts'. Yet all of these words are used in the West, which leads me to believe that the Maltese people came from North Africa.

Another such feature is the occasional appearance of the *u*-vowel in the suffix of the imperfect, as in ?*jaħsbok* and ?*jibdlok*.[56]

Another is the use of *wegħda* 'promise' and *wiżna*[57] 'weight', nouns derived from *wegħed* and *wiżen* respectively, and which, because they are not verbal nouns, retain their first consonant.[58] A similar thing happens in this line by the *Ḥamāsah*-poet:

> [65] If he returns from a journey [*min wijhatin*]
> carrying treasure
> I never go poking around behind his tent.

The commentator notes that the variant *min wajhihi* is also attested. Either way, the word means 'the journey he set out on'. The second hemistich is also attested with *mādhā* for *mimmā*. The

---

[54] I have not found this attested as a Maltese word, and Cassar does not suggest one.

[55] Both words are defined as 'to be disgusted or nauseated'.

[56] The expected forms are *jaħsbek* and *jibdlek*, both attested in the Korpus Malti. Cassar (al-Shidyāq 1985, 95) has *jaħsbuk* and *jibdluk*, which are plural forms—not what al-Shidyāq has in mind.

[57] The original says *wa-zinah*; emend to *wa-wiznah*.

[58] The standard forms of these words are *ʿidah* and *zinah*, from the roots WʿD and WZN.

line means 'I don't impose myself on him hoping to sniff out whatever he brought back so that he'll split it with me'.

Among their risible expressions is 'a man dog' and 'a woman donkey', meaning the male and female respectively, since they have no special term for these animals and so have to convey the idea using an awful paraphrase.[59]

'To do one's beard' [*għamel il-leħjaħ*] means 'to shave one's face' and 'to shave one's pubic hair'.

When one of them explains something to another, he says *jien inkellmek bil-Malti*, as if to say that he has expressed himself so clearly that his hearer cannot possibly misunderstand him.

They make frequent use of *qalli* 'he said to me', dropping it in repeatedly as they speak.

When they want to affirm some proposition, they will repeat the key word five or more times, saying, for example, *Ma rajtux* [*sic*] *qatt qatt qatt qatt qatt* [I haven't seen him at all, at all, at all, at all, at all];[60] or *ma kellix flus ħlief da biżż biżż biżż biżż biżż* [*sic*] [61] [I had no money except for this only only only only only],

---

[59] Maltese does have separate words for many masculine and feminine animals, but al-Shidyāq is right that "in the case of animals when there are no specific gender-designations, gender can be expressed by the words *raġel* 'male' or *mara* 'female' placed after the name of the animal" (Aquilina 1965, 55).

[60] Al-Shidyāq seems to have mis-remembered or mis-invented this sentence, as the *-x* suffix should drop when a negative complement (in this case, *qatt*) follows. In the last example in this series, he gets it right.

[61] Al-Shidyaq writes Maltese *biss* with a *ż* even though he writes the Arabic cognate with an *s*. As it happens, **biżż* would be pronounced *biss* because of final devoicing, but it still seems odd to spell it that way.

with *bizz* meaning *bass* 'only'; or *ħadu kollu kollu kollu kollu kollu* [He took all of it, all of it, all of it, all of it, all of it]; or *ma jiswa xej' xej' xej' xej' xej'* [it's not worth anything, anything, anything, anything, anything];[62] and so on.

They have their own morphological patterns, including *fāʿilah* used as a verbal noun. They say, for example, *għamiltu bil-wieqfa* 'I did it while standing' or *bil-qiegħda* '...while sitting'. According to the commentator on the *Shāfiyah*,[63]

> the verbal noun takes the form *fāʿilah* even less frequently than it takes the form *mafʿūl*. Examples include *ʿāfiyah* 'robust health', as in *ʿāfāhu l-Lāhu ʿāfiyah* 'God cured him completely'; *ʿāqibah* 'succession', as in *ʿaqaba Fulānu makāna abīhi ʿāqibah* 'he took his father's place'; *bāqiyah*, as in the verse *hal tarā lahum min bāqiyah* 'Do you see any remnant of them?';[64] and *kādhibah* 'denial', as in the verse *laysa li-waqʿatihā kādhibah*, 'There is no denying it will come to pass'.[65]

Speakers of Levantine, similarly, say *yiṭlaʿ biṭ-ṭāliʿ* 'go up', and *yinzil bin-nāzil* 'go down'.

---

[62] Al-Shidyāq writes the repeated word as *SHY*, by which he may mean *xi* 'thing', but since *xi* would be ungrammatical here, I assume he is transcribing *xej'*, a common variant of *xejn* 'nothing'.

[63] The *Shāfiyah* is a work on morphology by Ibn al-Ḥājib (d. 1249) and the commentary on it is by Raḍī al-Dīn al-Astarābādhī (d. c. 1285).

[64] Quran 69:8, referring to the tribe of ʿĀd, whom God punished with a mighty wind.

[65] Quran 56:2.

Another odd form is the pattern *fuʿul,* as in *sodod* [beds] and *soror* [bundles], which is rare.[66] Nouns containing three consonants[67] whose first vowel is *u* take *u* as the second vowel also, as in *għomor* and *xogħol.* This feature is based on a solid analogy. Nouns whose first vowel is *i,* similarly, take *i* in the next syllable, like *ʿij[i]l* [calf] and *rij[i]l* [foot].[68]

One of the bad habits they share with European Christians is using, without apology, expressions that might hurt the listener's feelings, or describe him as suffering some misfortune. For example, they might say, "I'll love you as long as you live," or "This heat can kill you," or "This plant will shred your guts" (*msaren,* meaning *maṣārīn* 'intestines'), or "This dust can blind you," or "When you die, the doctor will come and slice your limbs up one by one," or, when visiting a sick person, "Don't neglect your condition, because it can be fatal." In all these cases, one should instead speak in general terms. Did not the Prince of Eloquence[69] say "Love blinds and deafens," not "Love blinds and deafens *you,*" even though that is what he meant?

The tonality of their speech, or what the Franks call *emphasis* [*imfāzis*], will surprise anyone unaccustomed to it. They have

---

[66] Al-Shidyāq evidently means words of pattern *FʿL* where the second and third consonants are the same.

[67] Reading *thulāthiyyah* for *thalāthah.*

[68] Al-Shidyāq is speaking here of Arabic, where words of the pattern *FiʿL* may also take the form *FiʿiL.* The corresponding Maltese words are *għoġol* and *riġl.*

[69] The Prophet Muḥammad.

a way of drawing out [66] and lowering their voices that is unfamiliar to Arabic speakers. As if by contagion, the English born in Malta do this even when speaking their own language. This sort of thing may be a requisite for eloquence among the Franks, but not the way the Maltese do it, which is excessive. It does not seem to have a name in Arabic, except perhaps *lahjah* [way of speaking]. When a sheikh who is reading aloud comes across a passage he does not immediately understand, he might draw out his voice as he mulls over the difficulty. The Maltese intonation sounds something like that.

Another risible feature of their language is the way they repeat the word *smajtx* [Haven't you heard?], a corruption of *samiʿt* 'you heard' with the *-sh* suffix used as an interrogative, similar to the way it appears in negative constructions. The English, hearing them use this expression so often, have taken to using it to call people whose names they don't know, or to summon the boys who wait on them at table.

The survival of Arabic on the Maltese islands, albeit in a distorted form, and without being committed to writing, demonstrates the power of its hold over those peoples whom it reaches. Has Malta not witnessed a succession of rulers who sought to force its inhabitants to speak other languages? None have succeeded: generation after generation, the Maltese have clung to what Arabic they know. Although the English claim that their language will one day dominate all others, they have failed to spread it among the Maltese. The elite, admittedly, learn English, but with the awkwardness of late acquisition; among themselves they speak only Maltese.

It is said that the number of Arabic words, common or rare, used by the people of Malta amounts to some ten thousand. Note, however, that this estimate is based on counting words in the Frankish manner, that is, counting all the derived forms—active and passive participles, nouns of instrument, relative adjectives, and the like—as separate words. If, on the other hand, there were that many *roots*, that number would suffice to express the sorts of things one needs to say in conversation, though it would not be adequate for written composition. I imagine that the number of words used today in Egypt and Greater Syria is no greater, though the Syrians seem to have a wider vocabulary while the Egyptians express themselves better. But God alone knows best.

References

Agius, D.A. 1989–1990. 'Arabic Under Shidyaq in Malta, 1833–1848'. *Journal of Maltese Studies* 19–20: 52–57.

al-Shidyāq, Aḥmad Fāris. 2013 [1885]. الساق على الساق: *Leg over Leg*. Translated by Humphrey Davies. New York: New York University Press. (References to this work are by paragraph numbers, which are the same across the bilingual and English-only editions.)

———. 1985. *El-Wasita: Tagħrif dwar Malta tas-Seklu 19*. Translated by Francis Xavier Cassar. Malta: Ċentru Kulturali Islamiku f' Malta.

———. 1881. الواسطة في معرفة أحوال مالطة. Istanbul: Al-Jawāʾib.

Aquilina, Joseph. 1965. *Teach Yourself Maltese*. London: Hodder and Stoughton. Reprint, 1987.

———. 1987. *Maltese-English Dictionary*. Malta: Midsea.

Badawi, El-Said, and Martin Hinds. 1989. *A Dictionary of Egyptian Arabic: Arabic–English.* Beirut: Librairie du Liban.

Bou Ali, Nadia. 2012. 'In the Hall of Mirrors: The Arab Nahḍa, Nationalism, and the Question of Language'. Ph.D. dissertation, University of Oxford.

Cachia, Pierre. 1962. 'An Arab's View of XIX-C. Malta'. *Maltese Folklore Review* 1 (1): 62–69; 1 (2): 110–16; 1 (3): 232–43.

Cassar, Carmel. 2011. 'Malta and the Study of Arabic in the Sixteenth to the Nineteenth Centuries'. *Turkish Historical Review* 2: 125–54.

Cooperson, Michael. 2017. 'The Abbasid "Golden Age": An Excavation'. *Al-Uṣūr al-Wusṭā* 25: 41-65.

Mercieca, Simon. Forthcoming. 'Malta and Fāris al-Shidyāq's Political Thoughts: A Mazzinian Connection'.

Roper, Geoffrey. 1988. 'Arabic Printing in Malta, 1825–1845'. Ph.D. dissertation, University of Durham.

Vassalli, Michelantonio. 1827. *Grammatica della lingua maltese.* 2nd ed. Malta: stampata per l'autore.

ON THE ARABIC DIALECT OF THE JEWS OF QĀMIŠLI (NORTH-EAST SYRIA)

Aharon Geva-Kleinberger

1.0. Initial Research Information

In 1989, Otto Jastrow wrote an important article on the dialect of the Jews of Qāmišli. This article provided preliminary data on the dialect of this community, which originated in Nuṣaybin/Turkey. It belongs to the Arabic *Qəltu* group, which is widespread in Turkey.

In 2012, I began to conduct dialectological fieldwork among the Jews of this community, especially in Haifa and Kiryat Ata, north of Haifa,[1] where there is also a synagogue of the community where, in May 2013, I attended a yearly ceremony dedicated to Rabbi Yehuda Ben Batira. In the same month, I gave a lecture at a symposium held at the Mardin Artuklu University (Geva-Kleinberger 2013).[2] As part of this symposium, I had the opportunity to visit the City of Nuṣaybin on the border with Turkey—where the Syrian city of Qāmišli lies directly on the other side—and caught a swift glimpse of this city shortly before the

[1] There is also a relatively large community of Qāmišli Jews in the neighbourhood of Gilo in Jerusalem.

[2] My lecture was given in Arabic.

 https://doi.org/10.11647/OBP.0445.05

civil war in Syria began. About three years later, I began to supervise an MA study by my student Yehuda Tzuberi on the lexicon of the Jews of this community (Tzuberi 2020).

2.0. Short Historical Background

The Jews of Qāmišli (*Qāmišlo* in their own dialect; Avery and Bezmez n.d., 394–96) originate from the city of Nuṣaybin. Two hundred years earlier, some of them came as part of a wave of immigration to Nuṣaybin from Iraq, Kurdistan, Mardin, Diyarbakır, and Urfa (Turkish: Šanlıurfa), but others had already settled there after the destruction of the Second Temple, when a number of Tana'aim,[3] including Rabbi Batīra,[4] settled there. In the city of Qāmišli, there were also Assyrian Christians, Kurds, and Muslims. While the everyday language of the Jews was Arabic, the elderly spoke Kurmanji Kurdish and Turkish. The Jews used to live in *Ḥārt el-Yahūd* (= The Jewish Quarter), which was near to the Muslim Quarter.

In 1924, the French mandate in Syria built army camps in northern Syria in areas taken from Turkey. These lands were then given away free of charge on one condition: the recipient had to open a shop or build a house there. Soon the city's population reached approximately 10,000 persons. Among them were many Jews, mostly tobacco traders and textile shop owners. The com-

[3] Hebrew: תנאים 'repeaters', 'teachers' were the rabbinic sages active from approximately 10–220 CE whose views are recorded in the Mishnah.

[4] An eminent *Tanna* in Nsibis (= Nuṣaybin).

munity had a central synagogue which served as a spiritual centre. In the late 1930s, the population reached some 3,000 persons. However, after the Six-Day War in 1967, most of them left the city. Only 150 remained and most of them emigrated to Israel in the eighties and nineties of the last century.

Between the Six-Day War in 1967 and 1975, a curfew was imposed on the Jews of the city, in addition to a travel ban inside and outside Syria, causing a lack of contact between the different Jewish communities in Syria. The Jews of the Qāmišli and Aleppo Jewish communities tried repeatedly to escape from Syria through the Turkish border. Many of them failed and were arrested and tortured. At the same time, it should be noted that there were very good relations between the Jews and their neighbours from the other different communities of the city, and any problems were usually with Syrian Intelligence.

Since the establishment of the State of Israel in 1948, the Jews of the city suffered repeated antisemitic and political bullying and many were thrown into jail, especially after attempting to cross the Turkish border with the aim of reaching Israel, and some Qāmišli Jews were even killed or tortured after trying to flee. Generally, the Jews of the community described their life there as very difficult, not only from a security point of view but also economically, as most of the families in the community were poor. There was no Jewish school in Qāmišli and boys were sent to learn in the Christian school *Madras(a)t elKildaniyye.* Jews were able to learn Hebrew until 1967, when this was abolished by the authorities.

In Qāmišli, most of the Jews were merchants and pedlars, and many had clothing and fabric shops. According to my informants, among the famous rabbis of the Qāmišli community were the late rabbis Ishāq Mordechāy and Nissīm Brahīmo. One of the more recent rabbis of the community was Rabbi Ḥăxām Nisān Barūx, who also used to teach the Jewish children; a recent head of the Qāmišli Jewish community was Moshe Nāḥūm.

There was also internal migration of Qāmišli Jews to the Jewish community of Aleppo, which was much richer and better established. The Jews of Aleppo looked down on them because of their socio-economic status and even considered their dialect socio-linguistically low. They would rarely even allow marriages with them (an interesting phenomenon is that there were almost no divorces in the Qāmišli Jewish community as this was not tolerated). While many Qāmišli Jews made Aleppo a station before immigrating to Israel, almost no Aleppian Jews ever visited Qāmišli.

Today, most of the Qāmišli Jews live in Israel and not in the Diaspora. The Jews of Aleppo and Damascus (Ambros 1977, 1) do not tend to consider themselves Syrian Jews nowadays, either in Israel or in other Jewish communities around the world. They are not even represented in umbrella organisations or in other Jewish communities, which sometimes include even Lebanese Jewry, especially the Beirut Jewish community (Geva-Kleinberger 2017), which is considered intellectual and of a high economic status. In a way, they resemble the Jewish communities in Southwest Turkey in the cities of Antakya, Iskenderun (Arnold

1998), and even Gaziantep, which historically had some common roots or commerce relations with the Aleppo Jewish community.

Dialectologically, in Syria and Lebanon, and even in the Antakya region, the Jewish dialects belong to the Greater Syrian Arabic dialects (Geva-Kleinberger, 2021b), while the dialect of the Qāmišli Jews is an easy-to-diagnose *Qəltu*-dialect, which was socio-linguistically disdained, with these Jews considered to be Kurdish, mountain-dwelling, or even non-Syrian.

3.0. The Linguistic Informants

In this research, I base the dialectological data on four linguistic consultants who were born in Qāmišli: two women and two men. In order to maintain anonymity, I will use only initials: GIL (male, born 1967), AAC (female, born 1955), ZL (male, born 1958). There is also another very old woman whom I interviewed whose initials are GYḤ (born in 1929 or 1928, she is the mother of AAC). There are sometimes discrepancies among the informants, especially with ZL, who spent some of his life among the Jewish community of Aleppo and was therefore influenced by the Jewish dialect spoken there (Zenner 2000, 29).

4.0. Dialectological Data

4.1. General

The Arabic dialect of the Qāmišli Jews (henceforth QāJ) is undoubtedly a dialect of the *Qəltu* type, which stretches from southern Turkey through the Jazīra area in Syria on to Iraq and eastwards. Therefore, this dialect differs from the Jewish dialect of

Aleppo (henceforth AJ) and the Jewish dialect of Damascus (DJ). As previously mentioned, this led to socio-linguistic differences between the Jews of Qāmišli and the two other Syrian Jewish communities, especially with the Aleppo Jews. If there is a phenomenon that repeats among multiple informants, I will limit myself to giving only one example.

4.2. Phonology

4.2.1. Consonants

4.2.1.1. As with the Jews of Baghdad, /r/ tends irregularly to be shifted to /ġ/ (Jastrow 1980, 142) by genuine speakers of the dialect: *kintu... kān bi-lmadġase* 'I was... it was in school' (GIL), whereas in ZL's speech almost all the performances of /r/ stay unchanged, as /r/, since he spent the later phase of his life among the Jewish community of Aleppo. However, the /r/ in words that originate in Hebrew or belong to Jewish life remains as /r/ (Mansour 2011, 23–24): *nitʕallam tōra* [H] 'We used to learn the Bible' (GIL). The ancient /r/ also remains in the name of the Arabic language or to imitate the speech of Arabs: *ʕarabi* 'Arab' (GIL); the same situation exists with terms denoting Syria or Syrians: *min Suriyya* 'from Syria' (GIL). Israel, when mentioned in a religious context or in a context related chronologically to life in Syria before coming to Israel, is spoken with /r/. This differs from its form in modern contexts, which is with /ġ/, as in Modern Hebrew: cf. *ʕala Srāʔēl* 'to Israel' (GIL) vs *šaġġiġūt*[H] *Yisġaʔēl* 'the Embassy of the State of Israel' (GIL).

4.2.1.2. Like AJ, QāJ uses /ğ/ for the ancient /ج/: *ğaġġabna maġġa w kamān maġġa, tlat-maġġāt, ʔarbaʕ maġġāt, lamma eğīna ʕala*

Srāʔēl 'We tried [to escape] one time after the other, three or four times, until we finally came to Israel' (GIL). This /*ğ*/ differs from its equivalent in DJ, which is there overwhelmingly shifted into /*ž*/. This also applies to the situation among the non-Jewish population of the aforementioned cities (Behnstedt, 1997, 6–7).

4.2.1.3. Interdentals are irregularly preserved: *kān ʕindi ḏahab* 'I had gold' (AAC).

4.2.1.4. /*q*/ is preserved in QāJ:[5] *elbaṭan tabaʕ*[6] *elbaqara* 'cow's stomach' (AAC).

4.2.1.5. /*č*/ is found in several words that originate in foreign languages, especially Turkish and Kurdish (Mansour 2011, 25): *kān nsawwi čādəġ* 'We used to set up a tent' (GIL); *ʔabūy kān yilbəs ʕagāl w čafiyye* 'My father used to wear a headband and kufiyyeh' (ZL), maybe borrowed from a Bedouin dialect.[7]

4.2.1.6. /*k*/>/*g*/ in some words, e.g., *ʕindi ʔax miğğawwaz, gbīr* 'I have an elder brother who is married' (AAC); this is also applicable for the root √*k-b-r* in the second stem, e.g., *kānt lāzem tgabber lᵉwlād* 'She had to raise the children' (ZL); *ğamīʕ enniswān elʔagbariyye* 'all elderly women in Qāmišli' (ZL); *b-Suriyya kulləm gazzabīn w iSraʔēl taḥki bass eṣṣarīḥa* 'In Syria all of them [the media] are liars, while the Israeli Broadcast [in Arabic] tells only the truth' (ZL).

---

[5] See Karte 9, 'Reflexe von q', in Behnstedt (1997, 18–19).

[6] Cf. the genitive exponents in Haifa; see Geva-Kleinberger (2004, 85–86).

[7] See Map 062, 'Reflexes of *k*', in Behnstedt and Geva-Kleinberger (2019, 130), which pertains to the Galilee region.

4.2.1.7. */q/>/g/*: the stem √**q-b-r* is spoken as √*g-b-r*, e.g., *ˀabūy magbūr hunāk w ˀaˁmāmi magbŭrīn hunāk* 'My father is buried there and my uncles are buried there' (ZL); *w ilyōm, ˀiḏa ṣār salām, w rəḥna ˁa-lQāmišli, ˀen*[H8]*... fišš magbara tabaˁ lyihūd, mā fī, li-ˀanno killo zəfte, sawwūhəm killəm zəfte ˀarḍ* 'And today, if there will be peace [between Syria and Israel], and we will [be able to] go, there is no Jewish cemetery anymore, since they tarred everything, they tarred the road [instead of it]' (ZL); *el-gbūra tabaˁ lyihūd fišš* 'There are no more Jewish tombs' (ZL).

4.2.1.8. */k/>/q/* frequently in the word */yimkin/>yimqin* 'maybe' (AAC).

4.2.1.9. */p/* (Procházka 2002) exists in words that derive from foreign languages, e.g., *paṭāṭa maḥšiyye maˁa laḥam w rizz, hāy la-šŠabbatōt*[H] 'potatoes stuffed with meat and rice for the Sabbath' (AAC).

4.2.1.10. As in other Arabic dialects in Greater Syria, the Classical Arabic verb √**ġ-s-l* > √*xsl*, e.g., *kinna nxassel fiyyo* 'We were washing ourselves with it [with the well water]' (ZL).

4.2.2 Vowels

4.2.2.1 Diphthongs are irregularly used, e.g., *tīği ˀinti tᵉˁṭayn iḏḏahab tabaˁek* 'You will come and give me your gold' (AAC); *timšayn ˁal-bēt* 'Go home!' (AAC).

---

8 H is used to indicate a Hebrew word. In a whole Hebrew sentence, H appears at the beginning and at the end of the sentence, while in a single word it appears only once.

4.2.2.2 Pausal forms: one can locate a shift of /ī/ into /ē/ in pausal forms, e.g., *mešīna bi-ltaṛēq#* (< *ṭarīq*) 'We were travelling on the road' (GIL).

4.2.2.3 There are numerous examples of *Imāla* in QāJ, as also found in AJ (Nevo, 1991, 43–44): *ˀiğa wā̆ḥed ˁarabi* 'one Arab came' (GIL); *nsā̆feġ min aṣṣabā̆ḥ la-lmasā* 'We used to go out from the morning until evening' (GIL); *tlā̆t saˁāt*[9] 'three hours' (AAC).

4.2.2.4 Long vowels tend to be shortened, e.g., *ˀā̆š kānu yqulūn* 'What did they use to call them?' (AAC).

4.3. Morphology

4.3.1. In 1. sg.c., the ending /–u/ is preserved, e.g., *sawwaytu ˁīd ˁandəm* 'I have been with them during the holidays' (AAC).

4.3.2. The past tense of the first person ends with *-u*, as in other Qəltu dialects, e.g., *kintu zġīr* 'I was young' (GIL).

4.3.3. In the conjugation of the imperfect verb for 2. sg.f., the *-īn* is preserved, e.g., *lāzem tinzalīn#* 'You have to go down' (AAC); *timšayn ˁal-bēt* 'Go home!' (AAC; see McCarthy and Raffouli 1964, 201).

4.3.4. Even in 3. sg.f., there is /-n/, e.g., *ˀimmi kānt tsawwīn* 'My mother used to prepare' (AAC); as in Jewish Baghdadi, the suffixed *-n* is preserved also in the imperfect 3. sg.m., e.g., *ma-yeˁġfawn yeḥkawn Tərki* 'They do not know how to speak Turkish' (AAC).

4.3.5. Suffixed personal pronouns in QāJ, as in other Qəltu dialects, end with */-m/* and not with */-n/* as in AJ or DJ: *qalŭlna*

---

[9] The word 'hour' is without *Imāla*.

lēš ma-ğibtəm rāshum? qatatūhum! 'They said to us: Why didn't you bring their heads [with you]? You should have killed them!' (GIL); *elḥukūma ˀaxadítəm killəm* 'The [Syrian] government took them all' (ZL).

4.3.6. Interrogative particle: *ˀaš*,[10] e.g., *ˀaš kānu yqulūn* 'What did they used to call them?' (AAC).

4.3.7. As in some Bedouin dialects, the 1. sg.c. suffixed personal pronoun after consonants takes the form of a long vowel, e.g., *biddi ˀahlī! biddi ˀimmī! biddi ˀimmī* 'I want my family! I want my mother! I want my mother!' (AAC); this is also found sometimes in verbs, such as *ṣirt* [*sic*] *ˀabkī* 'I began to cry' (AAC).

4.3.8. Like various Qəltu dialects, and also Jewish Baghdadi, QāJ denotes the present tense with the prefix /qa-/ *immi kānt qa-tqilli* 'My mother used to tell me' (GYḤ).

4.3.9. Peculiar inner-plural forms (Grotzfeld 1965, 49–50): *kill el-ğiranīn* (< *ğīrān) *kānu yḥibbūna* 'All the neighbours used to love us' (ZL); *yišaˤ(ˤ)lu šmāˤ*[11] 'They used to light candles' (ZL).

4.4. Syntax

4.4.1. Sometimes the imperfect is used instead of the imperative, e.g., *timšayn ˤal-bēt* 'Go home!' (AAC).

4.4.2. As in Jewish Baghdadi, the structure of two combined imperfect verbs is used in 3. sg.m, e.g., *ma-yeˤğfawn yeḥkawn Tərki* 'They do not know how to speak Turkish' (AAC).

---

[10] The non-Jewish population of Qāmišli uses *ayšu*; see Behnstedt (1997, 569). The same form exists in JB; see Yona-Sweri and Rajwan (1995, 9).

[11] And not *šmūˤ*.

4.4.3. Numerals are sometimes used in irregular structures, especially in dual forms, e.g., *tnayn uwlād ibnu* 'the two sons of his son' (AAC); *ǧābət moniyót*[H] *tnēm* 'She called two taxis' (AAC).

4.4.4. Instead of using a direct object, the verb /*qtl*/ 'to beat' is used with the preposition /*bi-*/, e.g., *ṣāġu yəqtlūn* *ⁱbˀaxūy* 'They started beating my brother' (AAC).

4.4.5. Although *tabaˁ* is frequently used, possibly as a result of the influence of AJ, *māl*[12] is also used as an analytic genitive and is assumed to be the original QāJ form, e.g., *xaḻḻaset issine māl ˀabūh w tǧawwazna* 'The mourning year for his father finished and then we got married' (AAC).

4.4.6. Sometimes there are deviations in the normal word order of the sentence and the subject appears at the end as an afterthought, e.g., *kānu yrăqbūna dāyman, el-yihūd* 'We, the Jews, were always under [Syrian Intelligence] control' (ZL).

4.5. Glossary

4.5.1. General terms:

mšīna ***mašu***[13] *u ḥaṭṭ maṭaġ* 'We were going by foot and it was raining' (GIL; see Barthélemy 1935, 164);

karra 'once' (AAC), e.g., *karra*[14] *kān fi, w karra mā fi* 'once there was and once there was not' (AAC);

ǧābŭlna ˀakəl w šərəb w ***ˀaḥwās*** *w maṣāri* 'They brought us food, something to drink, clothes and money' (ZL);

---

[12] I have also observed the form *măliyye*.

[13] Normally, in other Syrian dialects, *maši*.

[14] Barthélemy (1935, 710): 'une fois'.

ezzōpa[15] *kānu ʕal-**bawāri** w dduxxān kān yoṭlaʕ barra* 'The stove was fired with wood and the smoke went outside' (ZL);

garabēṭa 'tie', e.g., *biʕmalu ṭaqəm w qumṣān w **garabēṭa*** 'They [the Jews of Qāmišli] used to make a suit, [elegant] shirts and ties [for the holidays]' (ZL);

*ʔimmi kānt mara **marḍāne** w ʕayyāne* 'My mother was a very sick woman' (ZL);

dann 'cooking pot' (ZL);

čuwwāl ḥinṭa 'sack of wheat' (ZL);

*el-ḥammām kān ʕinna ʕa-**lbabbōr*** 'We used to bathe ourselves with **water heated by a Primus stove**' (ZL);

*kān nḥammi bi-**difʔ** gbīr* 'We used to heat the water in a big **water tub**' (ZL);

zanbarīše[16] 'pillow' (ZL);

dawšäk 'mattress' (ZL);

yā dēkto![17] 'Oh, doctor' (ZL);

qālab būz (Barthélemy 1935, 68) 'ice block' (ZL).

4.5.2. Special dishes:

ğoqāt, stuffed intestines of beef, a special dish among the Jews of Qāmišli (AAC);

kip(p)āye, a dish made of cow's stomach (AAC);

ʕağīn kítal, raw bulgur[18] with kebab (ZL);

---

[15] Cf. *ṣṓba*, Barthélemy (1935, 449): 'un poèle'.

[16] Cf. *zambarīše* in Tzuberi (2020, 34).

[17] An honorific form said also to distinguished persons who are not doctors, e.g., professors.

[18] On the method of preparing *bulgur*, see Behnstedt (2000, 176–77).

kibab ʕaṣā̄fir,[19] kebab stuffed with bulgur and onion (AAC);

sambūrak,[20] a popular pastry in Iraqi and Middle Eastern cuisines, filled with hummus, meat, or cheeses (AAC);

qaliyye, bulgur stuffed with meat (ZL);

zbēbiyye, kebab filled with molasses and raisins (ZL);

klīča, rounded sweet cookies with cumin (ZL);

salīqa, a local dish in Qāmišli in all communities, made from wheat well roasted on a campfire, then ground in a flour mill (ZL);

sufrīto,[21] fried potatoes with meat (ZL);

pazzōta, pickled lemon, eaten especially on the Sabbath as an accompaniment to food (ZL).

4.5.3. As in Jewish Baghdadi, *lāx* (**al-ˀāxar*) is used (Sweri and Rajwan 1995, 233), e.g., *ˁabarna wāḥad xalf illāx* 'We crossed [the border] one after the other' (AAC).

4.5.4. Although the verb *šāf* 'he saw' is used, maybe as a result of AJ influence, it seems that the original verb in QāJ was *ˀara*,[22] e.g., ***ˀarayna*** *hēk irrǧāl mˁallaqīn* 'Thus, we saw some men

[19] And not *ˁasāfīr*.

[20] Normally *sambūsak*; maybe a compound word with the dish *börek*.

[21] A dish brought to Syria by Spanish Jews (Spanish/Ladino, pronounced *soˈfrito*). It typically consists of aromatic ingredients cut into small pieces and sautéed or braised in cooking oil for a long period of time over a low heat.

[22] The reflexes *ra* and *ara* of the verb 'to see' are found, according to Behnstedt et al. (2014, 330), in the region of Qāmišli and southern Turkey, as well as in Maltese. This verb exists in Kaˁbīye; see Jastrow (2021, 68).

who were hanged' (AAC); ***ˀarayna*** *ˁammi u wlādu, killa* ***ˀaraynāhəm*** *šāma*ᴴ 'We saw my uncle and his children; we saw all of them there' (AAC); but also *kān yiği* ***yrāni****, yšūfni* 'He came to see me, to look at me' (AAC).

4.5.5. Temporal and place adverbials:

la-bēn 'until' (ZL);

hunāke maˁak maṣāri—tākel, mā maˁak maṣār—mā btākel 'There [in Qāmišli], if you had money, you could eat; if you did not have money, you did not have anything to eat' (ZL);

ˀēmat *mă ˁəndo waqt* 'when somebody had time' (ZL).

4.5.6. Unlike in AJ or DJ, where the word for 'synagogue' is *knīs* (Stowasser and Moukhtar 1964, 233),[23] QāJ uses *ṣála* (Yona-Sweri and Rajwan 1995, 138),[24] e.g., *kān yruḥūn ˁa-ṣṣála* 'They were going to the synagogue' (AAC).

4.5.7. Special words to denote Jewish holidays, names and special uses:

ʕīd elMaġella[25] 'Purim' (AAC);

Bāṣlo 'Betzal'el' (AAC);

kinna ᴴ*níšmor šabbāt*ᴴ *w ma-kān* ᵉ*nsāfer, w lā kān* ᴴ***nḥállel***[26] *eššabbāt*ᴴ 'We used to keep the Sabbath and not travel and we did not desecrate the Sabbath' (ZL);

---

[23] Cf. *knīs* among non-Jewish speakers in Damascus.

[24] JB *ṣlā*; the very strange word *torât*, which was not used by the Jews, appears in Van Ess (1971, 234).

[25] Cf. Tzuberi (2020, 28): *əl-maġġilla*.

[26] The same use is found in Avishur (2001, 222).

kina ništəġəl šammūs bi-liknīs 'We used to work as beadles in the synagogue' (ZL);

Sikkōt 'Tabernacles' (ZL; see Piamenta 2000, 37);

huwwe ˀilli ˁallam w darras w ***qayyam***^{H} *ğīl ˀilli yitˁallam torā*^{H} 'He who taught and continued [the Jewish traditions] for those who learn the Torah' (ZL);

el-hilŭla tabaˁ Răbi Yihŭda Ben Batēra 'The public celebration in memory of the saintly Rabbi Yehuda Ben Batira' (ZL);

kāšêr^{H} (see Piamenta 2000, 259), e.g., *ˀiḥna lyehūd kina niˁmal kill ši bi-lbēt kāšêr*^{H} 'We, the Jews, used to prepare everything kosher at home' (ZL);

er-Rāb *tabaˁna bi****qaddis****əm bi-lbēt* '**Our Rabbi** used to **bless** them at home [during the Jewish marriage ceremony]' (ZL).

4.5.8. Hebrew words that were already in use in Qāmišli, as opposed to ones that penetrated into the speech of the Jews of Qāmišli after they emigrated to Israel: *kān* ***ˀannēv***^{H} 'He was modest' (GYḤ).

4.5.9. Euphemism: *la-bēn mā ˀimmi* ***miskená***^{H}*, kān lāzem tgabber lᵉwlād; ˀiḥna kina,* ***lbarake,*** *ˁašr wlād bi-lbēt* 'Until my poor mother, she had to raise the children; we were, [with God's] blessings, ten children at home' (ZL).

4.5.10. Turkish words: *kān ktīr-ktīr zengīn* 'He was very, very rich' (ZL); *zangīn*[27] 'rich' (AAC); *ğabŭlna lyúzbaš etTurki* 'They

---

27 This word is found in a text from Mardin; see Jastrow (1981, 4, first sentence).

brought the Turkish officer to us' (ZL; see Geva-Kleinberger 2004, 338).

4.5.11. Use of Hebrew fillers: a very intensive use of ^{ʔ}*ăz*^{H} by all my informants, e.g., ^{ʔ}*ăz*^{H} *qallo* ^{ʔ}*inno* ^{ʔ}*eḥna min Qāmišli* 'So, he told him, that we are from Qāmišli' (ZL).

4.5.13. Use of secret language: In QāJ, there was a use of pseudo-Hebrew words in order that non-Jewish speakers would not understand the meaning, yet the morphology seems near to the Arabic dialect, e.g., ^{Hʔ}*ibsílu w brāḥ*^{H}[28] 'Hit him and run away!' (ZL).

4.6. Unique Local Jewish Customs

According to AAC, among women in Qāmišli there used to be a unique Jewish custom related to ^{H}*Tish*^{ʔ}*a be-*^{ʔ}*Āv*^{H} (lit.: the ninth of Av),[29] to break a jar (*ğarra*) full of sugar, candies, and even salt, and to break it after the men returned from synagogue in order to represent the end of the mourning day commemorating the destruction of both the First and Second Temples. The Arab neighbours knew this custom and were waiting to eat the sweets. The jar had to be thrown in such a way as to cause a big explosion. This custom was not documented in Aleppo or Damascus. This day is called by AAC *Tís*^{ʕ}*a* (lit.: *the Ninth*):

[28] Cf. Matsa (2018, 202), who mentions the word *maḥanē*, which was used by the Jews of Damascus to denote Syrian Intelligence.

[29] In JD, the term is *ʾēxa* (The Book of Lamentations, Hebrew: אֵיכָה). Cf. QāJ *tša*^{c}*abōb*^{H} in Tzuberi (2020, 31).

be-Tísˤa, ˀabūy kān w uxwāni, kān yruḥūn ˤa-ṣṣála, w niḥnä nˤabbi ğarra, sikkar, w sikkar mlabbas, rizz, w sikkar ragíl^{H}*, w… lmilḥ; kān nˤabbīha lğarra. w kān yiğawn min aṣṣála ni-stanna…* ^{H}*ˀex… ˀex hayyínu*^{H} *nistannahəm hēk bi-lḥarr w yiğōn w nkibb al-ğarra qaddamən. w ˀabūy kān yiṭṭaḻḻaˤ "nū: ˀikibbīha yaḻḻa! kān nkibb al-ğarra,* ^{H}*ve-haytá mitpotṣētṣet!*^{H} *kān* ^{H}*ˀex ˀomġím*^{H} *tinfíğir bi-lˀarḍ w bi-sikkar. w lˤarab, kān yruḥūn ylummūn issikkar w* ^{H}*ze*^{H}*… kān yistannōn… yaˤġfūn ilˤarab yōm tabaˤ lyahūd.* ^{H}*ˀex*^{H} *kānu yaˤġfōn* ^{H}*ˀaní lo-ydat… hayú yodˤím*^{H} *Yōmət ykibbūn lğrār lyhūd. kān yruḥōn ystannōn ˤal-ⁱsṭūḥ ˀēmta yinkibb ilğarra.*

'On the ninth of Av, my father and my brothers used to go to the synagogue, while we [the women] used to fill the jar with sugar, candies, and rice: ordinary sugar and [even] salt. Then they [the men] came from the synagogue and we used to wait for them in the heat and then break the jar in front of them. My father used to look [at me] and say: "Go on! Break it!"; and then we broke the jar and it exploded on the ground with the sugar; the Arabs used to gather the sugar and wait. The Arabs knew that it was a special day for the Jews. How did they know it? I really have no idea… they used to wait on the roofs until the jar was thrown down.'

Another custom: During a Jewish marriage ceremony in Qāmišli, the invited guests used to place their presents on the bed of the new couple.

5.0. Conclusions

The Jewish dialect of Qāmišli, unlike the dialect of the non-Jews of the city, was short-lived, from the twenties of the twentieth century until the twenties of the twenty-first century. This period is even shorter if we take into account the time when the last

Jews left the city, during the nineties of the last century. Thus, the lifetime of this dialect is one of the shortest ever recorded, as Qāmišli was an artificial city established by the French for economic and political reasons.

There is a noticeable kernel of the QāJ community which originated in the nearby Turkish city of Nuṣaybin. The Jews of the city had come also from various other places in southern Turkey and Kurdistan, but soon, with the swift growing of the city, an urban dialect crystallised and was recognised as a different and peculiar dialect in Syria. The mixed origins of the Jews created a curious Jewish dialect which differs from the non-Jewish dialect of the city. Also, the use of many Hebrew words and a Jewish vocabulary created differences from the other dialects of the city. Unlike the other Jewish dialects in Syria, QāJ did not belong to the macro of Greater Syrian Arabic dialects; it was characterised as a *Qəltu*-dialect, belonging to a wider area in eastern Syria that is actually a continuum from southern Turkey, crossing the eastern strip of Syria and ending in southern Iraq. Therefore, QāJ has more linguistic features in common with Jewish Baghdadi than AJ and DJ. No wonder, then, that to this very day the Jews of Aleppo and the Jews of Damascus do not consider the Qāmišli Jews Syrians.

In the recordings, one can find deviations between the informants, specifically in the fields of phonology and morphology. This can be explained on the basis that one of the informants in this research had to make the Jewish community in Aleppo a stopover before emigrating to Israel. Nevertheless, it is easy to locate the original features of QāJ. It is characterised by the use of the suffix *-tu* in the verb in the perfect 1. sg.c, as in other Qəltu-dialects. The morphological suffixes tend always to be written with *-m* and not with *-n* as in many Greater Syrian Arabic dialects. The vocabulary is distinctive, both in QāJ and apparently also among the other communities of the city, as the city lies geographically in the north-eastern part of Syria, not far from south-east Turkey, where many Arabic dialects exist, and not far from Kurdistan and north Iraq. Thus, the influence of Kurdish and Turkish is traceable.

In contrast with AJ and DJ, which exist also in the Diaspora, there is almost no QāJ outside Israel, since most of the Qāmišli Jews immigrated to Israel. In the USA, especially in Brooklyn, DJ is still alive and even used by several rabbis in commentaries on the (Jewish ritual) section of the Torah read on the Sabbath in the synagogue (^{H}*Parăšāt ha-Šavūʕa*^{H}; Blau 1965, 273). In Latin America, where several Syrian Jewish communities live, especially in Panama, Mexico, Argentina, and Brazil, AJ and DJ are almost never used in daily life, and only very sporadically by elderly speakers (Assis et al. 2009, 205–21). It is the same in Israel, where most of the speakers of QāJ, AJ, and DJ speak Hebrew in their daily lives and thus all of these dialects are endangered.

A better situation exists in the preservation of traditional and religious chants in the various Arabic dialects, but these are also endangered. The fact that QāJ suffered in Syria because it was considered to be a low dialect socio-linguistically, especially by AJ speakers, made the Jewish speakers from Qāmišli feel inferior; no wonder that they tried to imitate the AJ dialect when waiting in a transitional location before emigrating to Israel.

Even thereafter, Jewish Syrian communities around the world did not and do not consider the Jews of Qāmišli to belong to the Syrian communities, and they prefer to welcome the wealthier Beiruti Jews into their communities.

In Greater Syria, there were in the past numerous Jewish communities (Geva-Kleinberger 2018, 570–71), and Jewish dialects therefore existed in many other geographical locations in addition to the known cities, such as in the Antakya region, which had previously belonged to Syria, especially in Antakya and Iskenderun, in Urfa (Šanlıurfa) and its vicinity; and in Lebanon, in Beirut, Tyros, and Sidon, and at one time also in Dēr ilQamar and Ḥāṣbayya in southern Lebanon. This was also the case in the Holy Land, in Haifa, Tiberias, Safed (Geva-Kleinberger 2000), Pqiʕīn (Geva-Kleinberger 2005, 45–61), and Jerusalem, where some dialects, like Haifa and Tiberias, existed only until the end of the twentieth century, while other Jewish dialects belonging to the Greater Syrian type, like Kfar Yāsīf and Shfarʕām, disappeared even earlier. Therefore, it is a high-priority mission to document the still living Jewish dialects of the region before they disappear, as Syria was one of the first Jewish diasporas outside Ancient Israel.

References

Abu-Haidar, Farida. 1991. *Christian Arabic of Baghdad.* Wiesbaden: Otto Harrassowitz.

Ambros, Arne. 1977. *Damascus Arabic.* Malibu: Undena.

Arnold, Werner. 1998. *Die arabischen Dialekte Antiochiens.* Wiesbaden: Harrassowitz.

Assis, Yom Tov, Miriam Frenkel, and Yaron Harel. 2009. *Aleppo Studies: The Jews of Aleppo—Their History and Culture*. Jerusalem: Ben-Zvi Institute, the Center for the Study of Aleppo Jewry and the World Center for Aleppo Jews Traditional Culture. [Hebrew].

Avery, Robert, and Serap Bezmez. n.d. *Redhouse Yeni Türkçe-İnglizce Sözlük*. Istanbul: Redhouse Yayınevi.

Avishur, Yitzhak. 2001. *Hebrew Elements in Judaeo-Arabic*. Tel Aviv: Archaeological Center.

Bar-Moshe, Assaf. 2019. *The Arabic Dialect of the Jews of Baghdad: Phonology, Morphology and Texts*. Wiesbaden: Harrassowitz.

Barthélemy. A. 1935. *Dictionnaire Arabe-Français: Dialectes de Syrie—Alep, Damas, Liban, Jérusalem*. Paris: Librairie Orientaliste Paul Gruthner.

Behnstedt, Peter. 1997. *Sprachatlas von Syrien*. Vol. 1, *Kartenband*. Wiesbaden: Harrassowitz.

———. 2000. *Sprachatlas von Syrien*. Vol. 2, *Volkskundliche Texte*. Wiesbaden: Otto Harrassowitz.

Behnstedt, Peter, Mahasin Abu Mansour, and Manfred Woidich. 2014. *Wortatlas der arabischen Dialekte*. Vol. 3, *Verben, Adjektive, Zeit und Zahlen*. Leiden: Brill.

Behnstedt, Peter, and Aharon Geva-Kleinberger. 2019. *Atlas of the Arabic Dialects of Galilee (Israel) with Some Data for Adjacent Areas*. Leiden: Brill.

Blau, Joshua. 1965. *The Emergence and Linguistic Background of Judaeo-Arabic: A Study of the Origins of Middle Arabic*. Oxford: Oxford University Press.

———. 1980. *A Grammar of Mediaeval Judaeo-Arabic*. Jerusalem: Magnes.

Driver, G. R. 1925. *A Grammar of the Colloquial Arabic of Syria and Palestine*. London: Probsthain & Co.

Fischer, Wolfdietrich, and Otto Jastrow. 1980. *Handbuch der arabischen Dialekte*. Wiesbaden: Otto Harrassowitz.

Geva-Kleinberger, Aharon. 2000. 'Living Amongst the Spirits: Death and Superstition as Reflected in the Arabic and Hebrew Vocabulary of the Jews of Safed'. *Mediterranean Language Review* 12: 18–40.

———. 2004. *Die arabischen Stadtdialekte von Haifa in der ersten Hälfte des zwanzigsten Jahrhunderts*. Semitica Viva 29. Wiesbaden: Harrassowitz.

———. 2005. 'The Last Informant: A Text in the Jewish Arabic Dialect of Pqīʕín'. *Wiener Zeitschrift für die Kunde des Morgenlandes* 95: 45–61.

———. 2009. *Autochthonous Texts in the Arabic Dialect of the Jews of Tiberias*. Semitica Viva 46. Wiesbaden: Harrassowitz.

———. 2013. 'Lexicon and Etymology Among the Arabic-Speaking Jews of Qāmišli'. Paper presented at the First International Symposium on Spoken Arabic Dialects and Their Oral Literature, Mardin, Turkey, 17–19 May 2013.

———. 2017. 'On the Dialectological Landscape of Arabic Among the Jewish Community of Beirut'. *Acta Orientalia Hungarica* 70: 31–47.

———. 2018. 'Judeo-Arabic in the Holy Land and Lebanon'. In *Languages in Jewish Communities, Past and Present*, edited by

Harry Benjamin and Sarah Bunin Benor, 569–80. Berlin: De Gruyter Mouton.

———. 2021. 'Historical Linguistic Remarks on Greater-Syrian Dialects from the Beginning of the Twentieth Century in Letters of Faraḥ Tābri, Gustaf Dalman's Most Important Informant'. *Zeitschrift der Deutschen Morgenländischen Gesellschaft* 172 (2): 327–45.

Grotzfeld, Heinz. 1965. *Syrisch-Arabische Grammatik (Dialekt von Damaskus)*. Wiesbaden: Otto Harrassowitz.

Harel, Yaron. 2015. *Syrian Jewry: History, Culture and Identity.* Ramat Gan: Bar-Ilan University Press.

Jastrow, Otto. 1978. *Die Mesopotamisch-Arabischen Qəltu-Dialekte.* Vol. 1, *Phonologie und Morphologie.* Wiesbaden: Deutsche Morgenländische Gesellschaft.

———. 1981. *Die Mesopotamisch-Arabischen Qəltu-Dialekte.* Vol. 2, *Volkskundliche Texte in Elf Dialekten.* Wiesbaden: Deutsche Morgenländische Gesellschaft.

———. 1989. 'The Judaeo-Arabic Dialect of Nusaybin/Qāməšli'. In *Studia linguistica et orientalia memoriae Haim Blanc dedicata*, edited by Paul Wexler, Alexander Borg, and Sasson Somekh, 156–69. Wiesbaden: Harrassowitz.

———. 2021. *Der arabische Dialekt der Christen von Kaʕbīye (Diyarbakir)*. Wiesbaden: Harrassowitz.

McCarthy, R. J., and Faraj Raffouli. 1964. *Spoken Arabic of Baghdad.* Part 1, *Grammar and Exercises.* Beirut: Librairie Orientale, Place de l'Étoile.

———. 1965. *Spoken Arabic of Baghdad.* Part 2 (A), *Anthology of Texts.* Beirut: Librairie Orientale, Place de l'Étoile.

Mansour, Jacob. 2011. *The Spoken Arabic Dialect of the Jews of Baghdad.* Jerusalem: Ben-Zvi Institute for the Study of Jewish Communities in the East; Yad Itzhak Ben-Zvi and The Hebrew University of Jerusalem.

Matsa, Shay. 2018. 'The Arabic Dialect of the Jews of Damascus: Distinctive Phonological, Morphological and Lexical Features'. Ph.D. dissertation, The Hebrew University of Jerusalem. [Hebrew].

Nevo, Moshe. 1991. 'The Arabic Dialect of the Jews of Aleppo: Phonology and Morphology'. Ph.D. dissertation, The Hebrew University of Jerusalem. [Hebrew]

Piamenta, Moshe. 2000. *Jewish Life in Arabic Language and Jerusalem Arabic in Communal Perspective: A Lexico-Semantic Study*. Leiden: Brill.

Procházka, Stephan. 2002. *Die arabischen Dialekte der Çukurova (Südtürkei)*. Wiesbaden: Harrassowitz.

Talay, Shabo. 1999. *Der arabische Dialekt der Khawētna*. Vol. 1, *Grammatik*. Wiesbaden: Harrassowitz.

Stowasser, Karl, and Ani Moukhtar. 1964. *A Dictionary of Syrian Arabic (Dialect of Damascus)*. Washington, DC: Georgetown University Press.

Tzuberi, Yehuda. 2020. 'The Judeo-Arabic Dialect of Qāmišli Between Two Macro-Dialectal Groups: The Qəltu Dialects and the Greater-Syrian Dialects—A Lexical Study'. MA thesis, University of Haifa.

Van Ess, John. 1971. *The Spoken Arabic of Iraq*. Oxford: Oxford University Press.

Yona-Sweri, Gila, and Rahamim Rajwan. 1995. *Dictionary of Iraqi Judeo-Arabic Dialect.* Dr Davide Sala's Library for Jewish Authors from Iraq 15. Jerusalem: Association for Jewish Academics from Iraq. [Hebrew].

Zenner, Walter P. 2000. *A Global Community: The Jews from Aleppo, Syria*. Detroit: Wayne State University Press.

INTERPRETING THE TRACES: ON THE GRAMMATICALISATION OF *ˀAṮAR*

Catherine Taine-Cheikh

In Arabic, the primary meaning of the lexeme *ˀaṯar* is that of 'trace', but it also has other meanings in 'literary' Arabic.[1] Moreover, there are in Arabic dialects various usages whose origins can be traced back to this nominal, even though they belong to other grammatical categories. This is notably the case in the Arabic dialect of Mauritania, Ḥassāniyya, where we find a pseudo-verb composed from the local form of *ˀaṯar*. Some Middle Eastern languages show a similar composition, while other languages have evolved separately, both semantically and morphosyntactically. The lexeme *ˀaṯar* is thus the object of several grammaticalisation phenomena, grammaticalisation being understood first and foremost in the general sense of moving from a major category (that of a noun) to a minor category (that of an auxiliary or adverb).

[1] Here I use the terminology adopted in the *Dictionnaire arabe–français–anglais*, which serves as our main reference for written Arabic, both classical and modern (see Blachère et al. 1967, iv–vii).

 https://doi.org/10.11647/OBP.0445.06

I will begin with a study of *ˀaṯar* and its cognates in Semitic, making reference to several works of scholarship and drawing upon, among others, Martin Zammit. I will then analyse the grammaticalisation of *ˀaṯar* in Ḥassāniyya, and further specify the ungrammaticalised uses of the lexeme in this formerly Bedouin society. Finally, in the third part, I will explore other cases of grammaticalisation reported in Arabic dialects, comparing their morphosyntactic behaviours and semantics.

1.0. *ˀaṯar* and its Cognates in Semitic

After a presentation of the various lexemes pertaining to the root ʔṮR in literary Arabic, I will focus more specifically on the cognates of the lexeme *ˀaṯar* in Semitic. I will conclude this overview with Hebrew, as it presents a case of grammaticalisation that has been discussed in the literature.

1.1. The ʔṮR Root in Literary Arabic

Without claiming to offer an exhaustive lexicographical analysis of the various lexemes belonging to the ʔṮR root, I feel it would be useful to present the word family in its grammatical and semantic diversity. For this reason, I have taken up the elements of analysis from the *Dictionnaire arabe–français–anglais* by Blachère, Chouémi, and Denizeau (1967), transcribing the Arabic into Latin characters and limiting myself to the definitions formulated in English.[2]

---

[2] I will not reproduce here the sentences and quotations given as examples in the dictionary (see Blachère et al. 1967, 29–33).

The choice of this reference was motivated, among other things, by the fact that the authors of this dictionary did not hesitate, on the one hand, to distinguish several conceptual fields for the same root (even when they appeared to be adjacent) and, on the other hand, to look for the fundamental concept found in the whole root (or a fragment of a root) and to start with that.

The root ʔṮR is precisely one of the cases taken as examples in the preface (Blachère et al. 1967, viii–ix), where it is stated:

> the fundamental concept was represented for us by 'track', from which are derived the secondary notions or meanings of 'vestige', 'influence', 'notoriety', 'handing down of a narrative, of an exploit'.

In the dictionary text itself, the entry *ˀaṯar*^{un} PL *ˀāṯār*^{un} provides the basic notion labelled A. The glosses are as follows:

> 'trace, print' || 'appearances' || 'ruins' || PL 'lands the same portions of which always belong to the same families' || 'exploits, memorable actions; traditions (handed down about Mahomet)' || 'clothes, worn clothes; furniture' || PL 'work(s) (of a writer)' (mod.) || 'effect, mark, impression' || 'influence (particularly of a star)' || 'authority' || 'trace, sequence, example'.

The entries that follow *ˀaṯar*^{un}—also under A—are:

- *ˀaṯariyy*^{un}: 'traditionist' || 'archaeologist' (mod.).
- *ˀiṯr*^{un}: 'trace'.
- *ˀiṯra*: prep. 'after' || loc. *ˀiṯra ʿalā*, *ˀiṯra fī* 'coming next after'.
- *ˀuṯr*^{un}/*ˀaṯr*^{un} pl. *ˀāṯār*^{un}: 'mark, scar'.
- *ˀuṯrat*^{un} pl. *ˀuṯar*^{un}: 'memorable fact'.
- *ˀāṯira*: loc. *ˀāṯiran mā* / *ˀāṯira ḏī ˀaṯīrin* 'before everything, first of all'.
- *ˀaṯārat*^{un}: 'remains, trace'.

- *ˀaṯīr*^{un}: ‘that leaves a deep foot-print (animal)’ || ‘illustrious, famous’.
- *maˀṯarat*^{un}/*maˀṯurat*^{un} ‘brilliant action, memorable fact’ || ‘favour, advantage’ || (ext.) ‘production of the spirit’.
- *māˀṯūr*^{un}: ‘handed down (story)’ || ‘transmitted tradition’ || ‘[sword] handed down from father to son’.
- *miṯṯarat*^{un}: ‘scraper (for the hoof of a soliped)’.
- I *ˀaṯara (i, u) min*: ‘to mention, to report a story after s.o.’ ||| + *ˁan*: ‘to hand down (a tradition)’ || (ext.) ‘to honour s.o.’ || ‘to scrape the inside of a horse’s hoof’.
- II—*fī*: ‘to leave a print, a trace on sth.’ || ‘to exercise an influence, to influence’ || (physics) ‘to put into the state of magnetic induction’ (mod.).
- *taˀṯīr*^{un} pl. *tāˀṯīr*^{u}: ‘influence’; *taˀṯīr*^{un} *maġnaṭīyy*^{un} ‘magnetic induction’ || (astr.) *al-tāˀṯīrāt* ‘astral influences’.
- *muˀaṯṯir*^{un}: ‘efficient’ || *muˀaṯṯirat*^{un}: ‘sarcastic (spirit)’.
- IV—: ‘to be serious, important (affair)’ || + *bi* ‘to make follow (s.o. or sth.) of’.
- V—*hu*: ‘to trail s.o.’ || ‘to be marked by a print’ || ‘to praise a dead man’ || ‘to be in a state of magnetic induction’ (mod.) || (fig.) ‘to undergo an influence’.
- *tāˀṯṯuriyyat*^{un}: ‘irritability’.

The lexemes grouped under label B are fewer in number. They are essentially verbs, like verbs III and IV, which give the basic notion ‘to choose’:

- I—*ˀaṯira (a) ˁalā*: ‘to have sth. in view; to decide sth.’ || + *li* ‘to begin, to broach sth.’.
- *ˀaṯarat*^{un}/*ˀuṯrat*^{un}: ‘preference’; loc. *bi-al-ˀaṯarat*^{un} ‘in preference’ || ‘selfishness’ || ‘altruism’.
- *ˀiṯrat*^{un}: ‘selfishness’.
- *ˀaṯīr*^{un}: ‘marked’ || ‘chosen, favourite’ || (ext.) ‘illustrious’ || subst. pl. *ˀuṯarā*^{ˀu} ‘chosen friends’.
- III—*bi* ‘to choose, to prefer s.o., sth.’ || ‘to value sth. highly’.

- IV—'to choose s.o., sth.' || 'to treat s.o. well; to honour s.o. (by inviting him in preference to other people)' || + *ʕalā* 'to prefer s.o., sth. to'.
- *ʔīṯār*^{un}: 'preference' || 'advantage'.
- V—*bi/ʕalā*: 'to appropriate sth., to monopolise sth. (to s.o.'s detriment)'.
- X—*bi*: 'to appropriate sth., to seize sth.' || 'to value highly sth., s.o.' || 'to give sth. to s.o. in preference' || 'to prefer solitude, to live aside'.

As for the entries appearing under labels C and D, they are both rare and marginal, being preceded by a reference to another root. These are:

- under C < WṮR: I—*ʔaṯara (i)*: 'to cover a female (stallion)'.
- under D < ʔŠR: *ʔuṯrun* 'sparkle of a sword's blade' and *ʔaṯīrun* 'sword' || 'dawn'.

Even if *ʔaṯīr*^{un} 'illustrious' is present under both A and B,[3] the concepts retained by the authors—'trace, print' on the one hand, 'to choose' on the other—do appear to be the basic notions of two relatively easy to distinguish series.[4]

1.2. The Cognates of *ʔaṯar* in Semitic

In the *Dictionnaire des racines sémitiques*, the root ʔṮR has six subdivisions. It is under the first that one finds what we are interested in here, the reconstructed form **ʔaṯar-*, glossed 'trace, step, vestige', which best represents the Semitic languages as a whole, with the verbal form meaning 'to choose' appearing only under

---

[3] Under B, however, the sense 'illustrious' is given as derived, unlike the other senses.

[4] On the verb, see Bettini (2014).

the fifth subdivision, with a much smaller set of tokens[5] (Cohen 1994: 37):

> *ˀaṯar-* 'trace, step, vestige': Akk. *aš(a)r-* 'place, location'; UG. *ˀaṯr*, 'to walk'; CAN. Heb. *ˀaš(š)ūr-*, Pun. *ˀšr*, Imp.Aram. Nab. Palm. Epig.JP *ˀtr*, Bibl. *ˀᵃtar-*, *ˀiṯr-*, ETH. Ge. *ˀašar* 'trace, vestige'; Tigrinya *ˀaššär* 'trace'; Arab. Saf. *ˀṯr* 'vestige, inscription'; UG. *ˀaṯr*, Aram. Nab. *bˀtr* (*b* + *ˀtr*), Syr. *botar*, Arab. *ˀaṯar*, South Arab. *ˀṯr* 'after'; Soq. *ˀihor* 'to follow'; UG. *ˀaṯr*, CAN. Moabite Epig.Heb. *ˀšr*, Heb. *ˀᵃšer*: relative 'who, that'.

This dictionary is one of the references cited in Martin R. Zammit's *A Comparative Lexical Study of Qurˀānic Arabic*, a major contribution on Qurˀānic Arabic, which Professor David Cohen (personal communication) had considered to be an under-researched field.

In the introduction to *A Comparative Lexical Study of Qurˀānic Arabic*, Zammit (2002, 3) sets out his aims:[6]

> The aim of this research is not to compile an etymological dictionary of Qurˀānic Arabic, nor does it suggest a new classification of the Semitic languages. This study offers insights into the internal lexical relationships characterizing nine Semitic varieties. A lexical corpus which takes into account nine cognate languages of the Semitic area is

---

[5] It comes after the subdivision relating to Arabic *ˀuṯr* 'flash of a sword blade' (appearing under D previously) and precedes only that relating to the name of a goddess (UG. *ˀṯrt*) whose sense 'Chosen' has been etymologically linked to the verb 'to choose'.

[6] The work also responds, as the author himself points out (2002, 28) to David Cohen's wish that lexicostatistical methods should be applied to a large corpus, and not just to reduced lists.

> bound to yield substantially reliable information about the Semitic lexicon. Such a quantitatively significant database makes it possible to determine, amongst others, whether certain meanings are specialized in one language and semantically unmarked in other cognate languages.

In the list of Qurˀānic lexemes in chapter 3, ʔṮR is doubly present: in the form of the nominal lexeme *ˀaṯar* and in that of the verb *āṯara* (Zammit 2002, 68). For reasons of space, I will place them one under the other.

Arab.	***ˀaṯar***	**'a trace, footstep'**
Ge.	*ˀašar*	'vestigium'
ESA	*ˀṯr*	'(on) the track (of s.o.)'; *(b-) ˀṯry* 'after'
Syr.	*ˀtrā*	'a place'
Aram.	*ˀtar*	BA 'a place'
Heb.	*ˀašūr*	'step, going'; *ˀašer* 'a place'
Ph.	*ˀšr*	'a place'
UG.	*ˀaṯr*	'a place'; 'to march'
Akk.	*ˀšru*	'Ort, Stelle, Stätte'
Arab.	***āṯara***	**IV 'to choose, prefer'**
ESA	*ˀṯr*	'to choose'

In the lexical grid (Zammit 2002, 447), *ˀaṯar* is the ninth and *āṯara* is the tenth of the lexical items listed (there are 1717 in all). Although they derive from homonymous roots,[7] they differ greatly in their number of cognates. While there is only one cognate for *āṯara*, there are 8 cognates out of 8 for *ˀaṯar*. With this maximum score, *ˀaṯar* belongs to a very select group: "In 82 cases, [the] cognates are shared by *all* of the languages" (Zammit 2002, 561).

---

[7] Out of 1504 roots, 121 are homonyms.

They also diverge in the areal distribution of their cognates: *ˀaṯar* has cognates in all four areas (South Semitic, North-West Semitic, Ugaritic, and East Semitic), while *āṯara* only has cognates in South Semitic. As Zammit (2002, 568) points out in Chapter 5, only 82 items are attested in all areas (corresponding to 4.8% of cases), whereas the presence of cognates only in South Semitic is almost twice as frequent (152 cases, or 8.9%).[8]

Finally, *ˀaṯar* and *āṯara* fall under different semantic classifications. *ˀaṯar* falls under domain B ("The physical being"), specifically B5 ("Actions on the body on the surrounding environment") and domain D ("Man—the social being"), specifically D7 ("Architectural and other constructions; the house and its furnishings"). *āṯara* falls under domain C ("The soul and the intellect"), specifically C1 ("Intelligence, perception, consciousness, memory, imagination, thought: reasoning and judgements") and C3 ("The will: desire and action").

Insofar as the lexicon common to all Semitic falls mainly under F, B, and D,[9] the case of *ˀaṯar*—attested in all languages—conforms to the general trend observed, since it falls under B and D. Similarly, *āṯara* is representative of its semantic categorisation, as C1 and C3 are two semantic categories where South Semitic

[8] These 152 cases, shared exclusively by Arabic and South Semitic, are to be set against the total of 765 cognates attested in South Semitic, whether or not they are found in other areas.

[9] "As regards the classification into semantic domains, most Common Semitic cognates fall under F (Man and the universe—27.2%), B (the physical being—18.8%), and D (Man—the social being—17.1%)" (Zammit 2002, 574).

provides a significant number of cognates with no correspondents elsewhere—higher even than North-West Semitic.

The data gathered by Zammit on *ˀaṯar* and *āṯara* give insight into the variety of cases encountered in the Qurˀānic lexicon, including for items falling under homonymous roots.

1.3. A case of Grammaticalisation in Hebrew

Attestations of the form **ˀaṯar-* in the *Dictionnaire des racines sémitiques* fall into several grammatical categories:

- nominal, most often (Akk. *aš(a)r-* 'place, location'; CAN. Heb. *ˀaš(š)ūr-*, Pun. *ˀšr*, Imp.Aram. Nab. Palm. Epig.JP *ˀtr*, Bibl. *ˀ^{a}tar-*, *ˀiṯr-*, ETH. Ge. *ˀašar* 'trace, vestige'; Tigrinya *ˀaššär* 'trace'; Arab. Saf. *ˀṯr* 'vestige, inscription');
- verbal (UG. *ˀaṯr*, 'to walk'; Soq. *ˀihor* 'to follow');
- prepositional (UG. *ˀaṯr*, Aram. Nab. *bˀtr* [*b* + *ˀtr*], Syr. *botar*, Arab. *ˀaṯar*, South Arab. *ˀṯr* 'after');
- relative (UG. *ˀaṯr*, CAN. Moabite Epig.Heb. *ˀšr*, Heb. *ˀašer*: 'who, that').

Of all these attestations, only the last has been the subject of discussion. Holmstedt (2007, 177–78) summarises the questions that have arisen over the centuries about Hebrew's relatives:

> Specifically, questions remain about the apparent linguistic novelty of *ˀăšer*: why were Hebrew and a few Canaanite sister-dialects (Moabite and Edomite) innovative in using *ˀăšer* as a relative word and not retaining any hint of nominal semantics? Also, is it plausible that Hebrew has *three* relative words, *ˀăšer*, *šeC-*, and *ze/zû/zô*, particularly when the typical derivation of the last two is from the same Proto-Semitic determinative-relative **ḏu/ṯu*?

Holmstedt (2007, 184) holds that, more recently, thinking has narrowed on the relationship between *ˀăšer* and *šeC-*[10] in Hebrew, but that, since the nineteenth century, this had been analysed in three different ways:

> All of the proposals fall into three basic camps: (1) those that derive one item from the other; (2) those that derive both items from a shared proto-form; and (3) those that conjecture no etymological connection between the two.

Holmstedt first demonstrates that, contrary to the proponents of the first hypothesis (the majority in the nineteenth century), *ˀăšer* could not be derived from *šeC-*, nor *šeC-* from *ˀăšer*. He then explains why the hypothesis of a shared proto-form like **ˀšl*, proposed by Ewald in particular,[11] is unconvincing. Finally, the author of the article concludes his overview by presenting Bergsträsser's position, which is representative of the third hypothesis, according to which the two relatives have different origins: "*ˀăšer* is connected to the Akkadian noun-cum-relative *ašru(m)/ ašar*, and... *šeC-* is connected to the Akkadian determinative-relative *ša*" (Holmstedt 2007, 185).

In the following paragraph, Holmstedt returns to Huehnergard's (2006) article, not because he agrees with his hypothesis

---

[10] "The *C* in *šeC-* indicates that with all nonguttural consonants, the consonant immediately following the relative word is geminated" (Holmstedt 2007, 177).

[11] Ewald (1844, 384) "suggests that this form began as the combination of three demonstrative particles, **ˀ*, **š*, and **l*, (by analogy with Arabic *allaṯī*)" (Holmstedt 2007, 184).

of a derivation of *šeC-* from *ˀăšer*,[12] but because the latter presents a renewed perspective on grammaticalisation that he deems it necessary to relate.

To conclude, after reaffirming the divergent origins of *ˀăšer* and *šeC-* and noting that it is not possible to deny the existence of two derivatives of the Proto-Semitic determinative-relative **dū/tū* (on the one hand *šeC-* and, on the other, *ze/zû/zô*), Holmstedt advocates seeing, in the exceptions to regular phonetic changes, the possible effects of language contact, interdialectal competition, and social registers.

Holmstedt's synthetic study confirms the hypothesis that only *ˀăšer* derives from **ˀaṯar-* 'trace, step, vestige'. Clarification of this evolution can be found in Israel's (2003) work, entitled 'Il pronome relativo nell'area Cananaica'.

While the use of *ˀăšer* as a relative pronoun in Hebrew, Moabite, and Edomite is an innovation, Israel wonders whether usages that might be considered its natural historical antecedents can be found not only in languages of the second-millennium Syro-Palestinian area, such as Ugaritic and the Canaanite of El Amarna, but also in Akkadian.

Israel (2003, 344) points out that, in Paleo-Babylonian and Paleo-Assyrian documentation, as well as in the Akkadian of El Amarna, *ašar* appears both as a conjunction 1) 'Where, whereto, where from' 2) 'as soon, while' 3) 'if, in case' 4) 'what' and as a preposition 'with, before, in the presence of, from, instead'. He

---

[12] Holmstedt (2007, 189) objects in particular: "A more serious problem for proposing that *šeC-* is a further grammaticalized form of *ˀăšer* is that *šeC-* already occurs at the earliest stage of Hebrew and Canaanite."

adds that in Akkadian there are several locative adverbs all derived from the noun *ašru* 'place', such as *ašarimma* 'at the same place', *ašaršama* 'elsewhere', *ašralanu/ašrakam* 'at this place', *ašrānu* 'from there, to there', *ašriš* 'there, on there'. Moreover, he points out that *ašrānu* appears, among others, in the peripheral documentation of Ugarit and Tell Amarna.

Israel does not dispute that the relative pronoun used in El Amarna texts is of the Akkadian type, nor that the form consistently used in Ugaritic is *d*, but he suggests that the attestations of Akkadian from El Amarna where *ašar* is clearly used as a locative conjunction have the merit of aligning this documentation with Mesopotamian Akkadian and Ugaritic within the Syro-Palestinian area. For him, the uses just mentioned in the Akkadian, Ugaritic, and Amarna spheres should be seen as the historical antecedents of *ˀašer*. The fact that adverbs have both temporal and locative values makes them favoured relay points in the process of grammaticalisation, where the endpoint is *ˀašer* used as a relative pronoun.

The grammaticalisation of *ˀašer* in Hebrew is not of the same type as in Arabic, but I am driven to mention it because it too has the form **ˀaṯar* as its starting point.

2.0. *äṯ̣ṛ/äṯ̣ᵊṛ-* in Ḥassāniyya Arabic

Before presenting the grammaticalisation attested in the Arabic dialect spoken in the Saharan West—notably in Mauritania, but also in Mali, southern Morocco and, very marginally, southern Algeria—I shall begin by specifying the area of use of the ungrammaticalised lexeme. I will conclude by comparing the grammaticalised auxiliary form with other auxiliary forms with the same or similar meaning.

2.1. Attestations of the Lexeme

With the exception of the verb *äṯṯaṛ iˀäṯṯaṛ* 'to influence' and its action noun *taˀṯīr*, which are borrowings from literary Arabic (as their forms indicate)[13]—but which, as we saw earlier, do not share the same base seme as *äṯṛ*—the only form to consider alongside *äṯṛ* is *wäṯṯaṛ* 'to favor, to prefer'. This verb appears under the root ?ṮR in the *Dictionnaire Ḥassāniyya–Français* (Taine-Cheikh 1988, 7); however, the presence of an asterisk marks it as unconfirmed.[14] In the same dictionary, the nominal *äṯṛ/äṯəṛ* has the plural form *äṯāṛi* when used with its dialectal meaning 'trace, imprint, track, mark on the ground', the plural *āṯāṛ* being reserved for the classical (hardly used) meaning of 'tradition, relics, folklore'.[15] In fact, *äṯṛ* is very frequently used in the singular, but quite rarely in the plural. For example, it remains in the singular in phrases like *v äṯṛ-u* 'on his trail' or *gaṣṣ əl-äṯᵊṛ* 'follow in tracks',

---

[13] Note, on the one hand, the presence of the laryngeal in the conjugated verb and the action noun (disappearing word-initially but retained internally), and on the other hand, the schema of the action noun in *tafˁīl* instead of *təfˁāl*.

[14] Recorded by Leriche (n.d.), this verb occurs in a plausible if unusual dialectalised form.

[15] *aṯāri* is also the plural given for 'imprint' and 'trace' by Pierret (1948, 317, 498) in his lexicon. In contrast, the plural given by Ould Mohamed Baba (2019, 37) in his dictionary is *äṯāṛ*.

where in English (and French) the plural would be used. Similarly, in the riddle purporting to depict the activity of divination (*lə-gzānä*) which, among the *Bīḍân* ('Moors'), is done mainly by means of strokes in the sand, animal tracks are named in the singular:

(1) *äṯᵊṛ nārəb w äṯᵊṛ lə-gṭūṭa* |
w äṯᵊṛ ˁžäylət-nä mən yāməs maṛbûṭa ||
'Traces of rabbits and traces of (wild) cats |
and traces of our heifer since yesterday tied up ||'[16]

While these particular traces require someone versed in their interpretation, the same cannot be said of other traces observable in nature. Among this nomadic population, individuals were indeed encouraged from an early age to study the various footprints left on the ground and, more broadly, to pay attention to all clues inscribed in the landscape. Herders needed to be able to recognise animals by their tracks, to catch up with them when they wandered off (sometimes in spite of their restraints), to find a lost or stolen animal, or to identify a beast that was not part of the herd. The 'pastoral riddles' (*əz-zärg*) reflect the shepherds' gift for observation and the knowledge they have acquired over the years, which enables the best of them to recognise the trail of a one-eyed camel (by the fact that it only eats the leaves on one side of the tree) as well as that of a white camel or white-legged

[16] It is indeed customary to hobble large calves to prevent them from leading young calves to pasture where they would join their mothers and suckle.

magpie (by the fact that the beast 'tramples its hair' *(z-zāylä lli) täwṭa və šaˁṛ-ha)*.[17]

Moreover, for all *Bīḏân* who had to travel in the desert, even if they were neither shepherds nor hunters, knowledge of tracks was necessary for survival—before the advent of GPS, and perhaps even after—and was also the best way to find one's bearings. The presence of *äṯᵊṛ* in many *amṯāl* (proverbial expressions, sayings, and proverbs) is a further indication of the importance of traces in *bīḏāniyyä* ('Moorish') culture:[18]

(2) *l-äṯṛ ällā mūlā-h*
'Traces are their owner' (lit. 'The trace...')

(3) *äṯṛ əs-sḥāb və t-tṛāb*
'(Like) the traces of rain on the ground'
Said of the positive consequences of s.th.[19]

---

[17] For more details on these special kinds of riddles, see Taine-Cheikh (1995).

[18] In *La fille du chasseur*, where Caratini interviews a Nmādi hunter's daughter and has her recount her childhood in the desert, the heroine explains why her mother had taught her, as a child, to recognise the mother's tracks in the sand and how this had enabled her, years later, to find her lost son on a Spanish beach (Caratini 2011, 60–61).

[19] This saying is also found in Ould Mohamed Baba (2019, 37). In addition, he notes two expressions related to witchcraft: *rvūd l-äṯəṛ* 'práctica de brujería que consistía en recoger arena pisada por la persona que se quiere embrujar y usarla para hacerle daño'; *vlān märvūd äṯṛ-u* 'fulano está embrujado'.

(4) *mā yūġəd däyn v-äṯṛ-u ṛ-ṛažžālä*
'A debt (= revenge) is not lost (when) on its trail (there are) men (to follow it).'

(5) *mši v-äṯṛ ᵊmgämmaḥ | lā təmši v-äṯṛ ᵊmräbbaḥ ||*
'Follow the one who pays badly, don't follow the one who provides a profit' (lit. 'walk in the footsteps of…').
This is the advice given to one who is not objective or is over-ambitious.

(6) *mnīḥət ʕanz v äṯᵊṛ-hä mbällḥa*
'(Like) the loan of a goat being followed (lit. on its trail) by a force-fed woman'
Said when s.o. gives s.th. but continues to use it as if it had not been given.

In the previous three *amṯāl*, *äṯr* is preceded by the preposition *v(ə)* (< *fī* 'in'), as in the following expression:

(7) *ʕayyaṭ v äṯṛ-u*
lit. 'to shout on one's trail'
When s.o. leaves, one must not call them back as this brings bad luck (to cancel the bad luck, the person must retrace their steps).

In the following expression, as well as in the final two *amṯāl*, *äṯr* is preceded by the preposition *ʕlä* (lit. 'on'):

(8) *ʕlä äṯᵊṛ ši*
'This is the sign, the result of s.th.' (lit. 'on the trail of s.th.').

(9) *ilä ṛayt mžaṛṛ ällā ʕlä äṯᵊṛ ši*
'If you see a particular action, there must be a reason.'

(10) *mā yəṣṭaḥbu t̠näyn kūn ʕlä ät̠r däygä*
'To be friends, you must have been former adversaries' (lit. 'two cannot be friends except on the trail of a fight').

2.2. Grammaticalisation of *ät̠r*

As regards Ḥassāniyya, I believe the first mention of a pseudo-verb with *ät̠r* 'trace' as its base is found in the *Dictionnaire Ḥassāniyya–Français* (Taine-Cheikh 1988, 7): it also appears in other dictionaries published since then (Heath 2004, 7; Ould Mohamed Baba 2019, 37).

Cohen shows in a 1975 article that, in what he then called 'quasi-verbs'—such as *ʕand-[hu…]*, used to express possession in many Arabic dialects (Ḥassāniyya *ʕand-[u, hä, hum…]* 'he has, she has, they have…')—the presence of the suffixed pronoun was equivalent to the personal index of the verb, and that it was one of the verbalisation indications by which one passed from a nominal (often prepositional) phrase to a 'quasi-verbal' phrase likely to assume the function of predicate.[20] *ät̠r-[u…]* is a rather special case in that *ät̠r* does not currently have any prepositional use in Ḥassāniyya—unlike the elements that most often form the basis of pseudo-verbs, starting with *ʕand*. Moreover, the nominal *ät̠r* undergoes no modification in the pseudo-verb.[21] There is therefore perfect homonymy between, for example, *ät̠r-u* 'its trace' and

[20] Other indications of verbalisation include the respective order of the predicative phrase in relation to the subject noun phrase, on the one hand, and the combination with verbal negation, on the other.

[21] It might be thought that truncation, frequent in grammaticalisation phenomena, is rarer when the base element is brief, but I found that in

the pseudo-verb *äṯr-u,* which is most often used to express doubt about an assertion, as in *äṯr-u mowžûˁ* 'it seems, it could be that he's ill', *äṯᵊṛ-hum mā žāw* 'it seems, it could be that they didn't come'.

Before returning to the semantic evolution that may explain the shift from the first to the second meaning, it should be stressed that it is solely the syntactic construction of the utterance that makes it possible to differentiate between the two uses, i.e. nominal or pseudo-verb. Exceptionally, however, a statement may be ambiguous. Thus the following example:

(11) *äṯr-u hūn*

a) 'his trace (is) here'

b) 'perhaps he (is) here'[22]

Below are the examples, quite varied, found in the *Contes arabes de Mauritanie* (Tauzin 1993). I have transcribed them for the sake of homogeneity, and underlined the pseudo-verb and its translation (Tauzin 1993).

(12) *"nxāmət mən?" gāl l-hä, "əhə, hāḏi mā-hi nxāmt-i ānä." "walla zād," gālət l-u, "<u>aṯᵊr-hä</u>* nxāmt-i ānä."*

"'Whose spit?" he told her. "No it's not my spit." "Or," she told him, "<u>maybe</u> it's my own spit."' (pp. 42–43)

Ḥassāniyya, grammaticalised lexemes also generally underwent little transformation compared to what was observed in other Arabic varieties (Taine-Cheikh 2004a; 2018; 2022).

[22] This example is found in Ould Mohamed Baba (2019, 37), but only with the second meaning ('podría estar aquí').

(13) *'…"yaqäyr äydī-hum mā nšäwv-hum. hāḏä," gālət l-hä, "aṯᵊr-hum məstätrīn."*
'…"but their hands, I didn't see them. They are," she tells him, "probably devils."' (pp. 54–55)

(14) *"mā-ni mlowwdā-l-u, ānä aṯr-i gəlt l-kum änn-i wārdä?"*
'"I refuse to fetch it [the bucket], did I tell you I was going to fetch the water?"' (pp. 70–71)

(15) *gāl l-hä: "lēh! ähl vlān aṯər-hum yaḥyāw l-hum ət-tərkä?"*
'He said to her, "What! So-and-so's family has living children?"' (pp. 104–5)

(16) *gālū-l-u: "naḥnä aṯᵊr-nä b owlād-nä?" gāl-l-hum: "b owlād-kum baˁd. aṛān-kum gāvḷīn ˁlī-hum ḏāk əl-bäyt."*
'They said to him: "Do we have children?" He told them, "Of course you do. You've locked them in this room."' (pp. 106–7)

(17) *gālət ˁazbət lə-bzūgä: "ānä aṯr-i lāhi nḏ̣ūg-u mā žā-ni mä l-gältä…?"*
'"Will I taste it before they bring me water from the pond…?" the Bzougue girl said.' (pp. 136–37)

(18) *gālət l-hum mənt əz-zolṭān:*[23] *"waḷḷāh mā tägᵊbḏ̣ū-h!". gālū-l-hä: "änti aṯr-u l-ək?"*
'The sultan's daughter said to them, "By God, you won't have it!" They said to her: "Is it yours (F)?"' (pp. 172–73)

---

[23] More frequently with *s* or *ṣ*: *əs-sulṭān/əṣ-ṣulṭān.*

When the pseudo-verb precedes a conjugated verb,[24] it functions as an auxiliary and the pronoun affixed to *äṯṛ* agrees in person, gender, and number with the personal index of the verb: there is 3PL agreement with *žāw* in *äṯᵊṛ-hum mā žāw* and *yaḥyāw* in (15), and 1SG agreement with *gəlt* in (14) and *nḏ̣ūg-u* in (17).

In the absence of a verbal form, the pronoun affixed to *äṯṛ* agrees with the participle (*məstätrīn* in (13)) or with the nominal (*nxāmt-[i]* in (12)) that follows. The nature of *äṯṛ-[u...]* is in this case less obvious, but the suffixed pronoun clearly takes on the function of subject (especially in (18), where there is no other possible candidate), as might the personal index of a verbal auxiliary such as *kān* 'to be' or *ʕād* 'to become' in a non-verbal predicate utterance.[25]

From a semantic point of view, we need to distinguish two types of occurrences, depending on whether the pseudo-verb is used in an affirmative statement ((12) and (13)) or in an interrogative statement ((14) to (18)).

---

[24] This is most often in the perfective form, but it can also be in the imperfective form, especially if preceded by the future tense modality (*lāhi*).

[25] Hence the obligatory presence of *hiyyä* in (i), whereas it is optional in (ii):

(i) *hiyyä mowžūʕa*
'she (is) ill'

(ii) *[hiyyä] kānət mowžūʕa*
'[she,] she was ill'.

In interrogative statements, the pseudo-verb is almost expletive.[26] Its presence only makes the uncertain nature of the hypothesis a little more obvious.[27]

In affirmative statements, the presence of the pseudo-verb carries more weight: it corresponds, for the enunciator, to the expression of a supposition, a probable but uncertain assertion, or a simple possibility.

In all cases, the meaning of the pseudo-verb is consistent with the idea of an utterance based on an appearance: the statement is made on the strength of indirect knowledge stemming from a trace (*äṯṛ*) left by s.o. or s.th., not from a person or thing seen directly.

2.3. Semantically Related Expressions

In interrogative contexts, *äṯṛ-[u...]* can be either deleted or replaced by the conjunctive phrase *mindṛa (yä)kān-* 'is it...?', where *(yä)kān-* is regularly followed by a suffixed pronoun.

In the examples (14) to (18) given above, we can therefore replace *äṯṛ-[u...]* without changing the meaning of the utterance; thus for (14):

---

[26] Heath (2004, 7), who found only interrogative uses in his texts, states in his dictionary that *aṯṛ-ha* can be the mark of a question tag ('isn't it?').

[27] There is redundancy syntactically too, except in (18), where deletion of *äṯṛ-u* would require its replacement by a pronoun (*huwwä* 'he', *ḥāḏä* 'this, this one') or a subject lexeme.

(14') *"mā-ni mlowwdā-l-u, ānä mindṛa (yä)kān-i gəlt l-kum änn-i wārdä?"*

"'I refuse to fetch it [the bucket], did I tell you I was going to fetch the water?'" (pp. 70–71)

On the other hand, the introduction of *mindṛa (yä)kān-[u…]* in place of *äṯṛ-[u…]* in an affirmative statement transforms it into an interrogative statement and thereby changes the interpretation. (12) thus becomes:

(19) *mindṛa (yä)kān-u hūn?*

'Is he here?'

If we now consider the uses of *äṯṛ-[u…]* in affirmative statements, we find as the main equivalents *kīv əlli/kīv ḥadd, ḑâḥər l-[i…] änn-[u…]*, and *ˁand-[i] ˁann-[u…].*[28]

(20') *huwwä kīv əlli/kīv ḥadd hūn*

'it looks like he's here' (lit. 'he's like who/like s.o. (was) here')

(20'') *ḑâḥər l-[i…] änn-u hūn*

'it seems to [me] that he (is) here'

(20''') *ˁand-[i] ˁann-u hūn*

'in [my] opinion (lit. at [me]) he (is) here'

---

[28] The use of *mumkin* is relatively recent (it is a borrowing from literary Arabic that was not traditionally used in Ḥassāniyya):

(iii) *mumkin žä*

'perhaps he came'

More frequent, however, are statements with a verbal predicate, with a verb in the completed form such as *žä* ‘he came’. Here are examples with the 3F.SG *žāt*:

(21') *hiyyä kīv əlli žāt*
‘she seems to have come’

(21") *ḏ̣âḥər l-[i...] änn-hä žāt*
‘it seems to [me] that she has come’

(21"') *ˁand-[i] ˁann-hä žāt*
‘[I] think (lit. at [me]) that she has come’[29]

Of the three expressions, that containing *kīv əlli/kīv ḥadd* is semantically the closest.[30]

3.0. Comparable Grammaticalisations in Arabic

3.1. Introduction

In the fourth and final volume of their rich and valuable *Wortatlas der arabischen Dialekte*, Behnstedt and Woidich (2021, 374–87) devote a large chapter to *vielleicht* ‘perhaps’, divided into three sub-sections, each illustrated by a map. The root ʔṮR and the form **ʔāṯārī* are examined in the third sub-section, and the authors make it clear in the introduction that not all particles derived from ʔṮR are likely to correspond to the definition they

---

[29] On the use of *ˁan(n)-* instead of *än(n)-* in Ḥassāniyya, see Taine-Cheikh (2022, 651–52).

[30] On the grammaticalisations of ‘as’ in Arabic and in particular those with *kīv*, see Taine-Cheikh (2004).

propose for *vielleicht* 'perhaps' at the start of their discussion (Behnstedt and Woidich 2021, 375):

> Mit 'vielleicht' ist hier das Satzadverb gemeint, das 'die Gewissheit einer Aussage' relativiert und angibt, dass der Sprecher die Satzaussage (Proposition) für ungewiss hält.
>
> 'Perhaps' here means the sentence adverb that relativises 'the certainty of a statement' and indicates that the speaker considers the sentence statement (proposition) to be uncertain.

The authors do not claim, however, that all 'perhaps' expressions are adverbial (Behnstedt and Woidich 2021, 375):

> Nicht alle dieser Möglichkeiten realisieren sich als Wortart 'Adverb', denn nicht selten treten sie auch als syntaktisch übergeordnete Ausdrücke auf, denen die Proposition untergeordnet folgt wie in 'es kann sein, dass...; peut-être que..., etc'.
>
> Not all of these possibilities are realised as a part of speech 'adverb', because they often appear as syntactically superordinate expressions, which are followed by the subordinate proposition as in 'it may be that...'

The present chapter largely builds on Behnstedt and Woidich, but examines the data from a slightly different perspective, looking more closely at the grammatical aspect of the problem, and above all making a comparison with the *äṯr-[u...]* found in Ḥassāniyya, whose existence seems to have escaped the authors.[31]

---

[31] They do refer to an article of mine, which is most certainly (despite errors in their reference) the one entitled 'Grammaticalized uses of the

In the Arabic dialects, the pseudo-verb *äṯr-[u...]* is used in different ways, though never exactly as in Ḥassāniyya. Some are morphosyntactically similar, while others are mostly semantically similar. I will consider the different cases in turn, starting with those that are only semantically close.

3.2. Adverbialised Uses

In a number of Middle Eastern Arabic dialects, the invariable form is used alone (without a pronoun suffix) at the head of a proposition.

It is often more or less similar to the plural form of *ˀaṯar* 'trace' in use in Ḥassāniyya (*ˀaṯāri*), whereas the usual plural in these dialects is *ˀaṯār* or *ˀāṯār* (with *ṯ*, *t*, or *s*), or *ˀatūra*.

Barthélémy (1935, 3) gives examples whence the interdental has often disappeared (*ṯ* > *t*): *ˀatēri* and *tēri*, with the adverbial meaning 'whereas in truth; but quite the contrary I see that', in Syro-Lebanese; and *ˀatāri* in Egyptian, with the same meaning. Reconciling these forms with the *ˀaṯāri* found in ˁAnaze, he suggests that the final *i* originates in the 1SG prominal suffix, since *ˀaṯāri* 'I find, I think' means lit. 'my traces or impressions are that...'.

This etymology corresponds well to the form noted in Iraq, in keeping with Meissner's (1903, 112) attestation of *ˀaṯāri* 'I

---

verb *ṛa(a)* in Arabic...', to which I shall return. A reference to the *äṯr-[u...]* in Ḥassāniyya does appear there (Taine-Cheikh 2013, 149 n. 16).

think' and according to Woodhead and Beene's (1967, 3) attestation of *ˀaṯāri* 'it seems, it turns out', their dictionary providing two further examples:

(22) *ˀaṯāri yrīdū-ni ˀaskun wiyyā-hum ḥatta ˀaṣruf ˁalē-hum*
'It seems they want me to live with them so I can spend my money on them.'

(23) *ˁabāli jīrānna muˁallim; ˀaṯāri ḏ̣ābuṭ*
'I thought my neighbor was a teacher; it turns out he's an officer.'

It also fits well with the case of Najdi Arabic (central Arabian). Ingham (1994, 174) translates *aṯāri* as 'it seems then, it seems therefore, it emerged that, am I right in thinking…' and defines it as "a sentence initial particle which introduces new information which explains something occurring previously in the text." Examples are lacking to understand exactly what *aṯāri* means in Najd. If it were semantically close to *cinn-* 'it seems'—"the equivalent of Classical *kaˀanna-* 'it seems', derivable from *ka-* 'like' and *ˀanna* 'that'" (Ingham 1994, 128)—then it could also be close to Ḥassāniyya *äṯṛ-[u…]*, even if it is not, like *cinn-*, "regularly followed by the object pronoun suffixes if it does not precede a noun" (Ingham 1994, 128). Indeed, Ingham's commentary makes *cinn-* a quasi-synonym of *kīv-änn-[u…]* and *äṯṛ-[u…]*.[32] Here is an example (Ingham 1994, 128):

---

[32] Ingham (1994, 128): "*cinn-* Speculative (1) 'it seems'… It is very similar in usage to the English 'I think' i.e. a statement based on unsure evidence, about which one is not expressing absolute commitment. It can also function as a polite form of enquiry signifying 'it is so… is it not?', being less blunt than a straight-forward question."

(24) *cinn-ih ma yi-fham wājid*
'he doesn't seem to understand much'

On the other hand, in Bahrain, it is a singular derived form that is used with the meaning 'perhaps, probably'. Indeed, Holes (2001, 5) has noted the adverbial use (typical of the Baḥārna village dialects) of *ˁafar*—a local form derived from *ˀaṯar*. Here are some examples (Holes 2016, 281):

(25) *ila l-ḥīn ˁafar iǧi ačfar min ifnaˁšar sana min twaffa abū-yi*
'Up until now it's probably around... more twelve years since my father died'

(26) *min zamān!... ˁafar min sanat mā ǧābat fiḍḍō ibrāhīm*
'(It was) ages ago!... I think in the year when Fiḍḍa gave birth to Ibrāhīm'

(27) *ˁind-hum ˁafar ˁiǧil mrabbīn-ah ila yōm xāmis*
'It seems they have a calf they've been raising for (slaughter on) the fifth day'

3.3. Uses with a Suffixed Pronoun

In Bahrain, the meaning remains unchanged when a pronoun is suffixed. On the other hand, the singular *ˁafar* is replaced by the form *ˁafarāt,*[33] as in the following examples (Holes 2016, 280–81):

(28) *sawwaw ḥiǧra zēna aṯarāt-ha arbaˁat ayyām yisawwūn fi-ha*
'They made a beautiful room, for perhaps four days they might work on it'

[33] Is it a plural of paucity? The plural of *ˁafar* 'track, trace' is *āṯār* (Holes 2001, 4).

(29) *il-awwal ana ˁafarāt-hum yiwaddūn, al-ḥīn ˁafar mā yiwaddūn*
'In the old days I think they used to take them, now I think they don't'

Holes emphasises the similarity in meaning with the modal particle *čūd* 'perhaps, probably, maybe' or 'it seems/it turns out that', but proximity to *činn-/kinn-* (< *kaˀann-*) 'I think' also exists here, not only semantically, but also morphosyntactically, since in Bahrain *ˁafarāt* can be followed by a pronoun suffix. Unlike the case described by Holes for Baḥarna, it can be the same form that is followed, or not, by a suffixed pronoun.[34] This is the case in Damascus Arabic, for which Salamé and Lentin's (forthcoming) dictionary distinguishes two *tāri* particles. The first has the meaning of

> 'ne voilà-t-il pas que' (à propos d'un événement avéré mais improbable, inattendu, ou simplement ignoré jusque là), 'et voilà qu'il apparaît que, qu'il se révèle que, qu'il s'avère que, que je découvre que etc.'
>
> 'well now it turns out that' (about an event that is known but improbable, unexpected or simply not known until now), 'now it would appear that, it is revealed that, I have discovered that, etc.'

It can be used on its own, as in (30), or with a suffixed pronoun, as in (31).[35]

(30) *tāri ˀAḥmad msāfer*
'I learned that [contrary to what I thought] Ahmed had left'

---

[34] As in Najd, *činn-* has been noted in interrogative utterances.

[35] The second particle is followed by the preposition *l* and a 2SG pronoun. It is used to communicate astonishment or surprise to the speaker.

(31) *fakkart-ak mˁammer bēt, tārī-k mˁammer ˀūḍa*
'I thought you had built a house, but in the end you only built a room'[36]

The existence of both possibilities in parallel (with or without a pronoun) seems to be quite frequent. This seems to be the case, for example, in Egyptian Arabic, where the two variants given by Badawi and Hinds (1986, 5) can be used with or without a pronoun (*ˁtābi* and *ˁtāri* on the one hand, *ˀtabī-* and *ˀtarī-* on the other).[37] Here are the two examples provided by Badawi and Hinds:

(32) *ˁtabī-k ma-get-š*
'so that's why you didn't come!'

(33) *ruḥt aqbad wi-ˀatāri l-filūs lissa ma-wiṣlit-š*
'I went to draw my salary and it turned out that the money hadn't arrived yet'

According to these examples, the pronoun seems to be absent when it precedes the subject nominal, as in (33).

The rule appears to be the same as in Damascus (see example (30) above), but there are dialects where the presence of the pronoun seems obligatory or at least more widespread.

---

[36] However, in the presence of a suffix, the usual form can be *tārīt-*. One could therefore have had *tārīt-ak* instead of *tārī-k* in (31).

[37] These variants diverge with respect to the place of the long vowel, and we can hypothesise that it is the placement of the accent that is responsible.

3.4. Presentative Uses

In his study of the Arabic dialect of the Bani Ṣaxar tribe,[38] Palva (1980, 134) devotes a special paragraph to "presentative particles" and identifies three different particles:

> The demonstrative pronoun *hâḏa* can also be used as a presentative: *hâḏa hû ğây* 'now he is coming', 'look, he is coming'. Another presentative is *harˁ-*, which I have attested with sing. 3. persons only: *harˁu* 'there he/it is' and *harˁi* 'there she/it is', [39] i.e. the suffixes are not suffixed pronouns but enclitic personal pronouns, cf. Ṣlūt *herˁu, herˁi, heraˁhåm, heraˁhen.* [note 82] The presentative *ˀaṯri* implies uncertainty: *ˀaṯrîhū* 'perhaps it is him' (I have attested the same form for al-Karak and aṭ-Ṭafīle, too).

The only example given with the particle derived from *ˀaṯri-* forms an independent utterance with the abbreviated form of the pronoun *-hū*—a possibility I have not noted elsewhere and which would not be possible in Ḥassāniyya (compare with example (11)).

A set of three presentative particles is also attested in Negev Arabic. In his article in the *Encyclopedia of Arabic Language and Linguistics*, Henkin (2008, 365) states: "The inflecting particle *iṯr*, primarily a modal-rhetorical evidential, has an additional presentative component," and gives the following example:

---

[38] Palva (1980, 112) says of them: "The Bani Ṣaxar moved to the area between Wādi Sirḥān and the cultivated lands of Transjordan mainly during the 16th and 17th centuries. They came from al-Ḥiğâz...."

[39] Here a note from Palva refers to Fischer (1959, 193–95) for the etymology and occurrence in different dialects.

(34) *al-gōm itrāt-ha jēyyih*
'[we found that] the enemies had apparently come up.'

In his book on Negev Arabic, Henkin (2010, 134) makes explicit the distinction between the three subcategories of presentatives, of which only (iii) is found in all environments (i.e., both "in a deictic conversational environment," as (i), and "in a retrospective narrative environment," as (ii)):

> (i) presentatives of conversational discourse, such as *arˁ*, *hay*, 'look here' and *hawēn* 'look over there';
>
> (ii) presentatives of narrative discourse, such as (*ġāṛ*) *win*, *wlin*, *willa*, *illa w* 'and lo';
>
> (iii) evidential presentatives, such as *iṯṛā(t)*, *iṯrīt* or *ṯarīt* 'apparently; it turns out that'

On the notion of evidentiality, she specifies (Henkin 2010, 141):

> Evidentiality, as a cross-linguistic category, combines several modal concepts, such as:
>
> (i) noncommitment to the information, which is secondhand knowledge ('apparently', 'it seems that', 'they say that');
>
> (ii) findings contrary to expectations ('turns out that').

The examples given illustrate these two possibilities:[40]

(35) *aḥsāb-ak mn-ⁱwlād aṣ-ṣgūrah tṣīd-niy ṯarīt-ak mn-ⁱwlād áṛ-ṛaxam wal-būm*
'I considered you a young falcon hunting me, turns out you're son of vultures and owls.'

---

[40] As Henkin (2010, 141) points out, other elements, both lexical and grammatical, help to express evidentiality—for example, the participles in (37).

(36) *halḥīn—al-gōm <u>iṯrāt-ha</u> jǣyyih. ulǣbdīn min šarg al-haṛāb fī Ṛās Fǣˁiy…*
'Now the enemy had <u>apparently</u> come up. And they must have hidden east of the Ṛās Fǣˁiy waterholes…'

As noted by Behnstedt and Woidich (2021, 387), the notion of possibility~probability is not present here. Negev Arabic therefore clearly differs on this point from Ḥassāniyya: in fact, they only share—apart from the obligatory presence of the pronoun and the consequent constitution of what I call here a pseudo-verb—the notion of 'noncommitment to the information'.

However, the second notion identified by Henkin is not new. We have already encountered it on several occasions—notably in Damascus and Egypt—often associated with a notion of suddenness. It would seem more logical for this notion to be expressed by presentatives derived from the literary Arabic verb *raˀā* 'to see',[41] but this is not observed in the data. It is with this second meaning ('findings contrary to expectations') that *w-ātəṛni* is recorded in the *Dictionnaire COLIN d'arabe dialectal du Maroc* (Iraqui-Sinaceur 1993, 3).[42]

---

[41] Contamination between the forms derived from *rāˀa* 'to see' and *ˀaṯar* 'track' has been considered by several authors, in particular Henkin (2010, 141), who stresses the intermediary role that *tara* 'you reckon? I wonder' may have played. I have followed this lead in Taine-Cheikh (2013, 144–154).

[42] De Prémare (1993, 12) also gives examples where the *w-ātəṛni* form (almost frozen) is used to express surprise at an unexpected fact.

The Moroccan attestation is the only one I have found in the Maghreb: although Morocco and Mauritania are geographically close, we cannot claim that there is notable semantic proximity between Moroccan and Ḥassāniyya on this point—at least not in the data currently available.

However, we also cannot claim that, as on other points, Moroccan Arabic is further away than others from its southern neighbor. In many dialects, the meaning of the forms derived from **aṯar* seems even more divergent: see, for example, among the attestations recorded by Fischer (1959, 197–98), the meanings of 'wirklich, gewiss, aber' (for *atāri, atarri*) recorded in Shuwa, Nigeria by Lethem (1920, 167); and, among those recorded by Seeger (2022, 6), the meaning of 'in Wirklichkeit'.

4.0. Conclusion

The nominal *ˀaṯar* 'trace' is a very old word, one of the 4.8% Qurˀānic items with cognates in the four Semitic areas (South Semitic, North-West Semitic, Ugaritic, and East Semitic) and in the eight Semitic languages covered by Zammit in his study of Qurˀānic Arabic. In some of these languages (Akkadian, Ugaritic, Aramaic, Hebrew…), the cognate means '(a) place'. This meaning is the source of adverbial uses, as well as, in Hebrew, the source of *ˀašer* as the relative pronoun 'who, that'.

In Arabic dialects, the grammaticalised form is *ˀaṯar* 'trace, imprint', in SG or PL. It is used in isolation or in a construction (followed—optionally or obligatorily—by a suffixed pronoun). Thus grammaticalisation has led to the emergence of a pseudo-verb in languages such as Ḥassāniyya and Negev Arabic (at least in some of the uses), but which functions rather as a sentence adverb in languages where the suffixed pronoun is absent or is completely fixed (as is possibly the case with the final *i* in *ˀaṯāri* 'I think', 'it seems, it turns out').

The grammaticalised form differs further in its meaning, which may be modal (possibility~probability) or evidential (uncertainty; secondhand knowledge). The notion of unexpected result, contrary to expectations, has been very frequently noted, but is absent from Ḥassāniyya. Conversely, that of possibility~probability, found in Ḥassāniyya and Bahraini Arabic, is absent in Moroccan, Damascus, and Negev Arabic.

In sum, one of the most consistently shared uses (even if not found everywhere) seems to be that of noncommitment to the information. Since it is also the one that follows most naturally from the original meaning of *ˀaṯar*—the path (literal or figurative) that can be followed from traces, the inference that can be made from a simple footprint—we can assume that this is the most likely route to grammaticalisation, especially when we think of the semi-desert areas from which many Arabic speakers originate.

I dedicate this little journey to Martin Zammit, following in the footsteps of his great study on Qurˀānic Arabic, in the hope that it will be of interest to him.[43]

[43] My sincere thanks go to Jérôme Lentin for the information and documents he kindly shared with me during the preparation of this article. I further thank the anonymous reviewer for the helpful remarks and Margaret Dunham for her copy-editing.

Abbreviations

Akk.	Akkadian	Imp.	Imperial
Arab.	Arabic	JP	Jewish-Palestinian
Aram.	Aramaic	Nab.	Nabatean
Bibl.	Biblical	Palm.	Palmyrene
CAN.	Canaanite	Ph.	Phoenician
Epig.	Epigraphic	Pun.	Punic
ESA	Epigraphic South Arabian	Saf.	Safaitic
ETH.	Ethiopian	Soq.	Soqotri
Ge.	Geʿez	Syr.	Syriac
Heb.	Hebrew	UG.	Ugaritic

References

Badawi, El-Said and Hinds, Martin. 1986. *A Dictionary of Egyptian Arabic: Arabic–English*. Beirut: Librairie du Liban.

Barthélemy, Adrien. 1935. *Dictionnaire Arabe–Français: Dialectes de Syrie—Alep, Damas, Liban, Jérusalem*. Vol. 1. Paris: Librairie orientaliste Paul Geuthner.

Behnstedt, Peter and Woidich, Manfred. 2021. *Wortatlas der arabischen Dialekte*. Vol. 4, *Funktionswörter, Adverbien, Phraseologisches: Eine Auswahl*. Leiden: Brill.

Bergsträsser, Gotthelf. 1909. 'Der hebräische Präfix שׁ'. *Zeitschrift für die Alttestamentliche Wissenschaft* 29: 41–56.

Bettini, Lidia. 2014. 'Le verbe arabe *ʾāṯara, yuʾṯiru* pour une fiche lexicographique'. In '*ʿĀmmiyya* and *Fuṣḥā* in Linguistics and Literature', *Romano-Arabica* 14: 59–76.

Cohen, David. 1975. 'Phrase nominale et verbalisation en sémitique'. In *Mélanges linguistiques offerts à Emile Benveniste*, 87–98. Paris; Leuven: Société de Linguistique; Peeters.

Cohen, David (with the collaboration of François Bron and Antoine Lonnet). 1976. *Dictionnaire des racines sémitiques ou attestées dans les langues sémitiques*. Vol. 2, *ˀTN–GLGL*. Paris: Peeters.

de Prémare, Alfred-Louis, et al. 1993. *Dictionnaire arabe–français de langue et de culture marocaines*. Vol. 1. Paris: L'harmattan.

Ewald, Heinrich. 1844. *Ausführliches Lehrbuch der hebräischen Sprache des Alten Bundes*. 5th ed. Göttingen: Dietrich.

Fischer, Wolfdietrich. 1959. *Die demonstrativen Bildungen der neuarabischen Dialekte: Ein Beitrag zur historischen Grammatik des Arabischen*. The Hague: Mouton and Co.

Heath, Jeffrey. 2003. *Hassaniya Arabic (Mali): Poetic and Ethnographic Texts*. Wiesbaden: Harrassowitz Verlag.

———. 2004. *Hassaniya Arabic (Mali)–English–French Dictionary*. Wiesbaden: Harrassowitz Verlag.

Henkin, Roni. 2008. 'Negev Arabic'. In *Encyclopedia of Arabic Language and Linguistics*, vol. 3, *Lat-Pu*, edited by A. E. Mushira Eid, Kees Versteegh, Manfred Woidich, and Andrzej Zaborski, 360–69. Leiden: Brill.

———. 2010. *Negev Arabic: Dialectal, Sociolinguistic, and Stylistic Variation*. Wiesbaden: Harrassowitz Verlag.

Holes, Clive. 2001. *Dialect, Culture and Society in Eastern Arabia*. Vol. 1, *Glossary*. Leiden: Brill.

———. 2016. *Dialect, Culture and Society in Eastern Arabia*. Vol. 3, *Phonology, Morphology, Syntax, Style*. Leiden: Brill.

Holmstedt, Robert D. 2007. 'The Etymologies of Hebrew *ʔăšer* and *šeC-*'. *Journal of Near Eastern Studies* 66 (3): 177–92.

Huehnergard, John. 2006. 'On the Etymology of the Hebrew Relative *šɛ-*'. In *Biblical Hebrew in Its Northwest Semitic Setting: Typological and Historical Perspectives*, edited by Steven E. Fassberg and Avi M. Hurvitz, 103–25. Publications of the Institute for Advanced Studies 1. Jerusalem; Winona Lake, IN: The Hebrew University Magnes Press; Eisenbrauns.

Ingham, Bruce. 1994. *Najdi Arabic, Central Arabian*. Amsterdam: John Benjamins.

Iraqui-Sinaceur, Zakia, dir. 1993. *Le Dictionnaire COLIN d'Arabe Dialectal Marocain*. Vol. 1. Rabat: Al Manahil.

Israel, Felice. 2003. 'Il pronome relativo nell'area Cananaica'. In *Mélanges David Cohen: Études sur le langage, les langues, les dialectes, les littératures, offertes par ses élèves, ses collègues, ses amis, présentées à l'occasion de son quatre-vingtième anniversaire*, edited by Jérôme Lentin and Antoine Lonnet, 31–46. Paris: Maisonneuve et Larose.

Leriche, Albert. n.d. *Lexique français-maure*. Unpublished typescript, 1765 pages.

Lethem, Gordon J. 1920. *Colloquial Arabic, Shuwa dialect of Bornu, Nigeria and of the region of Lake Tchad*. London: The Crown Agents for the Colonies.

Meissner, Bruno. 1903. *Neuarabische Geshichten aus dem Iraq*. Leipzig: J. C. Hinrich'sche Buchhandlung.

Ould Mohamed Baba, Ahmed-Salem. 2019. *Diccionario Ḥassāniyya–Español*. Libros de las islas 3. Cádiz: Editorial

UCA, Universidad de Cádiz; UCO Press, Editorial Universidad de Córdoba.

Palva, Heikki. 1980. 'Characteristics of the Arabic Dialect of the Bani Ṣaxar Tribe'. *Orientalia Suecana* 29: 112–39.

Salamé, Claude, and Jérôme Lentin. Forthcoming. *Dictionnaire d'arabe dialectal syrien (parler de Damas): Lettre ʔ.*

Seeger, Ulrich. 2022. *Wörterbuch Palästinensisch–Deutsch.* Vol. 1, *ʔ–Š.* Wiesbaden: Harrassowitz Verlag.

Taine-Cheikh, Catherine. 1988. *Dictionnaire Ḥassāniyya Français.* Vol. 1, *Introduction, hamza-bāʔ*. Paris: Geuthner.

———. 2004a. 'Le(s) futur(s) en arabe: Réflexions pour une typologie'. *Estudios de dialectologia notreafricana y andalusi* 8: 215–38.

———. 2004b. 'De la grammaticalisation de "comme" (comparatif) en arabe'. In *Approaches to Arabic Dialects*, edited by Martine Haak, Rudolf de Jong, and Kees Versteegh, 309–28. Leiden: Brill.

———. 2018. 'Grammaticalised Uses of the Verb *ṛa(a)* in Arabic: A Maghrebian Specificity?'. In *African Arabic: Approaches to Dialectology*, edited by Mena Lafkioui, 121–59. Berlin: De Gruyter.

———. 2018. 'La (poly)grammaticalisation des verbes de mouvement et de position en arabe: Tendances générales et faits spécifiques'. In *Fonctionnements linguistiques et grammaticalisation*, edited by Sylvie Hancil, 219–48. Limoges: Lambert-Lucas.

———. 2022. 'From Embedded Propositions to Complex Predicates: The Contribution of Arabic Dialects to Syntactic Typology'. *Language Typology and Universals* 75 (4): 643–84.

Tauzin, Aline. 1993. *Contes arabes de Mauritanie*. Paris: Karthala.

Woodhead, Daniel R., and Wayne Beene. 1967. *A Dictionary of Iraqi Arabic: Arabic–English*. Washington, DC: Georgetown University Press.

Zammit, Martin R. 2002. *A Comparative Lexical Study of Qurʾānic Arabic*. Leiden: Brill.

VARIATIONS IN THE WRITING SYSTEM AND STYLE OF THE MODERN JUDAEO-ARABIC OF LIBYA[1]

Sumikazu Yoda

1.0. Introduction

Most academic interest in so-called Judaeo-Arabic[2] has been focused on works of the relatively early stage, such as those of Rambam or Saadiya Gaon. And for this stage, a great number of studies looking at various aspects have been carried out. The tradition of Judaeo-Arabic continued at least until the period of WWII, and especially from the end of the nineteenth century, many newspapers began to be published in Judaeo-Arabic in many places. But

[1] This article is based on a presentation given at an online symposium 'Revisiting traditional isoglosses in the Maghreb: Methodology | Terminology | Classification Algeria | Tunisia | Libya', organised by the Department of Near Eastern Studies of the University of Vienna in cooperation with the Austrian Centre for Digital Humanities and Cultural Heritage (ACDH-CH) of the Austrian Academy of Sciences, 2–3 June 2022.

[2] 'Judaeo-Arabic' is here roughly defined as documents written in Arabic with Hebrew script.

 https://doi.org/10.11647/OBP.0445.07

studies on this language at this stage are not abundant.[3] As will be explained later, this kind of Judaeo-Arabic shows large variations in style on which it is worth carrying out research. From this point of view, this paper will discuss the writing system, which may be connected with the style, of texts written in Judaeo-Arabic published (i.e. manuscripts not included) in the Libyan area (mainly Tripoli) since the beginning of the twentieth century (henceforth JAL = (modern) Judaeo-Arabic of Libya). Note that this article aims towards a pure synchronic study, so no historical research is considered. In this article, words written in Hebrew scripts are transcribed in Arabic letters as necessary.

2.0. Judaeo-Arabic

2.1. Chronological Classification

'Judaeo-Arabic' is defined as any form of Arabic written in Hebrew script (Khan 2007, 526). According to Hary (1992, 75), Judaeo-Arabic is chronologically divided into five periods, whilst Khan (2007, 526) classifies it into three periods.

Hary 1992

(1) Pre-Islamic Judaeo-Arabic

(2) Early Judaeo-Arabic (8–10 c.)

(3) Classical Judaeo-Arabic (10–15 c.)

(4) Later Judaeo-Arabic (15–20 c.)

(5) Modern Judaeo-Arabic (20 c.)

---

[3] Among them are Avishur (2008–2010), Hary (1992), Khan (1979), Mor (2020), etc.

Khan 2007

(1) Early Judaeo-Arabic (–10 c.)

(2) Classical Judaeo-Arabic (10–ca 15 c.)

(3) Late Judaeo-Arabic (ca 15–20 c.)

Briefly speaking, the main difference between the periods is the contents of the language and the linguistic style, which will be explained in the following section.

2.2. Stylistic Varieties

In the early stage of Judaeo-Arabic, Jewish authors strove to write their texts based on the grammar of Classical Arabic (henceforth CA), so it was in fact a kind of CA written in Hebrew script. But as time went by, Judaeo-Arabic tended to be mixed with elements from the spoken language. In its latest stage, namely in the twentieth century, the style became much more based on spoken Arabic, with fewer elements from CA. Indeed, in Early and Classical Judaeo-Arabic (here following Hary's paradigm), the authors had good knowledge of CA and they could switch between varieties of the language, i.e. from "standard" to "close to colloquial," according to the literacy of the target readers (Hary 1992, 80).

On the other hand, the authors of Modern Judaeo-Arabic were also capable of writing in a wide range of styles, and sometimes we can find texts rather close to CA with hardly any dialectal elements. It is not clear, however, which level of education in CA these authors had received. In this period, was it possible for Jews to participate in Muslim schools teaching CA? Was there any educational system for Jewish men to learn to write in Judaeo-Arabic? We have to leave these questions for future research.

Although Modern Judaeo-Arabic is rather close to the spoken language, it contains elements from CA. The rate of occurrence of these elements depends on the text.

Figure 1: Model of the proportions of classical and dialectal elements in various documents

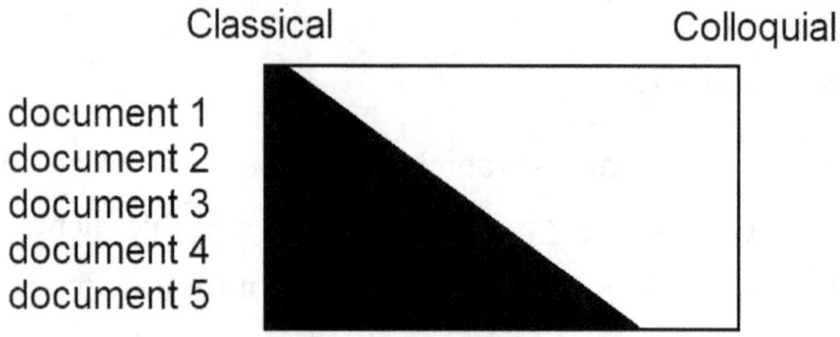

document 1 = almost dialectal

document 5 = nearly classical

Hary (1992, 79) uses the term 'Multiglossia' for this phenomenon. This concept is adapted from diglossia, spectroglossia, etc., which explain the situation for spoken Arabic, whilst Hary's Multiglossia is used for Judaeo-Arabic, which is a kind of literary Arabic.

The fact that Modern Judaeo-Arabic is based on the spoken language means that it differs from place to place.

As mentioned above, the documents defined as JAL are those printed in Libya since the beginning of the twentieth century. From here, the following two subjects concerning JAL are discussed:

(1) Variation in the writing system, especially for the letter *gimel* (§4.0);

(2) Variation in style, namely the Multiglossia situation (§5.0).

3.0. Materials

The following are the primary documents used in this paper (for detail, refer to References). Each document is referred to by the text number in the brackets.

Three newspapers:

Hahetorerot (Il Risveglio) (ההתעוררות) [Text 04]
Degel Zion (דגל ציון) [Text 07]
Il Messagerro Ebraico (המבשר העברי) [Text 11]

Two books:

a text book of Hebrew for Libyan Jews,
קבץ למדו עברית (*Qobets lamdu ʿivrit*) [Text 12]
and a book about Passover:
הגדה של פסח – ערב פסח עם תרגום בשפה הערבית וכן דינים הנחצים לחודש ניסן (*Hagada šel pesaḥ*) [Text 09]

Eight booklets:

three concerning legal matters,
Municipio di Tripoli, *Ordinanza 15 novembre 1936-XV relativa a norme per la circolazione stradale* [Text 08]
Comunita israelitica della Tripolitania [Text 10]
קואעד לאג'ל מועאמלאת קהל ישראל אלסאכנין פי עמאלת טראבלס (*Qawāʿid*) [Text 13]
and five for educational purposes (Zionism, immigration to Israel, civil education etc.):
שער העליה (*Šaʿar ha-ʿalya*) [Text 01]

הרצל ואלציונים (*Hertsel wa-l-ṣiyonim*) [Text 02]

פעלותיו בשנת התר'צב והתר'צג, מזכרת ליום חלקת הפרסים השנים (*Pe'ulotav*) [Text 03]

אלציוניסם (*al-Ṣiyonism*) [Text 05]

מסאיל אלדי בנאדם ילזם יערפהום (*Masāʾil*) [Text 06]

4.0. Variation in the Writing System

The first subject is variation in the writing system of JAL. Here I avoid using the term 'orthography', because this term implies a fixed writing system, whereas our target language in fact has no strict orthography, but only a wide range of ways of writing. A single word may have many variants in how it is written. For example, for the word 'newspaper', the following variants are found in the above-mentioned texts. Needless to say, these forms correspond to CA جريدة.[4]

גִרידא [Text 07:73b–7]
גִרידה [Text 11:1–5]
ג'רידה [Text 07:1a–21]
גִארידא [Text 07:1c–22]
גִארידה [Text 07:1c–13]
ג,ארידה [Text 02:3–12]

The difference among them is found in *gimel*, *aleph*, and the feminine ending corresponding to Arabic *tāʾ marbūṭa*.

[4] Considering the fact that, in the Arabic dialect of the Jews of Tripoli (henceforth TrJ), a word of Italian origin, *žŏrnālĕ*, is used for 'newspaper' (Yoda 2005, 347), it seems that جريدة was introduced to JAL from CA for a literary purpose.

(1) Hebrew *gimel* originally indicated the sound *g*, but in Judaeo-Arabic in general it is used in place of *jīm* and *ġayn*. In JAL, there are three different diacritic marks for *gimel* to distinguish it from the original *g* sound and indicate the *ž* and *ġ* sounds. In the examples above, the *ž* sound is indicated by three variants: 'ג, ג̣, and ,ג.

(2) *Aleph*, like *alif* in Arabic, indicates a short vowel in word-initial position and a long *ā* in word-medial and -final position. There are forms that contain *aleph* to indicate the vowel of the first syllable, which in CA is a short *a*. This phenomenon indicates that this word would be pronounced as *jārīda*, with a long *ā* in the first syllable. In Maghribi dialects in general, there is a widespread phonological rule that an unstressed short vowel in an open syllable is eliminated. According to this rule, the CA word *jarīda* should be **jrīda*; however, *a* in the first syllable is maintained as a long *ā* in order to reflect the two syllables of the CA form.

(3) The feminine ending -*a* is indicated by א or ה. In JAL, the feminine ending may be indicated by א or ה and the choice between them seems to be arbitrary.

The following table indicates the Hebrew letters used in the JAL texts and the corresponding sounds of the Jewish Tripolitanian dialect.[5]

---

[5] The system of transcription follows Yoda (2005); note that in this work phonological long vowels are represented as *a, i, u* without a macron, but in this paper, they are written with a macron: *ā, ī, ū*. For *ĥ*, see Yoda (2017).

Table 1: Table of Hebrew letters and corresponding sounds

letter	sound	letter	sound	letter	sound
א	*a, ā*	ז	*z*	ע	^{c}
ב	*b*	ח	*ḥ*	פ	*f*
ג	*ž, ġ, g*	ט	*ṭ*	פ̇	*f*
ג̇	*ž, ġ*	י	*y, i*	צ	*ṣ, ḍ*
גּ	*ž*	כ	*k, x*	צ̇	*ḍ*
ג'	*ž, ġ*	כ̇	*k, x*	צ'	*ḍ*
,ג	*ž*	ל	*l*	ק	*q*
ד	*d*	מ	*m*	ר	*r*
ה	*ɦ*	נ	*n*	ש	*š*
ו	*w, u*	ס	*s*	ת	*t*

The Hebrew alphabet consists of twenty-two letters, which do not cover the necessary distinction of the sounds of JAL, so, some letters are used to indicate two or three sounds:

ג is used to indicate *ž*, *ġ*, and *g*, with or without diacritic signs;
כ indicates *k* or *x* (usually כ̇ or כ' with a diacritic sign indicates *x*);
צ indicates *ṣ* or *ḍ* (usually צ̇ or צ' with a diacritic sign indicates *ḍ*);
פ indicates *f* (usually פ̇ with a diacritic sign).

Note that simple פ rarely appears in Arabic words, but in Hebrew words, simple פ is used to indicate *p* or in certain conditions *f*.

It is striking that ג has five variants. In some cases, different variants are used in one and the same text.

As stated above, JAL is a literary language based on the grammar of the spoken language, namely the Arabic dialect of the Jews of Libya. In TrJ, there are at least thirty-two phonemes, but some phonemes which do not exist in CA, for example emphatic ḅ, ḷ, ṃ, etc. (Yoda 2005, 6), are never distinguished in the published texts. This means that the basic writing system of Modern Judaeo-Arabic is within the continuum of CA.

The purpose of the diacritical marks is mainly to distinguish one sound from another. Although the choice of them is different from text to text, the readers, who are native speakers of TrJ, can immediately understand which variant indicates which sound in the text they are reading.

For example, in [Text 01] and [Text 02], *gimel* with a sign like a comma indicates *ž* and *gimel* with a dot above indicates *ġ*.

ג,	*ž*	ג,יאנךְ 'your coming' [Text 01: 1–14]
		ג,רידאת 'newspapers' [Text 02: 3–11]
ג̇	*ġ*	לג̇וותךְ 'your language' [Text 01: 2–10]
		סג̇רו 'his childhood' [Text 02: 3–6]

In [Text-03], [Text-04], and [Text-05], *gimel* with a dot beneath indicates *ž* and *gimel* with a dot above *ġ*.

ג̣	*ž*	יתוג̣דו 'they are found' [Text 03: 0–6]
		ג̣ארייא 'flowing (f.)' [Text 04: 1a–1]
		ג̣דידא 'new (f.)' [Text 05: 1–10]
ג̇	*ġ*	צג̇ארנא 'our children' [Text 03: 0–3]
		ג̇רצ̇הא 'its (f.) purpose' [Text 04: 1a–4]
		זג̇אר 'little (pl.)' [Text 05: 2–17]

And there are some other irregular cases. For example, in [Text-06], simple *gimel* is used for *ž* and *ġ*, while *gimel* with a dot above is also used for *ġ* at the same time.

ג	*ž*	אלחאגה 'the thing' [Text 06: 2–6]
	ġ	אלמגבונין 'the deceived (pl.)' [Text 06: 2–7]
ג̇	*ġ*	ג̇יר 'except' [Text 06: 4–9]

In this way, the five variants may indicate either *ž* or *ġ* and in some cases *g*. When reading a text, readers cannot predict which variant will be used for which sound.

In [Text-07], the usage of the diacritic mark is by no means consistent. We might imagine that each reporter writes his article in his own way, but there are cases where many variants are found in one and the same article.

ג	*ġ*	לנגלבו (لنغلبو) 'in order that we overcome' [Text-07: 1a–19]
	g	דגל (Heb. דגל *degel*) 'flag' [Text-07: 2a–14]
ג̇	*g*	דג̇ל (Heb. דגל *degel*) 'flag' [Text-07: 1b–12]
	ž	מג̇לס (مجلس) 'committee' [Text-07: 2a–30]
ג'	*ž*	אלג'ראיד (الجرايد) 'the newspapers' [Text-07: 1a–9]
גּ	*ž*	גּארידא (جاريدا) 'newspaper' [Text-07: 1b–13]

According to observations thus far, it seems that there is no strict rule for choosing the variants.

The five variants in general indicate the following sounds.

(1) Simple ג mainly indicates the sound *g*, and sporadically *ž* or *ġ*.

(2) ג̇ mainly indicates *ġ* and sporadically *ž*.

(3) ג' mainly indicates *ġ* and sporadically *ž*.

(4) גּ indicates *ž*.

(5) ג, indicates *ž*.

Table 2: Variations of *gimel* and its corresponding sounds

ž	ġ	g	Texts
ג,	ג̇		01, 01
ג,	ג'		08, 10
ג̣	ג̇		03, 04, 05, 11, 12
ג̣ ג̇	ג̇		13
ג̇	ג'		09
ג	ג ג̇		06
ג̣ ג̇ ג'	ג	ג	07

This table is a result of my observations of only fifteen texts, and different results may therefore appear as a result of more observation of more texts. As stated above, the choice seems to be arbitrary. According to my observations, no concrete criterion is found. It is possible, however, that the choice depends on the stock of types in printing houses. When 'Printing House A' does not possess a stock of ג̣, it uses 'ג, for example. In this case, the problem lies in the history of the printing houses.

5.0. Variation in Style

The second theme is variation in style. As mentioned above, Modern Judaeo-Arabic is based on the grammar of spoken Arabic but includes several elements used only for writing purposes; the typical words are, for example, function words, such as the negative particles ליס, לם 'not', the relative pronoun אלדי 'that, which', the conjunction אן 'that', etc. Their dialectal counterparts are מוש, מא ש-... 'not', and אלי, which is used as both relative pronoun and conjunction.

Table 3: Some characteristic words of literary and dialectal styles

	literary	dialectal
negative particles	(ليس) ליס (لم) לם	(ما ...ش) מא ...-ש (موش) מוש
relative pronoun	(الدي) אלדי	(الي) אלי
conjunctions	(ل) ל (ان) אן	(باش) באש (الي) אלי

It seems that, when a text contains such words as ליס (ليس), לם (لم), אלדי (الدي), אן (ان), it gives the impression that it would be literary in style, and on the contrary, when a text contains מא ...- ש (ما ...ش), מוש (موش), אלי (الي), it would be dialectal in style. But the situation is not so simple. In many texts, these literary and dialectal words co-exist, so it is necessary to examine the whole vocabulary in order to analyse the variation in the style.

Here I cite some exemplary passages with different contents, in which we can observe stylistic variations. Each text is followed by a rough translation.

(1) Passage from a booklet concerning legal matters [Text 08: 1]

חייתו אקתיצא מן ﭏזום צ̇ממאן ג,מיע אלתרתיבאת אלדי טלעו באואמר מן אלבלדייה אלדי תכץ אלמשי פ̇י אלשוארע ודאלך לאג,ל תחסין זבט אוצולאת אלמשי פ̇י אלטרק פ̇י דאכל חדוד מרכז ﭏבלדייה חתא מן ג,יהת ראחת אלנאס וסלאמתהם.

'When necessary, it is necessary to keep all the rules issued by the order of the municipality, which is concerned with the act of walking (or traffic) on the streets, and this is in order to improve the regulation of circulation of the walking (walkers) on the roads inside the city centre and also from the side of the comfort (for the comfort) and the safety of the people.'

This text is concerned with regulations for pedestrians in the city of Tripoli, to instruct them how to walk safely. Since it is an official announcement and includes juridical matters, the vocabulary and the expressions tend to be literary: חייתו (حيتو) 'as, due to', אקתיצ̇א (اقتيضا) 'necessity', לאג,ל (لاجل) 'for', זבט (زبط) 'regulation', אוצולאת (اوصالات) 'circulation', מן ﭏזום (من اللازوم) 'of necessity, it is necessary that…' (here the conjunction corresponding to CA أن is lacking). Note that in the word חייתו, the ending ו corresponds to the ending vowel of CA حيثُ. In addition, the *idāfa* construction is frequently used: צ̇ממאן ג,מיע אלתרתיבאת (ضممان جميع الترتيبات) 'keeping all the rules', תחסין זבט אוצולאת אלמשי (تحسين زبط اوصولات المشي) 'improvement of the regulation of the circulation of the walking (walkers)'. In other parts of this text, there are portions of text which contain many other literary words, such as קד (CA قَدْ), e.g., **קד** בטלו ג,מיע ﭏאומר (قد بطلو جميع الاوامر) 'All the rules were annulled' [Text 08: 01]; קטעיין (CA قطعيًّا), e.g., אישאראת אלתסמיע אלמדכורה הייא ממנועה **קטעיין** (ايشارات التسميع المدكوره هييا مملاوعه قطعيين) '(use of) klaxon (literally 'hearing signals') is strictly prohibited' [Text 08: 2]. It is true that this text is composed mainly of literary words, but some dialectal words and expressions also penetrate; the following are taken from other passages of the same text: מא …ש (ما …ش) 'not' in פי אלשוארע אלדי מא פיהמש האד אלכטוט (في الشوارع الدي ما فيهمش هاد الخطوط) 'in the streets in which these lines don't exist' [Text 08: 2–16]; באש (باش) 'in order to' in ממנוע עלה ﭏמאשיין עלא רג,ליהם באש ימשיו או יוקפו פי ג,יהת אלטרק… (الماشيين علا رجليهم باش يمشيو او اعقفو في جيهت الطرق) 'it is prohibited for the walkers to go or stop at the side of the roads…' [Text 08: 2–9]. On the other hand, this text assiduously avoids the use of מתע (متع) 'of' or אלי (الي) 'that' etc.

(2) Passage from an introductory booklet about Theodor Herzl and Zionism [Text 02: 4]
אלקתאל פי אֿמוסכו וצ̇̇יית אֿיהוד אלדי תוזזעת חתא פ̇י פ̇ראנצה לחררה ומסאלת דריפ̇וס פ̇ייקו פ̇י קלבו ג,מיע נואח קום אֿיהודי ועייט לג,מיע אֿדוול אֿמתמדנין אלדי חתא אחנאן קום ואחד וענדנא אֿחק באש נעישו מתל אלג̇יר ותכון תתאסס דולתנה.
'The massacre in Moscow and the hostility against the Jews which had spread even in free France and the Dreyfus affair raised in his heart all the lamentation of the Jewish people and he called to all the civilised country that we too are one people, and we have the right to live as others and for our state to be established.'

This passage contains many words seemingly borrowed from CA: קתאל (قتال) 'massacre', צ̇̇ייה (ضضييه) 'hostility', מתמדנין (متمدنين) 'civilised', תאסס (تاسس) 'to be established', דולה (دوله) 'state'. On the other hand, it contains relatively few dialectal words and expressions: חתא (حتا) 'even, also', אחנאן (احنان) 'we'—one of the key words that distinguishes JAL from other dialects (Mor 2020, 97; Yoda 2005, 115)—באש (باش) 'in order to', and in other parts of this text the preposition מתע (متع) 'of' is frequently used.

(3) Passage from a booklet for the enlightenment of the Jews of Libya for a better life by teaching scientific matter about everyday subjects such as water, hygiene, alcoholism, vaccination, etc. [Text 06: 2]

קדדאש מן יהוד בלאדנה אלדי מגבונין כאנו כאיפין מן אלבומבה מתאע
אלבאלון ארבו ללזאויה ולמטארח אכרין ותבאעהום ואחד עדו אכר
וקתלהום אלעדו הווא אלמיכרובו יעני זנז דוד אלדי נצר בנאדם לם יקדר
ישופו ואלדי תכשיפתהו תביינת פי וקת קריב בזנז מראיה...

'How many Jews of our country who are deceived were afraid of the bombs of the (combat) plain (and) fled to Zawiya and other places and there follows them another enemy and this enemy kills them, who is "microbe", namely a kind of worm which the view (eye) of the human being cannot see, and whose discovery appeared in close time (recently) with a kind of mirror.'

This passage contains a lot of dialectal words: קדדאש מן (قدداش من) '(how) many',[6] מתאע (متاع) 'of', מטארח 'places' (sg. מטראח), זנז (زنز) 'kind' (cf. *zəns*; Yoda 2005, 346). On the other hand, it also contains such literary elements as לם (لم) 'not' (used before a verb in the perfect or imperfect: Yoda 2015, 73–76), אלדי (الذي) '[relative pronoun]', אכרין (اخرين) 'others' (dialectal form is *čanyin*; see Yoda 2005, 319). As for the verb שאף (شاف) 'to see', here found in the form ישופו (يشوفو) 'they see it (m.)', it is not used, at least in Tripoli where *ṛa* is usually used (Yoda 2005, 188), so it may be considered a kind of literary word. There are many cases where dialectal words from dialects other than Libyan dialects (especially Tunisian) are found. A possible explanation for this phenomenon, namely the usage of Tunisian expressions in Tripolitanian texts, is that, as stated above, when the usual TrJ word for

---

6 The literary meaning is 'how many…', but in this case, the word does not have such an interrogative or exclamative meaning, but means merely 'many'; see example (6) below.

'to see' *ṛa* appears in written texts, it gives the impression that the passage is very colloquial or vulgar, and in order to avoid such a negative impression, a less familiar word שאף (شاف) is used. On the other hand, the CA word نظر is also found in some texts, e.g., משה נפטר מן ג̇יר מא נצ̇ר אלארץ (مشه نفطر من غير ما نظر الارض) 'Moses died without seeing the land' [Text 02: 3] (נפטר is a Hebrew word 'he died').

(4) Passage from a booklet concerning the legal affairs of Libyan Jews under Italian rule at the beginning of the twentieth century [Text 13: 18]
ﭏמג̣לס יג̣תמע בﭏאוציל מרתין פ̇אלעאם לאכן יצירלו ﭏאג̣תימאע כ̇ארג ﭏעאדא פ̇לוקת ﭏאזם ביאסתקראר ﭏכומסיון ﭏמוג̣ריא או תחת טלב מקסם לם ינקץ מן תלת לעצ̇אואת ﭏמתוצ̇פין.
'The assembly will be held usually twice a year, but an exceptional assembly may be held, when necessary, by the decision of the executive commission or under the shared request of members which is not less than three appointed members.'

The speciality of this booklet is that each sentence has two versions; both are Judaeo-Arabic, namely Arabic written in Hebrew script, but one in a style close to CA, which is referred to in the text as רסמי (رسمي) 'official', and another in dialectal JAL, which is referred to as שרח (شرح) 'explanation'. The above-mentioned passage is 'שרח' corresponding to the following 'רסמי' version (Yoda, 2016): יג̣תמע ﭏמג̣לס עאדתן מרתין פ̇אלסנא ולאכן יג̣וז להו ענד מסיס ﭏחאג̣א אן יעקד אג̣תימאעאת פ̇וק ﭏעאדא בקראר לג̣נת ﭏתנפ̇יד או טלב תלת ﭏאעצ̇אי ﭏמווצ̇פין עלא ﭏאקל.

Figure 2: [Text 13] p. 18

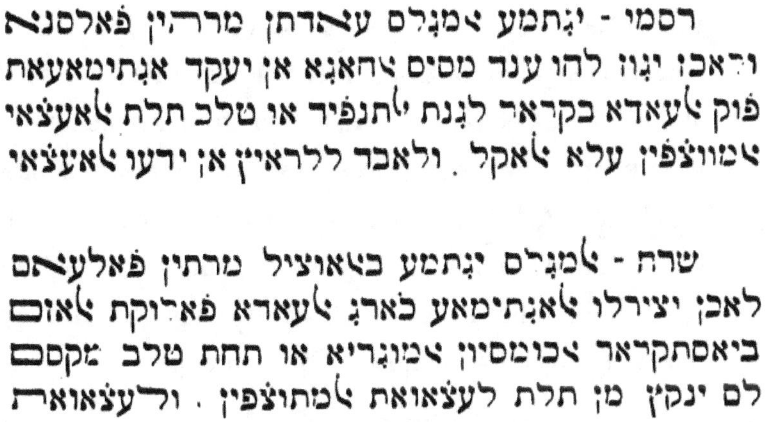
רסמי - יגתמע אלמגלס עאדתן מרתין פאלסנא
ואכד יגוז להו ענד מסיס אלחאגא אן יעקד אגתיטאעאת
פוק אלעאדא בקראר לגנת אלתנפיד או טלב תלת אלאעצ'אי
אלמוותצפין עלא אלאקל . ולאכד ללראיין אן ידעו אלאעצ'אי

שרח - אלמגלס יגתמע באלאוציל מרתין פאלעאם
לאכן יצירלו אלאגתימאע כארג אלעאדא פאלוקת אלאזם
ביאסתקראר אלכומסיון אלמוגריא או תחת טלב אלמקסם
לם ינקץ מן תלת לעצ'אואת אלמתוצפין . ולעצ'אואת

Comparing these two versions, only slight differences are found. For 'year' in שרח, the word עאם (عام), which is indeed dialectal, is used; on the other hand, in רסמי, the word סנא (سنا) is used. 'Exceptional' is expressed with different prepositions: כ̇ארג אלעאדא (خارج العادا), with כ̇ארג (خارج), in שרח, and פ̇וק כ̇ארג אלעאדא (فوق خارج العادا), with פ̇וק (فوق), in רסמי. In this passage, only a few dialectal words are observed, but in other passages, more dialectal words are found: מוש (موش) in מוש אקל מן תמניא ורבעין סאעא (موش اقل من تمنيا وربعين ساعا) 'not less than 48 hours' [Text 13: 18]; אלי in לעצאואת אלי נזאדו (لعصاوات الي نزادو) 'the added members' [Text 13: 14–19]; etc.

(5) Passage from a newspaper article [Text 4: 53–54]

מן אלגואב אלמרסול מן חצ̇רת ראייס אלכומוניטא לסי יעקב חדאד עבובי יבאן
אלי בניאן בית הכנסת גדידה פ̇י שארע מיזראן הווא יחב יציר מן טרף סי
חדאד אלמדכור יעני מן מאלהו ונסתגרבו כתיר לממא נשופו רציפ̇תנא
גרידת "דג̇ל ציון" תקול אלי אלבניאן אלמדכור יחב יציר בואסטת יעקוב חדאד.
תממא פ̇רק כביר פ̇לכלאם ומא נערפ̇וש יאהלתרא הדג̇ל געל דאך̇ בסהוו
אוו בע̇רץ̇.

> 'From the letter from Mr president of the community to Mr Yaqob Haddad Abubi, it seems that the construction of the new synagogue in Mizran street will be carried out by the above-mentioned Mr Haddad, namely from his money. And we are astonished when we see (saw) our fellow newspaper *Degel Zion* saying that the above-mentioned construction will be carried out by the agency of Yaqob Haddad. There is a big difference in the saying and we don't know if *Degel* put (wrote up) that by mistake or by intention.'

This passage contains relatively many dialectal words; the verb יחב (يحب) is used as auxiliary verb indicating the future (Yoda 2005, 194) and does not mean 'to like, to love'. סי (سي) 'Mr' is a dialectal word. תממא (تمما) 'there is, there are' (TrJ *čəmma*) corresponds to CA ثم. For the negation of verbs, מא ...ש (ما ...ش) is used. And the following literary words are found: a phrase יאהלתרא (ياهلترا) taken from CA يا هل ترى with the meaning of 'if, whether', corresponding to Tunisian dialect *yindṛa*;[7] לממא (لمما) 'when' (TrJ *wəqtli, kif*); גִעל (جعل) 'to put'; and כתיר (كتير) 'much' should be considered a literary word, since in TrJ *bzayd* is used for this meaning.

(6) From a newspaper article [Text 7: 60]

סמענא אלדי מוג'ודין קדאש מן שרכאננא קבלו לעדד אלאכ'יר מתע הדגל אכתר מוכ'כ'ר עלא אלעאדא ופיה מנהם אלדי מא קבלוש בלכל. סבב דאלך הווא מן ג'יהת ל̇עטלא ל̇די תעטטל פלמוראקבא (שנסורא) לנהו מא תסררח כאן מוכ'כ'ר בלכל יעני יום ל̇ג'מעא סאעתין קבל ל̇מגרב וזאדא מן ג'יהת אלדי אלמתכללף בתוזיע אלג'רידא כאן ג'דיד ומא ענדוש

---

[7] Singer (1984, 737) gives a meaning 'wer weiß (den) shon wie / was'.

מערפא כבירא פלשרכאן. בדאלך נטלבו אלעפו מן אחבאבנא לכראם ונקולו אומור מתל האדא לם יזידו יתעאודו פלמסתקבל.

'We heard that many of our subscribers received the last issue of the *Degel* (*Zion*) later than usual and there are among them some who never received it. The reason thereof is from the delay, which was caused by the censor, because it was only released completely late, namely two hours before sunset on Friday; in addition because the person in charge of the distribution of the newspaper was a new fellow and did not have enough knowledge about the subscribers. Therefore, we apologise to our dear friends and say (that) such a matter won't be repeated in the future.'

This passage is an announcement of a newspaper, from the editor to the readers. It contains many dialectal words: קדאש מן (قداش من) 'many' (see (3) above); מתע (متع) 'of'; אכתר מוכ'כ'ר (اكثر موخخر) 'later', which is a comparative composed of *kčər* + positive degree of adj. (Yoda 2005, 287); מא... כאן (ما... كان) 'only'. זאדא (زادا) 'also' is indeed a dialectal word mainly used in Tunisian dialects (see Singer 1984, 666), but not frequently used in TrJ, where *ḥətča* is more popular. For this phenomonon, see (3) above. At the same time, CA words are included: לנהו (لنهو) 'because' (CA لأنه), מתל (متل) 'as, like', לם (لم) 'not'. It is worthwhile to note that מוראקבא[8] (موراقبا) is followed by an Italian gloss (in Hebrew script) שנסורא (شنسورا; It. *censura* 'censor').

[8] ו in מוראקבא (موراقبا = CA مراقبة) reflects the same phenomenon explained above in §4.0. for the CA word جريدة.

(7) From a Hebrew textbook [Text 11: 1–1–3]

"המבשר העברי" ענד אנתשארהו אליום יקדדם סלאמהו אלצאפׄי ואלקלבי ללחכומה ולגׅמיע אלסלטאת ולקהלת טראבלס וללצחאפׄה. האדי אלגׅרידה אלנאתגׅה ברגׄבת גׅמאעה מן שבבאן אצחאב אגׅתהאד מקצודהא תהמז אלתקדדם אלעלמי בין יהוד טראבלס ומעא אלוקת נפׄסהו תתמים האדוך אלעלום אלאבתדאייה אלמפׄרוצׄה עלא כל יהודי צאלח.

'*The Hebrew Herald*, by its publication today, sends its sincere and heartful greetings to the government and all the authorities and the Jewish community of Tripoli and the press(es). The aim of this newspaper, (which was issued) as a result of the desire of the diligent young people, is to promote scientific progress among the Tripolitanian Jews and at the same time the perfection of this elementary science which is obligatory for each good Jew.'

This passage is literary in style and vocabulary, except for two dialectal words: האדי (هادي) 'this (f.)' and האדוך (هادوك) 'those'.

(8) From a newspaper [Text 11: 1–6–1]

גרידתנא תכללמת סאבק עלא עדדת מסאיל ילזם תצליחהם. וראינא נאס כׅתירא תלאחץׄ עליהא ונאס קדדמלתנא (= קדדמתלנא) תשכר ומדח עלא מא אחנאן מגׅתהדין פׄי וסאיט אמור תצליח בעץׄ נקסאת מכדדרה. וראינא נאס עדידא בדאת תפׄטן בסירתהא אלמאילה ותרגע באנפׄסהא.

'Our newspaper previously talked about a number of problems which have to be adjusted. And we saw many people observing them, (we saw) people who presented to us thanks and praise for that we are diligent in the matter of the improvement of some troublesome faults. And we saw many people begin to notice the tendency and reflect on themselves.'

The verb תכללמת (تكللمت) ‘it (f.) spoke’ is not a usual word in TrJ, where *dwa* is used, but it is usual in Tunisian dialects. This may be the same phenomenon mentioned above with respect to the verb שאף (شاف). At the same time, it is also a CA word; therefore it is probable that תכללמת (تكللمت) is taken from Tunisian dialect or CA.

(9) From a religious story contained in a book of Passover Haggada [Text 09: 51]

פי אייאם ניסן מליח יאסר אלי יכ̇רג̇ לסוואני באש ישוף אצ̇זר אלי פיהום אנוואר ויבארך̇ ברכת האילנות. אלי קאלו פזוהר הקדוש אלי פי האד לייאם מתאע ניסן יקאעדו הנשמות אלי מא זכ̇אוושי לגן עדן פוק אצ̇זר ולעשבים. ובהאד לברכה יצירלהום תיקון כ̇ביר ויזכ̇אוו למטראחהום.

‘In the day of Nisan, it is very good to go out to the field in order to see the trees in which (there are) flowers and to bless the blessing of the tree. What they said in the holy Zohar is that in these days of Nisan, the spirits which have not attained to the Gan Eden are on the trees and the grasses. And by this blessing a great reform occurs for them (the spirits) and they will attain to their place.’

This passage contains the typical dialectal words אלי ‘that’ (rel. pron.), באש (باش) ‘in order to’, and יאסר (ياسر) ‘very’, and no element from literary Arabic is found. אצ̇זר (اصّزر) ‘the tree’ is a transcription of the dialectal form *əṣ-ṣẓəṛ*. This text is deeply concerned with Jewish religious matters, so many Hebrew words are inserted.

(10) From a Hebrew textbook [Text 12: 49–4]

שמנדיפ̇יר מצאפר לפ̇יירה, פ̇טריק נזלו עליה קטעייא וגב̣רו אלמוצאפ̇רין
אלכול באש יקימו ידיהום לפ̇וק ובדאוו אלקטעייא יפ̇רג̇ו פ̇י ג̣יוב
אלמוצאפ̇רין. יהודי ואחד שיבאני לתפ̇ת לראייץ לקטעייא ימכנש תסררחני
אננזל ידייה? אנה ראג̣ל כביר ומא נקדרש נקימהום לפ̇וק. ראייץ
אלקטעייא סררחו, והאדאך פ̇יצע דכ̇כל ידדו פי ג̣יבו וטללאע 100 פ̇רנך
ועטאהום אלצאחבו אלדי ואקף פ̇י ג̣נבו. כיף הווא האיידאך,האוו אלמייאת
פ̇רנך אלדי תחב מנני ובררה כ̇לץ מא תטלב מנני שיי

‘A train was going to the fair, on the way a gang of robbers crashed into the train, assembled all the travellers to make them hold their hands up and began to empty the pocket of the travellers. An old Jewish man turned around to the chief of the gang of robbers (and said) “Can you allow me to put down my hand? I am an old man, and I cannot hold my hands up.” The chief of the gang of robbers freed him, then this man quickly put his hand in his pocket and took 100 francs and gave them to his friend who was standing by him. When he (did) so, (he said) “Here is the 100 francs which you want from me, now I paid you, so don’t ask me for anything.”’

This passage, a popular story (maybe a translation from a foreign language), is taken from a textbook for Hebrew published in Tripoli. It contains many dialectal words.

6.0. Conclusion

6.1. Variation in the Writing System

In this paper, only the variations of gimel, which represent the most complicated situation, are studied. The choice of the diacritic signs is arbitrary, but the same publication usually uses the same system.

6.2. Variation in Style

We mentioned above that some functional words have a literary form and a dialectal form. This distinction, however, in most cases does not clearly reflect the style and contents of the passage. Even texts which represent rather a literary style, for example Texts 08 and 13, contain dialectal words or expressions (see above). It is true that more literary passages contain fewer dialectal words and expressions, but cannot escape from them completely, and that more dialectal passages contain fewer literary words. Therefore, the relationship between the style and the literary-dialectal words is merely relative. The phenomenon whereby dialectal words that are not Tripolitanian (mainly Tunisian) are used for literary purposes is an interesting issue. The scale of publishing in Tunisia is far greater than that in Libya and the influence of publication culture from Tunisia on Libya should be considered with respect to this matter. It could be inferred that some authors are of Tunisian origin, but the fact that, except for those words in question, proper Libyan words and expressions are used may exclude this presumption. In order to deepen our knowledge of JAL, further analysis of the whole vocabulary, including expressions, of the texts at hand and a description of the grammar of JAL are necessary.

References

Documents in LJA

[Text 01] הסוכנות היהודית לא"י מחלקת הלקיטה, שער העליה. Tripoli, n.d.

[Text 02] הרצל וﭏציונים. Tripoli, n.d.

[Text 03] ההסתדרות הציונית בטריפוליטניה, פעלותיו בשנת התר'צב והתר'צג, מזכרת ליום חלקת הפרסיס השנים. Tripoli, 1933.

[Text 04] ההתעוררות *(Il Risveglio): Organo settimanale dell'Associazione Concordia e Progresso*. Tripoli, 14 March 1922.

[Text 05] אלציוניסם. Tripoli, 1920.

[Text 06] מסאיל אלדי בנאדם ילזם יערפהום. Tripoli, 1943(?).

[Text 07] דגל ציון *(Degel Zion): Unico Periodico Ebraico della Libia*. 3 July 1920.

[Text 08] Municipio di Tripoli. *Ordinanza 15 novembre 1936 XV relativa a norme per la circolazione stradale*. Tripoli, 1936.

[Text 09] Rabbi Haim ha-Kohen. הגדה של פסח—ערב פסח עם תרגום בשפה הערבית וכן דינים הנחצים לחודש ניסן. Jerusalem, 1989. [According to the biography of the author, Rabbi Haim ha-Kohen (1839–1905), the original book was published in Tripoli late in the nineteenth century (date not known)].

[Text 10] Comunita israelitica della Tripolitania, Tripoli. *Regolamento per le sinagoghe*. Tripoli, 1930.

[Text 11] המבשר העברי *(Il Messagerro Ebraico): Unico Quindicinale Ebraico della Tripolitania*. Year 1, no. 1, 19 March 1931.

[Text 12] קבץ למדו עברית: ללמוד השפה העברית ודקדוקה עם תרגום ערבית ואיטלקית ועזרה לבטוי בכתב לטיני. Tripoli, 1934.

[Text 13] Ministry of the Colonies. קואעד לאג'ל מועאמלאת קהל ישראל אלסאכנין פי עמאלת טראבלס (אמר ניאבי פי 26 אגוסט 1916 נומרו 1145) מתרג'ם מן אליאן בלערבי אלפקהי ומשרוח לסאן טראבלסי. Tripoli, 1917.

Secondary Sources

Avishur, Yitzhak. 2008–2010. *A Dictionary of the New Judeo-Arabic Written and Spoking* [*sic*] *in Iraq (1600–2000)*. 3 vols. Tel Aviv: Archeological Center Publication. [Hebrew].

Hary, Benjamin H. 1992. *Multiglossia in Judeo-Arabic with an Edition, Translation, and Grammatical Study of the Cairene Purim Scroll.* Leiden: Brill.

Khan, Geoffrey. 1992. 'Notes on the Grammar of a Late Egyptian Judaeo-Arabic Text'. *Jerusalem Studies in Arabic and Islam* 15: 220–39.

———. 2007. 'Judaeo-Arabic'. In *Encyclopedia of Arabic Language and Linguistics*, edited by Kees Versteegh et al, vol. 3, 526–36. Leiden: Brill.

Mor, Daniel. 2020. 'The Language of Tunisian Judeo-Arabic Journals (1885–1940)'. PhD dissertation, The Hebrew University of Jerusalem. [Hebrew].

Singer, H.-R. 1984. *Grammatik der arabischen Mundart der Medina von Tunis.* Berlin: Walter de Gruyter.

Yoda, Sumikazu. 2004. 'Notes on the Literary Idiom of the Tripolitanian Jewish Arabic'. *Kansai Journal of Arabic and Islamic Studies* 4: 63–75. [Japanese].

———. 2005. *The Arabic Dialect of the Jews of Tripoli (Libya)*. Wiesbaden: Harrassowitz Verlag.

———. 2015. 'Negation in Modern Tripolitanian Judaeo-Arabic'. *Journal of Arabic and Islamic Studies* 13: 63–86. [Japanese].

———. 2016. 'On Two Stylistic Varieties in a Modern Judaeo-Arabic Text from Tripoli, Libya'. *Studies in Language and Culture* 42: 195–217.

———. 2017. 'The Historical *h* in Some Eastern Maghribi Dialects Revisited'. In *Tunisian and Libyan Arabic Dialects: Common Trends–Recent Developments–Diachronic Aspects*, edited by Veronika Ritt-Benmimoun, 85–100. Zaragoza: Prensas de la Universitad ed Zaragoza.

SOME ARAB AND MUSLIM NAMES DISCERNIBLE IN MALTESE TOPONYMY

Mario Cassar

1.0. Introduction

Toponymy comprises the totality of toponyms (place-names) in a given region. A toponym, in turn, is a proper name applied to a geophysical or man-made feature.[1] The number of Maltese toponyms of Arabic origin is simply staggering. This Semitic treasure trove is notable for both its topographic and its anthroponymic repertoire. As a matter of fact, place-names may be divided into two broad categories: those including **descriptive** terms (e.g., *Ħal Saflieni, L-Għalqa l-Wistanija, Wied il-Kbir, Il-Baslija*) and those containing **personal** names (first names, surnames, and nicknames, e.g., *Għar Barka, Ġebel Jagħqub, Bir Buħaġar, Ħal Farruġ*). Arabic personal names of all types (both conventional and religious) are the point of interest of the present paper. Some names are secular, e.g., *Raqīq, Razīn,* and *Jaʿfar*; others have a Muslim (or Quranic) import, e.g., *Jabbār, Ḥamīd,* and *Salām*. The latter category includes **theophoric** epithets regarded as names of Allah.

[1] Actually, 'feature name' is a synonym of 'toponym'.

 https://doi.org/10.11647/OBP.0445.08

2.0. Essential Taxonymy

The first important distinction inherent in toponomastic studies is that between a **macrotoponym** and a **microtoponym** (Marcato 2009, 12). A macrotoponym is the name of a large place, such as a town, region, or vast agricultural estate. However, in some literature, the term is used to denote any inhabited area. Such a term is usually called a **polenym** (e.g., *Ħal Għaxaq, Bubaqra, Binġemma*). On the other hand, a microtoponym is the name of a very small place, such as a field, farm, or small agricultural district (e.g., *Il-Ġnien tas-Saqwi, Għalqet il-Qoton, Il-Wilġa tal-Fiddien*). However, in certain sources, the term is simply used to denote an uninhabited area. The vast majority of place-names listed in this paper fall in the second category.

There are several other ways of categorising place-names, but a typical method of classification is by semantic content. There are two main semantic categories, namely a **word-semantic** category (usually related to common nouns) and a **name-semantic** category (usually related to proper nouns). The former type is by far the more common one. The distinction can be exemplified in this manner: the Maltese place-names *Bir il-Qasab* 'the cistern or well beside the canes', *Wied il-Knejjes* 'the valley of the churches', and *Il-Wardija* 'watch post' are word-semantic toponyms; whereas *Ħal Safi* 'Sāfi's farmstead', *Għar Ħasan* 'Ḥasan's cave', and *Għajn Riħana* 'Rayhāna's spring' are name-semantic toponyms.

Another important distinction within the toponymic realm is that between **single-word** and **composite place names** (for definitions, see Kadmon 2002, 18–19). The former (often called simplex names) include *Il-Fawwara, Il-Balluta, Il-Miżieb* (Malta) and *Il-Qala, L-Għasri, L-Għarb* (Gozo); whereas the latter can be analysed as the compounding of a generic and a specific term (for definitions, see Kadmon 2002, 12, 24), e.g., *Għajn Fekruna, Ġnien il-Fieres, L-Andar tal-Ħafura, Wied Qirda, Raħal Tabuni.* The generic element names some topographic feature (*Għajn, Ġnien, Andar, Wied, Raħal*), whereas the specific element distinguishes it from others of the same feature class (*Fekruna, Fieres, Ħafura, Qirda, Tabuni*). In compound toponyms, personal names are hence always specific elements.

Toponymic nomenclature is so highly developed that special categories of names have to be designated. Some place-names related to geophysical features are derived from **hydronyms** (names of bays, lakes, springs, and rivers; hence *fawwara, għajn, miġra*, etc.), or **oronyms** (names of hills, mountains, caves, and valleys; hence *għolja, gudja, għaqba,* etc.). Some are derived from **geonyms** (meadows, plains, swamps, and grazing grounds; hence *xagħra, marġ, bur*, etc.), or **agronyms** (fields, orchards, gardens, and agricultural holdings; hence *ġnien, ħabel, raba'*, etc.). Some place-names are related to man-made structures, such as residential buildings (houses, farmsteads, huts; hence *dar, għarix, għorfa*, etc.) or thoroughfares (streets, alleys, pathways; hence *triq, sqaq, ħâra*, etc.; see Marcato 2009, 11). Others refer to rustic, religious, and military constructions (animal yards, cattle pens, sties; churches, chapels, abbeys; towers, forts, bastions; hence *mandra, mixta, merqad; dejr, knisja, misġed; qalgħa, qasar, sur*, etc.). Other miscellaneous man-made structures include tombs, windmills, and storerooms (hence *qabar, mitħna, maħżen*).[2] This rich taxonymy is enhanced by two other terms: **phytotoponyms** (toponyms with plant or tree names, e.g. *Il-Fulija, Il-Biżbiżija, Ix-Xewkija, Ta' Qronfla, Ta' Qasbi*) and **zootoponyms** (toponyms containing the names of animals of all kinds, e.g. *Ħabel tal-Għarnuq, L-Ibwar tal-Ħuttafa, Tal-Ġurdien, Ħal Għarux, Ta' Bir il-Lifgħa*; see Marcato 2009, 157, 159). It is quite evident that many designations in the later two categories were originally employed as nicknames, sometimes with ironic, humorous or mischievous connotations.

Within the Maltese toponymic repertoire, personal names are often made manifest either through the possessive preposition *Ta'* 'of' (e.g., *Ta' Mejmuna, Ta' Kemil, Ta' Ħalif*) or through the genitive function of the construct state (e.g., *Bir Ħamut, Ħabel Randan, Ġebel Selim, Xagħret Mewwija, Il-Bur ta' Ħirbit Baġar*).[3] Other names are harder to analyse. For example, within the mechanics of Maltese grammatical rules, the presence of the definite article preceding a personal name (e.g., *Il-Bir tal-Ferħa < Bir Ferħa, L-Għar tal-Bies < Għar Bies, Il-Ħabel tal-Ħanin < Ħabel Ħanin*) may sound baffling, but actually the phenomenon can be reasonably elucidated. When the anthroponymic value of the original name is no longer called to mind, the local population often tends to transform it into a recognisable word, either

[2] **Odonyms** are names given to roads, streets, pathways, and all types of thouroughfares; whereas **oikonyms** are names given to houses, villas, palaces, and all types of residential buildings.

[3] Note the use of the *t marbūṭa* (the 'tied' *t*, referring to the form of the Arabic letter ة as opposed to ت) in the latter examples.

through phonetic approximation or simply through common nominalisation. In the next stage of its evolution, the mutated term, now functioning as a noun, is intuitively appended to a definite article. In actual fact, some toponyms still survive in two parallel forms, one with the definite article and another without it (e.g., *Ta' Magħajjen/Tal-Magħajjen, Ta' Maħlula/Tal-Maħlula, Ta' Rajjes/Tar-Rajjes*). This confirms the aforementioned morphological progression.

Another conundrum arises from the fact that certain Arabic topographic terms are simultaneously attested as personal names; these include *Ayn* = *għajn, Wādi* = *wied, Ramlah* = *ramla, Jibal/Jabal* = *ġebel,* and *Marghah* = *mergħa.* Hence, toponyms such as *Wied il-Għajn* and *Il-Ġnien tar-Ramla* may be interpreted in two equally plausible ways. Are the second terms in each example topographic terms or personal names? Applying the abovementioned paradigm, the original place-names may have easily been *Wied Għajn* and *Ġnien Ramla,* in which case the construct state infers an anthroponym.

This takes us to the related realms of **deonomastics** and **folk etymology.**[4] The first field concerns the study of the process by which proper nouns are converted into common nouns. The second field (also known as 'popular etymology' or 'etymological reinterpretation') involves the change in a word (or phrase) resulting from the erroneous replacement of an unfamiliar form by

---

[4] For a definition of *deonomastics,* see https://www.garzantilinguistica.it/ricerca/?q=deonomastica, accessed 29 July 2024. For a comprehensive treatment of folk etymology, see Durkin (2013, 202–6).

a more familiar one. The form or the meaning of an archaic, foreign, or otherwise arcane word is reinterpreted so as to resemble more conversant words. Believing a word to have a certain origin, people begin to pronounce, spell, or otherwise use the word in a manner appropriate to that perceived or supposed origin.[5] By way of example, *Wied Xakura* was reanalysed as *Wied Xkora*, whereas *Ta' Ħumajra* was relexicalised as *Ta' Ħmajra*.

3.0. Arabic Nomenclature

In Arabic-Islamic usage, the full name of a person is usually made up of the following elements: *kunyah*, *ʾism*, *nasab*, and *nisba*. A certain number of persons are also known by a nickname (*laqab*)[6] or a pejorative sobriquet (*nabaz*), which, when the name is stated in full, comes after the *nisba*. In the present paper, more or less only the first three elements are taken into account, as *nisbas* and *laqabs* seldom translate into personal names.

The *kunyah* is usually an honorific compound name with *ʾAbū* 'father of' or *ʾUmm* 'mother of': *ʾAbū Dāwūd, ʾAbū Laylā, ʾUmm al-Ḥasān*.[7] It hence has the character of a **teknonym**,[8] that is, a name of a human being making reference to that person's child. Sometimes the *ʾAbū* loses its original sense completely and becomes a synonym of *dhū* 'the man with…', hence acquiring a

[5] See also https://en.wikipedia.org/wiki/Folk_etymology, accessed 29 July 2024.

[6] The Maltese word for 'nickname' is, incidentally, *laqam*.

[7] This kind of nomenclature is predominantly used in the Mashriq, far less in North African countries.

[8] Alternatively know as 'filionym' or 'paedonym'.

descriptive function, e.g., *ʾAbū Liḥya (bū laḥya)* means 'bearded person'. By extension, *ʾAbū* can also mean 'the master of', 'the holder of', 'the possessor of', 'the foremost of', 'the leader of', 'the first of', etc. Hence, *ʾAbū* (or *Dhū*) *ʾl-Yamīnayn* means 'the possessor of two right hands'. In other instances, it denotes proliferation/multiplicity, especially obvious in the dialects, as in the North African appellative *bū khamsa* 'master or possessor of five'.

The *kunyah* is often applied to certain animals, e.g., *ʾAbū Faris* 'lion', *ʾAbū Sulaymān* 'cock', *ʾUmm ʿĀmir* 'hyena'; to certain plants, e.g., *ʾAbū Farwa* 'chestnut'; or even to all sorts of things which are in some degree personified, e.g. *ʾAbū Qubays*, an oronym (EOI 5:396).

The *ʾism*, also called *ʿalam* or *ʾism ʿalam*, is the individual's personal or given name. It can be of several types. Some are ancient Arab names, mostly of pre-Islamic origin, and in the form of adjectives (e.g., *al-Ḥasān* 'good', 'handsome'), elatives (e.g., *Aḥmad* 'the most praised'), substantives (e.g., *ʾAsad* 'lion'), participles (e.g., *Muḥammad* 'praiseworthy'), or verbs of incomplete action (e.g. *Yazīd* 'he increases'). Some were originally used with the article (e.g., *al-ʿAbbās* 'stern', 'austere'), though many of those lost it in the course of time (e.g., *ʿAbbās*; EOI 4:179).

Others, such as *Ibrāhīm (Abraham)*, *Ishāq (Isaac)*, *Mūsā (Moses)*, *Yūsuf (Joseph)*, and *Ismāʿīl (Ishmael)*, are biblical names in their Quranic forms. Then there are compound theophoric names in two main patterns: (a) *ʿAbd* 'slave [of]' followed by *Allāh* or one of the divine names; (b) *Allāh* preceded by a construct substantive (e.g. *Hibat Allāh* 'gift of God').

The *nasab* is a lineage or pedigree name, comprising a list of ancestors, each name being introduced by the patronymic element *ibn* 'son of', e.g., *ibn ʿUmar.*[9] Arab historians quote as many generations as they feel to be necessary and sometimes go back a very long way when dealing with an eminent person or in order to avoid confusion, but the usual practice is to limit the *nasab* to one or two ancestors.

The *nisba* is an adjective ending in *-ī*, formed originally from (a) the name of the individual's tribe, clan, sect, dynasty, school of law, or eponymous ancestor (e.g., *al-Qurashī* 'of the Qurashi tribe'); (b) the place of birth, origin, or residence (e.g., *al-Māliṭī* 'the Maltese'); and occasionally from (c) a trade or profession (e.g., *al-Harīrī* 'the silk weaver'). In Arabic, the *nisba* is generally preceded by the definite article *al-* (see EOI 4:179, 8:53–6).

The *laqab* can be an honorific title or a distinctive epithet (e.g., *al-Rašīd* 'the one who rules rightly'), usually placed after the *nisba.* But in its simplest form, the *laqab* is a descriptive nickname with neutral connotations, usually referring to a physical characteristic (e.g., *al-Ṭawīl* 'the tall [one]'),[10] which follows the *ʾism.* These nicknames are felt to be less pejorative than the sobriquets (*nabaz*) such as *al-Ḥimār* 'the ass' (see EOI 4:180–1, 5:618–31). Names of animals and birds of prey are also common as *laqabs* (e.g., *al-ʿUqāb* 'the eagle').

---

[9] The *nasab* is always a patronymic; the only notable exception to this, a matronymic, was a special case: *ʿIsa ibn Maryam* 'Jesus, the son of Mary'.

[10] The termination *-ānī* is often used in an intensive or elative sense.

In this way, full Arabic names run like: ʾAbū ʾl-Faḍl Muṣṭāfa ibn Khālid al-Baġdādī, or ʾAbū Zayd ʿUmar bin Salem al-Ṣayrafī.

4.0. An Inventory of Names

Each entry is divided in two (sometimes three) parts: (i) the etymology and meaning of the relevant name (including alternative romanised forms); (ii) the toponym(s) bearing the said name (with their respective location and earliest attestation, whenever available); and (iii) further notes and alternative derivations (whenever appropriate). In some cases, I have referred to certain historical figures whose designations serve as proof that the relevant names truly exist.

Baġar: phonetic variant of Ar. male *ʾism Bajāl* (*r* < *l*) 'stately old man', 'prince' (PMI 313).

Tal-Baġar (Wied il-Għajn, 1537), Bir Baġar (Ħax-Xluq, 1557), Bjar Baġar (Qrendi, 1501), Ħirbit Baġar (Tal-Ħandaq, 1528), Ta' Ħirib Baġar (Tal-Ibjar, 1532), Meġil Baġar (Gozo, 1581), Il-Ħara ta' Meġil Baġar (id.).

Baħar: < Ar. *ʾism Baḥr* 'sea', 'ocean'. Less likely, (a) < Ar. fem. *ʾism Bahār* 'spring (time)', 'blossom' (DMN 245); or (b) < Ar. *ʾism Bahār* 'spice' (DAFN 1:83).

Il-Ħara ta' Meġil/Meġin Baħar (Gozo, 1578), Meġil Baħar (Gozo, 1720), Meġin il-Baħar (Gozo, 1578).

Baħrejn in the toponyms Il-Ħara ta' Meġil Baħrejn and Meġil Baħrejn (both found in Gozo) represents the dual form, quite common in Arabic toponymy.

Bakrat/Baqrat: < Ar. *ʾism Bakra* (+ 'tied' *t*). Unexplained. Cf. *Bubaqra* (q.v.).

Il-Ħabel ta' Bakrat (Tal-Qolla Bajda, Gozo, 1548), Tal-Baqrat (Il-Ħara tal-Imġarr, Gozo, 1577).

Bakr, incidentally, is an Arabic name for boys that arguably means 'new', 'innovative', 'untouched'. It is derived from the Quranic root *B-K-R*.

Baqqari: < Ar. *baqqār* (a) 'cattle-drover'; (b) 'ditch-digger'. The *-ī* suffix might be added to the name of a client or dependent of someone known as *(al-)Baqqār*. Wettinger (PMI 18) insists that it is habitually used as a personal name (in the former sense) among Arabophones. Less likely, a possible phonetic variant of the Romance surname *Vaccaro* (PMI 18). Cf. Mal. *baqra* 'cow'.

Baqqari/Tal-Baqqari (1419–20), Il-Ħara tal-Baqqari (Gozo, 1581).

Ar. male *ʾism Bakkāri* 'one who leaves early in the morning' provides another possible interpretation. Cf. Mal. *bakkâr* 'early riser'.

Barak/Beraq: perhaps a degeminated form of Ar. male *ʾism Barrāq* 'flashing', 'bright', 'brilliant', 'glittering' (DMN 35). Cf. Ar. male *ʾism Bāriq* 'shining', 'lightning', 'bright', 'illuminating' (DMN 29); Jewish name *Barak* 'lightning'; Mal. *beraq* (same meaning).

Is-Sined ta' Barak/Is-Sined ta' Beraq (Gelmus, Gozo, 1581), Ta' Beraq/Tal-Beraq (Għoxx il-Għorob, 1584).

Otherwise, a cognate form of *Barka* (q.v.).

Barka: < Ar. fem. *ʾism Baraka(h)* 'a blessing', 'the breath (essence) of life from which the evolutionary process unfolds'. Cf. *Barakāt* 'blessings', 'good fortunes', 'prosperities'; pl. of *Barakat* 'blessing' (DMN 34).

Għar Barka (near Rabat, Malta, 1436), Iċ-Ċagħkija ta' Għar Barka (id., 1539), Il-Ħamrija ta' Għar Barka (id., 1549). Cf. Tal-Berqa (Ħal Qadi, 1540). Cf. Gozitan top. Ta' Berqa/Tal-Berqa (PNG 1.1:21).

Bassar: < Ar. male *ʾism Bashshār* 'bringer of good news'.

Bjar Bassar/Bjar il-Bassar (Ħal Tigan, 1533).

Possible personal nickname. Mal. *bassâr* and *baxxâr* (same meaning) are interchangeable.

Battala: possibly the fem. form of Ar. male *ʾism Baṭṭāl* 'brave', 'hero', 'champion' (PMI 23).[11]

Ta' Battala (Ħal Luqa, 1502).

Less likely < male *ʾism Battāl* 'ascetic', 'virtuous'.

Bengħisa: Cf. *Bin Għisa* (q.v.).

Berqa: < Ar. fem. *ʾism Barqa(h)* 'flash of light', 'one flash of lightning'. Cf. *Barak* (q.v.).

Tal-Berqa (Ħal Qadi, 1540). Cf. top. Tal-Berqi.

Possible nickname meaning 'flash of lightning' (cf. Mal. *berqa*); or a phonetic variant of *birka* 'pond', 'pool', 'small lake' (unattested in Mal. dictionaries; see PMI 25). Otherwise, simply a lexical variant of *Barka* (q.v.), the interpretation favoured by Cooperson (p.c.).

Bies: < Ar. male *ʾism Bāz* 'peregrine falcon', 'northern goshawk' (DMN 37). The name is borne by, among others, Lebanese Christians. It is also found as a Spanish name, of the same origin (DAFN 1:118).

---

[11] In Arabic, it also occurs with a short vowel, *Baṭal*.

Tal-Bies (Siġġiewi, 1501), Ħaġret il-Bies (Ħal Kbir, 1531), L-Għar tal-Bies (San Dimitri, Gozo, 1746), Ir-Roqgħa ta' Ġebel Bies (Ħal Kirkop, 1688). Ħabel Pas (?) involves devoicing (*p* < *b*).

Possible ornithological nickname < Mal. *bies* (same meaning).

Binġemma/Benġemma: perhaps < Ar. *nasab Bin Jemmha* < fem. *ʾism Jammah,* arguably meaning 'well (full of water)'. The words *jammah* and *jummah* exist in various meanings but none are attested as personal names.

Binġemma (Mġarr, Malta, 1400), Ta' Benġemma/Ta' Binġemma (1473), Il-Ħara ta' Benġemma/Binġemma (Gozo, 1570), Wied Benġemma/Binġemma (Nadur, Gozo, 1525).

Otherwise, *Gemma* is a Romance fem. name meaning 'precious gemstone', 'jewel'; this interpretation is favoured by Cooperson (p.c.).

Bin Għali: < Ar. *nasab Ibn ʿAlī* or *Ibn Ghālī*. The male name, usually romanised as *Ali,* means 'high', 'lofty', 'sublime'; *al-ʿĀlī* is one of the Quranic names of Allah (DMN 13). Cf. *Għali* (q.v.).

Bin Għali (St Agatha, near Baqqari, 1536).

Benali still survives as a surname in Italy (DCA 76).

Bin Għisa: < Ar. *nasab Ibn ʿĪsā* (male name usually romanised as *Isa,* as well as *Eisa* or *Eesa*) 'Jesus, son of Maryam and messenger of Allah' (DMN 82). Cf. Heb. *Yeshua* 'saviour'. The name is borne by both Christian and Muslim Arabs (DAFN 2:235). Cf. *Għisa* (q.v.).

Bin Għisa/Bengħisa (Birżebbuġa, 1500), Il-Mellieħa ta' Bin Għisa (id., 1557).

Bin Naħla: Cf. *Naħla* (q.v.).

Bin Saliba: < Ar. *nasab Bin Ṣalībā* 'son of *Ṣalībā*' < Syriac *Salībā*—a Christian family name of Syriac–Aramaic origin used in the Levant, with obvious reference to the crucifixion of Jesus Christ.

Bin Saliba (unlocated, 1530).

The name survives to this day as a Maltese surname *Saliba.*

Bin Werrad: < Ar. *nasab Bin Warrād* 'son of *Warrād*'. The name in modern Arabic means 'florist', but its original meaning (from the root *W-R-D*) might have been different altogether. Cooperson (p.c.) cautiously suggests 'one who descends frequently to water'.

Bin Werrad (south of Salina Bay, 1361), Il-Ħabel Binwerrad/Il-Ħabel Binwarrad (Binwerrad, 1542), Il-Wileġ ta' Benwarrad (id, 1539).

Wettinger (PMI xviii) intimates that the top. Bin Arrad is a parallel form. *Werrad* may, on the other hand, be a reflex of a Romance surname of the type *Verratti.*

Bixir: < Ar. *ʾism Bishr* 'joy', 'happiness', 'cheerfulness' (DMN 38). Bishr ibn Maʿrūr was the name of a *sahābi.*

Ta' Bixir (Ta' Sammut, 1501), Ġebel Bixir (Birżebbuġa, 1539), Wied Bixir ta' Ħal Kbir (1586).

Another candidate is Ar. *ʾism Bashīr* 'bringer of good news', 'Messenger sent by Allah'—an epithet of Muhammad (DMN 35–36). *Bashīr*, however, works only if the stress is on the second syllable. Cf. Mal. *baxar* 'to bring news', 'to announce'; *bxara* 'announcement', 'news of an event'.

Bixrun: < Ar. male *ʾism Bishr* 'joy', 'cheerfulness', 'optimism', 'geniality' + Maghrebi suffix *–ūn.*[12] *Bishrūn* is extant in present-day Morocco and Algeria. Cf. *Bixir* (q.v.)

Ta' Bixrun (1497).

Bubaqra: < Ar. *kunyah Abū Bakra*. The meaning of *Bakra* remains unexplained.

Bubaqra (Żurrieq, 1419–20), Il-Kemmuniet ta' Bubaqra (id., 1507).

Some have tentatively proposed a reflex of the *kunyah ʾAbū Bakr* 'father of the young camel'. In that case, locally, *Bakr* may have acquired the final *-a* in the same way that *Sultana, Farrugia,* and *Saliba* developed respectively from *sulṭān, farrūğ,* and *ṣalīb,* reflecting the influence of Romance morphology.

Following Wehr, Caracausi (1:783) translates *Bū l-baqar* as 'that of the cows', but still does not ignore *Bū Bakr*. The element *baqra* in the present form of the place-name, is in all probability, a relexicalised form (through popular etymology).

Bufula: < Ar. *kunyah* of the *abū* type. The second element is either *fūla* 'broad bean' or perhaps *fulah* '(white) light', 'beam'.

Ta' Bufula (Wardija, St Paul's Bay, 1495), Wied Bufula (Wardija, St Paul's Bay, 1495).

Possible ornithological nickname meaning 'warbler', 'wren' < Mal. *bufula* (local formation); this is the interpretation favoured by Cooperson (p.c.).

---

[12] This usually has a hypocoristic value.

Buġibba: < Ar. *kunyah* of the *abū* type; the second element may reflect the fem. (non-Quranic) *ʾism Jabbā, Jabā* 'slim', 'slender'.

Buġibba (near St Paul's Bay, 1417).

Otherwise, the second element may be related to *jubba* 'long outer garment, open in front, with wide sleeves'. Reem Mehoudi (p.c.) reports that the garment is called *jibba* in Tunis and *jubba* in the Sahel. Jebba, on the other hand, is a city divided between two states, Kwara and Niger; the name means 'flowing water'. Cf. Ar. *jubb* 'well', 'cistern'; *jūba* 'watering trough'.

Buġimgħa: < Ar. *kunyah* of the *abū* type; the second element is probably the male *ʾism Jama* < *jumʿah* 'Friday, the Islamic holy day'.

Ta' Buġimgħa (Ħax-Xluq, 1501), Bur Buġimgħa (Mwieżeb, 1536).

Buciumì (< *Būjumʿah*) survives as a Sicilian family name (Caracausi 1:207).

Bugħarbiel: < Ar. *kunyah* of the *abū* type. The second element is presumably related to the male *ʾism Mugharbal* 'chosen', 'select', 'pure'. The cacographic mutation *Bu-* < *Mu-* cannot be excluded either.

Ta' Bugħarbiel (Ħal Bisqallin, Żejtun, 1486).

The Sicilian family name *Garboli* may derive from Ar. *gharbāl, ghirbal* 'sieve', 'sift', 'strainer' (Caracausi 1:681). Metaphorically, 'to sift' means 'to go through, especially to sort out what is useful or valuable'; hence the semantic correlation with *Mugharbal*. Cf. Mal. *għarbiel*. Salafia (p.c.) ponders the possibility of *għarbiel* being a cryptic form of *Grabiel* (*Gabriel*, via metathesis and hypercorrection).

Buħaġar: < Ar. *kunyah* of the *abū* type, comprising the term *ḥajar* 'stones', 'rocks' (Caracausi 1:212).

Bir Buħaġar (probably at Xwieki, 1538), Il-Ħamrija ta' Buħaġar (id., 1548).

The name survives to this day as a Maltese surname *Buhagiar*. *Buaggiaro* and *Boageri* are Sicilian surnames derived from the same source (Caracausi 1:204). Jebel ʾAbūhajr is a western Palestinian toponym meaning 'rocky mountain'. Bou Hajar is an Algerian toponym. Examples like these have led Cooperson (p.c.) to suppose that some of the *Bu*-names may actually refer to places, not people.

Buleben: < Ar. *kunyah ʾAbū Leben*, containing the *ʾism Laban* < 'buttermilk', 'yogurt', 'any food or beverage produced from fermented milk'. Cf. Ar. *labbān* 'milkman'.

Buleben (1465).

The Hebrew biblical name *Lābān* means 'white'.

Burix: < Ar. *kunyah* of the *abū* type. As it stands, the second element is probably *rīsh* 'feathers'. Cf. Mal. *rixa* 'feather', 'line'. If the original name included a final *-a*, it might have been derived from the affective personal name *Rīsha* (same meaning) or Tunisian Arabic *rīsha* 'prestige', 'charisma' (Reem Mehoudi, p.c.).

Ħabel Burix (unlocated, 1538), L-Ubwar ta' Burix (Ta' Burix, 1523).

Busewdien: < Ar. *kunyah* of the *abū* type, comprising the male *ʾism Sawdān* (*Saudan*) 'great', 'glorious', 'magnificent'.

Ta' Busewdien (San Pankrazju, near Wardija, 1486), Il-Qalgħa ta' Busewdien (Busewdien, 1560).

Otherwise, Mal. *sewdien* means 'darkish', 'blacklish'.

Busif: < Ar. *kunyah* of the *abū* type, comprising the male *ʾism Sayf* 'sword'. *Abū Sayf* (usually spelled *Abouseif* in Roman script) is a present-day Egyptian family name. Cf. Mal. *sejf* 'sword', 'dagger'.

Ta' Busif (Ħax-Xluq, 1547).

Another possible interpretation suggests the (non-Quranic) male *ʾism Sīf* < *sīf* 'coast', 'shore'.

Butiġieġ: < Ar. *kunyah* of the *abū* type, comprising the term *dajāj*, pl. form of *dajāja, dijāğa, dujāja* 'chickens', '(domestic) fowls' (Caracausi 1:223).

Ta' Butiġieġ (Ħas-Sejjieħ, 1537), Wied Butiġieġ (unlocated, 1556).

The name survives to this day as a Mal. surname *Buttigieg*.

Butomna: < Ar. *kunyah* of the *abū* type; *al-thumna* probably means 'the eighth (part)'. The Sicilian toponym Tumminu (Noto) derives from Sic. *tumminu* 'tumolo (an agrarian measure)' < Ar. *thumn* 'eighth part' (Caracausi 2:1664).

Ta' Butomna (Mellieħa, 1537, now known as Tat-Tomna), Għar Butomna (cave at Mellieħa, 1546).

Muhammad b. Ibrāhīm Ibn al-Thumna (d. 1062) was an independent *qāʾid* (provincial commander) of Muslim Sicily.

Buxibla: < Ar. *kunyah* of the *abū* type, comprising the Ar. (non-Quranic) *ʾism Shibl* 'lion cub'. The final *-a* may reflect the influence of Romance morphology.

Ta'/Tal-Ġnien Buxibla (Gozo, 1746), Il-Għajn ta' Ġnien Buxibla (id., 1746). Cf. Ta' Xibla (Xagħra ta' Prejna, 1543).

Wettinger (PMI 618) suggests a reflex of the fem. non-Semitic name *Sibilla.*

Buxiħ: < Ar. *kunyah ʾAbū Shaikh* 'chief', 'senior member or head of a community', 'old man'. Cf. *Xiħ* (q.v.).

(Ta') Għar Buxiħ (Mġarr ix-Xini, Gozo, 1557).

Bużellaq: < Ar. *kunyah* of the *abū* type, comprising the *ʾism Zallāq* 'fickle', 'inconstant', 'capricious' (Caracausi 1:219). Cf. the Sic. surnames *Busalacchi, Busilacchi,* which share the same etymology (DCA 93).

Ta' Bużellaq (Wied il-Għabid, 1538), Ta' Żellek (id., 1538), L-Għaqba ta' Żellek (unlocated, 1539), Ta' Żellieqa (Tal-Ħandaq, 1497).

Cooperson (p.c.) opts for a toponymic interpretation: a place where there is a *zallāqah*, 'ramp', 'shoot', 'slipway', with loss of the *-a*. Cf. Mal. *żellieqa* 'slippery place'. Zellaqa is a district in Casablanca, Morocco.

Dabrani: < Ar. *al-Dabrān* 'follower'—*al-Dabaran* (*Aldebaran*) is the Taurus constellation (*Alpha Tauri*), so called because it seems to follow the Pleiades.

Dabrani (Gozo, 1545), Ta' Dabrani/Tad-Dabrani (Marsalforn, 1585), Il-Ħara ta' Dabrani/Il-Ħara tad-Dabrani (Gozo, 1545).

Other star names in the Arabic world include *Thurayyā* 'Pleiades' and *Suhayl* 'Canopus'.

Dud: < Ar. male *ʾism Dāwud* (*Daud*), corresponding to the biblical name *David* (DMN 43). This Quranic name has Hebrew origins and means 'beloved friend', 'darling'.

Għar id-Dud (limits of Sliema).

The anthroponymic import of this name was suggested by Salafia (p.c.). Otherwise, it simply reflects Mal. *dud* < Ar. *dūd* 'worms', 'maggots', 'larvae', 'grubs', 'caterpillars'; this interpretation is favoured by Cooperson (p.c.).

Ferħ/Ferħa: < Ar. fem. *ʾisms Faraḥ* and *Farḥah* (*Farha*) 'joy', 'gladness', 'happiness', 'delight', 'good cheer', 'rejoicing' (DMN 255). Cf. Mal. *ferħ, ferħa* (same meaning).

Tal-Ferħ (unlocated, 1523), Tal-Ferħa (near Ħal Għargħur, 1544), Għadir Bir Ferħa (unlocated, 1558), Miġra Ferħa (Mtaħleb, 1647, cited by Abela).

Otherwise, a nickname meaning 'small animal' < Mal. *ferħ(a)* < Ar. *farkh(a)* 'chick', 'small bird'.

Ferħiet/Forkiet: < Ar. male *ʾism Farḥāt* 'joys', 'delights'; pl. of *Farḥah* 'joy'. It is derived from the root *F-R-Ḥ*, which is used in many places in the Quran, and has also been interpreted as 'happy events', 'joyous times'. Cf. *Ferħ/Ferħa* (q.v.).

Ta' Ferħiet/Tal-Ferħiet (Wied Kosta, 1537), Il-Ħara ta' Ferħiet/Il-Ħara tal-Ferħiet/Il-Ħara tal-Forkiet (Gozo, 1576).

Otherwise, a nickname meaning 'small animals' < Mal. *ferħiet* < Ar. *farkhāt* 'chicks', 'small birds'. *Forkiet*, on the other hand, is possibly a mistranscribed form of *Ferħiet*; otherwise, a sound plural of *forka* 'gallows', 'gibbet', although this is unlikely. Cf. top. Tal-Forok.

Fieres: < Ar. male *ʾism Fāris* (*Fares*) 'rider', 'horseman', 'knight'.

Tal-Fieres (*Rollo De Mello*, 1436), Ġnien Fieres/Ġnien il-Fieres (1418), Ħabel Fieres (Ħal Fuqani, 1537).

Possible nickname < Mal. *fieres* (same meaning).

Ġabar, Ġabbar: < Ar. male *ʾism Jabbār* 'powerful', 'mighty'; *Al-Jabbār* 'the All-Compeller' is one of the Quranic names of Allah (DMN 86). Cf. *ʿAbd al-Jabbār* 'servant of the All-Powerful'. The name also means 'giant', 'colossus', besides referring to 'Orion (the star)' (PMI 133, quoting Wehr).

Bjar Ġabar (unlocated, 1548; probably identical with Bjar Ġabbar listed by Abela, 1647), Ta' Ġabar (Marsa, 1501), Tal-Ġabbar (Ngieret, 1514).

There could have been some confusion with another Ar. *ʾism, Jābir* 'caregiver'. Cf. *Ġabrun* (q.v.).

Ġabrun: < Ar. male *ʾism Jabr* 'consolation', 'aid' + Maghrebi suffix *-un*. Cf. *Jābir* (*Jaber*) 'comforter', 'healer', 'restorer' (DAFN 2:237).

Bir Ġabrun (near Ħax-Xluq, 1475–76).

Ġagħfar: < Ar. male *ʾism Jaʿfar* '(water) spring', 'rivulet', 'source' (DMN 87). Locally, the name is nowadays written *Ġafar*.

Ta' Jagħfar (1529).

Ġulad: < Ar. male *ʾism Jālūt* 'Goliath' (PMI 76), with inversion of the vowels—the biblical name of the Philistine champion slain by David.

Ta' Bur Ġulad (Ħal Luqa and Bir Miftuħ, 1526).

Salafia (p.c.) opines that this term is rather a cryptic reflex of the personal name *Ġilard* (*Gerald*).

Għabdilla: < Ar. theophoric *ʾism ʿAbd Allāh* (*Abdallah, Abdullah*) 'servant or slave of Allah' (DMN 3–4). This sobriquet is compatible with the Islamic doctrine of total submission to God. *Abdallāh* was the name of Muhammad's father, who died before the birth of the Prophet in c. 570 AD. The name is also one of the many attributive titles of Muhammad himself.

Bir Għabdilla (unlocated, 1494), Wied Għabdilla (Bir Għabdilla, 1530).

The name survives to this day as a Mal. surname *Abdilla*.

Għabdun: < Ar. *ʾism ʿAbd* (romanised as *Abd*) '(male) servant' + Maghrebi suffix *-un* (DMN 3). The word *ʿAbd* is often used with attributes of Allah to form compound names (e.g., *Abd al-Azīz*).

(Ta') Għajn Għabdun (Gozo, 1445), Il-Ħara ta' Għajn Għabdun (Gozo, 1445).

Għabid: < Ar. male *ʾism ʿAbid* (*Abid*), pl. form of *ʿabd* '(male) slave'.

Tal-Għabid/Il-Għabid (Ħax-Xluq, 1530), Tal-Ġebel tal-Għabid (Ġebel Ciantar, 1567), Wied il-Għabid (near Burmarrad, 1497), Il-Ħbejjel ta' Wied il-Għabid (id, 1539), Qagħlet il-Għabid (1487), Il-Qasam ta' Qagħlet il-Għabid (1585).

Għabidnur (q.v.) and *Għabidirżeq* (q.v.) are both compound names with this element. Possible nickname < archaic Mal. *abid* 'slave', 'serf', 'servant'.

Għabidnur: < Ar. compound *ʾism ʿAbd al-Nūr* 'slave of the light', comprising the elements *ʿabd* '(male) slave' + *nūr* 'light', 'illumination' (DMN 4–5, 155)—one of the Quranic names of Allah.

Il-Bur ta' Għabidnur (unlocated, 1534), Ta' Għabidnur (Ħax-Xluq, 1532).

Għabidirżeq/Għabdrużaq/Għabid Riżeq: < Ar. compound *ʾism ʿAbd al-Razzāq* 'slave of the Provider (God)', comprising the elements *ʿabd* '(male) slave' + *razzāq* 'one who provides the necessities of life', 'giver of sustenance'. *ʿAbd al-Razzāq* is an indirect Quranic name for boys, as *al-Razzāq* is one of the names of Allah.

Ħal Għabdirżeq (Tal-Massar, 1541), Ta' Għabdrużaq (Żurrieq, 1476), L-Ibwar ta' Għabid Riżeq (Raħal Għorab, 1533).

Għadir: < Ar. fem. *ʾism Ghadīr* 'brook', 'rivulet', 'small stream' (DMN 258).

Ħabel Għadir/Il-Ħabel tal-Għadir (Ta' Xollixa, 1514).

Cf. Mal. topographic term *għadira* 'pool', 'lake'. Cf. Sic. top. Cala del Gadir (Milazzo) 'pond', 'swamp' (Caracausi 1:663). Less likely, a phonetic variant of Ar. male *ʾism Ghādil* (*l* < *r*) 'one who acts with justice and fairness', 'moderate', 'virtuous', 'excellent in character'.

Għajxa: < Ar. fem. *ʾism ʿĀʾishah*, colloquially pronounced *ʿĀysha* (romanised as *Ayisha, Aisha*) (a) 'living', 'alive'; (b) 'well-to-do', 'prosperous', 'fortunate', 'happy'—the name of one of Muhammad's wives (DMN 236; PMI 78). Cf. Mal. *għex, għaxja* (*ta' lejla*).

Ta' Għajxa (1501), Ħofret Għajxa (Wied il-Wiesa', near Ħal Għaxaq, 1498), Il-Bur ta' Għajxa (Gudja, 1535), Nadur Għajxa (Ħlantun, 1514), Għajn Għajxa/Ta' Għajn Għajxa (tenurial land belonging to the royal court in Gozo, 1490).

Għajxun/Għajxuna: < Ar. fem *ʾism ʿĀʾishah,* colloquially pronounced *ʿĀysha* + Maghrebi suffix *-un*(*a*). Cf. *Għajxa* (q.v.).

Ta' Għajxun/Ta' Għajxuna (1538), Ta' Ġebel Għajxun (Marsaskala, 1536).

Għali: < Ar. male *ʾism ʿĀli* (*Aliy, Ali*) 'high', 'exalted', 'superb', 'sublime'. The word *Ali* is used in many places in the Quran and it forms one of the names of Allah when it is prefixed with an *al-*, as in *al-ʿĀli* (DMN 13). Cf. Mal. *għoli* 'high'. Cf. *Bin Għali* (q.v.).

Ta' Bir Għali (perhaps at Qrendi, 1534), Iċ-Ċens ta' Għali (Ħal Lew, 1537), Ta' Għali (Santa Vennera, 1546).

Għalib: < Ar. *Ghālib* 'winner', 'victor', 'conqueror' (DMN 58). Ghalib ibn ʿAbd Allāh was the name of a *sahābi.* Cf. Mal. *għeleb* 'to overcome'.

Mtaħleb (1487) < *mita Ħalib, Ħalab* (where *mita* is an old notarial reflex of the preposition *ta'*), Ta' Ħalab, Ta' Ġebel Ħalab (unlocated, 1536), Ħabel Ħalib.

The anthroponymic import of Mtaħleb was first suggested by Salafia (p.c.). The author defends the shift from *GĦ* to *Ħ* by referring to the verbs *ħafer* and *ħasel,* which underwent the same phonetic transition.

Għamburi: < Ar. fem. *ʾism ʿAmbūr* (*Ambur*) 'amber'. Cf. Ar. *ʿambar* 'perfume', 'ambergris (fragrant material extracted from a type of whale)’, ‘precious stone (made up of fossilised tree resin)’ (DMN 238).

Ta’ Għamburi/Tal-Għamburi (Gozo, 1445), Il-Ħara ta’ Għamburi/Il-Ħara tal-Għamburi (Gozo, 1485, 1445).

Cooperson (p.c.) derives the name directly from Ar. *ʿanbarī* (pronounced *ʿambarī*) ‘seller of ambergris’, ‘perfumer’. Cf. *Għattar* (q.v.).

Għamiq: < Ar. male (non-Quranic) *ʾism ʿĀmiq* (*Ghāmik, Ghāmeq*) ‘dark’, ‘black’.

Wied Għamiq/Wied Għammieq (near Kalkara, 1504).

Popular etymology has interpreted the toponym as ‘deep valley’ (via Mal. *għamiq* < Ar. *ʿamīq* ‘deep’); however, the valley is far from bottomless. The term here is a proper noun, not an adjective.

Għamir: (a) < Ar. male *ʾism ʿĀmir* ‘prosperous’, ‘full of life’, ‘substantial’ (DAFN 3:16), hence related to *Għomor* (q.v.); or less likely (b) < Ar. male *ʾism ʾĀmir* (*Āmīr, Amīr*) ‘commander’, ‘ruler’, ‘leader’, ‘master’, ‘chief’, ‘superior’ (DMN 15), derived from the root *ʾ-M-R* ‘to command’ which is used in many places in the Quran.

Wied Għamir (Tal-Għargħar, 1647, listed by Abela).

The name *Amir* was adopted by Sephardi Jews (DAFN 1:35). Cf. Mal. *amar* ‘order’, *emir* ‘prince’. To complicate matters, the name *ʿUmm ʿĀmir* means ‘mother of hyena’.

Għammar: < Ar. male *ʾism ʿAmmār* (usually romanised as *Ammar*) ‘virtuous’, ‘pious’, ‘devout’, ‘religious’ (DMN 16). Ammar ibn Yāsir was the name of a *sahābi*.

Ta' Għammar (Gozo, 1450), Ħabel Għammar (Ħal Arrig, 1554), Ix-Xagħra ta' Għammar (Ta' Għodlien, Gozo, 1570), Il-Gudja ta' Għammar (id. 1576).

Għarib: < Ar. male *ʾism ʿArīb* 'poor', 'needy', 'humble', 'gentle' (DMN 59), hence synonymous with *Faqīr*. Cf. *Foqra* (q.v.).

Ġebel Għarib/Ġebel il-Għarib (Gozo, 1570), Qabar il-Għarib (militia post listed by Abela, 1647).

Possible nickname for 'stranger', 'someone living in a foreign land' < Mal. *għarib* < Ar. *gharīb* (a person from another city or country); incidentally, also used as a personal name with this meaning. This is the interpretation favoured by Cooperson (p.c.).

Għarifa: < Ar. fem. name *ʿArifah, ʿĀrifah (Arifa)* 'learned', 'expert', 'authority'; fem. form *of ʿArif, ʿĀrif* (DMN 234, 239–40). Cf. Mal. *għarfa, għaref* (same meaning).

Mtarfa (1362) < *mita Għarfa* (where *mita* is an old notarial reflex of the preposition *ta'*).

The anthroponymic import of Mtarfa was first suggested by Salafia (p.c.). The same author suggests that the top. Wied Għorof (Ogħrof) possibly contains the male name *Għarif* < *ʿArif,* which additionally means 'saint', 'the highest position a mystic can attain' (DMN 2).

Għasfur: < Ar. *ʾism ʿAṣfūr, ʿUṣfūr* (*Asfour, Osfur*) 'sparrow', 'little bird'.

Tal-Għasfur (Rabat, Gozo, 1558), Il-Ħara tal-Għasfur (Gozo, 1584), Għar Għasfur.

Possible ornithological nickname. Salafia (p.c.) ponders the possibility that the term *Għosfor* in toponyms like Ħabel Għosfor is a dialectal reflex of *għasfur*.

Għattar: < Ar. male and fem. *ʾism ʿAṭṭār* (*Attar*) 'perfumer' (DMN 23). Cf. Mal. *għattâr* 'apothecary', 'druggist'.

Bir Għattar (1487), Għar Għattar (1504), Il-Wileġ ta' Bir Għattar (Binwarrad, 1487), Il-Wileġ ta' Bjar Għattar (id. 1557).

Possible occupational name. Cf. *Għamburi* (q.v.).

Għaxaq: < Ar. male (non-Quranic) *ʾism ʿĀshiq* (*Ashik, Asheq*) 'ardent lover', 'paramour', 'suitor' (DMN 21).

Ta' Għaxaq (Marsalforn, Gozo, 1558), Il-Ġustpatronat ta' Għaxaq (id., 1558).

The name survives to this day as a Mal. surname *Asciak, Axiak, Axiaq* (cognate forms).

Another plausible interpretation links this name with *ʾIshāq* 'Isaac', borne by the biblical prophet. The medieval reference to Presbitero Bartholomeo de Ysac or de Aschac (d. 1390) seems to support this interpretation (Fiorni 1999, 46, 136).

Għażi: < Ar. male *ʾism Ghāzī* 'warrior', 'fighter'.

Tal-Għażi (Ħal Tmin, 1546), Ix-Xagħra tal-Għażi fuq Għajn Riħana (1651).

Wettinger (PMI 220, 604) explains the name as 'military campaigner', 'one who wages war in the cause of Islam', 'brave', 'conqueror'. The Libyan city of Benghazi drew its name from Ben (ibn) Ghāzī.

Għisa: < Ar. *ʾism ʿIsā* 'Jesus' (revered as a prophet by Muslims; DMN 82). Cf. *Bin Għisa* (q.v). *ʿIsā* is the name used by Muslims; Christian Arabs call him *Yasūʿ*.

Bir Għisa (near Ħal Millieri, 1495), Ħabel Għisa (Mqabba, 1516), Wied Għisa (Il-Ħara ta' Sant'Agata, Gozo, 1565).

Benisa is a Spanish toponym with the same import, whereas *Benisi* still survives as a surname in Italy (DCA 77).

Għomor: < Ar. male *ʾism ʿUmar* (usually romanised as *Omar*), of uncertain etymology, but often thought to be a cognate form of *ʿĀmir*—cf. *Għamir* (q.v., first derivation only; DAFN 3:16). The root word *ʿumr* means 'life' (DMN 214). Cf. Mal. *għomor* 'age', 'lifetime', 'span of life'.

Ta' Għomor (San Pietru tal-Ħerba, Naxxar, 1586), Ta' Ġebel Għomor (Fiddien, 1560), Tarġet Għomor (unlocated, 1544), Wied Għomor (valley running down to Spinola Bay, 1534).

The name is found almost exclusively among Sunni Muslims (DAFN 3:16). The Sicilian family names *Omari* and *Omero* are in most cases reflexes of the same anthroponym (Caracausi 2:1129).

Għul/Għula: < Ar. male *ʾism ʿUlā* (usually romanised as *Ula*) 'high rank', 'prestige', 'glory' (DMN 214). Cf. Mal. *għoli* 'high'.

Ħal Għul (Ta' Suffara, 1500), Il-Wilġa ta' Għar Għula (Gozo, 1576).

Otherwise, derived directly from Ar. *ghūl*, a kind of shape-shifting demon; this is the interpretation favoured by Cooperson (p.c.). Traditionally, the *għul* is an evil genie or ogre of legend that robs graves and feeds on corpses, or a person (like a grave robber) whose activities suggest those of a ghoul (itself of Ar. origin). Possible nickname for a contemptible person.

Ħafura: < Ar. male *ʾism Ghafūr* 'pardoner', 'merciful' (DMN 58)—*Al-Ghafūr* 'the Most Forgiving' is one of the Quranic names of Allah.

Ta' Ħafura (Ġibjet Selim, 1535), Ta' Ħafura l-Fuqqanija (id., 1517), Wied il-Ħafura/Il-Wied tal-Ħafura (Qala, Gozo, 1507), Il-Ħabel ta' Ħafura (Ġibjet Selim, 1506).

Possible botanical nickname from Mal. *ħafur* 'common wild oats', 'drake' < Ar. *Khāfūr*; this is the interpretation favoured by Cooperson (p.c.).

Ħajr: < Ar. *ʾism Khayr* (*Khair*) 'moral or physical good', 'wealth', 'prosperity', sometimes used in compound names such as *Khair-ul-Bashar* 'the greatest or best man'—an epithet of Muhammad (MED 1:479; DMN 35).

Ħabel il-Ħajr (Marsa, 1548).

Cooperson (p.c.) opts for a topographic interpretation: Ar. *ḥayr* 'park', 'enclosure', 'zoological garden', 'hunting-reserve'.

Ħakem: < Ar. male *ʾism Ḥākim* 'judge', 'ruler', 'governor', 'leader', 'chief'—*al-Hakim* 'the Judge' is one of the Quranic names of Allah (DMN 61). Cf. Mal. *ħakem* 'captain of the rod—head of the *Consiglio Popolare'*.

Tal-Ħakem (Bubaqra, 1559).

Ħalif: < Ar. male *ʾism Ḥalīf*, presumably meaning 'ally'. Cf. *Halif* 'one who takes an oath', 'one who swears', 'one who is under a solemn promise'.

Ta' Ħalif (Wied il-Busbies, 1535).

Otherwise, an apocopated form of Ar. *ʾism Khalīfah* 'successor', 'heir', 'viceroy', 'viceregent'—a title of the head of the Muslim Empire (DMN 97). It is a status name or honorific designation, often transliterated in English as *caliph*. The title was first adopted by ʾAbū Bakr, Muhammad's successor (DAFN 2:298).

Ħalima: < Ar. fem. *ʾism Ḥalīmah* 'patient', 'tolerant' (DMN 65); *al-Halīm* (male counterpart) 'the All-Forgiving' is one of the Quranic names of Allah.

Ta' Ħalima (Birżebbuġa, 1515), Misraħ Ħalima (Għajn Riħana, 1536).

Ħamdun/Ħandun/Ħandul: < Ar. male *ʾism Ḥamdūn*, presumably comprising *Ḥamd* 'praise', 'laudation (of Allah)' + Maghrebi suffix *-un*. Cf. *Hamdāni* (fem. *Hamdān*) 'much praise' (DMN 65, 263). *Ħandun* (*n* < *m*) and *Ħandul* (*l* < *n*) are merely phonetic variants.

Bir Ħandul/Ħamdun (Mrieħel, 1538), Wied Ħandun (= Wied il-Biżbież, 1510), Dejr Ħandul/Dejr Ħandun (near Rabat, Malta, 1399), Djar Ħandul (1517).

Ħamed/Ħamet: < Ar. male *ʾism Ḥāmed, Ḥāmid* 'praiser (of Allah)' (DMN 61). Cf. cognate forms *Ḥamad/Ḥammād* 'much praising' (DMN 65); *Ḥamīd* 'praised', 'commended', 'praiseworthy', 'commendable' (DMN 66); *al-Ḥamīd* 'the All-Laudable' is one of the Quranic names of Allah.

Bjar Ħamet/Bjar Ħamed (tenure of the bishop's fief, 1521), Għajn Ħamet/Għajn Ħommed (Miżieb ir-Riħ, 1629), Ta' Ħamed/Ta' Ħamet (Xewkija, Gozo, 1399).

The root *Ḥ-M-D* 'praise' is one of the most common elements in Arabic name forming; in addition to this name, it is also the basis of names such as *Aḥmad* and *Muḥammad* (DAFN 2:120).

Ħamut: < Ar. male *ʾism Ḥamūd* (with devoicing) 'praised', 'commended', 'praiseworthy', 'commendable' (DMN 66). Cf. cognate forms *Hamed/Hamet* (q.v.); *Ḥammūd* 'much praise to Allah'.

Bir Ħamut (a tenure belonging to the bishop, 1517).

The Sicilian family name *Camuti* shares the same etymology (Caracausi 1:266). The Gozitan toponyms Ta' Ħanut (San Lawrenz) and Tal-Ħanut (Għarb) may easily represent phonetic variants (*n* < *m*).

Ħanin: < Ar. male *ʾism Ḥanīn* 'yearning', 'desire' (DMN 67).

Ta' Ħanin (Ħal Tarxien, 1538), Il-Ħabel tal-Ħanin (id., 1514).

Possible nickname < Mal. *ħanin* 'kind', 'merciful', 'good-hearted'. The Sicilian family name *Canino* shares the same etymology (Caracausi 1:274).

Ħares: < Ar. male *ʾism Ḥaris* 'watchman', 'guardian'.

Ġnien il-Ħares (San Niklaw, 1564), Ħabel il-Ħares (Xagħret l-Imqalled, 1546).

Possibly a nickname < Mal. *ħares* '(prankish) ghost', 'house-haunting spectre', but etymologically it suggests an entity of a protective nature. It also means 'custodian', 'keeper', 'security guard' (MED 1:506–7).

Ħarfalla: elliptical form (via *Ħalfalla*) of the theophoric name *Khalaf Allāh* 'successor of Allah' (analogous to *Khalaf Ḥasan* 'successor of Hasan'), based on the belief that the khalifs were appointed as His viceroys on earth. Cf. *Ħalif* (q.v.). The term *khalaf* is sometimes translated as 'substitute provided by God (for someone lost)'.

Ta' Ħarfalla (Għasri, Gozo, 1577).

Ħaruf: (a) < Ar. male *ʾism Qarūf* 'dour', 'cruel'; or (b) < Ar. male *ʾism Gharūf* 'constant', 'perseverant', or (c) < Ar. male

ʾism Gharūf(ah) (*Arāfa*) 'one who knows', 'knowledgeable', 'learned', 'wise' (Caracausi 1:687; DAFN 2:19).

Ta' Ħaruf/Tal-Ħaruf (Qdieri, 1501), Ta' Djar Ħaruf (Ta' Djar Ħaruf, 1531), Misraħ il-Ħaruf (unlocated, 1536).

Possible nickname meaning 'lamb' < Mal. *ħaruf* < Ar. *kharūf* 'sheep (singular)'. The surname *Garuf* (comparable to Sicilian *Garufo*) features in the Maltese Militia List of 1419–20, while *Charuf* is attested in the 1480s.

Ħasan: < Ar. male *ʾism Ḥasan* 'handsome', 'beautiful', 'good-looking' (DMN 68). Cf. *Ḥassān* 'beautifier' (DMN 70). The name is popular among Sunni Muslims as well as Shiites (DAFN 2:138).

Ta' Ħasan (Bingħisa, 1509), Il-Ħabel ta' Ħasan (San Luqa ta' Bingħisa, 1535), Għar Ħasan (Bingħisa, 1517).

Ħawli: < Ar. male *ʾism Khawlī* (a) 'foreman', 'manager'; (b) 'gardener', 'farmer'.

Wied il-Ħawli (Bulebel, 1781), Il-Ħabel tal-Ħawli (Ħal Tmin, 1535), Tal-Ħawli.

Wettinger (PMI 577) explains the name as (a) 'overseer of a plantation', 'supervisor'; or (b) 'one year old animal', 'yearling'. Otherwise, in a topographic sense, Mal. *ħawli* means 'sterile', 'barren'. Cf. top. Il-Ħawlija.

Ħażrun: < Ar. male *ʾism Ḥasrūn*, of doubtful origin; the suffix *-un*, though, is typically Maghrebin.

Wied Ħażrun (Rabat, Malta, 1535).

Ḥasrūn is attested in modern-day Morocco. *Ḥaṣrūn* (Hasroun) happens to be the name of a village located in the Bsharri District in the North Governorate of Lebanon.

Ħida: < Ar. fem. *ʾism Hida,* arguably meaning 'present', 'gift', 'talent'. In Arabic, *Hidha* means 'having the gift of gab—the ability to persuade other people effortlessly'.

Il-Ħanaq ta' Ħida (Ta' Ħida Gozo, 1584), Il-Ħara ta' Ħida (Gozo, 1534), Ta' Ħida/Tal-Ħida (Tal-Brolli, 1505).

Possible nickname meaning 'falcon', 'kite' (ornith.). This plausibly covers toponyms such as Għoxx il-Ħida (1467) 'the falcon's nest'. Otherwise, Ar. *ḥida* means 'boundary'.

Ħira: perhaps < Ar. *ʾism Khīrah* 'the pick or best part of something'.

Ta' Ġnien Ħira (Xwieki, 1544).

Otherwise, *Ḥirā* (without the article) is a significant name in Islam, as in the Quran it is the name of a mountain and cave, near Mecca, where the Prophet Muhammad allegedly received revelations from Allah. Al-Ḥīrah (with the article), on the other hand, is the name of an ancient town in Iraq.

Ħmajra: presumably < Ar. fem. *ʾism Humayrāʾ* 'of red colour'—the name of Aisha, one of Muhammad's wives (DMN 266).

Ta' Ħmajra (1530).

Otherwise, simply a nickname reflecting the Mal. dim. noun *ħmajra* (< Ar. *ḥumayra*) 'little donkey'.

Ħosna: < Ar. fem. *ʾism Ḥusnā* 'best', 'most beautiful'. Cf. male *ʾism Ḥosni, Ḥusni* 'possessing beauty', 'handsome' (DMN 74); *Ħasan* (q.v.).

(Ta') Għajn Ħosna (Gozo, 1373), Il-Ħara ta' Għajn Ħosna (Għajn Xibla, Gozo, 1373).

Inġim: phonetic variant (*m* < *l*) of Ar. male and fem. *ʾism* (*al-*)*Injīl* 'the Gospels'. The word is originally from Greek εὐαγγέλιον, and means 'good news'. Cf. archaic Mal. *Inġir* 'gospel' (now superseded by *Vanġelu*).

Ta' Bir Inġim (Tal-Ħandaq, 1559).

Otherwise, Ar. *anjum* means 'stars' (pl. of *najm*), for a place with a particularly starry night sky.

Jagħqub: < Ar. male *ʾism Yaʿqūb* (*Yaqub*) 'Jacob, name of the biblical prophet' (DMN 222). *Yaqub* is an ancient name that means 'supplanter', 'successor', 'heir', 'following', as mentioned in the Bible.

Ġebel Jagħqub (Naxxar, 1495).

Jaħra: cryptic form of Ar. male *ʾism Yaḥyā* (*Yahia*), the Quranic name of John the Baptist. It is actually an adaptation of Heb. *Yohanan*, of contested interpretation, but plausibly meaning 'God is gracious'.

Għar Jaħra (Ras San Dimitri).

The anthroponymic value of *Jaħra* was first suggested by Salafia (p.c.). The connection with Mal. *jaħra* 'to defecate' is purely based on popular relexicalisation.

Kemil: < Ar. male *ʾism Kāmil, Kamīl, Kamel* 'perfect', 'complete', 'genuine' (DMN 94). Cf. *Kamāl* 'perfection', 'completion', 'integrity', itself a shortened form of *Kamāl-ud-Dīn* 'perfection of the faith (Islam)' (DMN 93).

Ta' Kemil (Ħal Għaxaq, 1501), Il-Ħabel ta' Kemil (Ħal Għaxaq, 1584).

Magħsur: (a) perhaps derived directly from Ar. *Maʿdhūr* (in some dialects pronounced *maʿzūr*) 'excused', 'forgiven'; or (b) presumably a phonetic variant of Ar. male *ʾism Maʿsūm* (*r* < *m*) 'innocent', 'sinless', 'blameless', 'infallible', 'protected'—an epithet of Muhammad (DMN 115).

Ħal Magħsur/Masur (near Siġġiewi, 1514).

Possible nickname from Mal. p.p. *magħsur* 'squeezed' < Ar. *maʾṣūr*, same meaning.

Maħluf: < Ar. male *ʾism Makhlūf* 'succeeded', 'replaced'.

Bjar Maħluf (Tal-Mintna, near Ħal Millieri, 1529), Ta' Bur Maħluf (unlocated, 1538), Djar Maħluf (unlocated, 1533).

Ar. *makhlūf* also means 'peak', whereas *mahlūf* means 'juror', 'constable', 'inspector', 'official'. The latter is the apparent etymon of the Sicilian toponym Magalufo (Caracausi 2:896).

Maħlula: fem. form of Ar. *ʾism Maḥlūl* 'untied', 'dissolved', 'absolved'; presumably here indicating 'someone released from the vows of marriage or from some contractual arrangement' (PMI 357).

Ta' Maħlula/Tal-Maħlula (Sieq it-Tarġa, Gozo, 1572).

Maqbul: < Ar. male *ʾism Maqbūl* 'accepted', 'acceptable', 'granted', 'approved' (DMN 113). Cf. Mal. p.p. *maqbul* 'agreed'.

Wied Maqbol (Tal-Baqqari, 1536).

Mawwija/Mewwija: < Ar. male *ʾism Muʿāwiyya* (*Muawiyah, Muāwiyah, Māwiyyah, Mawiyya*; PMI 609), a given name of disputed meaning. It was the name of the first and third Umayyad caliphs.

Xagħret Mewwija (site on which Valletta was built, cited by Abela, 1647), Ta' Mawwija (Għarb, 1497), Marġet Mewwija (near Mdina, 1775).

There are at least two places so called in Algeria, besides another one in Yemen. Muʿawiya, on the other hand, is an Arab village in Basma, Israel.

Mejmun/Mejmuna: < Ar. male *ʾism Maymūn* 'auspicious', 'prosperous', 'lucky', 'fortunate', 'blessed', 'thriving'; *Maymūnah* (*Maymuna*) is the fem. form—the name of one of Muhammad's wives (DMN 288).

Ta' Mejmun (Ta' Ranġisija, Gozo, 1398), Ta' Mejmuna (feudal land on Gozo belonging to the Grand Master, 1566), Għar Mejmun (Ħal Tmin, near Żejtun, 1579), Wied Mejmun (unlocated, 1522).

Dating from 1174, Maimuna's gravestone, discovered in Gozo around 1760, is a rare relic of the Arab period; its provenance is still far from certain. Nevertheless, it contains more than a hint of Fatimid Islam in Malta. The Sicilian family name *Maimone* and the historical toponym *Rahalmaymuni* reflect the same anthroponym (Caracausi 2:915, 1312).

Merżuq/Merżuqa: < Ar. male *ʾism Marzūq* (fem. *Marzūqah*) 'blessed (by God)', 'fortunate', 'prosperous', 'successful' (DMN 114, 287).

Ta' Merżuq (Ta' Qala, Malta, 1486), Ta' Merżuqa (unlocated, 1499; Santa Katarina, 1500), Bir Merżuq (unlocated land belonging to the Church, 1538), Il-Ħbula ta' Merżuq (Gozo, probably at Merżuq, c. 1565).

Mgħajjen: (a) < Ar. male/fem. *ʾism Muʿayyin*, itself a diminutive form of *maʿīn* '(water) spring', 'fountain', 'source of fresh water' (PMI 141; DMN 109); hence related to Mal. *għajn* (same meaning); (b) < Ar. male *ʾism Muʿayyin*, itself a diminutive of *Muʿīn* 'helper'.

Ta' Mgħajjen/Tal-Mgħajjen (Ħal Far, 1518), Ġebel Mgħajjen (Qlejgħa, 1467).

Maàni is the name of a spring near Salemi, Sicily (Caracausi 2:895).

Miftuħ: < Ar. male *ʾism Maftūḥ*, lit. 'opened', 'freed'; fig. 'one for whom the doors of good things are open', 'one whose heart is open to goodness'. Cf. Mal. *miftuħ* (same meaning).

Bir Miftuħ (*Rollo De Mello*, 1436), Santa Marija ta' Bir Miftuħ (id., 1496), L-Imnejqa ta' Bir Miftuħ (Ħal Kirkop, 1733).

Mikħal: < Ar. male *ʾism Mikhayl* (also *Mikayīl, Mīkāʾīl, Mikaīl*) 'Michael, one of the main angels of Allah'. In Islam, he is said to effectuate God's providence as well as natural phenomena, such as rain.

Il-Qala ta' Mikħal (Għajnsielem), Il-Ħara tal-Mikħal (Gozo, 1576), Il-Mikħal/Tal-Mikħal (Gozo, 1576).

Cooperson (p.c.) rejects this anthroponymic interpretation. Instead, he suggests the Ar. etymon *mikḥal* 'stick or pencil set for applying collyrium to the eyes'. In this sense, the term possibly indicates a place where collyrium was made or sold, or a nickname based on the appearance of the stick and the pot.

Otherwise, a possible nickname or a descriptive term derived from Mal. *ikħal* 'blue'. Geoffrey Hull (p.c.) actually opines that the term could well be some mimated form of the Arabic verb *ikḥāl* 'to be covered with plants just beginning to green': **mikḥāl*, which fits the phonetics of the Maltese name.

Miliet/Milied: < Ar. male *ʾism Mīlād* 'birthday', 'birth', 'nativity'.

Ta' Milied/Ta' Miliet (Gozo, 1468).

Misrija: < Ar. fem. *ʾism Miṣriyya* 'Egyptian (woman)' < *Miṣr* 'Egypt'.

Il-Misrija (unlocated, 1488).

Mlit/Mliet: Syncopated form of the Ar. *ʾism Milād*. Cf. *Miliet/Milied* (q.v.). Wettinger (PMI 394) affirms that *Milet/Milit* is a common Moorish name.

Ta' Mlit (Gozo, 1468), San Ġiljan ta' Mlit/San Ġiljan ta' Mliet (Gozo, 1570), Il-Ħara ta' San Ġiljan ta' Mlit/Il-Ħara ta' San Ġiljan ta' Mliet (Gozo, 1570).

Morr: < Ar. male *ʾism Murr* 'bitter', 'bitterness', 'myrrh'; 'severe', 'sharp', 'painful' (PMI 187; MED 1:858). Cf. Mal. *morr* 'bitter', 'unsweetened'.

Għajn Morr/Ta' Għajn Morr (Għammar, Gozo, 1583), Il-Ħara ta' Għajn Morr (Gozo, 1583).

Mosfar/Misfar: < Ar. male *ʾism Musfār* (*Musfer, Musfir, Mosfer, Mosfir*), arguably meaning 'bright', 'glowing', 'enlightened'.

(Ta') Ġnien Mosfar/Ġnien Misfar (Qala, Gozo, 1533).

Possible nickname meaning 'yellowish', 'pale' < Mal. *musfar* < Ar. *muṣfarr*; this is the interpretation favoured by Cooperson (p.c.).

Mqit: Syncopated form of Ar. *Muqīt* 'keeper', 'carer', 'nourisher', usually occurring in the compound name *Abdul Muqīt* 'servant of the Keeper'—*al-Muqīt* 'the Nourisher' is one of the Quranic names of Allah (DMN 135).

Tal-Imqit (Marsa, 1512), Andar l-Imqit (Ħal Qormi, 1544).

Possible nickname < Mal. *mqit* 'sullen', 'peevish', 'sour-faced' (MED 2:863) < Ar. *mqīt* 'hateful (person)'; this is the interpretation favoured by Cooperson (p.c.).

Msid(a): perhaps a syncopated form of Ar. male *ʾism Misʿid* (*Musʿad, Musid*), arguably meaning 'helper', 'one who makes others happy', 'one who brings joy'.

Tal-Imsid (1502), Għar Imsid (?), L-Imsida (1494), Il-Ħerba ta' Raħal Msida (?).

Cooperson (p.c.) rejects this interpretation and opts for either *maṣid* 'hunting or fishing place' or *mṣida* 'trap', 'snare'.

Muħammed/Mħammed: < Ar. male *ʾism Muḥammad* 'praised', 'lauded', 'commended', 'praiseworthy'—name of the Prophet, Messenger of Allah, founder of Islam (DMN 125). As expected, it is the most popular name throughout the Muslim world.

Il-Ġnejjen ta' Mħammed (Ħal Lew, 1549).

Musa: < Ar. male *ʾism Mūsā* (< Heb. *Mosheh*), name borne by the biblical prophet. According to Josephus, it means 'saved from the water'; other sources say it just means 'saved' or 'saviour'.

Ta' Musa (Xwieki, near Ħal Lija, 1496), Wied Musa (Tal-Ħandaq, 1541).

Ħal Muxi (Ħaż-Żebbuġ, 1467) comprises the Jew. reflex of the same anthroponym.

Nadir: < Ar. male *ʾism Nādir* (*Nader*) 'extraordinary', 'rare', 'exceptional', 'peerless', 'unique' (DMN 147).

(Ta') Għajn Nadir (Il-Ħara tal-Qabbieża, Gozo, 1612).

Naħla/Bin Naħla: (a) < Ar. fem. *ʾism Nahlah* (*Nahla*) 'a drink (of water)', 'a draught' (DMN 298); (b) < Ar. fem. *ʾism Nakhlah* (*Nakhla*) 'date palm tree'. *Bin Naħla* < *nasab Bin Nahlah* or < *nasab Bin Nakhlah.* Cf. top. In-Naħlija 'place abounding in palm trees'.

Ta' Naħla (1473), Ta' Bin Naħla (unlocated, 1525).

Possible entomological nickname < Mal. *naħla* 'honeybee'.

Pwales: < Ar. male *ʾism Buwālis*, seemingly a phonetic variant (*l* < *r*) of the *kunyah Abū Wāris*, in which *Wāris* (*Wārith*) means 'inheritor'. *Al-Wāris* is one of the Quranic names of Allah. Cf. Mal. *wirt, Werriet* (q.v.).

Il-Pwales (near Xemxija, 1372).

Cf. Sicilian historical toponym *Marsā al-Buwalis* 'Buwalis' port' (Caracausi 2:976). This interpretation infers an anthroponym, but Wettinger (PMI 426), following Saydon, albeit unconvincingly, suggests a Semitic pl. of Lat. *palus* 'swamp', 'marsh'.

Qabbieża: < Ar. *ʾism Qabisah* (most plausible interpretation) 'the almighty power (of Allah)'. Iyas ibn Qabisah was governor of al-Hirah, the capital of the Lakhmid kingdom, from 613 to 618.

Ta' Qabbieża/Tal-Qabbieża (Gozo, 1560, 1590), Il-Ħara ta' Qabbieża (Gozo, 1497), L-Armaġġ tal-Qabbieża (L-Għarb, 1575).

Otherwise, a nickname < Mal. *qabbieża* 'sprightly, energetic (woman)'; this is the interpretation favoured by Cooperson. Cf. Ar. *laqab qaffāzah* 'jumping', 'lively'.

Qadi: < Ar. male *ʾism Qāḍī* (*Qadi*) 'judge', 'magistrate', 'justice' (DMN 161). In Norman Sicily, the *qadis* presided over disputes among Muslim subjects (Caracausi 1:36).

Tal-Qadi/Il-Qadi (St Paul's Bay, 1500), L-Andar tal-Qadi (Tal-Qadi, 1508), L-Għalqa ta' Ħal Qadi (id., 1536), Il-Ħabel tal-Qadi (id., 1548), Għajn Qadi (Ġebel Ciantar, cited by Abela, 1647).

Possible nickname for a haughty or pretentious person, assuming the airs of a man in authority. *Bucaida* (< *Bū ʾl-Qāʾid*) survives as a Sicilian surname (Caracausi 1:204).

Qamar: < Ar. male and fem. *ʾism Qamar* 'moon'. *Al-Qamar* is the title of the 54th *sura* of the Quran. Cf. *Qamar-ud-Dīn* 'moon of religion (Islam)' (DMN 160).

Għajn Qamar (Gozo), Ta' Qamar id-Dar, Blatet il-Qamar.

Qawqla: < Ar. *ʾism Qawqal* (*Qauqal*) 'male sand-grouse or partridge' (PMI 209).

Għar Qawqla (Marsalforn, 1647, cited by Abela).

Possible ornithological nickname.

Rabib: < Ar. *rabīb* 'step-son', 'step-father'. Wettinger (PMI 603) actually interprets the name as 'foster son' or 'foster father', as well as 'slave'. Cf. It. surname *Arbib*.

Għajn Rabib (Marsa, 1533), Ix-Xagħra ta' Għajn Rabib (Corradino, 1536).

Less likely, *Rabib* represents the male form of the Ar. fem. *ʾism Rabība* 'queen', as well as 'one who is under oath', 'one who has given a promise'.

Raħeb: < Ar. *rāhib* 'monk', 'friar', 'hermit' (MED 2:1176; PMI 454).

Tar-Raħeb (unlocated, 1496), Il-Bajjada ta' Raħeb (Mrieħel, 1611), Il-Ħabel ta' Raħeb (Fiddien, 1720), Wied Raħeb (Gozo, 1564).

Less likely, it may be related to Ar. male *ʾism Rahīb* (fem. *Rahībah*) 'generous', 'big-hearted', 'forbearing', 'open-handed', 'spacious'.

Rajjes: < Ar. male *ʾism Raʾīs* (*Rayyes*, *Rayyis*, *Rayīs*, *Rais*) 'leader', 'chief', 'superior', 'master', 'the best fellow among a group of men' (DMN 168).

Ta' Rajjes/Tar-Rajjes (Mġarr, Gozo, 1578), Wied ir-Rajjes (Nadur, Gozo, 1746).

Possible nickname meaning 'commander', 'chief' < Mal. *rajjes* < *ras* 'head'.

Ramadan: < Ar. male and fem. *ʾism Ramaḍān*, 'the ninth month of the Islamic calendar' (DMN 169). Cf. Mal. *Randan* 'Lent'.

Ħabel Randan (Ħal Safi, 1526), Sqaq Randan/Randun (?), Wied Ramdan/Randun (?).

In this month, Muslims keep fast from early dawn to sunset. *Ramadan* originally meant 'great heat' (DMN 169).

Rażun/Rażul: < Ar. male *ʾism Rasūl* 'Messenger of Allah'—an epithet applied to the Prophet himself (DMN 171–72).

Għajn Rażun/Rażul (Tal-Veċċa, St Paul's Bay, 1663), Il-Ħara ta' Rasula/Il-Ħara ta' Rażula (Gozo, 1577), Ta' Rasula/Ta' Rażula (Gozo, 1577).

Possible nickname meaning 'apostle', 'prophet', 'envoy' < Mal. *rażul.*

Riħan/Riħana: < Ar. male *ʾism Rayḥān* (fem. *Rayḥāna* = *Rehana, Rihana*) (a) 'ease'; (b) 'fragrant herb', 'sweet basil' (DMN 172).

Il-Ħara ta' Riħan/Il-Ħara tar-Riħan (Gozo, 1570), Ta' Riħan/Tar-Riħan (Gozo, 1506), Għajn Riħana (Gozo, 1512), Ta' Għajn Riħana (Gozo, 1582).

Phytonym meaning 'myrtle' < Mal. *riħana.*

Riżin: (a) < Ar. male *ʾism Razīn* 'calm', 'composed', 'dignified' (DMN 311); or (b) < Ar. male *ʾism Raṣīn* 'firmly in place', 'deep-rooted', 'stable', 'upstanding'. Cf. Mal. *rżin* 'composed', 'respectable', 'virtuous', 'quiet', 'tranquil'.

Ta' Riżin (Żebbuġ, Gozo, 1565).

Rqiq: < Ar. male *ʾism Raqīq* 'delicate', 'fine', 'soft', 'slender', 'slim' (DMN 311). Cf. fem. *ʾism Raqīqah* (*Raqiqa*). The Sicilian family name *Richichi/Rechichi* shares the same etymolgy; however, *raqīq,* besides 'subtle' and 'tender', may also stand for 'slave' (Caracausi 2:1353).

(Il-)Ħabel ir-Rqiq/Ħabel Irqiq (Il-Qabbieża, Gozo, 1537).

Possible nickname (if referring to a person) or descriptive term (if referring to a topographic feature) meaning 'slim', 'thin' < Mal. *irqiq.*

Rummien(a): < Ar. fem. *ʾism Rummān*, pl. of *rummana(h)* 'pomegranate'—Umm Rumman was the mother of Aisha, one of Muhammad's wives (DMN 315). Cf. Mal. *rummien* (same meaning).

Ta' Rummiena (San Blas, 1522), Bur Rummien (?), Ħondoq ir-Rummien (Qala, Gozo, 1577).

The latter place-name may also be plausibly interpreted as a phonetic variant of Ħondoq ir-Rumin 'the ditch of the (Byzantine) Greeks' (Salafia, p.c.). Wettinger's (PMI 326) suggestion that it stands for 'the ditch by the pomegranate trees' now sounds far less convincing.

Ruxxieqa: presumably < Ar. fem. *ʾism Rashāqah* (*Rashaqa*) 'graceful stature', 'grace', 'elegance' (DMN 311).

Il-Ġebel ta' Ruxxieqa (Id-Dwejra, Gozo).

Safi: < Ar. male *ʾism Ṣāfī* 'pure', 'clear', 'untainted', 'honest' (DMN 179) < *ṣaffā* 'to make pure' (DAFN 3:249).

Ħal Safi (1419), Iċ-Ċens ta' Ħal Safi (1548).

The Sicilian toponym Safi shares the same etymology (Caracausi 2:1403), while the toponym Refalzafi (< *rahl Safī*) comprises the same Ar. *ʾism* (Caracausi 2:1341).

Sagħdun/Sagħduna: < Ar. male *ʾism Saʿdūn* (*Sādūn*, *Sadoun*) 'joyful', 'prosperous', 'lucky', from a hypocoristic form of *Saʿd* 'good fortune' (PMI 486).

Ta' Sagħdun (Ħal Tarxien, 1512), Ta' Sagħduna (Ħal Mann, 1500).

The surname *Sāʿdūn* was found among the Jews of medieval Malta.

Sajd: < Ar. male *ʾism Saʿīd* (*Saīd, Sayid*) 'happy', 'fortunate', 'blissful', 'prosperous' (DMN 182)—the name was borne by one of the most successful military commanders during the early years of Islam, a cousin of the Prophet.

Bir Sajd (Meġin, near Żurrieq, 1492), Ħabel Sajd (Għar Tiben, 1534), Ta' Ħaġar Sajd (Ħas-Saptan, 1535), Ħal Sajd/Ħas-Sayd (near Żabbar, 1504), Il-Wilġa ta' Sajd (Ħal Kbir, 1557).

The name survives to this day as a Mal. surname *Said*. Less likely, the name may be: (a) a reflex of the Ar. male *ʾism Sayyīd* (< *sayyīd* or or *sāʿid)* 'lord', 'master', 'chieftain' (DMN 191); or (b) a reflex of the Ar. male *ʾism Zayd* 'growth' < *ziyāda* 'increase', 'growth' (DMN 228).

Sajjied: (a) < Ar. male *ʾism Sayyād* 'worshipper of Allah' (DMN 184); (b) < Ar. male *ʾism Sāyed* (fem. *Sayyadah*) 'hunter'; or (c) < Ar. male *ʾism Sayyīd* < *sayyid* or *sāʿid* 'lord', 'master', 'chieftain' (DMN 191)—a title of honour conferred on the descendants of the Prophet through his daughter Fatima and his son-in-law Ali.

Ħas-Sajjied (Birkirkara, 1467), Ħabel is-Sajjied (Wied il-Barri, 1539).

Possibly an occupational name; this is the interpretation favoured by Cooperson (p.c.). Cf. archaic Mal. *sajjied* 'hunter'; via semantic restriction, the term now simply denotes a 'fisherman'.

Salaħ/Selaħ: < Ar. male *ʾism Ṣalāḥ* 'piety', 'righteousness', 'honesty', 'goodness', 'justice' (DMN 185). It also appears in several compound names such as *Ṣalāḥ ad-dīn* (*Saladin*). The name was also adopted by Sephardic Jews, and is sometimes romanised as *Tallāh* (DAFN 3:254).

Ta' Selaħ (Ħas-Saptan, 1499), Ħabel Salaħ (Marsa, 1361).

Sammut: < Ar. *ṣamūt* 'silent', 'taciturn', with gemination (Caracausi 2:1729).

Ta' Qortin Sammut (Buġibba, 1399).

The name survives to this day as a Mal. surname *Sammut.*

Since the above-mentioned place-name is also recorded as Ta' Qortin Sammat (Buġibba, 1399), one cannot ignore the influence of other names like *Sammad* (with devoicing) 'firm of will', 'strong in determination', 'persevering', 'steadfast'; and *Samad* (with gemination and devoicing) 'everlasting', 'eternal'. Cf. Ar. male *ʾism Samūd* (with devoicing) 'firmness', 'durability', 'steadfastness', 'perseverance', 'endurance' (DMN 189).

Sannat: < Ar. male *ʾism Sanad* 'support', 'prop' (DMN 189) with gemination and devoicing.

Ta' Sannat (Gozo, 1468).

Geoffrey Hull (p.c.) ponders the possible connection with Sicilian *sinnatu, assinnatu* (It. *assennato*) 'sensible'.

Sawd: < Ar. male *ʾism Suʿūd* (sometimes romanised as *Suʿud*) 'happy', 'lucky', 'blessed'; pl. form of *Saʿd* 'felicities', 'good fortune'.

Ta' Sawd (unlocated ecclesiastical benefice, 1436).

Sarġ: < Ar. male *ʾism Sirāj* 'lamp', 'light'. The name also features in compounds, such as *Sirāj-ud-Dawlah* 'lamp of the state' and *Sirāj-ud-dīn* 'lamp of the faith' (DMN 203).

Ħal Sarġ, Ħaġar Sarġ, Wied Sarġ, Il-Ħbula ta' Sarġ.

Salafia (p.c.) explains the phonetic mutation thus: *Sarġ* < *Srāġ* (via metathesis) < *Sirāj*. The same author is also convinced that the terms *sruġ* (in the top. Il-Ħotba ta' Sruġ) and *srejġu* (in the top. Ta' Srejġu) are respectively pl. and dim. forms.

Sbejjaħ: < Ar. male *ʾism Ṣubayḥ,* itself a diminutive form of *ṣabīḥ* 'handsome', 'comely', 'glowing'.

Ta' Sbejjaħ (Sannat, Gozo, 1581).

Possible nickname meaning 'attractive', 'pretty' < a dim. of Mal. *sabiħ.*

Semaħ: < Ar. male *ʾism Ṣamāḥ* 'generosity', 'bounty', 'good-heartedness', 'magnanimity' (DMN 188).

Ta' Semaħ (Qala, Gozo, 1575).

Less likely, < Ar. male *ʾism Samiʿ* (*Samiʕ*) 'hearing', 'listening' (DMN 188)—*Al-Samiʿ* 'the All-Hearing' is one of the Quranic names of Allah.

Seqer: < Ar. male *ʾism Ṣaqr* 'falcon', 'hawk'.

Tas-Seqer (Mrieħel, 1467), Wied Seqer (Gozo, 1575). Cf. Ta' Sejqer (a house at Attard, 1569).

Possible ornithological nickname meaning 'falcon' < Mal. *seqer, sejqer* (dim.).

Serija: < Ar. fem. *ʾism Sariyah* (*Sāreyah*), of dubious import.

(Ta') Ħabel Serija (Gozo, 1565, 1569), Il-Ħara ta' Ħabel Serija (Gozo, 1569).

Possibly a reflex of Ar. fem. noun *sarriyya* 'concubine'.

Sejba: < Ar. fem. *ʾism Ṣāiba* (pronounced *Ṣayba*) 'striking the mark', 'straight', 'pertinent'.

Ta' Sejba (San Ġwann, 1528), L-Ibwar ta' Sejba (unlocated, 1541), Rqajja' Sejba (1505), Il-Bur ta' Sejba (unlocated, 1555), Ħabel Sejba (Għajn Riħana, 1542).

Sejma: < Ar. fem. *ʾism Ṣāima* (pronounced *Ṣayma*) 'pious woman who fasts often', 'a person who gives up pleasures for the sake of Allah'. Cf. *Ṣayim* (male), *Ṣaymīn* (pl.) < Ar. *sawm* 'fasting'.

L-Irqajja' ta' Sejma (unlocated, 1537).

Cf. Mal. *sajma, sajjem* (same meaning).

Siekel: < Ar. male *ʾism Shakīl* 'well formed', 'handsome', 'comely' (DMN 197).

Wied Siekel (?).

The mutation *S* < *Sh* is not problematic. Salafia (p.c.) interprets *Sejkel* and *Sejkla* in the toponyms Ta' Sejkel and Il-Wied ta' Sejkla as dim. forms. Other interpretations explaining the Mal. surname *Seychell* are, however, conceivable.

Sielem, Selim/Selem: < Ar. male *ʾisms Sālim, Salām, Salīm, Salem* 'safe', 'unharmed', 'sound', 'healthy'—*al-Salām* 'the All-Peaceable' is one of the Quranic names of Allah (DMN 185). Cf. *Sliema* (q.v.).

Ġebel Selim/Ta' Ġebel Selem (Għammar, 1542), Ta' Għajn Sielem (Gozo, 1587), Wied Sielem (Gozo, 1562).

Sifa: possibly an aphaeretic form of *waṣīfa* 'female servant', with loss of the *wa-*.

Ta' Qabar Sifa (unlocated, 1539), Ta' Qbur Sifa (Andar il-Blat, 1559).

Less likely < Ar. fem. *sifa(h)* 'trait', 'characteristic', 'state'.

Slajten: < Ar. male ʾ*ism Sulaytān* (*Sulaitan*), dim. form of *Sultān* 'sultan', 'king', 'ruler'.

Ta' Slajten/Tas-Slajten (Il-Ħara ta' San Anard tal-Għarb, 1570).

Possible nickname meaning 'little king' < Mal. *slajten* < *sultan*.

Sliema, Slima: < Ar. fem. ʾ*ism Salāmah* (*Salamah, Salīmah, Salema*) 'peace', 'safety', 'security', 'integrity' (DMN 321–22). Cf. *Umm Salama* and *Salima Sultana* (compound names). Ar. *salāmah* (dial. *slāma*) properly means 'safe arrival'.

Ta' Sliema (Ħal Kirkop, 1529), Ta' Slima (Gozo). Modern-day Ta' Sliema is first recorded in 1758: *Visitatio Beatae Mariae Virginis ta' Caortin, sive ta' Sliema* (PMI 537).

Salīma also means 'righteous', 'true', 'perfect', 'unblemished', 'unharmed', 'in good health'. *S-L-M* is the root for many common Quranic words, like *Islam, Muslim*, and *Salām* 'peace'. Cf. *Sielem* (q.v.).

Sultan: < Ar. male ʾ*ism Sultān* 'sultan', 'ruler', 'authority', 'power' (DMN 206). Cf. Mal. *sultan* 'king'.

Ħabel Sultan (Ħas-Sejjieħ, 1525).

The fem. form *Sultānah* begot the Mal. family name *Sultana*, which survives to this day; otherwise, the surname derived directly from *sultan* (+ *-a*, entailing Romance morphological influence).

Tmim: Syncopated form of Muslim male ʾ*ism Tamīm* 'well formed', 'solid' (DMN 209). Cf. (a) Abu Ruqayya Tamīm, a *sahābi*; (b) a ruler so called in North Africa (1062–1108).

Ħal Tmim (Żejtun, c. 1419).

The toponym is often wrongly transcribed as *Ħal Tmin* or (via popular etymology) *Ħal Tmiem.*

Tuffieħa: < Ar. *tuffāḥa* 'apple'. Wettinger (PMI 191) managed to trace the fem. *ʾism Toffecha/Toffiecha* in seventeenth-century records.

Għajn Tuffieħa (1299).

Otherwise, a relexicalised form (through popular etymology) of the Ar. fem. *ʾism Toufikah* (*Tawfiqah, Tawfiqa, Taufiqa*) 'prosperity', 'good luck', 'good fortune', 'success (granted by Allah)' (DMN 337).

Tuta: < Ar. fem. *ʾism Tūta*(*h*) meaning 'mulberry (fruit and tree)'.

Għajn Tuta (Gozo, 1565), Santa Duminka ta' Għajn Tuta (id., 1590).

Possible botanical nickname < Mal. *tuta* (same meaning).

Twil/Twila: < Ar. male *ʾism Ṭawīl* (fem. *Ṭawīla*) 'tall', 'lanky'. The name is also Jewish (mainly Levantine) and its Arabic bearers are both Muslim and Christian.

Ta' Twil (Żebbuġ, Gozo, 1580), Ta' Twila (Siġġiewi, 1535), Ta' Twila t-Taħtenija (id., 1540).

Possible nickname < Mal. *twil* (same meaning). The Sicilian toponym Realtavilla (< *Racaltavilla* < Ar. *raḥl ṭawīl*) comprises the same anthroponym (Caracausi 2:1340).

Warda: < Ar. fem. *ʾism Wardah* 'rose', 'flower', 'fresh', 'glowing' (DMN 341). Cf. Mal. *warda* (same meaning).

Ħal Warda (Ħ'Attard, 1680), L-Andar tal-Warda (Qrendi, 1621), Tal-Warda (Ħal Għaxaq, 1535).

Wettinger (PMI 291), alternatively, suggests a reflex of the non-Semitic name *Guaglarda*.

Werriet: < Ar. male *ʾism Wārith* (*Wāris*) 'heir', 'inheritor', 'successor'—*al-Wāris* 'the Inheritor' is one of the Quranic names of Allah (DMN 220). Cf. Mal. *werriet* (same meaning) < Ar. *wārith* (pl. *wurrāth*)

Tal-Werriet (Tal-Qasar, 1540), Tal-Werrieta (unlocated, 1524).

Wieli/Wieri: Phonetic variants of Ar. male *ʾism* (a) *Walī* 'guardian', 'custodian', 'protector', 'helper'; also 'lord', 'saint', 'friend' (DAFN 3:576), or (b) *Wālī* 'governor', 'ruler', 'prefect'. *Walī Allāh* 'friend of God' is an epithet of the Prophet Muhammad.

Wied Wieli (near Ħal Tarxien, 1494), Tal-Wieli (id., 1538), Tal-Wieri (Għarb, Gozo, 1487).

In the English-speaking world, *wali* most often means a Muslim saint or holy person. It has sometimes been extended to mean the tomb or shrine of such a man. *Wāli* may also refer to an Islamic legal guardian. Toponyms Għajn Dwieli and Ġnien Dwieli may respectively stand for **Għajn di Wieli* and **Ġnien di Wieli*—presumably contracted from idiosyncratic notarial forms (Salafia, p.c.).

Xaħam/Xaħma/Xħajma: (a) Ar. male *ʾism Shaham*, *Shahim* 'thick'; or (b) < Ar. fem. *ʾism Shahama* 'beautiful', 'peaceful'. *Xħajma* presumably represents a dim. form.

Ta' Xaħam (Dwejra, Gozo, 1572), Ta' Xaħma (Ta' Bajdun, 1558), Roqgħa Xaħma (unlocated, 1529), Ta' Xħajma (Nadur, Gozo, 1575).

Possible nickname < Mal. *xaħam/xaħma* < Ar. *shaḥm* 'fat', 'lard', *shaḥmah* 'piece of fat'.

The above-mentioned names could have been reanalysed by popular etymology.

Xakla: Ar. fem. *ʾism Shaklah, Shaklā/Shuklah, Shuklā* 'beautiful', 'well-shaped', 'well-formed'.

Ta' Xakla (Ħal Millieri, 1431).

Otherwise, Ar. *shaklā* also means 'of mixed hue', a possible reference to soil colour.

Xaqra: (a) < Ar. fem. *ʾism Shaqra(h)* 'blonde', 'fair-skinned'; or (b), albeit less likely, a syncopated form of the Ar. fem. *ʾism Shākirah* (*Shakira, Shakera*) 'thankful', 'grateful', 'appreciative' (DMN 329). Cf. *Xkora* (q.v.).

Ta' Xaqra (Torbit Garfagna, 1535), Il-Ħabel ta' Xaqra (Santa Marija ta' Raħal Tabuni, 1585).

Cf. Ar. *Shaqriyyah* 'blonde', 'fair-skinned'. Otherwise, Ar. *shuqra* means 'light red', 'bay-coloured', especially if referring to the colour of the local soil.

Xejba: (a) < Ar. fem. *ʾism Shaybah, Shaybā* 'grey-haired', 'aged'; (b) < Ar. fem. *ʾism Shayba* 'goddess of the moon and hunting, equivalent to Artemis'.

Għajn Xejba (Gozo, 1449), Ħal Xejba (unlocated, 1527), Ta' Xejba (Ramla, Gozo, 1539), (Ta') Għar Xejba (Gozo, 1746).

Also attested as a medieval Maltese surname, *Xejba* (*Xeiba*) is actually recorded in Gozo during the fifteenth century (PMI 192).

Xemx: < Ar. male and fem. *ʾism Shams* 'sun'. *Al-Shams* is the title of the 91st *sura* of the Quran. The name also features in compounds, such as *Shams-ud-Dīn* 'sun of the faith' and *Shams-ud-Dawlah* 'sun of the kingdom' (DMN 198).

Għar ix-Xemx, Tax-Xemx, Il-Bur tax-Xemx u l-Qamar. Cf. *Qamar* (q.v.).

Salafia (p.c.) is convinced that the element *xmejxi* (in the top. It-Tafal ta' Xmejxi) represents a dim. form.

Xewka/Xewk: < Ar. male *ʾism Shawka(h)* 'thorn', 'spine', 'barb', 'fork'. However, the Ar. *ʾism Shawkat* (*Shaukat*) means 'power', 'bravery', 'valour' (DMN 199).

Xewka (Ix-Xagħra ta' Sannat, Gozo, 1437), Bir Xewka (1524), Tax-Xewk (Ta' Nwadar, 1529), Andar Xewk (Għajn Riħana, Gozo, 1582), Ħabel Xewk (Bingħisa, 1535).

Salafia (p.c.) is convinced that *Xewk* is just an apocopated form of *Xewka* and hence rejects the botanical connection with thorns.

Xieref/Xaraf/Xurraf: *Xieref* and *Xaraf* (a) < Ar. (non-Quranic) male *ʾism Sharaf* 'honour', 'dignity', 'greatness'. The co-radical *Xurraf* is related to the Ar. male *ʾism Musharraf* 'honorable', 'worthy of honour'.

Ġnien Xieref/Ġnien ix-Xieref (Mrieħel, 1543), Ħabel Xieref (Ħal Bajda, 1531), Tax-Xieraf (Wied is-Sewda, 1518), Xaraf il-Far (Bubaqra, 1523), Ta' Xurraf (*Rollo De Mello*, 1436).

Possible nickname < Mal. *xieref* 'tough', 'hard-hearted', 'very old' (MED 2:1549). Cf. *Xurraf* (q.v.). A place called al-Shārif (usually spelled Charef) exists in Algeria.

Xiħ/Xejħ: < Ar. male *ʾism Shayk* (*Shaikh, Sheikh*) 'title of a political or spiritual leader of a Muslim community', 'chief', 'head', 'old man' (DMN 200). Cf. *Buxiħ* (q.v), *Mart ix-Xiħ*—presumably, the only instance in the Mal. toponymic repertoire in which the *nasab* refers to a wife, rather than to a son.

Tax-Xiħ/Ix-Xiħ (Żurrieq, 1506), Għar ix-Xiħ (Tabrija, 1518), Ħabel ix-Xiħ (It-Torri tal-Għassiewi, 1487), Tax-Xejħ (Gozo, 1539), Tax-Xiħa (Għadir Bordi, 1534), (Ta') Ħabel Xiħa (Ħas-Sejjiegħ, 1545), Ta' Mart ix-Xiħ (Tal-Ħandaq, 1521).

Possible nickname for an old man < Mal. *xiħ* < Ar. *shaykh.*

Ximlan: < Ar. *ʾism Shamlan,* presumably meaning 'illuminating', 'complete man'.

Ta' Ximlan (Xlendi, Gozo, 1568).

Xirek: < Ar. male *ʾism Sharīq* 'the Sun'. Literally, it means 'that which rises from the East', derived from the root *SH-R-Q* 'sunrise', 'East'. *Sharīq,* presumably, also means 'glowing', 'happy', 'hopeful'.

Il-Barrani ta' Xirek (unlocated, 1538).

Cf. Mal. *xerq/xarq* 'East'. Wettinger (PMI 21; see also MED 2:1574) suggests a possible nickname < Mal. *xrik/xriek* 'partner', 'associate', but also 'hired hand', 'apprentice'.

Xkora: Presumably a syncopated form of Ar. *ʾism Shakūra* 'very thankful', 'much obliged', 'extremely appreciative', 'deeply grateful'. It is derived from the Quranic root *SH-K-R* 'thankfulness' and is the fem. form of the male name *Shakur*. Cf. *Xakra* (q.v.).

Ta' Xkora (Il-Ħamimiet, Gozo, 1474), Ta' Wied Xkora (Siġġiewi, 1508), L-Irqajja' ta' Xkora (Mosta, 1538).

Possible nickname meaning ‘sack’, ‘bag’ < Mal. *xkora*; otherwise, relexicalised through popular etymology.

Żabur/Żibur: < Ar. (non-Quranic) male *ʾism Zabūr, Zebūr* ‘lion’, ‘lion-like’.

Ta’ Żabur (San Martin, 1581), Ta’ Għar Żibur (Ġnien il-Far = Tabrija, 1525).

Żagħfran: < Ar. fem. *ʾism Zāfarani* < *zaghfarān* ‘saffron’.

Ta’ Żagħfran (Il-Ħara tal-Qortin, 1574).

Possible phytonym meaning ‘saffron’. The Sicilian toponym Zafarana shares the same etymology (Caracausi 2:1725).

Żahra: (a) < Ar. fem. *ʾism Zahrāʾ* ‘bright’, ‘radiant’, ‘shining’, ‘luminous’ (DMN 343); or (b) < fem. *ʾism Zahrah* ‘flower’, ‘blossom’, ‘beauty’ (DMN 343). *Zahrāʾ* is an epithet of Fatima, daughter of Muhammad.

Wied Żahra (Gozo, 1580), Il-Ħara ta’ Wied Żahra (Gozo, 1580).

The name survives to this day as a Mal. surname *Zahra*. The Sicilian toponym Zagara derives from Ar. *zahr* ‘orange blossom’ (Caracausi 2:1726).

Żejjed: phonetic variant of *Zayyād* < Ar. male *ʾism Zāʾid* ‘increasing’, ‘exceeding’, ‘excessive’, ‘growing’, ‘surplus’ (DMN 225). Cf. *Zayd* ‘growth’, ‘increase’, ‘increment’, ‘addition’ (DMN 228); *Zayed* ‘prospering’, ‘in abundance’, ‘progessing’; *Ziyad* ‘enlarging’, ‘superabundance’.

Ta’ Żejjed (Mwieżeb, 1500), Il-Ħabel ta’ Żejjed (Ħal Qormi, 1499).

Less likely, an occupational name < Ar. *zayyāt* 'maker or seller of oil'; hence, a cognate form of Ar. *ʾism Zayit* 'olive'.

Żejjen: < Ar. male *ʾism Zayyān* (*Zeyyan, Zayan*) 'beautifier', 'one who makes things beautiful or improves things'. Cf. Mal. *żej-jien* 'decorator' < *żejjen* 'to adorn', 'to beautify', 'to decorate' (MED 2:1606).

Ta' Żejjen (Ħerba, 1540).

Żejtun/Żejtuna: < Ar. fem. *ʾism Zeitun, Zaytun* (*Zaitun*), *Zaytuna* (*Zaituna*) < *zaytūn* 'olive', 'olive tree'.

Ta' Żejtuna (Ħirbit ir-Riħ, 1499), Għajn Żejtuna (Mellieħa, 1479).

The Sicilian toponym Zaituni (Noto) shares the same etymology (Caracausi 2:1727). Possible nickname or descriptive term meaning 'olive (tree)'.

Żerqa: < Arabic fem. *ʾism Zarqā* (*Zerqa, Zerka*) 'blue-eyed'. It is sometimes appended to another personal name as in *Zarqa Sultana* and *Zarqa Habiba*.

Ta' Żerqa (Bir Abdilla, 1494), Wied iż-Żerqa (?).

Possibly a nickame from the fem. form of *iżraq* (q.v.).

5.0. Conclusion

The inventory of Arabic names discussed in this paper is quite ample (around 170 entries),[13] but it is definitely not exhaustive.

[13] The present author surmises that, in all, there must be well over 300 Muslim names lurking in the Maltese toponymic pool. Henceforth, this inventory may easily be doubled, in good time, by more rigorous researchers.

Less plausible candidates have been cautiously omitted, as they call for additional scrutiny, while others possibly survive in camouflaged forms and must have eluded the present author's attention.

Salafia (PNG 2:326–27) suggests the inclusion of *Aħżien, Barmil(i), Barrani, Bellula, Biljun, Boros, Bullara, Dbieġi, Errin, Fekruna, Foqra, Futni, Għadir, Għasejla, Għasir/Għasri, Ġifra, Ħalluf, Ħanżir(a), Ħarrat, Ħarrax, Ħurrieqa, Klejba, Kortoll, Kotob, Lelluxa, Lewż(a), Monġur/Minġur, Mrik, Qaddisa, Qadim, Qanfud, Qatet/Qatta, Qaws, Qawwi, Qortil, Sanab, Semaq, Xemgħan, Xemgħat, Xini, Żanqur*, and *Żewwarija*. On the other hand, Wettinger (PMI xvi–xviii) mentions *Bixrub, Biżbud, Budaqq, Buġineħ, Bugħarien, Bunuħħala, Bunixeb, Buqana, Busif, Buskieken, Busrawel, Ħalil, Ħsejjen, Jaħlef, Mhelhel, Midbuħ*, and *Tlieli*. Other possible nominees are *Bilbla, Għajn, Għarab, Għorof, Ħamiem(a), Ħamran, Ħanżir, Kantra, Kbir, Manara, Mellieħa, Mergħa, Miġlus, Nisa, Qorrot, Ramla, Riqudi, Rokna, Sabat/Sabbat, Sawd, Sidra, Simar, Sined, Snien, Sufa, Torba, Tarġa, Xarolla/Xirolla, Żahruna*, and *Żebbiegħ*.

Abyad, Ahmar, Akhdar, Asmar, Ashqar, and *Azraq* are all attested as Arabic personal names. However, Maltese *Abjad* (e.g., Tal-Abjad), *Aħmar* (e.g., Ġebel l-Aħmar), *Aħdar* (e.g., Tal-Aħdar), *Ismar* (e.g., Tal-Ismar), *Ixqar* (e.g., Ħirbit l-Ixqar), and *Iżraq* (e.g., Ta' Għar l-Iżraq) have been deliberately omitted from this paper as they could easily represent a personal nickname or even a topographical (descriptive) label. The same criterion applies to *Sawdah* (Maltese *Sewda*, e.g., Wied is-Sewda).

Hence, this can only be considered a work in progress. Further research may unearth a string of surprising specimens which would enhance this already abundant repertoire.

Author's Note

This paper could not have been written without the indispensable input of my trusted colleagues, Michael Cooperson and Simon Salafia. I thank them for kindly agreeing to read a previous draft of this paper. Their comments and suggestions have proved very valuable, but, obviously, full accountability for the final version, including any inaccuracies and misinterpretations which might have slipped through, lies entirely on me.

Abbreviations

*	reconstructed form
?	dubious
<	derived from
Ar.	Arabic
dial.	dialectal
dim.	diminutive
fem.	female/feminine
fig.	figuratively
Heb.	Hebrew
It.	Italian
Jew.	Jewish
Lat.	Latin
lit.	literally
Mal.	Maltese
ornith.	ornithology
p.c.	personal communication
p.p.	passive participle
Sic.	Sicilian
top.	toponym

References

Caracausi = Girolamo Caracausi. 1993–1994. *Dizionario onomastico della Sicilia*. 2 vols. Palermo: Centro di Studi Filologiche e Linguistici Siciliani; L'Epos Società Editrice.

DAFN = Patrick Hanks (ed.). 2003. *Dictionary of American Family Names*. Oxford: Oxford University Press.

DCA = Giuseppe Staccioli and Mario Cassar. 2017. *Dizionario dei cognomi italiani di origine araba*. Pisa: Pacini Editore.

DMN = Salahuddin Ahmed. 1999. *A Dictionary of Muslim Names*. London: Hurst & Company.

Durkin, Philip. 2013. *The Oxford Guide to Etymology*. Oxford: Oxford University Press.

EOI = P. J. Bearman et al. (eds). 1960–2004. *The Encyclopaedia of Islam*. 2nd ed. 12 vols. Leiden: Brill.

Fiorini, Stanley (ed.). 1999. *Documentary Sources of Maltese History*. Part 2, *Documents at the State Archives, Palermo*. No. 1, *Cancelleria Regia 1259–1400*. Malta: Malta University Press.

Kadmon, Naftali (ed.). 2002. *Glossary of Terms for the Standardization of Geographical Names*. New York: UN Publication.

Marcato, Carla. 2009. *Nomi di persona, nomi di luogo: Introduzione all'onomastica italiana*. Bologna: Il Mulino.

MED = Joseph Aquilina. 1987–1990. *Maltese-English Dictionary*. 2 vols. Malta: MidSea Books.

PMI = Godfrey Wettinger. 2000. *Place-Names of the Maltese Islands, ca 1300–1800*. Malta: PEG.

PNG = Simon Salafia. 2020–2022. *The Place-Names of Gozo*. 2 vols. Malta.

Wehr, Hans. 1979. *A Dictionary of Modern Written Arabic*. Edited by J. M. Cowan. 4th ed. Wiesbaden: Harrossowitz Verlag.

KOINEISATION AND LANGUAGE CONTACT IN SYRIAN ṬUROYO[1]

Bruno Herin

1.0. Introduction

The goal of the present contribution is to investigate koineisation and language contact phenomena in Ṭuroyo as spoken in north-eastern Syria, around the city of Qamishli. Usually classified as a central neo-Aramaic language, the original homeland of Ṭuroyo is an area in the south-eastern part of modern Turkey known as Ṭūr ʿAbdīn. The region is centred around the town of Midyat and includes a few dozen villages and settlements around it. All the speakers of Ṭuroyo belong originally to the Syriac Orthodox Church. There is a strong feeling of correlation on the part of the speakers between language, religion, and ethnicity, to the point that a single adjective *suryoyo* 'Syriac' is used to refer to all three. As far as the language is concerned, the adjective *suryoyo* often collocates with the noun *lišono* 'language': *lišono suryoyo* 'the Syriac language'. This term refers primarily to Classical Syriac, which is the liturgical language of the Syriac Orthodox Church,

[1] I would like to thank Bachar Malki, without whom the present contribution would have been impossible. Heartfelt thanks also to Alice Croq for helping me with Classical Syriac.

 https://doi.org/10.11647/OBP.0445.09

and by extension, to the vernacular. A common opinion among speakers is that their vernacular is a corrupted version of Classical Syriac, mostly because of contact with Arabic and Kurdish. To disambiguate between the classical language and the vernacular, the glossonym *ṭuroyo* is in use. The original homeland Ṭūr ʿAbdīn is refered to in the vernacular as *ṭuro*, whose literal meaning is 'mountain'. The word *ṭuroyo* is therefore the relational adjective derived from *ṭuro* by suffixation of the adjectiviser morpheme *-(o)yo*. It should be added, however, that the term *ṭuroyo* may be perceived pejoratively because of the connotations it carries (rurality, remoteness, etc.). Another glossonym also in use is *surayt*, which derives from the feminine form of the adjective *suryoyo* (*surayto* in Ṭuroyo). Despite this, the term *ṭuroyo* is now well established in the scholarly literature and will be used throughout this paper.

Prior to the genocide against the Christians in 1915 (referred to as *sayfo*), Ṭuroyo was restricted to Ṭūr ʿAbdīn. The first wave of migration to the northern parts of Syria and beyond (Aleppo and Damascus, Lebanon and Palestine) happened after the genocide. Migration outside Ṭūr ʿAbdīn increased after the establishment of the French mandate over Syria and Lebanon in the aftermath of the First World War (Gabriel 2023). Many families, mostly from rural areas, did not feel safe any more because of repeated land-related conflicts with surrounding Kurdish tribes. Oral history also records a number of cases of abduction of women, which significantly contributed to the feeling of lack of safety for those who lived in remote areas. Consequently, many took the opportunity given by the security provided by the

French mandate and settled in and around the city of Qamishli in northern Syria. From a linguistic perspective, the migration changed the linguistic ecosystem from a mostly bilingual Ṭuroyo–Kurdish setup in Ṭūr ʿAbdīn into a trilingual Ṭuroyo–Arabic–Kurdish setup in Syria, with the difference being that Arabic was now the majority language and Kurdish a minority language.

Ṭuroyo is one of the few descendant languages of Aramaic that are still spoken today. These languages are classified into three groups: Western Neo-Aramaic, Central Neo-Aramaic, and Eastern Neo-Aramaic. Western Neo-Aramaic is spoken in three villages in the Anti-Lebanon mountains and is known to us mostly due to the work of Arnold (1989; 1990a; 1991a; 1991b; 1990b; 2019), although more recent data collection seems to be underway (Duntsov et al. 2022). Eastern Neo-Aramaic subdivides into Mandaic, historically spoken in Southern Iraq and Iran (Häberl 2009), and North-Eastern Neo-Aramaic, which comprises a myriad of varieties originally spoken across eastern Turkey, Iraq, and Iran (Coghill 2019). Central Neo-Aramaic is composed of Ṭuroyo and Mlaḥso, which is reported to have gone extinct some decades ago (Jastrow 2011). Ṭuroyo therefore remains the sole member of Central Neo-Aramaic. The language has been known to the scholarly community for quite some time, with the first descriptive account dating back to the end of the nineteenth century (Eugen and Socin 1881), followed by Siegel (1923). An important documentary and descriptive work is that of Ritter (1967; 1979; 1990), which consists of the Boasian triad of grammar, dictionary, and texts. The main descriptive reference work is that of Jastrow (1993), which focusses on the variety of Mīdən. More recent documentary work is found in Lahdo (2017), Jastrow and Talay (2019), Häberl et al. (2020), and Demir et al. (2022). Based for the most part on secondary sources, studies on Ṭuroyo syntax can be found in Waltisberg (2016) and Noorlander (2021). The works mentioned here are only the most salient monographs and it goes without saying that there is a significant number of other publications that deal with all aspects of Ṭuroyo ranging from sociolinguistics to historical linguistics, a review of which are of course beyond the scope of the present contribution. It appears, however, that none of these works are based on data collected in Syria or from speakers that originate from Syria. The material on which the present work draws is therefore novel. It consists of family recordings carried in the cities of Qamishli and Qaḥṭāniyye during the summer of 2010. The goal was of course to go on with data collection *in situ*, but because of the war that started in 2011, this became impossible. Much of the Syriac population of northern Syria found refuge in Europe, to the point that very few individuals are left, mostly to avoid expropriation by the local Kurdish administration. Consequently, we decided to carry on with data collection in Belgium with individuals who had recently arrived from Syria.

Ṭuroyo as spoken in northern Syria is interesting primarily from two perspectives. The first one is koineisation, or the emergence of new varieties, and the second is language contact. From a koineisation perspective, it appears that Qamishli was populated by speakers who hailed from different places in Ṭūr ʿAbdīn such as Arbo, ʾḤwo, Babəde, ʿEwardo, and also the town of

Midyat. Some neighbourhoods eventually took the name of the place of origin of the newcomers. A case in point, for instance, is a neighbourhood in Qamishli called *ḥārt il-ʾarbāwiyye* 'the neighbourhood of the people from Arbo' (*arboye* in Ṭuroyo, plural of *arboyo* 'from Arbo'). Speakers report that the people who originated from the villages around Midyat quickly gave up their dialectal specificities, but those from Midyat itself maintained some of their original features, because of the prestige associated with this form of speech in the context of an urban versus rural linguistic dichotomy. From a language contact perspective, Syrian Ṭuroyo and more precisely Qamishli Ṭuroyo is described by the speakers themselves as highly influenced by Arabic. What our data suggest is that this is indeed the case. Ṭuroyo–Arabic bilingualism has been generalised and the degree of intertwining between both languages is well advanced. The questions raised in the present paper are therefore twofold: what the effects of koineisation are on Syrian Ṭuroyo and how language contact, mostly with Arabic, materialises in actual speech.

2.0. Koineisation

Koineisation refers to the emergence of a new variety when speakers of closely related dialects come together and form a new linguistic community. The stabilisation of this new variety, also called focussing, usually happens over three generations. The linguistic output of this process involves four potential phenomena: levelling, simplification, reallocation, and interdialectal forms (Britain and Trudgill 1999; Trudgill 2020). What happens precisely is that variants of one linguistic variable collide. This collision results in one of these four phenomena. Levelling means that one variant is left out altogether. Simplification refers to the loss of distinction, whether phonological, morphosyntactic, or semantic. Reallocation means each variant is reallocated to a specific function, whether morphosyntactic, semantic, or even pragmatic. Interdialectal forms occur when the two variants hybridise and give birth to a form not found in any of the input varieties.

2.1. Levelling, Linearisation, and Morphological Structure of the Predicate

Ṭuroyo possesses two sets of subject markers: one that grammaticalised from independent pronouns (Table 1) and one that grammaticalised from the dative preposition *l-* 'to, for' and bound pronouns (Table 2). These markers do not have the same morphosyntactic status. Predicative markers are clitics, whereas subject markers are affixes, both morphosyntactically and phonologically. Phonologically, predicative markers have no influence on stress assignment. Compare, for example, [ˈharke] 'here' and [ˈharkeːno] 'I am here', in which the stress does not move. This is not the case with subject markers (the *ko-* prefix marks indicative mood): [ko-ˈʃoːməʕ] 'he listens' vs [ko-ʃoːˈmaʕno] 'I listen'. Morphosynactically, predicative markers are not selective as far as the host is concerned, since they attach to nominals,[2] adjectives,

[2] It may be argued that *harke* 'here' is an adverb of time and not a noun, but it substitutes for a noun phrase and, as such, it is a nominal or a nominoid (Creissels 1988).

and prepositional phrases, whereas subject markers only attach to verbs.

Table 1: Grammaticalisation of independent pronouns

	Independent pronouns	Predicative markers and *harke* 'here'	Subject markers and *š-m-ʿ* 'listen' in the imperfective
1ms	*ono*	*harke-no*	*šōmaʿ-no*
1fs			*šəmʿo-no*
2ms	*hat*	*harke-hət*	*šəmʿ-ət*
2fs		*harke-hat*	*šəmʿ-at*
3ms	*hiye*	*harke-yo*	*šōməʿ-Ø*
3fs	*hiya*		*šəmʿo-Ø*
1pl	*aḥna*	*harke-na*	*šəmʿi-na*
2pl	*hatu*	*harke-hatu*	*šəmʿ-utu*
3pl	*hənne*	*harke-ne*	*šəmʿī-Ø*

Table 2: Grammaticalisation of *l-* and bound pronouns

	l- + bound pronouns	Existential *kit* + *l-* + bound pronouns	Subject markers and *f-t-ḥ* 'open' in the perfective
1sg	*-l-i*	*kət-li*	*ftəḥ-li*
2ms	*-l-ux*	*kət-lux*	*ftəḥ-lux*
2fs	*-l-ax*	*kət-lax*	*ftəḥ-lax*
3ms	*-l-e*	*kət-le*	*ftəḥ-le*
3fs	*-l-a*	*kət-la*	*ftəḥ-la*
1pl	*-l-an*	*kət-lan*	*ftəḥ-lan*
2pl	*-(l)-xu*	*kət-xu*	*ftəḥ-xu*
3pl	*C-Ce*	*kət-te*	*ftəḥ-ḥe*

Although this has been noted many times, from a Semitic perspective, the most striking evolution in the verbal system of these Neo-Aramaic languages is the loss of the inherited prefix and suffix conjugations in favour of perfective and imperfective conjugations based respectively on the old passive and active participles. The new imperfective arose from the grammaticalisation of the active participle CōCəC (of course cognate with Arabic CāCiC) and reduced forms of the independent pronouns. The first-person singular form *šōmaʿ-no* is therefore the result of the coalescence of *šōməʿ* and *ono*. Classical Syriac is of course well known for having marginalised the inherited prefix conjugation to an irrealis mood and recruited the active participle to mark indicative mood, but embryos of these evolutions are also found in earlier stages of the language, such as Biblical Aramaic: *yādaʿ ʾana dī* 'I know that…'. The active participle *yādaʿ* of the root *y-d-ʿ* 'know' is followed by the 1sg pronoun *ʾana*. This construction is straightforwardly reminiscent of Ṭuroyo *ōḏaʿ-no* '(that) I know'. The new perfective, based on the old passive participle CCīC and the subject marker composed of *l-* and bound pronouns, is not a typological oddity. Indeed, evolutions of the type *ftīḥ l-i* 'opened by me' > *ftəḥ-li* 'I opened' are well-attested across Indo-Iranian and may well be a contact-induced evolution in these varieties of Aramaic (here Central Neo-Aramaic and North-Eastern Neo-Aramaic). Moreover, traces of this development can already be found in Classical Syriac: *qrēn lux* 'read by you' > 'you read' (Ṭuroyo *qrē-lux* 'you read')

As far as tense is concerned, Ṭuroyo has the past-marking morpheme *-wa*. It harks back to *hwā* 'he was' (< *h-w-y* 'be, become'). In conservative varieties of Ṭuroyo, two orders exist. It is either placed between the stem and the subject index or at the right edge of the predicate. When placed between the stem and the subject index, the allomorph is *-way-*: *harke-wa* 'he was here' vs *harke-way-no* 'I was here' and *šoməʿ-wa* 'he was listening' vs *šoməʿ-way-no* 'I was listening'.

Table 3: Predicative and subject markers and *-wa*

	Pronoun	Predicative markers and *-wa*	Subject markers and *-wa*
1sg	*ono*	*harke-way-no*	*šōmaʿ-way-no*
2ms	*hat*	*harke-way-t*	*šəmʿ-ət-wa*
2fs			*šəmʿ-at-wa*
3ms	*hiye*	*harke-wa*	*šōməʿ-wa*
3fs	*hiya*		*šəmʿo-wa*
1pl	*aḥna*	*harke-way-na*	*šəmʿī-way-na*
2pl	*hatu*	*harke-way-tu*	*šəmʿ-ūt(u)-wa*
3pl	*hənne*	*harke-way-ne*	*šəmʿī-wa*

The use of *(h)wa* used as a past-tense auxiliary in post-predicate position is well attested already in Classical Syriac: *koṯeḇ-way-t* 'you were writing' (Mīdən Ṭuroyo *kəṯwət-wa* (m.) or *kəṯwat-wa* (f.), Qamishli Ṭuroyo *kəṯwat-wa*). Here again, these trends are found even in earlier stages of the language. In Biblical Aramaic, in this case the book of Daniel, structures such as these are indeed common: *ḥāzē hawēṯ* 'I was seeing' (see.AP.MS be.PFV.1SG). Adding the first person pronoun to the right yields *ḥāzē hawēṯ ʾana*. Compare this to Ṭuroyo *ḥōze-way-no* 'I was seeing'. Except for the shift from /ā/ to /ō/, the Ṭuroyo form appears to be a contraction of the structure already attested in Biblical Aramaic.

As far as the subject markers derived from the dative preposition *l-* are concerned, the same allomorphy is found, but the order is always stem + *way* + subject marker: *kət-way-li* 'I had' and *ftəḥ-way-li* 'I had opened'.

Table 4: Subject markers, *-wa* and *l-* + pronouns

	Existential *kit* + *wa* + *l-* + pronouns	Subject markers and *-wa* in the perfective
1sg	*kət-way-li*	*ftəḥ-way-li*
2ms	*kət-way-lux*	*ftəḥ-way-lux*
2fs	*kət-way-lax*	*ftəḥ-way-lax*
3ms	*kət-way-le*	*ftəḥ-way-le*
3fs	*kət-way-la*	*ftəḥ-way-la*
1pl	*kət-way-lan*	*ftəḥ-way-lan*
2pl	*kət-wa-lxu*	*ftəḥ-wa-lxu*
3pl	*kət-wa-lle*	*ftəḥ-wa-lle*

As far as Qamishli Ṭuroyo is concerned, the order stem + *way* + subject marker is attested, but only marginally and only in the speech of elderly speakers (example 1), most likely because their speech reflects a pre-koineisation stage. Overwhelmingly, the order attested in the data is stem + subject marker + *-wa*, as shown in (2).

(1) Qamishli Ṭuroyo
*wa̤l̤la šwaʿ tmone qurṭi-**way**-na*
by_God seven eight crunch.IPFV.PL-PST-1PL
'We would crunch seven (or) eight [of those carrots]'

(2) Qamishli Ṭuroyo
*ayko d-yotaw-no-**wa** məğġoli-**wa** ʿal-i-mādde*
where REL-sit.IPFV-1SG-PST speak.IPFV.3PL-PST on-DEF-matter
'Wherever I would be they would speak about money'

It appears, therefore, that the morpheme *-wa* has been displaced to the right bound of the verbal word and that the allomorph *-way* was levelled out in favour of *-wa*. In the case of non-verbal predication, only the 3sg form remains identical. The rest of the paradigm is restructured (Table 5).

Table 5: Non-verbal predication and *-wa*

	Predicative markers and *-wa* (Mīdən)	Predicative markers and *-wa* (Qamishli)
1sg	*harke-way-no*	*harke-no-wa*
2ms 2fs	*harke-way-t*	*harke-hat-wa*
3ms 3fs	*harke-wa*	*harke-wa*
1pl	*harke-way-na*	*harke-na-wa*
2pl	*harke-way-tu*	*harke-hatu-wa*
3pl	*harke-way-ne*	*harke-ne-wa*

As far as the subject markers that grammaticalised from the independent pronouns are concerned, only the 1sg and the 1pl change, because in the other persons, the morpheme *-wa* already occurs rightward of the verb even in Mīdən (Table 6): *šomaʿ-way-no* 'I used to listen' in Mīden vs *šomaʿ-no-wa* in Qamishli and *šəmʿī-way-na* 'we used to listen' in Mīdən vs *šəmʿī-na-wa* in Qamishli.

Table 6: Subject markers and *-wa*

	Subject markers and *-wa* (Mīdən)	Subject markers and *-wa* (Qamishli)
1sg	*šōmaʿ-way-no*	*šōmaʿ-no-wa*
2ms	*šəmʿ-ət-wa*	*šəmʿ-at-wa*
2fs	*šəmʿ-at-wa*	
3ms	*šōməʿ-wa*	*šōməʿ-wa*
3fs	*šəmʿo-wa*	*šəmʿo-wa*
1pl	*šəmʿī-way-na*	*šəmʿī-na-wa*
2pl	*šəmʿ-ūt(u)-wa*	*šəmʿ-utu-wa*
3pl	*šəmʿī-wa*	*šəmʿī-wa*

The paradigms with the markers that grammaticalised from the preposition *l-* are completely restructured, because *-wa* is placed between the stem and the subject marker.

Table 7: Possessive predication and *-wa*

	kit + *-wa* + *-l-* (Midən)	*kit* + *-wa* + *-l-* (Qamishli)
1sg	*kət-way-li*	*kət-li-wa*
2ms	*kət-way-lux*	*kət-lux-wa*
2fs	*kət-way-lax*	*kət-lax-wa*
3ms	*kət-way-le*	*kət-le-wa*
3fs	*kət-way-la*	*kət-la-wa*
1pl	*kət-way-lan*	*kət-lan-wa*
2pl	*kət-wa-lxu*	*kət-xu-wa*
3pl	*kət-wa-lle*	*kət-te-wa*

It appears, therefore, that the morphological layout of the verbal complex in Qamishli Ṭuroyo has stabilised and has the following shape (Table 8). The first slot is occupied by indicative *k(o)-* or future *g(əd)*, followed by the verbal stem, subject index, object index, dative index, and finally the past tense marker *-wa*.

Table 8: Morphological layout of the verb in Qamishli Ṭuroyo

Pre-verb	stem	subject	object	dative	*-wa*	
g	*maḥke*	*no*	*la*	*lux*	*wa*	'I was going to tell it to you'
	maḥruwi	*na*	*la*		*wa*	'We would have destroyed it'
	mər	*li*		*le*		'He said it to me'
k	*ōbaʿ*			*la*		'It/he/she needs'

It seems, however, that forms in which all the slots are filled are rather rare. Elicited forms were not straightforwardly accepted as speakers showed hesitations in processing them. This is especially the case with forms that embed object and dative indices of the same person. For instance, *g-maḥke-no-la-lux-wa* (FUT-tell.IPFV-1SG-OBJ.3FS-DAT.2MS-PST) 'I was going to tell it to you' was processed without much difficulty, seemingly because the object index *la*, which is in the 3fs, and the dative index *lux*, which in the 2ms, are different enough. More problematic was *g-maḥke-no-la-le-wa* (FUT-tell.IPFV-1SG-OBJ.3FS-DAT.3MS-PST) 'I was going to tell it to him', in which the object index *la* 'it' and the dative index *le* 'to him' are in the same person, and even more so the sequence *g-maḥke-no-la-la-wa* (FUT-tell.IPFV-1SG-OBJ.3FS-DAT.3FS-PST) 'I was going to tell it to her', where the object and the dative index have the same form. In these cases, speakers favour extracting the object index and moving it to the postverbal position in the shape of the 3sg index *yo*, which is unmarked for gender: *g-maḥke-no-la-wa-yo* 'I was going tell it (m./f.) to her'. Consequently, it appears that Qamishli Ṭuroyo has two layouts:

(a)

preverb	stem	subject	object	dative	*wa*
g	*maḥke*	*no*	*la*	*lux*	*wa*
FUT	tell	1SG	3FS	2MS	PST

'I was going to tell it to you'

(b)

preverb	stem	subject	dative	*wa*	*yo*
g	*maḥke*	*no*	*la*	*wa*	*yo*
FUT	tell	1SG	3FS	PST	3SG

'I was going to tell it to her'

The homophony between the object indices and dative indices is due to the fact that, in previous stages of the language, definite direct objects were differentially marked with the dative preposition *l-*, as exemplified in (3), where the definite object *ḵawkaḇ ṣaprā* 'the morning star' is marked with the preposition *l-*. The language has since lost differential object marking and the homophony between object indices and dative indexes is therefore the sole remnant of it in Ṭuroyo.[3]

(3) Classical Syriac, Revelation 2:28

w-ettel	*lē-h*	*lə-ḵawkaḇ*	*ṣaprā*
and-give.IPFV.1SG	to-3MS	OBJ-star	morning

'And I will give him the morning star'

2.2. Simplification and Pronominal Indices

Careful readers may also have noticed another difference between Mīdən Ṭuroyo and Qamishli Ṭuroyo, reported below:

Table 9: Subject markers and *-wa* in the 2sg

<table>
<tr><th></th><th>Subject markers and -wa (Mīdən)</th><th>Subject markers and -wa (Qamishli)</th></tr>
<tr><td>2ms</td><td>šəmʕ-ət-wa</td><td rowspan="2">šəmʕ-at-wa</td></tr>
<tr><td>2fs</td><td>šəmʕ-at-wa</td></tr>
</table>

Unlike Mīdən, Qamishli Ṭuroyo lacks gender distinction in the second person singular. What is striking is that this gender dis-

[3] Some dialects of Ṭuroyo are reported to have kept or recreated differential object marking with the dative preposition *l-*. While Qamishli Ṭuroyo has *ḥzēli u-Gabi* 'I saw Gabi', other dialects may exhibit *ḥzēli l-u-Gabi* (see also Noorlander 2021, 308). As for pronominal objects, *l*-less forms are also possible: *ko-roḥam-n-a* ~ *ko-roḥam-no-la* 'I love her'.

tinction in Mīdən is available for subject markers, but not independent pronouns (Table 10), out of which the subject markers grammaticalised.

Table 10: Independent pronouns

	Pronouns (Mīdən)	Pronouns (Qamishli)
1sg	*ono*	*ono*
2ms	*hat*	*hat* ~ *hate*
2fs		
3ms	*hiye*	*hiye*
3fs	*hiya*	*hiya*
1pl	*aḥna*	*aḥna*
2pl	*hatu*	*hatu*
3pl	*hənne*	*hənne* ~ *hənnək*

Table 11: Subject markers in the imperfective (*š-m-ˁ* 'listen')

	Subject markers (Mīdən)	Subject markers (Qamishli)
1sg	*šomaˁ-no*	*šomaˁ-no*
2ms	*šəmˁ-ət*	*šəmˁ-at*
2fs	*šəmˁ-at*	
3ms	*šoməˁ-Ø*	*šoməˁ-Ø*
3fs	*šəmˁ-o*	*šəmˁ-o*
1pl	*šəmˁ-ina*	*šəmˁ-ina*
2pl	*šəmˁ-utu*	*šəmˁ-utu*
3pl	*šəmˁ-i*	*šəmˁ-i*

Gender distinction is also maintained in all varieties of Ṭuroyo in the second-person singular bound pronouns, with masculine *-ux* and feminine *-ax*. Consequently, gender distinction is also available in the subject markers that grammaticalised from the preposition *l-* and bound pronouns: *ftəḥ-lux* 'you (m.) opened' vs *ftəḥ-lax* 'you (f.) opened'. I showed above that the verbal system of

Central and North-Eastern Neo-Aramaic was completely restructured around the active and passive participles—roughly, active particple + independent pronouns and passive participle + *l-* + bound pronouns (although certain verbs are formed from the passive participle + independent pronouns). This radical transformation introduced gender distinction where it was previously unknown, such as in the first person singular. The feminine marker in Aramaic is *-ā* (< Proto-Semitic *-at*). In older stages of the language, there was therefore a masculine active participle *šāməʿ* 'listening' and a feminine *šāmʿ(ə)-ā*. After the shift from /ā/ to /ō/ that happened in the western parts of the Arameo-sphere, we have *šōməʿ* and *šōm(ə)ʿ-ō*. One phonotactic constraint later, which shortens long vowels in closed syllables, we have Ṭuroyo *šoməʿ* and *šəmʿo*. The coalescence with bound pronouns produces synthetic forms such as *šōmaʿ-no* 'I (m.) listen' vs *šəmʿo-no* 'I (f.) listen'. This distinction is stable in the language and not subject to variation: *ko-mətzakro-no* 'I (f.) remember', *ko-dəmxo-no* 'I (f.) sleep', etc.

In the second person, the phonotactic constraint that prevents long vowels in closed syllables hides the stem allomorphy: both *šoməʿ + *-at* and *šəmʿ-o + *-at* yield *šəmʿ-at*. In more conservative varieties, of course, gender distinction is ensured by vowel alternation (*šəmʿət* vs *šəmʿat*). This, however, is not the case for every type of verb. Verbs whose last consonant is/y/ exhibit stem allomorphy in the second person. Consider, for example, the roots *b-x-y* 'cry' and *ḥ-z-y* 'see'. The stem in the masculine is CoCe (*boxe*, *ḥoze*) and in the feminine CəCyo (< CoCy-o, *bəxyo* and *ḥəzyo*). In conservative varieties, gender distinction is carried both by stem allomorphy and by vowel alternation: *box-ət* 'you (m.) cry' vs *bəxy-at* 'you (f.) cry' and *hōz-ət* 'you (m.) see' vs *ḥəzyat* 'you (f.) see'.

Table 12: Imperfective of weak roots in the 1sg and 2sg (Mīden)

Root	Stem (m.)	Stem (f.)	1ms	1fs	2ms	2fs
b-x-y	*boxe-*	*bəxyo-*	*boxe-no*	*bəxyo-no*	*box-ət*	*bəxy-at*
ḥ-z-y	*ḥoze-*	*ḥəzyo-*	*ḥoze-no*	*ḥəzyo-no*	*ḥoz-ət*	*ḥəzy-at*

In Qamishli, however, although gender distinction is well maintained in the first person singular, the feminine form of the stem was levelled out in the second person singular, and gender distinction neutralised altogether: *box-at* 'you (m./f.) cry' and *ḥōz-at* 'you (m./f.) see'.

Table 13: Imperfective of weak roots in the 1sg and 2sg (Qamishli)

Root	Stem (m.)	Stem (f.)	1ms	1fs	2ms	2fs
b-x-y	*boxe-*	*bəxyo-*	*boxe-no*	*bəxyo-no*	*box-at*	
ḥ-z-y	*ḥoze-*	*ḥəzyo-*	*ḥoze-no*	*ḥəzyo-no*	*ḥoz-at*	

2.3. Non-stabilised Levelling and Bound Pronouns

Ṭuroyo has two sets of bound pronouns whose distribution depends on the consonantal shape of the host. The difference is only apparent in the second and third person plural. In the first set, the stem is modified because of the same phonotactic rule that shortens long vowels in closed syllables: *[e:bxu] → [apxu] 'in you'. In the second set, three-consonant clusters are resolved by the insertion of an anaptytic segment [aj]: *[aʕm-xu] → [aʕmajxu] 'with you'.

Table 14: Two sets of bound pronouns

	b- 'in' Set 1: C-	*ʿam* 'with' Set 2: CC-
1sg	*eb-i*	*aʿm-i*
2ms	*eb-ux*	*aʿm-ux*
2fs	*eb-ax*	*aʿm-ax*
3ms	*eb-e*	*aʿm-e*
3fs	*eb-a*	*aʿm-a*
1pl	*eb-an*	*aʿm-an*
2pl	*ap-xu*	*aʿm-ayxu*
3pl	*ap-pe*	*aʿm-ayye*

What can be observed in the speech of some speakers is the creation and generalisation of a third set, which primarily draws on the second set, after it went through paradigmatic levelling and the generalisation of the segment *-ay-* in the plural, as shown in Table 14. In the 1pl, *-an* is replaced by *-na*, possibly extracted from verbal paradigms (cf. *šəmʿ-īna* 'we listen'). This innovation has not spread to all the linguistic community, so it is not focussed in sociolinguistic terms.

Table 15: Bound pronoun paradigmatic levelling

	b- 'in' + bound pronouns	*ʿam* 'with' + bound pronouns
1sg	*eb-i*	*aʿm-i*
2ms	*eb-ux*	*aʿm-ux*
2fs	*eb-ax*	*aʿm-ax*
3ms	*eb-e*	*aʿm-e*
3fs	*eb-a*	*aʿm-a*
1pl	*eb-ayna*	*aʿm-ayna*
2pl	*eb-ayxu*	*aʿm-ayxu*
3pl	*eb-ayye*	*aʿm-ayye*

2.4. Conclusion of Koineisation

Three developments in Qamishli Ṭuroyo that are linked to koineisation have been highlighted:

(a) the levelling of the morphological structure of the predicate and the generalisation of the rightward placement of the past tense marker *-wa*;

(b) the further loss of gender distinction in the second person singular, which is now only available with subject markers that grammaticalised from the preposition *l-* and bound pronouns;

(c) the creation of a new innovative paradigm of bound pronouns, which appears to be an interdialectal form.

From the four possible linguistic outcomes of koineisation singled out above, namely levelling (a), simplification (b), interdialectal forms (c), and reallocation, only reallocation was not found in Qamishli Ṭuroyo. In terms of focussing, the first two innovations appear to have focussed, but not the last one.

3.0. Language Contact

As far as the linguistic ecology is concerned, it was noted above that the main contact languages of Ṭuroyo in Ṭūr ʿAbdīn were primarily Kurmanji Kurdish and to a lesser extent Turkish, whereas Arabic was not part of the immediate landscape, being itself a minority language. In spite of this, Ṭūr ʿAbdīn Ṭuroyo already exhibits borrowings from Arabic. There are of course lexical items, such as *ʿaṣriye* 'evening', *faqiro* 'poor' (< *faqīr*), *ḥakəm* 'judge' (< *ḥākim*), *ḥərma* 'woman' (< *ḥurma*), *kiso* 'bag' (< *kīs*), *maʕlum* 'known' (< *maʕlūm*), *fahəm* 'understand' (*f-h-m*), *maqbəl* 'accept' (*q-b-l*), *məstaʕməl* 'use' (< *istaʕmal*), *mğarəb* 'try' (< *ğarrab*), *ṭoləb* 'request' (*ṭ-l-b*); but there are also grammatical items, such as *ənkān* 'if' (< *ʾin kān*), *laqəddām* 'forward' (< *la qiddām*), *lāzəm* 'must' (< *lāzim*). These borrowings indicate that contact with Arabic had already occurred in the past. This situation changed in Syria, where Arabic became the primary contact language and contact with Kurdish was downgraded. Virtually all the Syrian speakers of Ṭuroyo are bilingual in Arabic and Ṭuroyo. Arabic is normally acquired in early childhood. Many individuals also have native or near-native command of Kurmanji Kurdish, but there is a great level of individual variation. It is therefore expected that, after a century or so of intense contact, Syrian Ṭuroyo be, as speakers themselves frame it, highly 'arabised'.

The terminology used here follows that introduced in Sakel (2007). She distinguishes between two types of loan: matter replication and pattern replication. Matter replication occurs when "morphological material and its phonological shape from one language is replicated in another language" (Sakel 2007, 15), whereas pattern replication refers the borrowing of "the organization, distribution and mapping of grammatical or semantic meaning, while the form itself is not borrowed" (Sakel 2007, 15).

3.1. Matter Replication

All the consonants found in Arabic are also part of the phonology of Ṭuroyo. The vowel system is only slightly different. Jastrow (1992) gives five long vowels /a, i, u, e, o/, three short vowels /ə, ŭ, ă/, and two diphthongs /aw/ and /ay/. This means that virtually no phonological adaptation is needed when Arabic material is replicated into Ṭuroyo. Ṭuroyo and Arabic have similar morphologies, as they use the same root-and-pattern system. Some patterns are cognate, such as Arabic $C_1aC_2C_2\bar{a}C_3$, which is cognate with Ṭuroyo $C_1aC_2oC_3o$. As far as the integration of open word classes goes, nouns and adjectives should be treated differently from verbs. Arabic nouns and adjectives are usually not integrated into native consonantal patterns, as shown in (4). The Arabic noun *masʾūliyye* 'responsibility' is replicated without any change. It is also assigned the same grammatical gender as in Arabic, as shown by the feminine allomorph of the article *i-*.

(4) Qamishli Ṭuroyo
g-mǝtḥaman-no ***i-masʾūliyye***
FUT-bear.IPFV-1SG DEF.F-responsabilité
'I'll bear responsibility'

Bound morphemes such as demonstratives and possessives normaly attach the right of the host, whose final vowel drops: *i-qaṣīd-aṯe* 'this poetry' (DEF.F-poetry-DEM.F < Arabic *qaṣīde*), *u-daftar-ayḏe* 'his notebook' (DEF.M-notebook-3SG < Arabic *daftar*). Arabic plurals are also integrated without change: *am-mašākil* 'the problems' (DEF.PL-problems < Arabic *mašākil*, plural of *muškile*), *aḍ-ḍurūf* 'the conditions' (DEF.PL-conditions < Arabic *ḍurūf*, plural of *ḍarf*). Native nouns and adjectives are pluralised by changing the ending *-o* into *-e* (*qadišo* 'saint' pl. *qadiše*). This does not apply to loans that are not morphologically integrated into a native template, although one recorded exception is *malyōn-e* 'millions', plural of *malyōn* (the Arabic plural is *malāyīn*). The Ṭuroyo article inflects for number and gender. The plural form has the shape *aC-C*, where the initial consonant of the noun is geminated, e.g., *am-maye* 'water' (always plural in Aramaic). It is possible to use the plural article and an Arabic noun in the singular if it is augmented with a bound morpheme to the right (possessive or demonstrative), as shown in (5).

(5) Qamishli Ṭuroyo
tāǧir *m-at-**tāǧir**-ayḏi*
salesman from-DEF.PL-salesman-1SG
'One of my salesmen'

Arabic adjectives are also not normally integrated morphologically. Moreover, they retain their original number and gender inflections, which is expected since speakers are also fully proficient in Arabic. In (6), the adjective *tārīxiyye* is the feminine form of *tārīxi* 'historic(al)'. It agrees here with the noun *sahra* 'evening' which in Arabic is feminine. In (7), the adjective *məmtāz* 'excellent' keeps its Arabic plural form *məmtāzīn*.

(6) Qamishli Ṭuroyo
wa̤l̤la ***tārīxiyye**-wa*
by_God historical.F-COP.3SG.PST
'[the evening] was unforgettable'

(7) Qamishli Ṭuroyo
***məmtāzīn**-hatu-wa*
excellent.PL-COP.2PL-PAST
'You (pl.) were excellent'

There are, however, a handful of morphological integrations. A one-to-one correspondence is impossible, because Ṭuroyo has fewer nominal and adjectival templates than Arabic (around twenty, according to Jastrow 1993). Examples are *taʿbo* 'fatigue' (pattern CaCCo) from Arabic *taʿab*, *ʿaṭoro* 'merchant' (CaCoCo) from Arabic *ʿaṭṭār*, and *šaġolo* 'worker' (CaCoCo) from Arabic *šaġġīl* or *šaġġāl*. An interesting borrowing is *waroqe* 'Syrian pounds', plural of *warəqto*, from Arabic *waraqa* (literally 'page' but also 'banknote', by extension a one-Syrian-pound banknote). Arabic *waraqa* is feminine. It was integrated using the pattern CaCoCo, whose feminine form is CaCəCto and plural CaCoCe (the plural is formed from the masculine): *ḥamšo u šawʿi waroqe* 'seventy-five pounds' (Arabic *xamse u sabʿīn waraqa*). Another example of morphological integration is *ḥoḍure* 'people attending'. Here the speaker replicates Arabic *ḥāḍirīn* 'the people who are present', inserting the Arabic root *ḥ-ḍ-r* into the native pattern CoCuCo. The adaptation of Arabic agentive active participles with this pattern is already attested in Ṭūr ʿAbdīn Ṭuroyo: *šohudo* 'witness' (Arabic *šāhid*), *xodumo* 'servant' (Arabic *xādim*; Jastrow 1993, 188).

Integration of Arabic adjectives into native templates is also attested, but with a certain degree of intraspeaker variation, as shown in (8), where the speaker alternates between the Arabic adjective *ġalṭān* 'wrong' and its integrated counterpart *galṭo* (pattern CaCCo).

(8) Qamishli Ṭuroyo

***ġalṭān**-no*	*mərli-lux*	*hawxa*	***ġalṭo**-no-wa*
wrong-COP.1SG	say.PFV.1SG-DAT.2SG	so	wrong-COP.1SG-PST

'I'm wrong, I told you I was wrong'

The data also provide another example of variation between Arabic *barī* 'innocent' and integrated *bariyo*. The pattern CaCiCo is often used to integrate the Arabic adjectival pattern CaCīC (with which it shares cognacy): *ġašimo* 'naive' (Arabic *ġašīm*), *qawiyo* 'strong' (Arabic *qawi*).

Verbs are usually integrated into native patterns. Verbal morphology is probably the most complex grammatical sub-system in Ṭuroyo.[4]

Table 16: Verbal patterns in Ṭuroyo (Jastrow 2011, 701)

Middle-Aramaic	Form	Ṭuroyo	Imperfective	Perfective
Peʿal	I.	Active	*qoṭəl* 'he kills'	*qṭəlle* 'he killed'
Eṯpeʿel		Passive	*məqṭəl* 'he is killed'	*qṭīl* 'he was killed'
Paʿʿel	II.	Active	*mzabən* 'he sells'	*mzabanle* 'he sold'
Eṯpaʿʿal		Passive	*mizabən* 'he is sold'	*mzabən* 'he was sold'
Afʿel	III.	Active	*madməx* 'he causes to sleep'	*madmaxle* 'he caused to sleep'
Ettafʿal		Passive	*mitadməx* 'he is caused to sleep'	*mtadməx* 'he was caused to sleep'

Table 17: Integration of Arabic verbs in the imperfective

Ṭuroyo form		Imperfective	Arabic	Arabic form
I.	Active	*ko-šoġal-no* 'I work'	*aštaġil*	VIII
	Passive	*ko-məʿrəḍ* 'it is exposed'	*yinʿariḍ*	VII
II.	Active	*mqarar-no* 'I decide'	*aqarrir*	II
	Passive	*miṭabqo* 'it applies'	*tiṭṭābaq*	VI
III.	Active	*ko-maḥko-wa-li* 'she used to tell me'	*kānat tiḥkī-li*	I
	Passive	*mitaḥke* 'it is told'	*yinḥaka*	VIII

[4] More than one third of Jastrow's (1993) grammar is devoted to the description of verbal morphology.

Table 18: Integration of Arabic verbs in the perfective

Ṭuroyo form		Perfective	Arabic	Arabic form
I.	Active	*ṭləb-le* 'he requested'	*ṭalab*	I
	Passive	*ʿriḍ* 'it was exposed'	*inʿaraḍ*	VII
II.	Active	*mqarar-li* 'I decided'	*qarrart*	II
	Passive	*mwansi-na* 'we had fun'	*twannasna*	V
III.	Active	*malqe-lan* 'we pronounced'	*alqēna*	IV
	Passive	*mtaḥke* 'it was told'	*inḥaka*	VIII

It appears from the tables above that borrowed verbs are integrated in all categories. Ṭuroyo active form I integrates Arabic form I verbs, except when anomalous, like Arabic *ištaġal*, which is transitive but in the form VIII. Ṭuroyo passive form I integrates Arabic form VII, which is predictable because it has a medio-passive value. Ṭuroyo active form II integrates Arabic verbs of form II, with which it is cognate. Ṭuroyo passive form II integrates form V, VI, and VII Arabic verbs, which is also predictable because Arabic form V is the reflexive-passive of form II and form VI is the reflexive-passive of form III. Ṭuroyo form III integrates transitive Arabic verbs of form I or form IV, with which it is cognate.

Speakers may also integrate Arabic verbs without using native templates. The Arabic stem is adapted to the phonotactics of Ṭuroyo by degeminating geminates and compensatorily lengthening preceding vowels. The prefix *m-* (cognate with Arabic *mu-*, as found on the participles of derived verbs) is added and subject markers are suffixed. The imperfective selects markers that grammaticalised from independent pronouns, whereas the perfective selects the subject indices that grammaticalised from the preposition *l-* + bound pronouns. The Arabic stem *tḥammal* 'bear, suppor' (form V) undergoes the following adaptations: *tḥammal* → *tḥamal* → *mətḥaməl*. The first person singular imperfective becomes *mətḥamal-no* [mətħa:manno] 'I bear, support'. The Arabic verb *iʕtaraf* 'admit' is integrated in this way: *iʕtaraf* → *ʕtaraf* → *məʕtarəf-*. The first person singular perfective becomes *məʕtaraf-li* 'I admitted'. As far as Arabic form X is concerned, the following instance was recorded: *məstaʕmlə-nne-wa* (use.IPFV.PL-OBJ.3PL-PST) 'they would use them' from Arabic *istaʕmal*. Speakers extract the stem *staʕmal* and add the prefix *mə-*: *məstaʕməl*. The integration of these Arabic verbs creates new hybrid Arabic–Ṭuroyo patterns: *mətCaCəC* (Arabic form V and VI), *məCtaCəl* (Arabic form VIII) and *məstaCCəC* (Arabic form X).

Although not a majority, it is not uncommon to come across utterances that are composed entirely of integrated Arabic roots, as shown in (9): *ğ-b-r* 'force', *b-l-ʕ* 'swallow', *b-r-ʾ* 'clear', the nominal *ğurum* 'crime', and the complex conjunction *fi sabīl* 'in order to'.

(9) Qamishli Ṭuroyo

*ko-**ğobar**-li* *d-**bolaʕ**-no* *u-**ğurum***

IND-force.IPFV.3SG-OBJ.1SG COMP-swallow.IPFV-1SG DEF-crime

fi sabīl *d-**mbare**-no-le*

in way COMP-clear.IPFV-1SG-OBJ.3SG

'He forces me to take the rap in order to clear him'

As far as closed classes are concerned, many morphemes are replicated for Arabic, such as the complementiser *inno* (although not the Arabic relativiser *illi*), the adversative *bass* 'but', the conditional conjunctions *iza* and *law*, and more. One native way to form conjunctions in Ṭuroyo is to use the versatile inherited Aramaic subordinator *d-* after a lexical element: *meqəm d-* 'before'. Hybrid forms with both the Arabic subordinator *mā* and Aramaic *d-* are found, as shown in (10). Qamishli Ṭuroyo also borrows many of Arabic's discourse markers and narrative devices, such as *tara* (used to redirect the hearer's focus of attention towards the upcoming utterance) or the much-employed assertion marker *wal̤l̤a*.

(10) Qamishli Ṭuroyo

meqəm ***mā d*** *məǧġol-at*

before that that speak.IPFV-2SG

'Before you speak'

(11) Qamishli Ṭuroyo

yā xi ***wal̤l̤a*** *layt eb-a mede*

VOC brother by_God EXIST.NEG in-3FS thing

'My friend, I swear there is nothing wrong about it'

(12) Qamishli Ṭuroyo

ono ***tara*** *kit mede b-leb-i*

1SG DM exist thing in-heart-1SG

'As far as I am concerned, you know, there is something in my heart [I would like to talk about]'

3.2. Pattern Replication

Pattern replication is usually more difficult to identify. In the case of Arabic and Ṭuroyo, things are also less clear cut because they are closely related both genetically and typologically. In spite of this, it appears that this type of replication is already attested in Ṭūr ʿAbdīn Ṭuroyo. Jastrow (1993, 242), for instance, notes that it is possible to apply the Arabic comparative derivation template ʾaCCaC to adjectives borrowed from Arabic and also a handful of native adjectives: *xašuno* 'thick' (< Arabic *xišin*) → *axšan* 'thicker', *noquṣo* 'few' (Arabic *nāqiṣ*) → *anqaṣ* 'fewer', *komo* 'black' (inherited) → *akyam* 'blacker'. What is interesting is that, although Syrian speakers of Ṭuroyo are notoriously more arabised than their Ṭūr ʿAbdīn coreligionists, this transfer is not attested in Syrian Ṭuroyo, and not even accepted. Speakers resort to the inherited strategy, which consists of reducing the penultimate syllable, to which the Kurdish comparative suffix *-tər* may attach: *komo* 'black' → *kəm-tər* 'blacker', *noquṣo* 'few' → *noqəṣ-tər* 'fewer', *rabo* 'big' → *răb-tər* 'bigger'.

A possible case of pattern replication already found in Ṭūr ʿAbdīn Ṭuroyo is the grammaticalisation of existential *kit* (negative *layt*) and the preposition *b-* 'in' into a modal predicate 'can'. This parallels the use of the grammaticalisation of the preposition *fi* 'in' + bound pronouns in Syrian Arabic (*fī-ye* ~ *fī-ni* 'I can', *fī-k* ~ *fīn-ak* 'you can', etc.): *kīb-i* 'I can' (< *kit eb-i*), *kib-ux* 'you can' (< *kit eb-ux*), etc. In (13), *layb-an* is the result of the coalescence of *layt* 'there is not' and *eb-an* 'in us'. Other possible forms involve the *l*-subject markers: *kəp-li* 'I can', *kəp-lux* 'you can', *kəp-le* 'he can' and negative *lap-li* 'I can't', *lap-lux* 'you can't', *lap-le* 'he can't'. This is in likelihood a later formation created through analogy with the possessive predicate *kit* 'there is' + *l-*: *kit* 'there is' + *l-i* 'for me' yields *kət-li* 'I have'. A form such as *kəp-li* is therefore the reduction **kib-li*, created from *kib-i* and *kət-li*.

(13) Qamishli Ṭuroyo

layb-an *fəyšīna* *baynoṯ-ayye*

can.NEG-1PL stay.SBJV.1PL between-3PL

'We can't stay amongst them'

Another case of transfer, which does not seem to have been available in the pre-Syrian history of the language, is that of the verb *hawi* 'he became' as an inchoative auxiliary, replicating one of the uses of the verb *ṣār* 'he became' in Arabic. In (14), *hawən ko-dərsi* is reminiscent of Levantine Arabic *ṣāru yudursu* (become.PFV.3PL study.SBJV.3PL). There is one salient difference with Arabic, though, namely the form of the auxiliated verb, which in Ṭuroyo is marked for indicative and not subjunctive as in Arabic. The Ṭuroyo construction more resembles a serial verb construction, as there is no syntactic dependency between the auxiliary and the auxiliated verb. Arabic *ṣār* also has the lexical meaning of 'happen, occur', which also appears to have been replicated in Ṭuroyo, as shown in (15).

(14) Qamishli Ṭuroyo

hawən *ko-dərsi*

become.PFV.3PL IND-study.IPFV.3PL

'They started to study'

(15) Qamishli Ṭuroyo

kul *mede* *d-**hawi***

every thing REL-become.PFV.3SG

'Everything that happened'

Another construction that has been replicated in Ṭuroyo is what is known in Arabic grammar as *ǧumlat al-ḥāl*. It is a clausal combining device that indicates concomitance, and whose linear order is the conjunction *w* 'and', then the subject, followed by the predicate, as shown in (16). The phrase *w ono b-u-sižən* is reminiscent of Arabic *w ana bi-s-sižən* (lit. 'and me in prison'). It is remarkable that no predicative marker surfaces in Ṭuroyo, although technically the construction falls within the reach of non-verbal predication: **w ono b-u-sižən-**no***. The copula on non-verbal predicates is compulsory in Ṭuroyo, so the replication of this construction bypasses the Ṭuroyo copula marking constraint and fully converges towards Arabic, which exhibits zero-marking for this type of predicate.

(16) Qamishli Ṭuroyo

i-qaṣid-aṯe	*kṯiwo-li*	***w***	***ono***	***b-u-sižən***
DEF.F-poem-DEM.F	write.PFV.F-1SG	and	1SG	IN-DEF.M-prison

'(As for) this poem, I wrote it while I was in prison'

As far as relativisation is concerned, Ṭuroyo did not replicate the Arabic relativiser *illi*. Instead, it kept the inherited jack-of-all-trades *d-*. Moreover, Ṭuroyo did not replicate the conditions of appearance found in Arabic, in which the relativiser *illi* is selected with definite nouns. In Ṭuroyo, even when the relativised noun is indefinite, the use of *d-* is compulsory. Ṭuroyo, however, like Arabic, makes use of the pronoun-retention strategy (also called resumptive), compulsorily at least for obliques but optionally for objects.

(17) Qamishli Ṭuroyo

ayy	*muğtamaʿ*	***d-ko-yotaw-no***	***eb-e***
any	society	REL-IND-stay.IPFV-1SG	in-3SG

'Any society in which I stay'

Another evolution that appears in the speech of some speakers is the adoption of the Arabic definite marking on the adjective when it modifies a definite noun. In Arabic, both the noun and the adjective are marked for definiteness: *il-bēt l-kbīr* (DEF-house DEF-big) 'the big house'. The normal construction in Ṭuroyo is for the adjective to be unmarked: *i-dərto rabṯo* 'the big courtyard' (DEF.F-courtyard big.F), except with a small set of nominals such as kinship terms: *aḥun-i u-naʿimo* 'my younger brother' (brother-1SG DEF.M-small). In (18), the speaker marks the adjective *mawǧūdīn* 'present' with the plural form of the article although no marking is expected: *u-ʿamo mawǧūd* 'the people who were present'. Note also the Arabic plural suffix *-īn*.

(18) Qamishli Ṭuroyo

u-ʿamo	***am**-mawǧūdīn*	*gaḥxi*	*aʿl-i*
DEF.m-people	DEF.PL-present.PL	laugh.IPFV.3PL	on-1SG

'The people who were present would laugh at me'

Finally, Qamishli Ṭuroyo tends to replicate the argument structure of the verbs it borrows. This can be illustrated by the Arabic root *f-h-m* 'understand'. When the patientive argument of the verb denotes a person, it is coded obliquely with the preposition *ʿala* 'on'. This, as exemplified in (19), is also the case in Ṭuroyo. The clause *fahimat aʿl-i* 'you understood me' is reminiscent of Arabic *fhimt ʿalayye* (understand.PFV.1SG on.1SG)

(19) Qamishli Ṭuroyo

fahim-at	*aʿl-i*
understand.PFV-2SG	on-1SG

'You understood me'

3.3. Code-switching and Arabic Insertions

The best way to capture how Arabic integrates into Ṭuroyo is to present a piece of spontaneous speech. The following text was recorded in July 2010 during a casual family conversation in the town of Qaḥṭāniyye, located thirty kilometres east of Qamishli. The speaker recounts how he tasted for the first time braised cheese (*ğibne məšwiyye* in Arabic) while on a visit to Aleppo. Arabic insertions are highlighted in bold face.

(1) ***waḷḷa*** *ṭləble muklo,* ***mašāwi ṭabʿan*** *u-medone u-xabro d-fahamno,* ***ğīb-inna šawi ğibne, ğibne məšwiyye sīx ğibne məšwiyye,*** *ono b-aḥ-ḥay-ayḏi* ***ṭabʿan waḷḷa*** *lo kobaʿno mwaṣafno ruḥi* ***waḷḷa*** *l-axili u lo ḥzeli omanno* ***yabu ğīb-inna ğibne mašwiyye, waḷḷa*** *amṭele* ***ğibne mašwiyye,*** *gweto xəd kuxlina-la b-u-bayto aḏiʿat gweto* ***ʿādi yaʿni***

(1) I ordered food, grilled meat of course. The words I understood were "bring us braised cheese, a skewer of braised cheese." Of course, never in my life, I can't describe (it) myself, I had not eaten nor seen (it), so I said "bring us braised cheese." He brought braised cheese. It was cheese like the one we eat home you know, normal cheese.

(2) ***waḷḷa*** *i-gwet-ayḏi koxanno-la k-madno* ***i-šawke,*** *qoṭaʿno-la –* ***waḷḷa*** *gweto-yo-* ***yā xi waḷḷa*** *haṯe gweto-yo, kmoḥeno koxanno,* ***yā xi waḷḷa*** *layt eba mede gweto-yo haṯe,* ***bass walākin*** *rakəxto-yo* ***xayyo*** *basəmto-yo*

(2) My (piece) of cheese, I eat it, I take the fork, I cut it. It was cheese, this was cheese. I eat (it), man I swear there was nothing wrong about it, it was cheese, but it was tender and good.

(3) *k(i)t eba* ***ṭarāwe,*** *basəmto-yo u košotina ʿaraq i-naqqa-yo lo šoteno-wa wiski* ***ṣarāḥa*** *ʿaraq šotena-wa, mətyaqnat* ***ṭabʿan*** *falqe latne-wa raqiqe xəd kəmqaṭʿina hani ḥləm hani hawxa ḥlime* ***šawi,*** *komqaṭaʿno*	(3) It has a nice texture, it's good. And we drink arak. At that time, we didn't use to drink whiskey, honestly, we used to drink arak. Believe me, the slices were not thin, like those that we cut, (even) thicker, thick like that, but braised, I cut (it).
*(4)*** kosamno ruḥi* ***madani*** *ono-ste xayyo, qayy ktoweno ġašimo aḏiʿat,* ***ğibne*** *omanno ē* ***ğibne šawi walaw, kill əsbūʿ bnākil, yā xi waḷḷa*** *ṭawto-yo haṯe rakəxto ṭawto-yo aḏiʿat*	(4) I pretend to be an urbanite myself, why would I make my-self look naive you know, cheese, I said, braised cheese, of course, I eat it every week, man I swear it's good, tender and good you know.

This short excerpt shows that the speaker borrows from Arabic a wide range of Arabic discourse managing devices, such as *waḷḷa* 'I swear, by God', which is now best interpreted as an assertion marker given its very high frequency of use; *ṭabʿan* 'of course', the reformulation marker *yaʿni* 'I mean', the adversatives *bass* and *walākin*, the nominal *ṣarāḥa* used adverbially 'frankly', and vocative formulas such as *yā xi yā bu* to catch the audience's attention. There are also insertions of full clauses in Arabic, but these are actually reported speech because Arabic was the language in which the interaction took place and are not code-switching per se. These insertions are, however, clear evidence that Arabic is an integral part of the linguistic repertoire of the audience. As far as pattern replication is concerned, two instances can easily be identified. The first one is the utterance *layt eb-a mede* 'there is nothing in it', which parallels Arabic *mā fī-ha ši*, and the second is the way of expressing 'pretend' that consists in using the verb 'do' and a reflexive: *kosamno ruḥi madani*, literally 'I do myself urbanite', i.e. 'I pretend to be a city-dweller', which is strictly parallel to Arabic *basawwi* (or *baʕmil*) *ḥāli madani*.

4.0. Conclusion

As far as language contact is concerned, Syrian speakers of Ṭuroyo frequently insert Arabic items that belong to open classes (nouns, adjectives, and verbs). These borrowings are not always morphologically integrated, depending on the proximity between the Ṭuroyo pattern and the Arabic pattern. Arabic nouns and adjectives normally keep their original inflections. Arabic lexemes that are not integrated into the Aramaic template were never found to bear Aramaic inflectional markers. Arabic inflectional markers are also not attested within the native lexicon. The separation between the two sets of inflections therefore seems to be solid. As far as verbs are concerned, they are either integrated into one of the native templates or lead to the creation of hybrid templates. As far as closed classes are concerned, it was shown that Ṭuroyo borrows a wide range of clause-combining devices but, interestingly enough, relativisation is left untouched. Numerous cases of pattern replication were also identified. Some are old, such as the grammaticaliation of the preposition *b-* into a modal predicate, while others are more recent, such as the *w-*

subordinate clause, the inchoative construction, and the semantics and argument structure of verbs. It was also shown that code-switching, although attested and permitted, is not generalised. It would therefore be inaccurate to characterise speakers of Syrian Ṭuroyo as being in 'bilingual mode', a mode in which there would be no restrictions as far as the use of the whole linguistic repertoire is concerned. The numerous cases of pattern replication indicate that convergence towards Arabic is ongoing, but by no means complete. As for koineisation, it was shown that the process is in indeed underway in Qamishli, where there are clear signs that specific features are in focus, giving birth to a new variety of Ṭuroyo.

As a final note, it should be added that the account given here of koineisation and language contact in Syrian Ṭuroyo was probably valid until 2011. Since then, almost all the Syrian speakers of Ṭuroyo have migrated to Western Europe. Although the community ties are still strong even in diaspora, the sociolinguistic setup and ecosystem of these speakers has radically changed. Future studies will enable researchers to check to what extent the state of affairs described here has evolved.

References

Arnold, Werner. 1989. *Das Neuwestaramäische*. Vol. 1, *Texte aus Baxʿa*. Semitica viva 4. Wiesbaden: O. Harrassowitz.

———. 1990a. *Das Neuwestaramäische*. Vol. 2, *Texte aus Ǧubbʿadīn*. Semitica viva 4.2. Wiesbaden: Harrassowitz.

———, ed. 1990b. *Das Neuwestaramäische*. Vol. 5, *Grammatik*. Semitica viva 4.5. Wiesbaden: Harrassowitz.

———. 1991a. *Das Neuwestaramäische.* Vol. 3, *Volkskundliche Texte aus Maʿlūla.* Semitica viva 4.3. Wiesbaden: Harrassowitz.

———. 1991b. *Das Neuwestaramäische.* Vol. 4, *Orale Literatur aus Maʿlūla.* Semitica viva 4.4. Wiesbaden: Harrassowitz.

———. 2019. *Das Neuwestaramäische.* Vol. 6, *Wörterbuch: Neuwestaramäisch–Deutsch.* Semitica viva 4.6. Wiesbaden: Harrassowitz.

Britain, David, and Peter Trudgill. 1999. 'Migration, New-Dialect Formation and Sociolinguistic Refunctionalisation: *Reallocation* as an Outcome of Dialect Contact'. *Transactions of the Philological Society* 97 (2): 245–56. https://doi.org/10.1111/1467-968X.00050.

Coghill, Eleanor. 2019. 'Northeastern Neo-Aramaic : The Dialect of Alqosh'. In *The Semitic Languages*, edited by John Huehnergard and Na'ama Pat-El, 711–47. London: Routledge. https://urn.kb.se/resolve?urn=urn:nbn:se:uu:diva-382397, accessed 31 July 2024.

Creissels, Denis. 1988. 'Quelques propositions pour une clarification de la notion d'adverbe'. *Cahiers d'Études Hispaniques Médiévales* 7 (1): 207–16. https://doi.org/10.3406/cehm.1988.2123.

Demir, Gulsuma, Nikita Kuzin, and Yulia Furman. 2022. '"Metran Îsa! Do Not Stir Up Trouble, Trouble Is Bad", A Kurdish Folk Song through a Christian Lens'. *Oral Tradition* 35 (2): 441–62.

Duntsov, Alexey, Charles Häberl, and Sergey Loesov. 2022. 'A Modern Western Aramaic Account of the Syrian Civil War'.

WORD 68 (4): 359–94. https://doi.org/10.1080/00437956.2022.2084663.

Eugen, Prym, and Albert Socin. 1881. *Der Neu-Aramäische Dialekt Des Ṭūr ʿAbdīn.* 2 vols. Göttingen: Vandenhoeck & Ruprecht.

Gabriel, Fikri. 2023. *Le Génocide des Syriaques et le Vatican (1890–1920).* Cerf Patrimoines. Paris: Les éditions du Cerf.

Häberl, Charles. 2009. *The Neo-Mandaic Dialect of Khorramshahr.* Semitica Viva 45. Wiesbaden: Harrassowitz.

Häberl, Charles, Nikita Kuzin, Sergey Loesov, and Alexey Lyavdansky. 2020. 'A Neo-Aramaic Version of a Kurdish Folktale'. *Journal of Semitic Studies* 65 (2): 473–93. https://doi.org/10.1093/jss/fgaa008.

Jastrow, Otto. 1992. *Lehrbuch Der Ṭuroyo-Sprache.* Semitica Viva 2. Wiesbaden: Harrassowitz.

———. 1993. *Laut- und Formenlehre des neuaramäischen Dialekts von Mīdin im Ṭūr ʿAbdīn.* 4th ed. Semitica viva 9. Wiesbaden: Harrassowitz.

———. 2011. 'Ṭuroyo and Mlaḥsô'. In *The Semitic Languages*, edited by Stefan Weninger, Geoffrey Khan, Michael P. Streck, and Janet C. E. Watson, 697–707. Berlin: De Gruyter Mouton. https://doi.org/10.1515/9783110251586.697.

Jastrow, Otto, and Shabo Talay. 2019. *Der neuaramäische Dialekt von Midyat (Midyoyo).* Semitica viva 59. Wiesbaden: Harrassowitz.

Lahdo, Ablahad. 2017. *A Traitor Among Us: The Story of Father Yusuf Akbulut, a Text in the Turoyo Dialect of 'Iwardo.* Semitica viva 56. Wiesbaden: Harrassowitz.

Noorlander, Paul M. 2021. *Ergativity and Other Alignment Types in Neo-Aramaic: Investigating Morphosyntactic Microvariation.* Studies in Semitic Languages and Linguistics 103. Leiden: Brill.

Ritter, Hellmut. 1967. *Ṭūrōyo: Die Volkssprache der Syrischen Christen des Ṭūr ʿAbdīn.* Vol. A, *Texte.* Wiesbaden: Steiner.

———. 1979. *Ṭūrōyo: Die Volkssprache der Syrischen Christen des Ṭūr ʿAbdīn.* Vol. B, *Wörterbuch.* Wiesbaden: Steiner.

———. 1990. *Ṭūrōyo: Die Volkssprache Der Syrischen Christen Des Ṭūr ʿAbdīn.* Vol. C, *Grammatik: Pronomen, 'Sein, Vorhanden Sein', Zahlwort, Verbum.* Stuttgart: Steiner.

Sakel, Jeanette. 2007. 'Types of Loan: Matter and Pattern'. In *Grammatical Borrowing in Cross-Linguistic Perspective*, edited by Yaron Matras and Jeanette Sakel, 15–30. Berlin: De Gruyter Mouton. https://www.degruyter.com/document/doi/10.1515/9783110199192.15/html.

Siegel, Adolf. 1923. *Laut- und Formenlehre des Neuaramäischen Dialekts des Ṭūr ʿAbdīn.* Hannover: Heinz Lafaire.

Trudgill, Peter. 2021. 'Dialect Convergence and the Formation of New Dialects'. In *The Handbook of Historical Linguistics*, vol. 2, edited by Richard D. Janda, Brian D. Joseph, and Barbara S. Vance, 123–44. Chichester: Wiley. https://doi.org/10.1002/9781118732168.ch6.

Waltisberg, Michael. 2016. *Syntax des Ṭuroyo.* Semitica Viva 55. Wiesbaden: Harrassowitz.

LOCATIVES IN THE SPOKEN ARABIC OF MARDIN (TURKEY)

George Grigore

It is a great honor and joy for me to contribute to the *Festschrift* occasioned by the 65th birthday of Prof. Martin Zammit, a first-rate name in the field of Semitic studies, especially in Arabic dialectology.

1.0. Introduction

This article is concerned with description of the locatives, words or phrases indicating place or direction (we included both in this study, under this denomination), in the spoken Arabic of Mardin. This study is based on a corpus of data recorded on the spot, in Mardin, from 2002 up until today. A portion of these data was used to supplement the monograph *L'arabe parlé à Mardin: Monographie d'un parler arabe 'périphérique'* (Grigore 2007), as well as a series of articles that expand upon the mentioned monograph, as is the case with the current study.

The proposed analysis has been formalised within the framework of the work of Arlette Roth (2006), which deals with the locatives in another variety of Arabic, that spoken in

 https://doi.org/10.11647/OBP.0445.10

Kormakiti (Cyprus), because of their similarities as peripheral dialects, and implemented according to the general study on the preposition in Arabic dialects by Stephan Procházka (1993).

2.0. Locatives in the Spoken Arabic of Mardin

In the studied corpus, I have identified two types of locative markers: the ones that are independent from a semantic point of view, namely the locative adverbs, and, on the other hand, the ones that are dependent from a semantic point of view, i.e., the locative prepositions.

2.1. Locative Adverbs

The independent locative markers are adverbs of place that have a meaning; hence they do not require other determiners and express where the verb action is carried out.

The numerous adverbs and adverbial phrases place the event in space by putting it in relation to a (fixed) point which can be found either in the text of the message (anaphoric), or in the situational context of communication (exophoric).

If the point can be found in the textual context, it is represented by an element of the message. In relation to this type of point one can express:

- inferiority or superiority: *taḥt* 'under', 'below', 'beneath', 'down'—*fōq* 'on (top)', 'up', 'upstairs', 'above'
- anteriority or posteriority: *qəddām* 'in front of'—*ḫalf* 'behind';
- the quality of being indoors or outdoors: *baṛṛa* 'out(side)'—*ğawwa* 'in(side)'.

It is worth noting that all these adverbs also work as prepositions, which, combined with a noun, result in a prepositional phrase with the syntactic function of an adverbial one, of place. When the noun is taken out of the prepositional phrase, the preposition becomes free, independent, with meaning of its own, *ergo* an adverb:

(1) *ḥəṭṭ ṯmān-ək taḥt əl-ḥawīs!* → *ḥəṭṭ ṯmān-ək taḥt!*
'Put your money under your clothes!' → 'Put your money beneath!'

Remark: the two adverbs *baṛṛa* 'outside' and *ğawwa* 'inside' have as correspondents the prepositions *baṛṛāt* and *ğawwāt*:

(2) *astanḍər-ək ğawwāt əd-dəkkān.* → *astanḍər-ək ğawwa.*
'I'm waiting for you inside the shop.' → 'I'm waiting for you inside.'

If the point can be found within the situational context, then it either represents the same place where the emitter is, or the place where another point in the communication space can be located:

- *hawn / hawne* 'here'—*hawnak / hawnake* 'there';
- *qarīb* 'close'—*baʕīd* 'far';
- *ʕal-yamīn* 'on the right'—*ʕač-čəppe* 'on the left'.

For example:

(3) *əl-yawme ğītu la-hawne, lākən ġadde mō-ği čənki nġabantu mən-ki.*
'I came here (place that can only be identified within the situational context) today, but tomorrow I won't come any more because I got upset with you.'

As for the adverbs *hawn* and *hawnak*, they cannot become prepositions, which does happen in all other varieties of Arabic, but unlike these, the spoken Arabic of Mardin introduces an innovation: the two adverbs can be the second term of the *status constructus*:

(4) *hārūn hawn.*
'The tomcat here.' [literally 'Here's tomcat.']

(5) *kalb hawnak.*
'The dog there.' [literally 'There's dog.']

(6) *ḥāṛṛ hawnake mo kama ḥāṛṛ hawne we; hāke nēšəf we.*
'The heat there (in Mardin) is not like the heat here (in Istanbul); that one is dry.' [literally 'There's heat (in Mardin) is not like here's heat (in Istanbul); that one is dry.']

2.2. Locative Prepositions

A locative preposition describes a spatial relationship between two entities. In the spoken Arabic of Mardin, the prepositions are always combined with other words, a pronoun or noun (with or without adjectives), as determiner. As a result, the prepositional phrase acts as an adjective or an adverb, locating something in space, modifying a noun, or relating when or where or under what conditions something happened.

The locative prepositions in the spoken Arabic of Mardin are:

2.2.1. The Preposition *ʿala*

The preposition *ʿala* suffixed with the personal pronouns (before pronouns, the preposition *ʿala* becomes *ʿalay*): *ʿalay-i; ʿalay-k; ʿalay-ki; ʿalay-u; ʿalay-a; ʿalay-na; ʿalay-kən; ʿalay-ən.*

This preposition is used to indicate the position of an object in relation to another object that is lower on the same vertical direction (etymologically, the preposition originates from a root, *ʿlw*, which also conveys the meaning *height*). The either concrete or abstract spatial usage of *ʿala* is no different from using *fōq* 'on (top of)'. When it precedes nouns defined with the definite article, the pronoun reduces its form to *ʿa*.

(7) *ḫārūf mašwi ʿa-n-nāṛ.*
'Lamb broiled over a fire.'

(8) *qabər ʿala qabər, w la bayt ʿala bayt.*
'Tomb over tomb, but not house over house.'

(9) *Aḷḷa yəktəb ʿalay-k əs-səlāme.*
'May God give you peace.' [literally 'May God write peace upon you.']

2.2.2. The Preposition *ʿand/ʿənd*

The preposition ***ʿənd*** suffixed with the personal pronouns: *ʿənd-i; ʿənd-ək; ʿənd-ki; ʿənd-u; ʿənd-a; ʿənn-na; ʿənd-kən; ʿənd-ən.*

This preposition indicates adjacency, spatial proximity: 'at', 'by', 'near', 'beside', 'around', 'next to', 'near to':

(10) *ʿənd abū-hu mō-yəšṛab čəġāṛa.*
'He doesn't smoke around his father.'

This leads to a territorial meaning ('at'):

(11) *əl-layle, abīt ʿənd-kən.*
'Tonight, I'll sleep in your (house).'

Moving forward from this last value, the preposition also indicates property, possession, as it is equivalent to the verb 'to have' (the same goes for *li* and *maʕ*):

(12) *sabbət əğ-ğēye ʿənd-ək waqt fārəġ?*
'Do you have time next week?'

(13) *yṣēr ʿənd-ək əl-ktēb.*
'You will have the book.'

The preposition *ʿənd* combines with the prepositions of movement *mən* 'from' and *la* 'to', 'towards':

(14) *ağı la-ʿənd-ək.*
'I'm coming to you.'

(15) *aṛōḥ mən ʿənd-ək.*
'I'm going away from you.'

2.2.3. The Preposition *baṛṛāt*

The preposition *baṛṛāt* suffixed with the personal pronouns: *baṛṛāt-i; baṛṛāt-ək; baṛṛāt-ki; baṛṛāt-u; baṛṛāt-a; baṛṛāt-na; baṛṛāt-kən; baṛṛāt-ən.*

This preposition introduces a spatial reference, as it is marking the exteriority of an action:

(16) *əl-kalb mō-yṣēr yfūt əl-bayt, yəlzəm yəbqa baṛṛāt əl-bayt.*
'It doesn't do for the dog to enter the house; he must remain outside the house.'

(17) *baṛṛāt əl-bayt təstanḍər-ni!*
'Wait for me outside the house!'

2.2.4. The Preposition *bayn*

The preposition *bayn* suffixed with the pronouns:

a) singular (the form *bayn* 'between' is used): *bayn-i; bayn-ək; baynki; bayn-u; bayn-a* (e.g., *bayn-i w bayn-ək* 'between me and you');
b) plural (the form *baynat* 'among' is used): *baynat-na; baynat-kən; baynat-ən.* In Ṭuroyo, there are also two forms for this preposition: *bayn*, which precedes a noun, e.g., *bayn li-arʿo w li-šmoyo* 'between the earth and the sky'; and *baynoṯ*, when it is followed by a bound pronoun, e.g., *baynoṯi w...* 'between me and...', *baynoṯan w...* 'between us and...' (Jastrow, 1992, 99).

This preposition indicates a space that separates two or more objects, an interval defined by several points that create a limit (the form *bayn* 'between'):

(18) *bayn əṭ-ṭəyyār w əl-gērgēf fīyu ǧaṛṛat ṃayy.*
'Between the spindle and the sewing frame there is a water pot.'

(19) *bayn-i w bayn-ək mā-fi ši.*
'There is nothing between me and you.'

This preposition also indicates a collectivity, of which some entities can be distinguished (the form *baynat* 'among'):

(20) *baynat-na kəllət-na mā-fi aḥḥad ḫərāb.*
'Among us there is no one bad.'

Nonetheless, this preposition (especially the form *baynat*) also combines with other prepositions, especially *mən*: *mən baynat* 'from among', 'from the midst of'.

2.2.5. The Preposition *fōq*

The preposition *fōq* suffixed with the personal pronouns: *fōq-i; fōq-ək; fōq-ki; fōq-u; fōq-a; fōq-na; fōq-kən; fōq-ən.*

This preposition has a spatial value, as it means 'on (top of)':

(21) *ana aqʿad fōq əl-bayt*
'I am sitting on the house.'

(22) *mērdīn fōq əl-ǧabal ye.*
'Mardin is located on the mountain.'

(23) *mā-fi ši fōq əl-maṣa.*
'There is nothing on the table.'

The preposition *fōq* combines with the prepositions *mən* and *la*:

- *mən fōq* 'from above', 'from atop';
- *la-fōq* '[to the] top of'.

2.2.6. The Preposition *fi/fə*

The preposition *fi/fə* suffixed with the personal pronouns: *fī-yi; fī-k; fī-ki; fī-yu; fī-ya; fī-na; fī-kən; fī-yən.*

This preposition is generally used for showing either the space or the time, that is, it indicates a situation that is happening in a certain place or during a certain time span ('in'):

(24) *ana fə-maktab əl-ġāzi ana.*
'I am in the al-Ghazi school.'

(25) *baramtu fə-l-balad w ḥələqtu.*
'I wandered the town and I am exhausted.'

(26) *əl-barġūṯ yəlʿab fə-ḏ-ḏaqən.*
'The flea is playing in [his] beard.'

It can also indicate stability, steadiness, fixity:

(27) *əd-dīk ymūt, təbqa ʿayn-u fə-z-zbāle.*
'The rooster is dying, but he keeps gazing at the (pile of) trash.' [literally 'The rooster is dying, but his eye is on the (pile of) trash.']

(28) *taʿān vēya ḫallī-k fə-l-bayt! kama trīd!*
'Come or stay home! Do as you like!'

2.2.7. The Preposition *ǧamb*

The preposition *ǧamb* suffixed with the personal pronouns: *ǧamb-i*; *ǧamb-ək*; *ǧamb-ki*; *ǧamb-u*; *ǧamb-a*; *ǧamb-na*; *ǧamb-kən*; *ǧamb-ən*.

This preposition indicates proximity, adjacency: 'beside', 'near', 'next to', 'at':

(29) *taʿān w qʿad hawne ǧamb-i!*
'Come and sit here next to me!'

2.2.8. The Preposition *ǧawwāt*

The preposition *ǧawwāt* suffixed with the personal pronouns: *ǧawwāt-i*; *ǧawwāt-ək*; *ǧawwāt-ki*; *ǧawwāt-u*; *ǧawwāt-a*; *ǧawwāt-na*; *ǧawwāt-kən*; *ǧawwāt-ən*.

This preposition introduces a spatial reference by marking the interiority of an action:

(30) *mən ǧawwāt əl-bayt kān təǧi rīḥat akəl kwayyəs.*
'From inside the house came a smell of tasty food.'

The preposition *ǧawwāt* is the opposite of the preposition *baṛṛāt* 'out(side)'.

2.2.9. The Preposition *ḥawl*

The preposition *ḥawl* suffixed with the personal pronouns: *ḥawl-i*; *ḥawl-ək*; *ḥawl-ki*; *ḥawl-u*; *ḥawl-a*; *ḥawl-na*; *ḥawl-kən*; *ḥawl-ən*.

This preposition indicates the surrounding space or close proximity:

(31) *lā-tṛōḥīn-təğīn ḥawl əl-bayt.*
'Stop fidgeting around the house.'

(32) *yəkfa təbrəmīn ḥawl-i!*
'Stop swirling around me!'

(33) *dəṛtu ḥawl əl-maktab.*
'I went around the school.'

2.2.10. The Preposition *ḫalf*

The preposition *ḫalf* suffixed with the personal pronouns: *ḫalf-i*; *ḫalf-ək*; *ḫalf-ki*; *ḫalf-u*; *ḫalf-a*; *ḫalf-na*; *ḫalf-kən*; *ḫalf-ən*.

The preposition *ḫalf* indicates posteriority; something that lies beyond another thing, 'behind', 'beyond':

(34) *ḫalf bayt-i*
'behind my house'

(35) *ḫalf əl-wəlāya*
'beyond the town'

Between nouns or pronouns that refer to animates and the spatial preposition *ḫalf*, the preposition *mən* 'from' always interposes so that any obscene connotations be avoided.

(36) *ḫalf mən-ni fīyu mərе.*
'Behind me there is a mirror.'

(37) *əẖt-i ẖalf mən-ni ye.*
'My sister is behind me.'

2.2.11. The Preposition *əla*

The preposition *əla* suffixed with the personal pronouns (the form *lay* is used): *lay-(y); lay-k; lay-ki; lay-u; lay-a; lay-na; lay-kən; lay-ən.*

This preposition indicates the limit, the end of an action, the destination 'to', 'at', 'towards':

(38) *baʿaṯū-hu la-bayt ẖāl-u.*
'They sent him to his uncle's (mother's brother) house.'

(39) *ham aṛōḥ la-ʿənd ǧīrānāt-i, ham ze ağī la-ʿənd-kən.*
'I'm going to my neighbours' and I'm coming to you as well.'

(40) *rəǧǧāl yədfaʿ w yrīd yfūt la-qəddām.*
'A man is pushing (forcing the line) and wants to enter in the front.'

2.2.12. The Preposition *mən*

The preposition *mən* suffixed with the personal pronoun: *mən-ni*; *mən-nək*; *mən-ki*; *mən-nu*; *mən-na*; *mən-na*; *mən-kən*; *mən-ən.*

When followed by the definite article, the preposition *mən* sometimes, but not always, drops its final consonant /n/, so as to form, with the /l/ in the article (or with the consonant that results after its assimilation), a closed syllable:

(41) *mə-š-šawke warde, mə-l-warde šawke.*
'From the thorn, a rose, from the rose, a thorn.'

This preposition indicates:

- the starting point:

  (42) *mən hawn əla hawnake.*
  'From here to there.'

- the place of origin:

  (43) *əl-qatəl mə-ğ-ğanne kəṭ-ṭalaʿ.*
  'Beating comes from heaven.'

2.2.13. The Preposition *qəddām*

The preposition *qəddām* suffixed with the personal pronouns: *qəddām-i; qəddām-ək; qəddām-ki; qəddām-u; qəddām-a; qəddām-na; qəddām-kən; qəddām-ən.*

This preposition usually marks anteriority in space: 'in front of', 'ahead':

(44) *qəddām dəkkān-i fīyu tūṯe gbīre.*
'In front of my store there is a big mulberry tree.'

(45) *bayt-na qəddām bayt nūri.*
'Our house is in front of Nuri's house.'

The preposition *qəddām* combines with the prepositions *mən* 'from' and *la* 'to': *mən qəddām* '[from] in front', e.g., *mən qəddām əl-bāb* '[from] in front of the door'; *la-qəddām* '[towards] in front', e.g., *la-qəddām əl-bāb* '[towards] in front of the door'.

2.2.14. The Preposition *taḥt*

The preposition *taḥt* suffixed with the personal pronouns: *taḥt-i; taḥt-ək; taḥt-ki; taḥt-u; taḥt-a; taḥt-na; taḥt-kən; taḥt-ən.*

This preposition marks the position of an object in relation to a second object that is higher on the same vertical direction, hence it means 'under':

(46) *ḥaṭṭaytu məftāḥ-ək taḥt əl-məre.*
'I placed your key under the mirror.'

(47) *taḥt bayt-i fīyu ğəwērīn mlāḥ.*
'Below my house there are some good neighbours.'

The preposition *taḥt,* like its opposite *fōq,* combines with the prepositions *mən* and *la* as follows: *mən taḥt* 'from under', 'from beneath'; *la-taḥt* '[towards] under (beneath)':

(48) *hārūn-ī mā yrīd yəṭlaʿ mən taḥt əč-čarpāye.*
'My tomcat doesn't want to come out from under the bed.'

3.0. Conclusion

The system of locatives in the spoken Arabic of Mardin is highly stable, since it is very little influenced by the languages spoken in the area, Turkish and Kurdish, which put very much pressure on it. This is probably due to the fact that Turkish has a whole different system of locatives made up of postpositions and not prepositions as is the case in Arabic. Both the adverbs and the prepositions analysed retain the signified and the signifier (De Saussure 1959) just as they appeared in old Arabic.

References

de Saussure, Ferdinand. 1959. *Course in General Linguistics.* New York: McGraw Hill.

Grigore, George. 2007. *L'arabe parlé à Mardin: Monographie d'un parler arabe 'périphérique'*. Bucharest: Editura Universităţii din Bucureşti.

———. 2012. 'La deixis spatiale dans l'arabe parlé à Bagdad'. In *Dynamiques langagières en Arabophonies: Variations, contacts, migrations et créations artistique—Hommage offert à Dominique Caubet par ses élèves et collègues*, edited by Alexandrine Barontini, Christophe Pereira, Ángeles Vicente, and Karima Ziamari, 77–90. Estudios de dialectología árabe 7. Zaragoza: Universidad de Zaragoza.

Grigore, George, and Gabriel Biţună. 2012. 'Common Features of North Mesopotamian Arabic Dialects Spoken in Turkey (Şırnak, Mardin, Siirt)'. In *Bilim Düşünce ve Sanatta Cizre: Uluslararası Bilim Düşünce ve Sanatta Cizre Sempozyumu Bildirileri*, edited by M. Nesim Doru, 545–55. Istanbul: Mardin Artuklu Üniversitesi Yayınları.

Jastrow, Otto. 1969. 'Die arabischen Dialekte des Vilayets Mardin (Südosttürkei)'. In 'XVII. Deutscher Orientalistentag', *Zeitschrift der Deutschen Morgenländischen Gesellschaft* supplement 1 (2): 683–88.

———. 1992. *Lehrbuch der Ṭuroyo-Sprache.* Semitica Viva, Series Didactica 2. Wiesbaden: Otto Harrassowitz.

Procházka, Stephan. 1993. *Die Präpositionen in den neuarabischen Dialekten.* Vienna: VWGÖ.

Roth, Arlette. 2006. 'Les localisateurs spatiaux dans le parler arabe de Kormakiti (Chypre)'. In *L'arabe dialectal: Enquêtes, descriptions, interprétations*, edited by Salah Mejri, 395–410.

Actes d'AIDA 6. Tunis: Centre d'Etudes et de Recherches Economiques et Sociales.

PERCEPTIONS OF MALTA IN ARABIC PROVERBS AND IDIOMS

Kurstin Gatt

1.0. Introduction

This paper delves into the realm of paremiology, the scientific study of proverbs, shedding light on both proverbs and idioms in different varieties of Arabic that specifically mention Malta, the Maltese people, or the Maltese language. This research aims to provide a list of such expressions and examine the perceptions that Arabic proverbs impart about Malta, its inhabitants and its language. The study consists of four main sections; the first one discusses the role of proverbs in the long-standing Arabic–Islamic tradition, and is followed by an overview of existing literature and research in the field. The third section provides a discussion on the collection of the proverbs taken into consideration in this research, assembling a list of these linguistic expressions and presenting them in transcription and their translated versions. Subsequently, a thematic analysis is presented in the final section, which features the central themes that are prevalent in the collected Arabic expressions about Malta. The paper concludes by summarising key findings and implications from this inquiry.

 https://doi.org/10.11647/OBP.0445.11

2.0. The Role of Proverbs and Idioms

Often rooted in folklore and tradition, proverbs serve as conduits for imparting age-old perceptions from one generation to the next. Proverbs are short, traditional sayings with a generally fixed structure that offer advice, wisdom, or a moral lesson. They often convey universal truths or cultural values. According to Wolfgang Mieder (1993, 5), a proverb is “a short, generally known sentence of the folk which contains wisdom, truth, morals, and traditional views in a metaphorical, fixed and memorable form and which has been handed down from generation to generation.” Far beyond their pithy nature, proverbs serve as repositories of information and may, at times, impart deeply rooted stereotypes with reference to other national, linguistic, or religious communities, wielding influence on how consumers of a particular language perceive other groups. While proverbs find usage in literate societies, their significance is amplified in non-literate societies, where the oral transmission of traditions prevails.

When embedded in discourse, proverbs fulfil several functions, such as advising, warning, satirising, educating, motivating, and summarising an argument. At times, proverbs are used as part of the argument. They may lend “support and force to the statement” if quoted at the right moment in a discussion (Freyha 1974, xvii). Moreover, a proverb “has the authority to settle a dispute or solve a vexing problem” or may be used to settle a dispute in “quarrels over verbal agreements or binding contracts” (Freyha 1974, xvii). Some proverbs include everyday observations on the weather and seasons, knowledge about customs, manners, laws, traditions and superstitions, medical advice, prescriptions, and health regulations (Freyha 1974, xiv–xx).

This study takes into consideration a number of idioms in addition to proverbs. Structurally, idioms are expressions that often have a fixed structure as well, but their meanings can be opaque or nonsensical when interpreted literally. They may originate from historical or cultural contexts but are not always as universally recognised or employed as proverbs. Functionally, idioms are expressions whose meanings cannot be understood from the literal definitions of the individual words. They convey a figurative meaning that is unique to the specific phrase. Idioms tend to add colour or emphasis to language but typically lack the didactic content found in proverbs.

Arabic proverbs are a testament to the heritage of the Arabic language, showcasing centuries of wisdom and cultural idiosyncrasies. These sayings have been passed down through generations, forming a remarkably well-documented branch of Arabic prose literature (Leder 1998, 616). In Arabic poetry, the technique of intertextuality may be explicitly achieved by alluding to proverbs. Poets may evoke a well-known earlier proverb "to create an enigmatic line which can only be understood with reference to the original line" (Heinrichs 1998, 82).

The closest term to 'proverb' in Arabic is *mathal* (pl. *amthāl*), which expresses different meanings, including "likeness; metaphor, simile, parable; proverb, adage" (Wehr 1979). Proverbs may also indirectly impart knowledge by alluding to historically or socio-culturally known facts or persons, and their meaning is considered wisdom (*ḥikma*). Proverbs appear in various literary genres, including classical Arabic poetry, *adab* works, folk literature, and the *Maqāmāt* of al-Hariri (d. 1122 CE). In the premodern period, knowledge of proverbs was integral to one's education; "to know and use a certain amount of proverbs was part of the ideal of the civilised and educated *adīb*" (Walther 1998, 622). Their value lies in their ability to capture truths and societal values in concise and memorable phrases.

The famous Arab philologist al-Maydani (d. 1124 CE), who provided a voluminous compilation of proverbs, considered proverbs to be "the summit of rhetoric" and claimed that proverbs were popular due to their "concise formulation, their apt expression, their beautiful comparisons and their excellent allusions" (Walther 1998, 623). The study of proverbs provides a glimpse into the consciousness of various Arabic-speaking cultures, exposing "socio-religious, anthropological and cultural conceptions, some conditioned by special social and historical circumstances" (Walther 1998, 623).

While the origins of proverbs remain enigmatic due to the inherent challenge of attributing their authorship, Anis Freyha, who compiled a list of modern Lebanese proverbs, posits that, while it is impossible to trace the origins of the proverb, it is feasible to infer, in a broad manner, the contextual factors, events, and conditions that conceivably led to the emergence of a particular proverb. These factors include proverbs derived from day-to-day encounters or observations of the natural world, those rooted in allegorical tales and anecdotes, riddles and answers to riddles, expressions referring to classical literature, emulations of existing proverbs, and expressions that seemingly originated around some historical incident (Frehya 1974, xii).

3.0. State of the Art

There are several collections of proverbs in Classical Arabic; the earliest documented is *Kitāb al-amthāl* by Abu ʿUbayd (d. 838 CE). Later, the Arab philologist Ahmad b. Muhammad al-Maydani (d. 1124) prepared a well-known collection of proverbs known as *Majmaʿ al-amthāl*, which was based on fifty previous collections (Walther 1998, 520). In Western scholarship, the German Arabist Georg Wilhelm Friedrich Freytag undertook the production of an edition of al-Maydani's compilation of proverbs, accompanied by a Latin translation, between 1838 and 1843 (Freytag 1838–1843). Collections of proverbs in regional varieties of Arabic became popular from the thirteenth century onwards. The Tunisian scholar Abu Yahya al-Zajjali (d. 1294) wrote *Amthāl al-ʿawwām fī al-andalus* (see Zajjālī 1975).

While the researcher acknowledges the extensive scholarship on Arabic proverbs in Arabic and other languages, this review shall exclusively reference sources that are directly pertinent to this study. Crucial for analysing perceptions about Malta in Arabic proverbs is the work of the Lebanese author and scholar Anis Frehya (d. 1993), who compiled *A Dictionary of Modern Lebanese Proverbs* (Frehya 1974). This publication consists of a list of Lebanese proverbs, which are presented in Arabic script, transliteration, and English translation. In the preface of this compilation, Frehya states that he collected the proverbs in his native village, Ras al-Matn, which is a predominantly Druze village in the district of Matn, to the east of Beirut.

Similarly, Ferdinand-Joseph Abela's (1981) *Proverbes populaires du Liban sud: Saïda et ses environs* consists of Arabic proverbs collected from southern Lebanon with French translation and comments.[1] There are also multiple collections of proverbs in Moroccan Arabic. One of the earliest collections was compiled by the Finnish sociologist Edward Alexander Westermarck (d. 1939) in his book *Wit and Wisdom in Morocco: A Study of Native Proverbs* (Westermarck 1930).

In spite of the wealth of documented collections of Arabic proverbs in Classical and dialectal Arabic, along with extensive Western scholarship in this area, there remains a notable gap in the realm of research about how specific countries, cultures, or people are portrayed in Arabic proverbs. This research aims to bridge this gap by delving into the interplay of linguistic and cultural dynamics to examine the representation of Malta and the Maltese within Arabic expressions.

4.0. Collection of Proverbs

One of the main challenges in analysing the Arabic proverbs referencing Malta is contextualisation, because of the frequent lack

---

[1] Ferdinand-Joseph Abela was born in Sidon in South Lebanon in 1887. After finishing his studies in Oriental studies and archaeology, he became the vice-consul of Spain and Britain in Sidon. While his surname may suggest that he was of Maltese origin, the researcher could not find any information about Abela's family background.

of details or explanations accompanying these linguistic expressions. To mitigate the potential misunderstandings related to specific proverbs, and given that the researcher is not intimately connected to the vast communities where these proverbs are commonly employed, the researcher reached out to several scholars in various disciplines related to particular communities and asked for their insights and explanations. Additionally, any anecdotes or incidents linked to a specific proverb are included in the discussion. Nevertheless, it is essential to clarify that this study does not aim to trace the origins of these proverbs. Since cultural traditions are primarily passed down orally from one generation to another, often with varying degrees of accuracy, it is impossible to attribute a particular proverb to a specific historical event.

Central to our inquiry are the following research questions: What are the Arabic proverbs that mention Malta or the Maltese, and how are Malta and its people portrayed in Arabic proverbs and sayings? In order to systematically analyse the portrayal of Malta, its inhabitants, and its language within Arabic proverbs, the following approach was adopted. Firstly, proverbs were gathered from various sources, including books on famous sayings and proverbs, popular songs, and other elements of popular culture. Subsequently, these proverbs were documented both in transcription and in transliteration to ensure clarity and accessibility for readers. The next step entailed categorising these proverbs thematically based on their overarching impressions about Malta, its inhabitants, and its language. Finally, each proverb's usage was elucidated, accompanied by any relevant comments or anecdotes that were associated with it.

The proverbs considered in this study are gathered in the following list, with the country to which each proverb is attributed indicated in parentheses. It is important to note that the country mentioned in the brackets corresponds to the attribution provided in the collection of proverbs, and this does not imply that variations of the same proverb do not exist in other communities, particularly in neighbouring ones. In the translation of the proverbs, the researcher attempted to preserve the original as faithfully as possible. Additionally, while these expressions serve as key focal points, this compilation is not exhaustive, and the possibility of encountering additional expressions within the broader context of the topic exists. However, the chosen proverbs constitute this research study's primary body of text.

4.1. Transcription

1. *riğlayh* (var. *əğrayh*) *b-təlḥaʾ mālṭa* (or *ʾObroṣ*) (Lebanon)
2. *yḫallī ʿawwāk yaṣil l-mālṭa* (Syria)
3. *əʾdaḥ ʿalayh hawn b-yūlaʿ bi-mālṭa* (Lebanon)
4. *mālṭa yōk* (Lebanon)
5. *baddu yuqīm d-dīn fī mālṭa* (Palestine)
6. *bi-l-aḏān fī mālṭa* (Egypt)
    a) *lā āḏān fī mālṭa*
    b) *ğāy yuʾaḏḏin fī mālṭa*
    c) *miṯla l-muʾaḏḏin fī mālṭa*
    d) *āḏḏan baʿda ḫirāb mālṭa*
7. *l-mālṭī wŭ l-fār lạ tswurrîhum bạ̄b ḍ-ḍār* (Morocco)
8. *hānī bach nəğbəd men mālṭa* (Tunisia)
9. *mālṭa l-ḥnīna ḫubza w-sardīna* (Tunisia)

4.2. English Translation

1. [He is so agile that] his feet would reach Malta (or Cyprus).
2. He will let your shouting reach Malta.
3. Light the (lighter) here, and it will catch fire in Malta!
4. There is no Malta.
5. He wants to uphold religion in Malta.
6. Calling to prayer in Malta.
   a) There is no call to prayer in Malta.
   b) He's coming to call for prayer in Malta.
   c) Like the muezzin in Malta.
   d) He called for prayer after the destruction of Malta.
7. Don't show the house-door to the Maltese and the mouse.
8. I am going to get [my words] from Malta.
9. Malta is kind, bread and sardines.

5.0. Themes

The proverbs listed above include a range of themes that shed light on perceptions and cultural perspectives related to Malta and the Maltese. The main themes that are discussed henceforth include Malta as a relatively distant or unreachable and potentially unfamiliar location, Malta as a non-existent place, Malta as non-Islamic, the Maltese people as untrustworthy, and the Maltese language as enigmatic or incomprehensible.

5.1. Theme 1: Malta as a Distant/Unreachable and Potentially Unfamiliar Location

One of the recurring themes present within Arabic lore is the portrayal of Malta as a geographically remote destination, which reflects a geographical understanding and carries deeper cultural and symbolic meanings. Introducing this theme about Malta, the Palestinian-born scholar Nawaf al-Tamimi (2018) writes in a blog post that:

> تحضر مالطا في ذاكرة الطفولة مرادفة لبُعد المسافة. كان الطفل منا يتهدّد قرينه بالقول: "أضربك أجيبك في مالطا"، أو يصف الطفل المسافة البعيدة أو المكان البعيد، فيقول "مشينا حتى وصلنا إلى مالطا"، أو قوله "بعيد مثل هنا ومالطا". لا ندري من أي جاءت هذه الكناية، علماً أن هذه الجزيرة المتوسطية أقرب إلى الشرق والمغرب العربيين من الصين أو اليابان أو أستراليا، أو كأن خيال الطفل منا لم يكن يقدر على التحليق أبعد من مالطا.
>
> In childhood memory, Malta was synonymous with distance. Children among us used to taunt their peers by saying, "I will hit you (so hard), you will end up in Malta," or when describing a far-off place or a distant location, they would say, "We walked until we reached Malta," or use the phrase, "as far away as here and Malta." We do not know the origin of this metaphor, even though this Mediterranean island is closer to the Arab Eastern and Western regions than China, Japan, or Australia. It is as if our childhood imagination could not soar farther than Malta.

The concept of distance also appears in other proverbs in the Levant. A Lebanese proverb reads رجليه (اجريه) بتلحق مالطة (قبرص) *riǧlayh* (var. *əǧrayh*) *b-təlḥaʾ mālṭa* (or *ʾObroṣ*), which translates to '[He is so agile that] his feet could carry him as far as

Malta (or Cyprus)' (Abela 1981, 50). The mere mention of 'Malta' or its variant 'Cyprus' suggests that the inhabitants of Lebanon are knowledgeable about these two islands. Moreover, this expression implies shared geographical similarities between Malta and Cyprus. The most apparent similar features include the fact that they are both islands, separated from the mainland by sea and varying in distance from the Levant.

Historically, both Cyprus and Malta were pivotal to the maritime trade routes that connected the eastern and western Mediterranean during the ancient and pre-modern eras. They were sought-after territories due to their strategic positions, serving as trading hubs and centres of cultural exchange. This interconnectedness led to the presence of various cultures, including the Phoenicians, Greeks, Romans, Byzantines, Arabs, and Crusaders, influencing the islands' historical past. Especially in an era predating modern air travel, embarking on a journey across the Mediterranean by sea was arduous and dangerous. The Mediterranean Sea was often perceived as a barrier, creating a sense of distance and separation between these islands and the mainland. The idea of walking to these islands highlights the arduousness of the journey and the extraordinary, if not impossible, abilities of the person in question. The proverb, therefore, demonstrates the imaginative lengths to which individuals would go to emphasise the exceptional qualities of someone's attributes.

The perception of Malta as a distant location also features in a satirical Syrian comedy series known as *ḍayʿa dāyiʿa*. This concept is notably highlighted in the twenty-sixth episode of the series' second season (Sama Art International 2015). In this particular episode, one of the main characters, known as assistant Muhsan, becomes aware of a corruption case involving Joudah, another main character in the series. Upon arresting Joudah, assistant Muhsan addresses him by saying والله ليخلي عواك يصل لمالطا *w-allāhi li-yḫallī ʿawwāk yaṣil l-mālṭa*, which translates to 'By God, he will let your shouting reach Malta' (Darawshe 2023), implying that assistant Muhsan is so fed up or unbothered by the other person's angry or aggressive behaviour that he is willing to go to extreme lengths. The term *ʿawwā*, which is generally accompanied by the preposition *ʿalā*, means 'to bark' in Syrian Arabic (Stowasser and Ani 2004, 18), and is translated as 'to shout' in this context. It is worth mentioning that, in previous cases in this series, assistant Muhsan uses Cyprus to symbolise a remote place. However, in this particular case, the usage of Malta is intended to convey an even greater sense of distance, underscoring the gravity of the situation.

On a similar note, the Lebanese proverb اقدح عليه هون بيولع بمالطه *əʾdaḥ ʿalayh hawn b-yūlaʿ bi-mālṭa*, which translates to 'light the (lighter) here, and it will catch fire in Malta!' also depicts Malta as a distant geographical location. It is metaphorically used to describe something that will ignite or spread very quickly. Abela provides additional comments with this proverb, comparing the dry man with dry tinder; the man is so dry that he catches fire in Malta from a distance (Abela 1981, 280).

5.2. Theme 2: Malta as a Non-existent Place

Malta as a non-existent place is another perception about Malta which may be related to a historical incident involving Malta and the Arab world. The proverb مالطه يوك *mālṭa yōk*, meaning 'Malta does not exist', is an expression that features in different collections of Lebanese proverbs. The Turkish term *yōk* ('does not exist') encapsulates the concept of outright denial of an existing reality. According to one account, this proverb is related to a tale involving the Grand Admiral of the Turkish fleet during the sixteenth century. The admiral was tasked with visiting Malta, but after weeks of navigation, he returned empty-handed to his sultan, claiming that he had been unable to find the island (Abela 1981, 250). This narrative humorously stresses the notion of disbelief in the face of undeniable facts. In another anecdote, a Turkish captain assigned to recapture Malta similarly reported back to Constantinople that there was no such place as Malta after extensively sailing across the Mediterranean to no avail (Freyha 1974, 616). In another version of the anecdote, *mālṭa yōk* is believed to relate to the Ottoman Sultan Suleyman, who failed multiple times to conquer Malta, leading to his decree to erase any mention of the island's military resistance and institution of a death penalty for those who referred to it. Therefore, the statement *mālṭa yōk* was embedded in Turkish and neighbouring cultures as signifying a deliberate rejection of reality, a denial so intense that it becomes farcical.

5.3. Theme 3: Malta as a Symbol of Religious Devotion

Several variants of Arabic proverbs depict Malta as a bastion of Christian devotion. The term 'Malta' features in one of the 5000 Arabic proverbs collected from Palestine by Saʿid ʿAbbud and translated by Martin Thilo. The proverb reads بَدُّه يقيم ٱلدّين في مالطه *baddu yuqīm d-dīn fī mālṭa*, which translates to 'he wants to establish religion in Malta' (Thilo 1937, 59), implying that someone wants to accomplish something that is practically impossible. Malta was deemed a bastion of Catholicism; hence it was absolutely impossible to establish Islam on the island. The proverb carries a contextual meaning that revolves around an individual's actions and reactions in a specific situation, often linked to nonconformity or going against the prevailing norms. While it is challenging to trace this proverb's origins, an anecdote that accompanies this proverb links it to a particular historical incident.

According to Saʿid ʿAbbud, the underlying story behind this proverb centres around a non-Roman Catholic man's presence in Malta during a religious procession involving a body, presumably a funeral procession. It is narrated that everyone around the procession, when it approached them, would kneel or prostrate themselves as a sign of respect or devotion. However, this particular man chose to remain standing, not participating in the customary gesture of reverence. Others who were part of the crowd noticed his refusal to kneel and attempted to influence him to conform by physically pushing and urging him to kneel (Thilo 1937, 59). This proverb is used with reference to an individual who, in the midst of a prevailing practice or social convention, resists conformity and persists in their beliefs or actions, even in the face of intense pressure from others to conform. It is a metaphorical way of referring to someone who goes against the grain or stands firm in their convictions despite the majority's expectations. Therefore, a plausible meaning would be that someone wants to accomplish something that is actually undoable.

This proverb perceives Malta as a place where religious customs and practices hold importance within the cultural and societal context. The story underlying the proverb, involving a non-Roman Catholic man's refusal to kneel during a religious procession, highlights the reverence for and devotion to religious traditions that people in Malta show; it also portrays a cultural milieu where religious observance is not just a personal choice but a communal and expected behaviour. The non-conformist behaviour of the man who chooses to stand upright instead of kneeling is an example of deviating from this norm. This highlights a perceived cultural expectation for individuals to adhere to religious customs, with the story emphasising the community's firm response to non-conformity.

Other proverbs also refer to Malta as a devout Christian country, such as the proverb لا أذان في مالطا *lā āḏān fī mālṭā*, which translates to 'there is no call to prayer in Malta'. Other similar proverbs include جاي يؤذن في مالطا *ǧāy yu'aḏḏin fī mālṭa* (see Al-bāb al-awwal), which means 'he's coming to call for prayer in Malta' and the proverbial comparison مثل المؤذن في مالطا *miṯla l-mu'aḏḏin fī mālṭa*, which translates to 'like the muezzin in Malta'. The Lebanese-born author Saqr Abu Fakhr provides a counterpart to this comparison, that is, *miṯla baṭrīark fī makka*, which translates to 'like a patriarch in Mecca' (Fakhr 2016). Which Muslim believer would listen to the muezzin's call to prayer on a Catholic island isolated by the Mediterranean Sea? Likewise, which Catholic believer would listen to the Patriarch in Mecca, Islam's holiest city? These expressions, therefore, are used when one needs to express the impossibility of accomplishing a task (al-Tamīmī 2018). One needs to stress the point that the potentially skewed and unreliable version of events is here being interpreted through Levantine eyes.

Other proverbial variants include أذّن بعد خراب مالطا *ā̱d̠d̠an baʿda ẖirāb mālṭa*, translated as 'he called for prayer after the destruction of Malta', or its variant جاء بعد خراب مالطا *ğāʾ baʿda ẖirāb mālṭa*, translated as 'he came after the destruction of Malta'. The expression *ẖirbit mālṭa* 'the destruction of Malta' is also the name of a popular Egyptian song by the pop singer known by the stage name Sandy (2010), who laments that her lover 'came after the destruction of Malta' (*gāy baʿd mā ẖirbit mālṭa*). The proverb conveys a situation where there is an attempt at reform but no hope of success or when efforts to reform come too late.

In popular folklore, the 'destruction of Malta' is often attributed to the French occupation of Malta between 1798 and 1800. The French army, under the leadership of Napoleon Bonaparte, brought about the island's destruction (ʿAlwān 2018). Even though the French occupation of the Maltese islands barely lasted two years, the islands were left in complete ruins. The French occupation is believed to have looted, plundered, and destroyed the islands to such an extent that the inhabitants were forced to flee for their lives to the island of Sicily. Malta's residents returned to their city following its liberation by the English army, led by Commander Sir Alexander Ball, in 1800. However, by that time, the city had already been reduced to ruins. According to the blog writer Amal al-Attum (2020), this gave rise to the famous and enduring phrase, 'after the destruction of Malta'.

5.4. Theme 4: The Maltese as Importunate

On a different note, there are proverbs that express perceptions about the Maltese people. A Moroccan proverb reads لمالطي والفار لا توريهم باب الدار *l-mālṭī wŭ l-fār lą̄ tswurrîhum bą̄b ḍ-ḍār*, which translates to 'don't show the house-door to the Maltese and the mouse'. Westermarck (1930, 134) explains this proverb by arguing that this formulaic expression refers to people, in this case the Maltese, who are perceived as both importunate and addicted to pilfering. The proverb serves as a cautionary expression about being mindful of who one trusts and allows into one's personal space or affairs, suggesting that if one welcomes them into one's home, they may take advantage of one's hospitality, potentially causing trouble.

This proverb emulates the structure of existing proverbs that follow the same formula and meaning but replace the word 'Maltese' (*l-mālṭī*) with other variants. For example, Westermarck notes another variant of this proverb, which is *l-filâli wŭ l-fār lą̄ tswurrîhum bą̄b ḍ-ḍār*. The term *filâli* refers to someone from Tafilalt, a region in southeastern Morocco. Another Moroccan variant is بْنَادَمْ وَالْفَارْ لاَ تْوَرِّيهُمْ بَابْ الدَّار *bną̄dam wŭ l-fār lą̄ tswurrîhum bą̄b ḍ-ḍār*, in which the variant *bną̄dam* means 'human' (see Amthāl šaʿabiyya maġribiyya). The formulaic structure of this proverb also appears in Maltese; Joseph Aquilina (1972, 488) claims that the people on the sister island of Gozo say the following about their fellow Maltese:

> *Il-Malti u l-far iddaħħlux id-dar* (or *turihx bieb id-dar*), 'Let not a Maltese or a rat enter your house'. Var. (i) *Il-Malti u l-far iddaħħlux id-dar għax jaħxilek il-mara u t-tfal*, 'Do not let a Maltese or a rat enter your house for he will dishonour your wife and your children'. Var. (ii) *Il-Malti u xriku aħxih u niku*, 'Never spare a Maltese or his companion'. In Gozo there is an old strain of anti-Maltese prejudice. One hears there: *Malti tajjeb aħarqu, aħseb u ara ħażin*, 'Burn a Maltese even if he is good, let alone if he is bad'. Of course, the Maltese adapt a changed form of the proverb to the Gozitans.

It is interesting to note that Aquilina also provides other variants of this proverb, such as *l-ʿarbī wa-l-fār lā twerrilhum bāb d-dār*; in this case, 'the Arab' refers to the Arab from the countryside (Aquilina 1972, 488). These different variants depict the versatility of these proverbs, whose formulaic structure can be adapted by speakers in a particular community to reflect their xenophobic perceptions.

5.5. Theme 5: The Maltese Language as Incomprehensible or Vulgar

Another perception about Malta is that its language is incomprehensible or even vulgar, even though research shows that asymmetric mutual intelligibility exists, especially between Tunisian and Libyan speakers and Maltese. It is estimated that speakers of Tunisian and Libyan Arabic can understand about 40% of the

Maltese language (Čéplö et al. 2016, 584). The Tunisian journalist Lubna al-Harbawi, who contributes to the Alarab blog, opens her article on Malta (al-Harbawi 2021) by introducing a local Tunisian proverb هاني باش نجبد من مالطا *hānī bach nəğbəd men mālṭa* which translates to 'I am going to get [my words] from Malta'. Al-Harbawi explains that this expression is often used in moments of anger, signalling that the speaker is about to switch to a kind of speech where some words may not be understood or that could contain inappropriate or out-of-context language. According to al-Harbawi, this phenomenon might be attributed to several vulgar Tunisian words that have entered common parlance in the Maltese language.

5.6. Theme 6: Malta as a Poor Country

A famous Tunisian proverb reads مالطا الحنينة خبز وسردينة *mālṭa l-ḥnīna ḫubz w-sardīna*, which roughly translates to 'Malta is kind, bread and sardines'. This Tunisian phrase is employed in times of adversity, specifically recalling the period when Maltese individuals faced severe hardships, prompting them to migrate to Tunisia (and other North African countries such as Algeria) in significant numbers (see al-Harbawi 2021). It is interesting to note that this proverb is also found in Maltese. According to Aquilina, the proverb *Malta ħanina, ħobża u sardina* 'our beloved Malta, a loaf and a sardine' and its variant *Malta ommna l-ħanina* 'Malta is our beloved mother' depict Malta as "the well-loved country of a people destined to wrest their living from a resourceless soil" (Aquilina 1972, 488).

6.0. Conclusion

This study set out to determine the perceptions about Malta and the Maltese conveyed through Arabic proverbs. First, this paper provided a list of the proverbs with potential variants accompanied by their English translation. Subsequently, six perceptions about Malta, its people and language were identified, namely:

1. Malta as a distant/unreachable and unfamiliar location: The notion of Malta as a far-off and potentially unfamiliar place is consistently portrayed in the Arabic proverbs of Lebanon, Palestine, and Syria.
2. Malta as a non-existent place: The Lebanese proverb *mālṭa yōk*, which translates to 'Malta does not exist', reflects the denial of Malta's existence as part of a historical incident involving Malta and the Arab world. This proverb humorously illustrates the concept of disbelief in the face of undeniable facts and highlights the endurance of such tales in shaping societal perspectives.
3. Malta as a symbol of religious devotion: Some Arabic proverbs in Egypt and Palestine depict Malta as a bastion of Christian devotion, emphasising the importance of religious customs and practices within the Maltese cultural context. These proverbs also convey the expectation of conformity to religious norms, even in the face of nonconformity.
4. The Maltese as importunate: The Moroccan proverb *l-mālṭī wŭ l-fār lā̤ tswurrîhum bā̤b ḍ-ḍār* characterises the Maltese people as importunate and prone to pilfering. It

serves as a cautionary expression about being cautious of whom one trusts and invites into one's personal space.

5. The Maltese language as incomprehensible or vulgar: Perceptions of the Maltese language as incomprehensible or containing vulgar elements are reflected in the Tunisian expression *hānī bach nəǧbəd men mālṭa*. This proverb suggests that the Maltese language may be challenging for speakers of Arabic dialects to understand fully.
6. Malta as a poor country: The Tunisian proverb *mālṭa l-ḥnīna ḫubz w-sardīna* highlights the historical adversity faced by the Maltese people, who migrated to Tunisia in significant numbers during challenging times. It portrays Malta as a symbol of resilience in the face of hardship.

In examining these themes, this paper focussed on the intricate web of perceptions and cultural conceptions surrounding Malta, its language, and its people within the Arabic-speaking environment. Furthermore, this study underscored the need for further research in this field, as there are undoubtedly more proverbs that can help us understand how particular groups are perceived in the oral folklore of specific communities. Scholarship about linguistic and cultural expressions can help us better understand the intricate interplay between language, culture, and perception. Future studies may focus on the portrayal of Malta in other non-Arabic languages, the portrayal of other cultures and peoples in Arabic proverbs, and the portrayal of foreign cultures in Maltese proverbs.

References

Abela, Ferdinand Joseph. 1981. *Proverbes populaires du Liban sud: Saïda et ses environs*. Vol. 1. Les littératures populaires de toutes les nations, n.s., 28. Paris: GP Maisonneuve et Larose.

al-Attūm, Amal. 2020. 'ذاع صيته واشتهر بين الناس - إليكم قصة مثل بعد خراب مالطا'. E3arabi (blog), 15 October. https://tinyurl.com/3bse453n, accessed 4 September 2023.

'الباب الاول'. Palestiniangirl (website). Accessed 2 September 2023. https://palestiniangirl.tripod.com/amthal.html.

al-Harbawi, Lubna. 2021. 'مالطا الحنينة خبز وسردينة'. Alarab (newsportal), 2 October. https://tinyurl.com/t29n4uj6, accessed 2 September 2023.

al-Qurṭubī, ʿUbayd Allāh b. Aḥmad Zajjālī. 1975. أمثال العوام في الأندلس. Edited by Muḥammad bin Šarīfa al-Nāshir. Fez: Mohammed V Press.

al-Tamīmī, Nawāf. 2018. 'لا أذان في مالطا'. Alaraby (blog), 10 August. https://tinyurl.com/542m2z6c, accessed 2 September 2023.

ʿAlwān, Nūr. 2018. 'جزيرة مالطا: ملامح تاريخية إسلامية تكشفها اللغة والعمارة'. Noonpost (blog), 21 September. https://tinyurl.com/cpwyc7ve, accessed 4 September 2023.

'أمثال شعبية مغربية'. Faynaq (blog). https://faynaq.blogspot.com/2019/01/12_13.html, accessed 31 August 2023.

Aquilina, Joseph. 1972. *A Comparative Dictionary of Maltese Proverbs*. Malta: Royal University of Malta.

Čéplö, Slavomír, Ján Bátora, Adam Benkato, Jiří Milička, Christophe Pereira, and Petr Zemánek. 2016. 'Mutual Intelligibility of Spoken Maltese, Libyan Arabic, and Tunisian Arabic Functionally Tested: A Pilot Study'. *Folia Linguistica* 50 (2): 583–628.

Chaabi, Chedi. 2021. 'قصة مثل: بعد خراب مالطا!'. YouTube video, 18 December. https://www.youtube.com/watch?v=4dk7j-rIPxU, accessed September 20, 2023..

Darawshe, Rafat. 2023. 'مالطا'. YouTube video, 7 February. https://www.youtube.com/watch?v=1q3WYR24b8A, accessed 2 September 2023.

Fakhr, Saqr Abu. 2016. 'مالطا يوك'. Alaraby (blog), 27 April. https://tinyurl.com/s2kwj566, accessed 2 September 2023.

Freyha, Anis. 1974. *A Dictionary of Modern Lebanese Proverbs: Collated, Annotated and Translated into English.* Beirut: Librairie du Liban.

Freytag, Georg Wilhelm Friedrich. 1838–1843. *Arabum Proverbia: Vocalibus Instruxit, Latine Vertit, Commentario Illustravit.* 3 vols. Bonn, Germany: A. Marcus.

Heinrichs, W. P. 1998. 'Allusion and Intertextuality'. In *Encyclopaedia of Arabic Literature*, edited by Julie Scott Meisami and Paul Starkey, 1:81–83. London: Routledge.

Leder, S. 1998. 'Prose, Non-Fiction, Medieval'. In *Encyclopaedia of Arabic Literature*, edited by Julie Scott Meisami and Paul Starkey, 2:615–18. London: Routledge.

Mieder, Wolfgang. 1993. *Proverbs Are Never out of Season: Popular Wisdom in the Modern Age.* Oxford: Oxford University Press.

Sama Art International. 2015. 'إلى مالطا مسلسل ضيعة ضايعة - الجزء الثاني . الحلقة 26 السادسة والعشرون كاملة'. YouTube video, 1 December. https://www.youtube.com/watch?v=vhl0iRHU9UM, accessed 30 August 2023.

Sandy. 2010. 'Kherbet Malta'. YouTube video, 18 June. https://www.youtube.com/watch?v=TZ-v7Nf9GLQ&list=RDTZ-v7Nf9GLQ&start_radio=1, accessed 20 September 2023.

Stowasser, Karl, and Moukhtar Ani (eds). 2004. *A Dictionary of Syrian Arabic: English–Arabic*. Washington, DC: Georgetown University Press.

Thilo, Martin (trans.). 1937. *5000 Sprichwörter aus Palästina*. Berlin: Reichsdruckerei.

Walther, W. 1998. 'Proverbs'. In *Encyclopaedia of Arabic Literature*, edited by Julie Scott Meisami and Paul Starkey, vol. 1:622–24. London: Routledge.

———. 1998. 'Al-Maydānī, Aḥmad ibn Muḥammad (d. 518/1124)'. In *Encyclopaedia of Arabic Literature*, edited by Julie Scott Meisami and Paul Starkey, vol. 2:520. London: Routledge.

Wehr, Hans. 1979. *A Dictionary of Modern Written Arabic (Arabic–English)*. Edited by J. Milton Cowan. 4th ed. Wiesbaden: Harrassowitz.

Westermarck, Edward. 1930. *Wit and Wisdom in Morocco: A Study of Native Proverbs*. London: George Routledge & Sons Ltd.

RECOGNISABLY ARABIAN: A LEVANTINE/SOUTH-ARABIAN MORPHOSYNTACTIC BUNDLE IN MALTESE

David Wilmsen

Martin Zammit speaks cautiously but convincingly of shared Levantine features in Maltese (2006; 2009; 2009–2010), less cautiously of South Arabian elements (2009), and quite confidently of the relationship between Andalusi Arabic and Maltese (2009–2010; 2020). His caution notwithstanding, drawing a connection between Levantine Arabic, South Arabian, southern peninsular Arabic, and Andalusi varieties and Maltese is a bold stance, motivated by compelling evidence emerging from Professor Zammit's careful comparisons between Maltese and other varieties of Arabic. Taken together, these attest, as he says, "to the remarkable diachronic depth of the Maltese language" (Zammit 2009–2010, 29)

Much of Professor Zammit's work involves skilful lexical comparisons in the mode of the classic comparative method for establishing relationships between members of a language family. Bearing in mind that words can be borrowed from adjacent languages, the Arabic and South Arabian borrowings—if that is

 https://doi.org/10.11647/OBP.0445.12

what they are—in Maltese indicate proximity to or descent from source languages that are at a far remove from Maltese in place and time.

So, too, with morphosyntactic traits. An examination of a bundle of those vindicates Professor Zammit's conception of the development of the features of Maltese from South Arabian sources by way of the Levant. These are grammatical constructions formed with an enclitic *-š* or *-šī* alone. One of these is the unusual prohibitive so formed, which appears occasionally in Egyptian Arabic dialects, characteristically and frequently in some varieties of Levantine Arabic, and obligatorily in Maltese. It also appears a few times in one of the earliest documentations of an Arabic dialect, that of Oman (Reinhardt 1894, 178, 183). Another is the posing of polar questions—to which the answer is either 'yes' or 'no'—with a phrase- or sentence-final *-š/šī*. This, too, is shared by Maltese (Wilmsen 2016a) and Levantine Arabic (Holes 2004, 192), and it is attested also in Egyptian Arabic of the nineteenth century (Wilmsen and Al-Sayyed 2019, 11) and in the early documentation of Omani Arabic (Reinhardt 1894, 16, 220–21, 283). Yet a third is what has been called a partitive, distributive, or quantifier *šī* (Reinhardt 1984, 29, 69, 291, 416). It happens that an analogue of *šī* also performs these functions in the so-called 'Modern' South Arabian languages (Wilmsen 2022a; Wilmsen and Al-Taei 2022–2023, 105–9).

It is thus possible to trace the movement of the feature bundle from southern Arabia to the Levant and points westward, notably Muslim Iberia and Malta. It happens that Andalusi Arabic texts also show a few instances of polar interrogative *-š/šī*. The implication is that Maltese does, indeed, exhibit remarkable diachronic depth.

1.0. Enclitic *-š* in Maltese and Arabic

1.1. Negations with *-š* in Maltese and Arabic

The usual negation of the indicative in Maltese follows the pattern that is widespread across North Africa, Egypt, and some Levantine Arabic varieties, with a pre-posed negator *mā* (or *ma*) and an enclitic *-š*:

(1a) Maltese[1]

ma smajtx l-istoria kollha

Neg. heard.1sg. the-story all

'I [did] not hear the whole story' (Borg and Azzopardi-Alexander 1997, 88)

(1b) Egyptian Arabic

ma simiʿ-š hāḏa l-kalām

NEG heard.3MSG-NEG DEM DET-talk

'He [did] not hear this talk' (own data)

These Arabic varieties form the prohibitive with *mā* or *lā*, with some of them usually affixing an enclitic *-š*:

---

[1] The interlinear glosses and transcriptions of the authors of the Maltese examples are retained, with some modifications for the purposes of clarity. The glosses of the Arabic examples will conform to the Leipzig Glossing Rules. A list of the abbreviations follows the chapter.

(2a) Moroccan Arabic

ma ti-mši-š

NEG 2-go-NEG

(2b) Moroccan Arabic

lā ti-mši-š

PRH 2-go-PRH

(2c) Moroccan Arabic

lā t-rōḥ

PRH 2-go

'[Do] not go' (Wilmsen 2016b, 136)

A few Arabic dialects optionally form their prohibitives with an enclitic *-š* alone. Egyptian Arabic dialects may exercise this option, but it is especially common in southern Levantine Arabic varieties, that is, southern Syrian, Jordanian, and Palestinian dialects. Maltese obligatorily forms its prohibitive in the same way (Borg and Azzopardi-Alexander 1997, 27; Wilmsen 2016b, 136–38):

(3a) Jordanian Arabic

ti-nsā-š

2-forget-NEG

(3b) Maltese

ti-nsie-x

you-forget-NEG

'[Do] not forget' (Wilmsen 2016b, 137–38)

Reinhardt attests this quality in his 1894 study of a dialect of Omani Arabic, one of the earliest thorough documentations of an Arabic dialect, in which the prohibitive is an enclitic *-ši* alone:[2]

(4) Omani Arabic (nineteenth century)
ti-xrug-ši
2-exit-PRH
'[Do] not go out' (Reinhardt 1894, 178)

Notable, however, is the fact that, in the Omani Arabic of the nineteenth century, the negator enclitic *-ši* is used to negate all parts of speech, not only verbs and not only in the prohibitive (Reinhardt 1894, 137). A few examples should suffice to illustrate this (for others, see Morano 2022, 247–48; Wilmsen and Al-Taei 2023, 95–96).

(5a) Omani Arabic (nineteenth century)
Negating a participle
ġaḍbān-ši *ʿalī-k*
angry.PTCP.MSG-NEG PREP-PRO.MSG
'[He is] not angry with you' (Reinhardt 1894, 96)

(5b) Omani Arabic (nineteenth century)
Negating a preposition
ʿalī-k-ši *xōf*
PREP-PRO.MSG-NEG fear
'Fear not' [lit. 'on you not fear'] (Reinhardt 1894, 96)

---

[2] Forming the prohibitive with *lā*, as do some varieties of Arabic, including other Gulf Arabic dialects, is an alternative (Reinhardt 1894, 152)

(5c) Omani Arabic (nineteenth century)
Negating a demonstrative
kitāb-ek *hinā-ši*
book-PRO.MSG here-NEG
'Your book [is] not here' (Reinhardt 1894, 102)

Also worth noting is that negation with enclitic *-ši* has almost completely disappeared from the Omani Arabic of the twenty-first century. Sentential negation is now carried out with *mā*, which was always an option (Reinhardt 1894, 137). Morano (2022, 250), who revisits the same dialects that Reinhardt documented, proposes "that the clitic /-ši/ was probably the original negative construct used in the region, before being almost entirely replaced by *mā* under the influence of non-š-dialects as the ones spoken in the Arabian Peninsula." Compare, for example, (5b) and (5c) from the nineteenth century with (6a) and (6b) from the twenty-first:

(6a) Omani Arabic (twenty-first century)
Negating a demonstrative
hiya *mā* *hinā*
PRO.FSG NEG here
'She [is] not here' (Morano 2022, 244)

(6b) Omani Arabic (twenty-first century)
Negating a preposition
mā *ʿind-i* *flūs*
NEG PREP-1SG money
'I [do] not have cash' [lit. 'not at me money'] (Morano 2022, 246)

For their part, prohibitives are now formed with *lā* in the manner of other Gulf Arabic varieties:

(7) Omani Arabic (twenty-first century)

lā t-rūḥ-i

PRH 2-go-FSG

'[Do] not go' (Morano 2022, 246)

Negation with enclitic *-ši* alone appears only in relicts. Morano (2022, 250–51) notes its occurrence in a folk song, which may be expected to preserve older speech styles, and in negative existentials (Morano 2022, 252). She also mentions Reinhardt's documenting the negation of personal pronouns in copular utterances, which apparently do not appear in her data.

(8) Omani Arabic (nineteenth century)

Negating a personal pronoun

hūwā-ši sekrān

PRO.3MSG-NEG drunk.PTCP

'[He is] not drunk' (Reinhardt 1894, 282; Morano 2022, 247)

Its absence in Morano's data notwithstanding, this type of pronominal negation remains attested amongst Arabic speakers from the interior of Oman west of Muscat, the same dialect area that Reinhardt documented.

(9) Omani Arabic (Dakhiliyya Governorate)

hūwā-š ʿumāni

PRO.3MSG-NEG Omani

'He [is] not Omani' (Wilmsen 2022b, 166; Wilmsen and Al-Taei 2022–2023, 115 n. 2)

Reinhardt (1894, 21–22) provides an almost complete list of negated personal pronouns. These are shown in Table 1:

Table 1: Reinhardt's (1894, 21–22) negation of personal pronouns

enā-ši	*nicht ich*	not I
ntā-ši	*nicht du*	not you (M)
ntī-šši[3]	*nicht du*	not you (F)
huwā-ši	*nicht er*	not he
hiyā-ši	*nicht sie*	not she
ḥenā-ši	*nicht wir*	not us
ntū-šši	*nicht ir*	not you (PL)

Remarkably, the same construction occurs in Andalusi Arabic in a fifteenth-century collection of folk proverbs:

(10) Andalusi Arabic

ʾism-u *ʿalay-ya*

name-PRO.3MSG PREP-PRO.1SG

wa ***hūwā-š*** *yi-ġaṭṭi* *riǧlay-ya*

CONJ PRO.3MSG-NEG 3-cover legs-PRO.1SG

'His name [is] on me but it [does] not cover my legs'[4]

---

[3] Reinhardt notes that *Bei den auf ursprünglich lange Vocale ausgehenden Formen wird das š verdoppelt* 'In forms based on originally long vowels, the *š* is doubled'.

[4] The meaning of this maxim becomes clear when it is compared to its modern Moroccan counterpart, in which it is the ears that are uncovered, not the legs. It is couched as spoken by a servant whose master is rich and would be expected to earn a decent salary but who laments, "It does not even cover my ears" (Wilmsen 2014, 70).

Another instance of pronominal negation in Andalusi Arabic appears around a half century earlier in a *kharja*, a genre of colloquial poetry, usually involving lovers' complaints, which gives voice to this lament and warning:

(11) Andalusi Arabic

qāl *li-y* *man* *rā-k*

said.3MSG PREP-PRO.1SG PRO saw.3MSG- PRO.2SG

wa *lis* *min* *asrā-k*

CONJ NEG PREP captives-PRO.2SG

mira *iyyāk* *yā* *nāẓir* *iyyāk* ***ʾanī-š*** *na-dri*

look.3MSG beware VOC viewer beware PRO.1SG-NEG 1SG-know

'He said to me, "Who has seen you and is not among your captives? Look, [but] beware, O you who look, beware. I know not"'

It is possible to interpret these negators as rhetorical polar interrogatives of the type that are common in spoken Arabic, in which a question is used to negate a presupposition, as in the common Levantine Arabic expression (see discussion in Wilmsen 2014, 75–81):

(12) Levantine Arabic

šu *b-ya-ʿrif-ni*

Q DUR-3-inform-PRO.1SG

'What do I know?' [lit. 'What informs me?'] = 'I don't know'

As such, the negations in (10) and especially (11) can be understood as rhetorical questions 'Do I know? [what might happen to you if you look?]'.

Remarkably, personal pronouns with enclitic -*š* also function as polar interrogatives in Maltese.

1.2. Polar Interrogative -*x* in Maltese

Polar interrogative pronominals in Maltese have been documented from some of the early grammars of the language, Vassalli's *Grammatica della Lingua Maltese* (1827, 142), Vella's *Maltese Grammar for the Use of the English* (1831, 249–51), and Sutcliffe's *A Grammar of the Maltese Language* (1936, 211). Indeed, according to these sources and to later descriptions of the language, an enclitic -*š* may also be attached to other parts of speech to form a polar interrogative. Vella (1834, 249) actually misstates the matter in his grammar for the English: "In our interrogative phrases, we affix *x* [*š*] to the end of the verb." It is *polar* interrogatives that are so formed, and the -*x* is affixed to other parts of speech as well, notably pronouns. Following his intial statement, Vella does give an example of a perfective verb phrase, 'Have you eaten?', which he writes as *Chiltux?* Immediately following that, he gives what he calls 'Conjugation of an interrogative verb', giving the pronominal paradigm in Table 2.

Table 2: Vella's (1834, 249) pronominal polar interrogative paradigm

Jieniex?	Am I?	*Ah'niex?*	Are we?
Intix?	Art thou?	*Intomx?*	Are you?
Hujex?	Is he?	*Humiex?*	Are they?
Hijiex	Is she?		

Vella gives but one example of a sentence with a pronominal polar interrogative:

(13) Maltese
Intomx tah'seb fuku
'Do you think of it?' (Vella 1831, 251)

He does, however, provide a complete paradigm for the verb 'to be' in the past tense and the future.[5] He also gives examples of a few other verbs (Vella 1834, 250–51), noting further that negating any of these constructions involves *ma*:

(14a) Maltese
Affirmative
Th'obbnix?
'Do you love me?' (Vella 1831, 251)

(14b) Negated
Ma th'obbnix int?
'Do you not love me?' (Vella 1831, 252)

Notice that even with the negator, the question remains a polar interrogative. By the time Sutcliffe was writing about Maltese, a full century after Vassalli and Vella, polar interrogative *-š* had become optional, as is evidenced by his explanation that "an interrogation is *frequently* indicated by the addition of the particle -x" (Sutcliffe 1936, 211, emphasis added). Some sixty years after Sutcliffe, in their grammar of Maltese, Borg and Azzopardi (1997, 3–4) document a further delimiting of usage, such that neutral yes–no questions, as they call them, "are characterized by a rising

[5] Vassalli (1827, 1420) gives the paradigm, too, using a script of his own invention to indicate the sound [š], but his examples of usage are all verbs, including *geuš?* 'sono eglino venuti?', *mortuš?* 'siete andati?', *kyltš?* 'hai mangiato?'.

intonation contour," but that it is possible to add what they call "the negative suffix -x to the verb," giving the example *Ħriġtux min l-forn* 'Did you take it out of the oven?'. According to them, it also functions as a tag, and as an obligatory element of indirect questions in the invariable third-person pronoun *hux* meaning 'is it?'.

The reality is more complex. An examination of a Maltese corpus (Wilmsen 2016a) shows that any of the personal pronouns may be used in indirect questions and that they may continue to pose direct polar questions as well:

(15a) Maltese

Pronominal interrogative in indirect question

Ma n-af-x intom-x aware minn-u

not 1SG-know-NEG you(PL)-Q aware PREP-it

'I don't know if you are aware of it' (Wilmsen 2016a, 182)

(15b) Maltese

Pronominal interrogative in direct question with tag

Inti-x ta-ra hux

you.SG-Q 2-see Q

'You do see, don't you?' (Wilmsen 2016a, 185)

Here, the tag *hux* retains the quality of a negator, meaning something like 'is it not?' and, indeed, other such pronominal constructions must be interpreted as negators:[6]

---

[6] See the detailed discussion of negator and interrogative *-x* in Wilmsen (2014, 90–101) and Wilmsen (2016a).

Bħala poplu nistgħu naffordjaw li nħaddnu l-abort, id-divorzju, il-konsumiżmu u l-egoiżmu? Humiex dawn il-perċimeż għad-diżażtri spiritwali li jeżiżtu f' pajjiżna?

As a people, can we afford to embrace abortion, divorce, consumerism, and selfishness? *Are these not* precursors to the spiritual disasters in our country?

(16) Maltese

Humie-x?	*dawn*	*il-perċimeż*	*għa-d-diżażtri*	*spiritwali*
they.are-NEG	these	the-precursors	PREP-the-disasters	spiritual

'[Are] these not precursors to the spiritual disasters?' (Wilmsen 2016a, 185)

Many Arabic dialects also exhibit a polar interrogative *šī*, and some Moroccan Arabic dialects use *wāš*, surely an analogue of the Maltese *hux/huiex* (Procházka and Dallaji 2020, 234). It is evidently an archaic feature dating back at least to Andalusi Arabic and probably earlier.

1.3. Polar Interrogative *šī* in Arabic

Reinhardt (1894, 16, 32) specifically identifies what he calls *fragenden šy* 'question [marker] *šī*' and *die Frage verstärkende ši* 'the question reinforcer *šī*' in the Omani Arabic of the late nineteenth century, a function that it retains to the present day in the dialects that Reinhardt describes.

(17a) Omani Arabic (nineteenth century)

šrub-ti	*ṭāse*	*qahwe*	*waḥdā-ši*	*llé*
drunk-2SG	cup	coffee	one-PQ	ADV

'[Did] you drink one cup of coffee only?' (Reinhardt 1894, 136)

(17b) Omani Arabic (twenty-first century)

waǧaʿ šay fi īdē-š

pain PQ PREP hands-PRO.FSG

'[Is there] pain in your (f)[7] hands?' (Holes 2016, 27)

The same polar interrogative is so common in Levantine dialects of Arabic as to be a hallmark feature.

(18a) Levantine Arabic

ḥāsis bi waǧaʿ ši

feel.PCPT PREP pain PQ

'[Are you] feeling pain?' (own data)

(18b) Levantine Arabic

ʿāmil-ik ši ḍarba ši

do.PCPT-PRO.2FSG QUANT blow PQ

'[Has he] struck you any blow?' (own data)

The first *ši* in (18b) is what has variously been called a partitive (Wilmsen 2014, 51–53), a distributive (Holes 2016, 113), a quantifier (Vanhove 2009), or all three (Wilmsen 2017), corresponding to the English 'some, any', 'certain', 'about/approximately', and even the indefinite determiner 'a'. That, too, is a feature of the bundle in Maltese.

1.4. Quantifier *šī* in Maltese and Arabic

In an exploration of the same phenomenon in Maltese, Vanhove (2009) undertakes an in-depth analysis of its various functions, providing numerous examples (see also Wilmsen 2017, 292–97).

---

[7] The *-š* in *īdē-š* is a palatisation of the second-person possessive feminine pronoun *-ik* 'yours.'

(19a) Maltese

Irrid xi bellus fin

I want some velvet delicate

'I want some delicate velvet' (Vanhove 2009, 22)

(19b) Maltese

Meta kien jara xi għasfura

when he was he sees some bird

'Whenever he saw a bird' (Vanhove 2009, 22)

In example (19b), she glosses *xi* as 'some', but she translates it as the indefinite article 'a' with no inconsistency, as indefinite pronouns and indefinite determiners overlap in meaning. As she observes, "the quantifier *xi* refers to part of a subset of a class and does not pick out the individuals of which it is made up" (Vanhove 2009, 25). This is almost identical to the way Holes (2016, 132) defines what he calls distributives, of which Arabic *šī* is one, as "as denoting 'particular ones from a large group', each defined by some characteristic." This is essentially the same definition as that for partitives (Wilmsen 2014, 51–52).

Hence, Vanhove (2009, 25): "Like in Moroccan Arabic, depending on the context or the extra-linguistic situation, *xi* may highlight more a value of quantitative determination, meaning 'some, a certain number':"

(20) Maltese

xi nies kienu jużawhom

some people they were they use them

'Some people would use them' (Vanhove 2009, 25)

Notably, *xi* can indicate an approximation of numerical values:

(21) Maltese

kien hemm xi mitejn ruħ jisimgħu

was there some hundred.DU soul they listen

'There were about two hundred people listening' (Vanhove 2009, 27)

Notice that, in all these examples, the range of meanings is somewhat interchangeable: '*a certain amount* of velvet', 'he saw *some* bird', '*certain* people use them', and '*some* two hundred people'.

Vanhove provides a convenient summary of the range of values of quantifier *xi* in Maltese, modified here as Table 3.

Table 3: Vanhove's (2009, 32) values of quantifier *xi*

semantic value	syntax
possible element of a class: 'some'	*xi* + sg. noun
indefinite article	*xi* + sg. noun
subset of a class: 'certain'	*xi* + pl. noun
quantitative approximation: 'about'	*xi* + numerals
indefiniteness of noun: 'some'	*xi* + numerals

These are the same values quantifier *šī* expresses in the various Arabic dialects in which it occurs. Among these is Levantine Arabic, in which, as with polar interrogative *šī*, quantifier *šī* is a hallmark feature, and, as in Maltese, can be interpreted as expressing a range of values, as a quantitative, an indefinite determiner, a distributive or partitive, and an approximator.

(22a) Levantine Arabic

b-t-axd-i ši dawā li-l-ġudda?

DUR-2-take-FSG QUANT medicine PREP-DET-gland

'[Do] you take a/any/some medicine for the thyroid?' (own data)

(22b) Levantine Arabic

y-kūn fī ši xabar ʿan-hum yi-farriḥ

3-be EXIST QUANT news PREP-PRO.3PL 3-gladden

ʾalb ahālī-hum

heart families-PRO.3PL

'There may be any/some news about them to gladden the hearts of their families' (own data)

(22c) Levantine Arabic

naṭar-t ši xamas daʾāyiʾ wa mā ḥadā ajā

waited-1SG QUANT five minutes CONJ NEG one came

'I waited about/some five minutes, and no one came' (own data)

The same usage is documented in Omani Arabic from the nineteenth century to the present.

(23a) Omani Arabic (nineteenth century)

fi-l-bistān šay sébö' šegrāt ṯāmrāt

PREP-DET-garden QUANT seven trees fruiting

'In the garden [there are] some seven fruiting trees' (Reinhardt 1894, 69)

(23b) Omani Arabic (nineteenth century)

e-lqa šay xlāf mekān

1SG-find QUANT afterwards place

'I'll find some place later' (Reinhardt 1894, 291)

(23c) Omani Arabic (twenty-first century)

lo kān ʿand-i šē flūs

if was-3MSG to-me some money

'If I had some money' (Davey 2016, 207)

In Omani Arabic too, quantitative *šay* is amenable to alternative readings: 'In the garden there are *about* seven trees', 'I'll find *a* place later', 'If I had *any* money'.

These similarities in function and semantic values are unlikely to have arisen independently in the widely disbursed Arabic sister varieties where they appear. They point in the direction of a common origin in the southern Arabian Peninsula, reaching their dispersal points at various times in the prehistory and sparsely documented history of the migrations of Arabic speakers throughout the Arabian Peninsula, including the Fertile Crescent, and the Mediterranean Basin. It is likely that the bundle of features shared amongst Maltese, Levantine Arabic, and southern peninsular Arabic, represented by Omani Arabic but not restricted to the geographical boundaries of the modern Sultanate of Oman, predates the Islamic era. It happens that the so-called 'Modern' South Arabian languages, the ancestor or ancestors of which are undoubtably older than the so-called Old South Arabian languages, exhibit the same bundle of features as their Arabic and Arabic-derived sisters.

2.0. A South Arabian Analogue

The extant South Arabian languages, the so-called 'Modern' South Arabian languages, possess an analogue of Arabic *šī* (Simeone-Senelle 1997, 419) realised with a lateral fricative [ɬ], which is traditionally represented as [ś] in writings about Semitic languages.

The current homeland of the Modern South Arabian languages is delimited to an area of southern Oman and the south-eastern Yemen, as well as the island of Socotra off the southern coast of the Yemen, but their traditional territories likely encompassed a large part of southeastern Arabia before the Islamic era. The largest and best studied of the Modern South Arabian languages is Mehri, with an estimated current population of some one hundred thousand speakers.

2.1. Quantifier *śī* in Mehri

One of the most frequent uses of the grammatical particle *śī* in Mehri is as a quantifier (Wilmsen 2022a, 633–37 and 661–62)

(24a) Mehri

šī-häm	*śī*	*śaʿār*	*wlī*	*śī*	*šī-häm*	*ḳṣāb*
PREP-PRO.3MPL	QUANT	hay	CONJ	QUANT	PREP- PRO.3MPL	straw

'They have some hay or they have some straw' (Sima 2009, 292)

(24b) Mehri

t-axxarīj	*śī*	*śählīṯ*	*tḥām*	*arbaʿ*
2MSL-extract	QUANT	three	charcoal	four

'You take out three [or] four [pieces of] charcoal' (Sima 2009, 312)

2.2. Polar Interrogative *śī* in Mehri

Less common is the use of *śī* as a polar interrogative (Watson 2012, 241; Wilmsen 2022a, 639–40, 662), but when it does occur, it mirrors Arabic usage.

(25) Mehri

šū-k *mḥanēt* *śī*

PREP-2MSG problem Q

'You have a problem?' (Watson 2012, 241)

2.2. Negations with *śī* in Mehri

The Modern South Arabian languages negate with a reflex of the common Semitic negator *lā* (Sjörs 2018), but they are unusual amongst their Semitic sisters in that standard (that is to say verbal) negation is usually performed by a post-positioned *lā̈*.[8] Negations are often associated with an adjunct *śī*, when they take the configuration V + *śī* + *lā̈*, V + *śī* + N + *lā̈*, or N + *śī* + *lā̈*.

(26a) Mehri

y-ḥasräm *hēh* *lā̈*

3-guard PRO.3MSG NEG

'They don't guard it' (Sima 2009, 298)

(26b) Mehri

nä-woḳfän *śī* *lā̈*

1PL-stop ADJ NEG

'We [do] not stop' (Sima 2009, 516)

[8] Watson (2012, 310–37) gives a detailed explanation of negation in Mehri, noting that the negated element is often, although not always, preceded by an anticipatory negator *al-* or *l-*, which pertains to the discussion below.

(26c) Mehri

n-ḥōmal śī ḳṣāb lā̆

1PL-carry ADJ straw NEG

'We [do] not carry straw' (Sima 2009, 446)

3.0. Discussion: On Cycles and Contacts

Analysing the similarities in negation between Mehri and Arabic varieties, including Maltese, requires interpretation. Recall that those spoken Arabic varieties that use the common Semitic *lā* generally restrict it to prohibitives, undertaking standard negation with *mā*, which is itself unusual in Semitic languages (Sjörs 2018, 242–49, 395–96), and some of them, including Maltese, affix *š(i)* to the end of the verb.

3.1. A Jespersen Cycle in Arabic?

The prevailing opinion in Arabic dialectology is that negation with post-positioned *-ši* or reflexes thereof constitutes a stage of a cycle that is operable in standard negation, dubbed the Jespersen cycle after the Danish linguist Otto Jespersen, who proposed that, over the life of a language, as verbal negations become associated with adjuncts, such as *pas* 'step' in French (the characteristic example), those adjuncts may eventually overtake the entire process of negation (Lucas 2007, 398–400). Although the assumption has long been that negation in the Arabic dialects resembles that in French, the Arabic phenomena were not specifically identified as a Jespersen cycle until Lucas (2007) named them as such.[9]

[9] Watson (2012, 310–11) embraces the notion as applying to *al* + V + (*śī*) + *lā̆* negations where they occur in Mehri.

It is unnecessary here to outline the dynamics of the cycle as it is assumed to operate in Arabic in depth, because its contours have by now become thoroughly familiar in the discourse of Arabic dialectology, as recently summarised by Diem (2014, 100–2), who expresses some reservations about it. In brief, it is said in Arabic to follow an arc from negation with *mā* alone, through negation augmented with the adjunct *š(i)*, to negation with *š(i)* alone, as follows:

Stage I: *mā* + V > Stage II: *mā* + V + *š(i)* > Stage III: V + *š(i)*

Amongst themselves, Arabic varieties do exhibit all these forms of standard negation, some exhibiting all of them together. Palestinian Arabic is held to be the characteristic example of this latter type (Lucas 2010), but the reality is that it occurs throughout Levantine varieties of Arabic in Lebanon, Syria, Jordan, and Palestine (see discussion and references in Khairallah 2014, 25–37). The following are all from a northern Lebanese dialect of Arabic, the mountain village dialect of Zeitoun, about an hour's drive north of Beirut:

(27a) Northern Lebanese Arabic (Zeitoun)

mā šil-nā-hon

NEG lift/carry/take1PL-PRO.3PL

(27b) Northern Lebanese Arabic (Zeitoun)

mā šil-nā-hon-š

NEG lift/carry/take1PL-PRO.3PL-NEG

'We [did] not take them' (Khairallah 2014, 42)

It is notable that the prohibitive in the spoken Arabic of Zeitoun may be formed by an enclitic *-š* in the same configuration as the

Maltese prohibitive, but it may also be formed without the second-person marker *t-*.

(28a) Northern Lebanese Arabic (Zeitoun)

ti-ns-ī-š *amīṣt-ik*

2-forget-FSG-PRH shirt-PRO.2FSG

'Don't forget your shirt' (Khairallah 2014, 46)

(28b) Northern Lebanese Arabic (Zeitoun)

xāf-ī-š *ʿa* *Maureen*

scared-FSG-PRH PREP personal name

'Don't worry about Maureen' (Khairallah 2014, 46)

Verbs in both the imperfective and the perfective may also be negated with an enclitic *-ši* alone (Khairallah 2014, 29–30, 46–47).

In the context of a Jespersen cycle, the variability in this dialect would be interpreted as exhibiting a transitional stage between negation with a preposed element alone and negation with a postposed element alone. Indeed, it is taken as *prima facie* evidence of the working of the cycle in Arabic. In that regard, Reinhardt's presentation of negation in the Omani Arabic of the late nineteenth century presents something of a conundrum. He documents only two types of negation: either with *mā* or *lā* alone or with enclitic *-ši* alone (Reinhardt 1894, 137):[10]

---

[10] Lucas (2007, 403) misreads Reinhardt as representing Omani Arabic as negating with the discontinuous *mā* + V + *š(i)*: "A stage II construction is (generally speaking) the unmarked structure for expressing sentential negation in Arabic varieties spoken… in parts of Oman and on Zanzibar."

> *Das Zeitwort wird verneint 1. durch* mā *oder* lā. *Das erstere steht vor dem Perfect* [sic] *und Imperfect, des letztere nur vor dem Imperfect; 2. durch angehängtes* ši.
>
> The verb is negated 1. by *mā* or *lā*. The former comes before the perfect and imperfect, the latter only before the imperfect; 2. by added *ši*.

For example:

(29a) Omani Arabic (nineteenth century)

mā tü-fhem h-al-kelām

NEG 2-understand DEM-DET-talk

'You [do] not understand this talk' (Reinhardt 1894, 145)

(29b) Omani Arabic (nineteenth century)

hāḏā il-xaṭṭ yu-n-qrī-ši

NEG DET-handwriting DEM-DET-talk

'This handwriting [is] not read' [= 'cannot be read'] (Reinhardt 1894, 231)

Had negation with enclitic *-ši* alone been the end state of a Jespersen cycle in Omani Arabic, remnants of an intermediary stage II, exhibiting the bipartite construction *mā* + V + *š*(*i*), would be expected. But there are none. So, too, might it be expected that all but a few remnants of negation with a preposed *mā* would have vanished. Instead, it is negation with enclitic *-ši* that has largely vanished, leaving a few relicts behind, and negation with *mā* that predominates. This change has apparently come about through contact with an inter-regional Arabian Gulf idiom to which the dialects of Oman are gradually succumbing (Holes

2012, 245; Morano 2022, 250), a process that would be external to and disruptive of the operation of a Jespersen cycle.[11]

Be that as it may, Reinhardt's documentation of negation effectuated solely with enclitic *-ši* in a variety or varieties of Omani Arabic of the nineteenth century, with no trace of a presumed intermediary stage of a Jespersen cycle, might be interpreted as indicating that the cycle had proceeded to a stage III in so remote a past that relicts of an intermediate stage had long since disappeared from the dialect(s). This explanation would leave the stages of a Jespersen cycle in other Arabic dialects as requiring further explication.

The hypothesis that stages II and III of a Jespersen cycle arose in or around the Mediterranean multiple times independently and relatively late and spread to Oman by means of trade (Lucas 2007, 415) is uncongenial. It is highly unlikely that a feature that is so similar across the Arabic dialects in which it appears arose independently over and over again. Owens (2006, 156) maintains that in historical linguistics of Arabic, "unless the high degree of similarity is due to chance independent development, it has to be assumed that the similar contemporary populations must have at one time shared a common ancestor." As for the feature spreading to Oman by way of coastal entrepots (Lucas 2007, 215–16), Reinhardt describes dialect(s) from the interior, which in his day would have been remote from the coast and

[11] Diem (2014, 102) suggests that a completion of the cycle might involve a return to negation with *mā* alone. Compare Watson and Rowlett (2012, 207), who propose that Mehri is "showing signs of moving to a stage I."

singularly isolated, although they are nowadays reachable from Muscat by paved roads within about an hour and a half (Holes 2012, 241).

3.2. Contact Phenomena—Which Way?

Recent work with Mehri (Wilmsen 2022a; Wilmsen and Al-Taei 2022–2023) suggests that negation with enclitic *šī* may well have come into the Arabic dialects of southern Arabia through contact with ancestors to the Modern South Arabian languages. It happens that Lucas (2020, 653–60) partly agrees with this, regarding the stages of a Jespersen cycle arising where they did in Arabic as a contact phenomenon. He identifies five contact languages, the speakers of which are and indeed have been in contact with Arabic: Berber varieties, with a bipartite structure *ul… kra*; Coptic, whose negators are *en… an*; Domari, with negators *n… eʾ*, Kumsari with a sole post-positioned *…na*; and, tellingly, Modern South Arabian, which may sometimes negate with *al …laʔ*. There are complicating circumstances, which Lucas acknowledges, with the languages in question mutually reinforcing their respective negation patterns.

Regardless, assuming five separate contacts as motivating a Jespersen cycle in Arabic is problematic. If contact really were the motivator for the development of bipartite negation in Arabic, the dialects utilising bipartite negation or negation with an enclitic -*š*(*i*) will not have arrived at those stages—or more correctly *states*—by undergoing cyclic change but by coming into contact with languages that exhibit those states. What is more, it is unlikely that all varieties in which bipartite negation or enclitic negation occurs will have converged upon the same enclitic -*š*(*ī*), when none of the negative enclitic negators of the contact languages resembles it. It also assumes that the contact in southern Arabia must have taken place after the beginning of the Islamic era.

In this regard, Lucas (2020, 655) envisions a mechanism by which speakers of Modern South Arabian languages will have imposed a bipartite construction on Arabic, their second language, by reanalysing a presumably borrowed Arabic *šī/šay* as a negator. Aside from the fact that *śī* is not a negator in Modern South Arabian languages, there is new evidence for Arabic speakers living close to or amongst speakers of languages ancestral to the Modern South Arabian languages in the centuries before the Islamic era (Wilmsen 2022a, 646–48). This provides a deeper diachrony for contact-induced change to appear and a simpler mechanism for a borrowing to occur.

Arabic speakers who were in the habit of negating with *mā* alone, when hearing negation in Modern South Arabian languages with V + *śī* + *lā̆* and V + *śī* + N + *lā̆*, could easily have misinterpreted *śī* as the verbal negator, with *lā̆*, derived from a common Semitic negator that they both share, as a pro-sentential negator placed at the end of the utterance for emphasis. Hearing things thus, they could have adopted *śī*, which they would have realised as *šī*, as an alternative negation pattern to their native *mā*.[12] This would explain the presence of the enclitic -*šī* negator

[12] An indication that *śī* is a borrowing into Arabic is that Modern South Arabian Languages possess [š] as well as [ś], whereas Arabic has [š] only (Wilmsen 2022a, 645).

with verbs in the Omani Arabic of the nineteenth century: it was a feature incorporated into Omani Arabic, and, indeed, other Arabic varieties of the southern Arabian Peninsula, where similar features are attested (Wilmsen 2022a, 652), by exposure to languages ancestral to the Modern South Arabian languages.

This in turn can explain the otherwise extraordinarily odd negation patterns in nineteenth-century Omani Arabic, which, according to Reinhardt's attestations, can negate anything with an enclitic *šī* (see also Morano 2022, 247–48). This type of negation is so vanishingly rare in other varieties of Arabic as to be nonexistent. In Modern South Arabian languages, on the other hand, for whatever reason, the negator may often be paired with an adjunct *śī* to form *śī lā̆*, which appears at the end of the sentence, adjacent to any part of speech. Watson (2012, 310) observes, "the main *l*-based negative particle generally follows the whole proposition even where the negated term is the initial element." In such constructions, it is difficult to assess the intended meaning of *śī*, but *śī lā̆* constructions are, nevertheless, common in Mehri.

(30a) Mehri

lā̆kan	*lyōmäh*	*y-näfʿam*	*män*	*śī*	*lā̆*
but	DEM	3-benefit	PREP	ADJ	NEG

'But these are of no use' (Sima 2009, 58)

(30b) Mehri

y-ḥōkam	*ḥābū*	*śī*	*lā̆*
3-judge	people	ADJ	NEG

'People [did] not judge' (Sima 2009, 250)

3.3. Original Modern South Arabian *śī*

Quite possibly the original function of Modern South Arabian *śī* was as an existential particle, bearing a meaning analogous to English 'there is/was' (Wilmsen 2022a, 648–56). In Mehri, N + *śī lǟ* and *śī* + N + *lǟ* constructions are often existential negations.

(31a) Mehri

xadmǟt śī lǟ

work EXIST NEG

(31b) Mehri

śī xadmǟt lǟ

EXIST work NEG

'There was no work' (Sima 2009, 422)

Less often, *śī* appears in affirmative existential predications.

(32) Mehri

śī xarrayt būmäh

EXIST hole DEM

'There [is a] hole here' (Sima 2009, 156)

Omani Arabic and other dialects of the southern Arabian Peninsula have an exact analogue, realised variably as *šay*, *šē*, or *šī* (Davey 2016, 171, 180, 223; Holes 2016, 24–26). Reinhardt attested it in the Omani Arabic of his day, and it was attested in all dialects of the southern and eastern Arabian Peninsula soon afterwards (see discussion and references in Wilmsen and Al-Taei 2022–2023).

(33a) Omani Arabic (nineteenth century)

mā šay yi-ṭlaʿ ʿan-i minn-he ʾlle rabb-i

NEG EXIST 3-elevate PREP-PRO.1SG PREP-PRO.3MSG PREP lord-PRO.1SG

'There [is] not [anyone to] lift from me from it except my Lord' (Reinhardt 1894, 297)

(33b) Omani Arabic (nineteenth century)

šay baʿdo tāife saġīra

EXIST ADV tribe small

'There [is] still [a] small tribe' (Reinhardt 1894, 423)

It is worth noting that Reinhardt attests *mā šī* less often than the odd construction *šīši*, comprising both an existential particle *šī* and a negator *ši*. This is the negative existential that Morano (2022, 252) reports as surviving in modern interior dialects of Oman.

(34) Omani Arabic (twenty-first century)

šī ši šay hnā

EXIST NEG CONJ DET

'There [is] nothing here' (Morano 2022, 252)

The more common negative existential throughout the Omani Arabic of the twenty-first century is *mā ši*, which Reinhardt (1894, 30) also attests.

(35) Omani Arabic (twenty-first century)

šay šāy wallā mā šī

EXIST tea CONJ NEG EXIST

'[Is] there tea or [is] there not?' (Wilmsen and Al-Taei 2022–2023, 100)

It is also worth noting that the perception is that *mā šay/šē/šī* is less common than *mā fī*, but recent work shows the opposite. Affirmative existential predications are more common with *fī*, but their negations are more common with *mā šī* (Wilmsen and Al-Taei 2022–2023, 100–2).

The reasons for this are of little relevance to the matter at hand (see the discussion in Wilmsen and Al-Taei 2022–2023, 102–3). More relevant is that an existential particle *šay/šē/šī* is highly unusual in Arabic, almost entirely restricted to the varieties of the southern peninsula, in the dialects of the Yemen, Oman, the United Arab Emirates, and Bahrain. This is perhaps the best indicator that it and the bundle of features associated with it are original to the Modern South Arabian languages, or, more precisely, to their ancestor or ancestors, and that it and they were adopted by Arabic speakers resident in the same areas of the southern Arabian Peninsula in which the ancestors to the Modern South Arabian speaking peoples lived.

Relevant, too, is that a polar interrogative and partitive or quantifier *šay/šē/šī* can derive from the existential, by way of a tag question 'is it?', and a subjunctive 'be it' (Wilmsen and Al-Taei 2022–2023, 97, 109).

4.0. Closing the Cycle: Maltese Connections

Of course, existential *šī* is not part of this particular South Arabian/Lebanese bundle in Maltese, which possesses another unusual existential particle: *hemm*, meaning both 'there' and 'there is/are' (Vanhove 2009, 19–20). This is itself a feature of apparent southern peninsular origin, deriving from an archaic Arabic distal demonstrative *ṯamma* 'there', reflexes of which are found only in writing and in spoken southern peninsular dialects of Arabic (Behnstedt 2016, 164–65). It may have come to Maltese either by way of Tunisian Arabic, which has *ṯamma* or *famma*, or Andalusi Arabic, which had the two as well (Institute of Islamic Studies of the University of Zaragoza 2013, 22, 106). Aside from Maltese, they are the only other Arabic varieties to use it existentially.

This, too, is a testament to the diachronic depth of Maltese, or, to put it more precisely, to the diachronic depth of features of Maltese. The earliest evidence of the use of an Arabic existential particle is, in fact, *ṯamma*, in Qur'ān 2:115: 'Wherever you turn, *there* is the face of Allah' فَأَيْنَمَا تُوَلُّواْ فَثَمَّ وَجْهُ اللهِ. In the other three instances of ثَمَّ in the Qur'ān, it is unambiguously a deictic adverbial, and, indeed, it may be so interpreted here too. It is, nevertheless, unambiguously an existential form in Tunisian and Andalusi Arabic, and it may have reached Malta's shores from either of those sources or both.

With regard to possible Andalusi sources of features of Maltese, Professor Zammit (2009–2010, 57) makes a trenchant point and sounds a cautionary note regarding the possibility of multiple sources for the Arabic matrix of Maltese:

> Andalusi Arabic and Maltese had access to common and rather archaic sources of Arabic. However, they were not necessarily exposed to the same diffusion patterns, nor did they inevitably follow the same evolutionary paths. Nevertheless, in view of the role played by the Aragonese in Malta's medieval past, and given that Andalusi Morisco elements interacted with the Maltese islands, and some even settled in these islands, one cannot exclude the eventuality

> that a number of Andalusi Arabic elements must have reached Malta directly through these channels.

The bundle of features in Maltese that have evidently derived from the South Arabian *śī* may have been reinforced by input from al-Andalus or Tunisia. Tunisian Arabic does exhibit a distributive and polar interrogative *šī* (Wilmsen 2014, 111–115; 2017, 292), but they seem to be developing along their own evolutionary paths, as Professor Zammit names them. For example, the use of *šī* as a polar interrogative in Tunisian Arabic appears to be on the wane as compared to its usage from fifty years ago (Procházka and Dallaji 2020, 239). Regardless, the features of *šī* likely did come to Maltese from Tunis, and likely from Andalusi Arabic, too. Nevertheless, they are also likely to have come from the input of Levantine Arabic dialects, where reflexes of *šī* remain vital.

The Levantine Arabic dialects themselves were surely influenced by influxes of Arabic speakers from the southern peninsula. It is known that there were population pulses from the southern peninsula into the Fertile Crescent in the centuries before Islam. The same sorts of population influxes will have informed the Arabic matrix of Maltese. The Aghlabids, who entered Sicily and likely Malta from Tunisia in the ninth century, were originally from Najd, the north central plateau of the Arabian Peninsula. The Fatimids replaced the Aghlabids in North Africa and Sicily, which they ruled briefly, before appointing the Kalbids as governors of Sicily (Jiwa 2024). The Kalbids, who established an independent emirate there, and who controlled the islands for the longest period, came from Syria and in pre-Islamic times were members of a tribal confederacy of southern peninsular origin. They were also involved in the conquest of al-Andalus.

Little is known about the Arabic of Sicily, but it should be clear from this brief review of the successive Arab dynasties to rule in Sicily that the Arabic spoken there would itself have received multiple inputs, as Manwel Mifsud (2008, 146) says of Maltese, "from different Arab stations and at different points in the island's history." So, too, of Maltese, which, it is generally accepted, descended from the varieties of Arabic spoken on Sicily.

The early formation of the Arabic regional dialects, too, involved contact with, and the absorption of multiple influences from, numerous varieties of Arabic. In such a situation, it is meaningless to speak of a cyclic development of bipartite or solely post-positioned negation within the language. There are too many competing influences militating against a linear progression of stages. It would have been, and likely was, a natural process for Arabic speakers in the Levant, who were accustomed to form negations with *mā* or *lā*, when encountering emigrant speakers of southern Arabian dialects negating with *mā* alone or *šī* alone, to adopt those negations and to begin applying their own *mā* to the enclitic *šī* negations that they were hearing, retaining the negation with enclitic *šī* as an alternate form.

That is as good an explanation as any for the high variability in negation forms throughout Levantine varieties of Arabic. It also goes a long way towards explaining the South Arabian and Levantine elements in Maltese.

The bundle of features derived from existential *šay/šē/šī* is found variously in varieties of Arabic outside the southern Arabian Peninsula, but only the Levantine dialects and Maltese exhibit all of them consistently. Egyptian Arabic can form an enclitic *šī* prohibitive, but apparently not as consistently as do Levantine dialects; it has a disjunctive *iši*, but one that is not otherwise used as a quantitative or partitive; and it had a polar interrogative *šī* attested in the nineteenth century (Wilmsen and Al-Sayyed 2019, 11). North African dialects of Arabic do variously retain a polar interrogative and a partitive *šī*, but no enclitic *šī* prohibitive.

5.0. Conclusions

Regardless of their origin, the consistency in form and function of the bundle of features of reflexes of *šī* in Levantine varieties of Arabic and of reflexes of *xi* in Maltese, along with their attestation in an Arabic variety of the southern Arabian Peninsula of the nineteenth century and their survival in the entire dialect area of the southern peninsula, do, indeed, attest to the diachronic depth of Maltese. To put it more correctly, they attest to the diachronic depth of the individual features or bundles of features of Maltese. Maltese itself cannot extend any further back in time than the ninth century, but its many Arabic elements are older. The Arabic elements of Maltese are unlikely to have a linear descent from any single Arabic variety. Professor Zammit's work with the many Arabic lexical forms of diverse origins had already suggested this.

Abbreviations

ADJ	adjunct	NEG	negator
CONJ	conjunction	PL	plural
DEM	demonstrative	PRH	prohibitive
DET	determiner	PRO	pronoun
DU	dual	PTCP	participle
DUR	durative aspect particle	PQ	polar interrogative
		Q	interrogative
EXIST	existential particle	QUANT	quantifier
FSG	feminine singular	SG	singular
IMP	imperative	1	1st person
MPL	masculine plural	2	2nd person
MSG	masculine singular	3	3rd person

References

Behnstedt, Peter. 2016. *Dialect Atlas of North Yemen and Adjacent Areas*. Leiden: Brill.

Borg, Albert, and Marie Azzopardi-Alexander. 1997. *Maltese*. London: Routledge.

Davey, Richard J. 2016. *Coastal Dhofari Arabic: A Sketch Grammar*. Leiden: Brill.

Diem, Werner. 2014. *Negation in Arabic: A Study in Linguistic History*. Wiesbaden: Harrassowitz.

Holes, Clive. 2004. *Modern Arabic: Structures, Functions, and Varieties*. Washington, DC: Georgetown University Press.

———. 2012. 'The Omani Arabic Dialects in Their Regional Context: Yesterday, Today, and Tomorrow'. In *Building Bridges: Integrating Language, Linguistics, Literature and Translation in*

English Studies, edited by Najma Al Zidjaly, 233–48. Newcastle upon Tyne: Cambridge Scholars.

———. 2016. *Dialect, Culture, and Society in Eastern Arabia*. Vol. 3, *Phonology, Morphology, Syntax, Style.* Leiden: Brill.

Institute of Islamic Studies of the University of Zaragoza (ed.). 2013. *A Descriptive and Comparative Grammar of Andalusi Arabic.* Leiden: Brill.

Jiwa, Shainool. 2024. 'The Kalbids of Sicily: Stalwarts of Fāṭimid Ifrīqiya'. In *Muslim Sicily: Encounters and Legacy*, edited by Nuha Alshaar, 73–95. Edinburgh: Edinburgh University Press.

Khairallah, Natalie Maroun. 2014. 'Negation in the Lebanese Dialect of Zeitoun, Keserwan: An Examination of Claims, Concepts, and Usage'. MA thesis, American University of Beirut.

Lucas, Christopher. 2007. 'Jespersen's Cycle in Arabic and Berber'. *Transactions of the Philological Society* 105 (3): 398–431.

———. 2010. 'Negative *-š* in Palestinian (and Cairene) Arabic: Present and Possible Past'. *Brill's Annual of Afroasiatic Languages and Linguistics* 2: 165–201.

———. 2020. 'Contact and the Expression of Negation'. In *Arabic and Contact-induced Change,* edited by Christopher Lucas and Stefano Manfredi, 643–67. Berlin: Language Science Press.

Mifsud, Manwel. 2008. 'Maltese'. In *Encyclopedia of Arabic Language and* Linguistics, edited by Kees Versteegh, Mushira

Eid, Alaa Elgibaly, Manfred Woidich, and Andrzej Zaborski, 146–59. Leiden: Brill.

Morano, Roberta. 2022. *Diachronic Variation in the Omani Arabic Vernacular of the Al-ʿAwābī District: From Carl Reinhardt (1894) to the Present Day*. Cambridge: Cambridge University Press.

Owens, Jonathan. 2006. *A Linguistic History of Arabic*. Oxford: Oxford University Press.

Procházka, Stephan, and Ines Dallaji. 2020. 'Polar Question in Tunis Arabic'. In *Studies on Arabic Dialectology and Sociolinguistics: Proceedings of the 13th International Conference of AIDA*, edited by Guram Chikovani and Zviad Tskhvediani, 233–40. Kutaisi: Akaki Tsreteli State University Press.

Reinhardt, Carl. 1894. *Ein arabischer Dialekt gesprochen in ʿOman und Zanzibar, nach praktischen Gesichtspunkten für das Seminar für orientalische sprachen in Berlin*. Stuttgart: W. Spemann.

Sima, Alexander. 2009. *Mehri-Texte aus der jemenitischen Sharqīyah: Transkribiert unter Mitwirkung von ʿAskari Saʿd Hugayrān*. Wiesbaden: Harrassowitz.

Simeone-Senelle, Marie-Claude. 1997. 'The Modern South Arabian Languages'. In *The Semitic Languages*, edited by Robert Hetzron, 378–423. London: Routledge.

Sjörs, Ambjörn. 2018. *Historical Aspects of Standard Negation in Semitic*. Leiden: Brill.

Sutcliffe, Edmond. 1936. *A Grammar of the Maltese Language: With Chrestomathy and Vocabulary*. London: Oxford University Press.

Vanhove, Martine. 2009. 'The Nominal Quantifier *xi* in Maltese'. In *Maltese Linguistics: A Snapshot—In Memory of Joseph A. Cremona (1922–2003)*, edited by Ray Fabri, 17–34. Bochum: Brockmeyer.

Vassalli, Michelantonio. 1827. *Grammatica della Lingua Maltese*. Malta: Stampata per l'Autore.

Vella, Francis. 1831. *Maltese Grammar for the Use of the English*. Leghorn: Glaucus Masi.

Watson, Janet C. E. 2012. *The Structure of Mehri*. Wiesbaden: Harrassowitz.

Watson, Janet C. E., and Paul Rowlett. 2012. 'Jespersen's Cycle and Negation in Mehri'. In *Grammaticalization in Semitic*, edited by Domenyk Eades, 205–25. Oxford: Oxford University Press.

Wilmsen, David. 2014. *Arabic Indefinites, Interrogatives, and Negators: A History of Western Dialects*. Oxford: Oxford University Press.

———. 2016a. 'Polar Interrogative *-š* in Maltese: Developments and Antecedents'. In *Shifts and Patterns in Maltese*, edited by Gilbert Puesch and Benjamin Saade, 79–102. Berlin: De Gruyter Mouton.

———. 2016b. 'The Dehortative in the Spoken Arabics of the Eastern Mediterranean'. *Romano-Arabica* 16: 133–50.

———. 2017. 'Grammaticalization and Degrammaticalization in an Arabic Existential Particle *šay*'. *Folia Orientalia* 54: 279–307.

———. 2022a. 'The Enigma of Mehri and South Peninsular Arabic Existential *Śī* and *Šī*'. *Journal of Semitic Studies* 67 (2): 627–63.

———. 2022b. 'Extensions and Commonalities of Negative Existential Cycles in Arabic'. In *The Negative Existential Cycle*, edited by Arja Hamari and Ljuba Veselinova, 141–72. Berlin: Language Sciences Press.

Wilmsen, David, and Amany Al-Sayyed. 2019. 'On Morpho-Syntactic Levantisms in Maltese'. In *Studies on Arabic Dialectology and Sociolinguistics: Proceedings of the 12th International AIDA Conference*, edited by Catherine Miller, Alexandrine Barontini, Mari Aimeé Germanos, Jairo Guerrero, and Cristophe Pereira. Aix-en-Provence: Institut de recherches et d'études sur le monde arabe et musulman. https://books.openedition.org/iremam/4180?lang=en, accessed 28 September 2023.

Wilmsen, David, and Al-Baylasan Al-Taei. 2022–2023. 'Revisiting Reinhardt: The Status of Omani Arabic Grammatical *šay/šē/šī* in the Early Twenty-first Century'. *Al-ʿArabiyya* 56: 93–119.

Zammit, Martin. 2006. 'Unrecognizable Arabic-Maltese: The Innovative "Maltese" Element in the Maltese Language'. In *L'arabe dialectal: Enquêtes, descriptions, interprétations—Actes d'AIDA 6; Travaux offerts au Professeur Taieb Baccouche*, edited by Salah Mejri, 487–98. Tunis: Imprimerie Officielle de la République Tunisienne.

———. 2009. 'South Arabian Loanwords'. In *Encyclopedia of Arabic Language and Linguistics*, edited by Kees Versteegh, Mushira Eid, Alaa Elgibali, Manfred Woidich, and Andrzej Zaborski, 295–97. Leiden: Brill.

———. 2009–2010. 'Andalusi Arabic and Maltese: A Preliminary Survey'. *Folia Orientalia* 45–46: 21–60.

———. 2020. 'Andalusi Arabic Catechisms and the First Maltese Catechisms'. In *Studies on Arabic Dialectology and Sociolinguistics: Proceedings of the 13th International Conference of AIDA*, edited by Guram Chikovani and Zviad Tskhvediani, 498–507. Kutaisi: Akaki Tsreteli State University Press.

SOUL INSPIRATION FROM WADI EL NATRUN: OSTRICH EGGS AS REMINDERS OF VIGILANCE IN PRAYING

Ioana Feodorov

1.0. Introduction[1]

For the symbolism of the egg as matrix of life, the researcher has at his disposal numerous dictionaries of symbols, where the conventional information is often repeated. However, there are considerably fewer written sources on the symbolism of the ostrich and the ostrich egg. Michel Cazenave's *Encyclopédie des symboles* does not mention the ostrich egg *s.v. Oeuf*, a section otherwise rich in information collected from all cultures and times (Cazenave 1996, 469–70). In the *Birds* section by Manabu Waida included in *The Encyclopedia of Religion* edited by Mircea Eliade, the symbolism of many birds (eagle, hawk, falcon, pigeon, raven,

[1] I extend warm thanks to all who provided me with insights, sources, and images during this research: Mihai Țipău, Archim. Policarp Chițulescu, Emanuela Timotin, Maria Magdalena Székely, Ioana Munteanu, Andrei Timotin, Ovidiu Olar, Fr Anania at the Putna Monastery, Oana Iacubovschi, Adina and Marius Ristea.

 https://doi.org/10.11647/OBP.0445.13

nightingale, goose, etc.) is explained, but not that of the ostrich (Waida 1987, 2:225–26).

In a recent study, Nile Green (2006, 29) called ostrich eggs and peacock feathers “the most wonderful and mysterious products of the animal world.” Yet, the ostrich is a creature misunderstood since ancient times. Its behaviour in the colony it creates for itself and how it ensures the perpetuation of the species have given rise to fanciful explanations and contradictory attitudes towards it, from criticism of its indifference to its young to admiration of its dedication to their care. The ostrich’s way of ensuring the perpetuation of its species is so clever and elaborate that it has become a topic of extensive surveys, including applied research. A study funded by the Food and Agriculture Organisation of the United Nations (FAO) appeared in *Ostrich Production Systems* by Dr M. M. Shanawany and Dr John Dingle (1999). So, let us start with scientific information.

2.0. The Ostrich and Its Eggs

2.1. The Ostrich, a Remarkable Bird

The wild ostrich is a huge bird (weighing up to 120 kg) that has always lived in the desert and on the arid plains of Africa, particularly in the region south of Alexandria, where the first communities of Anchorites, founded by Paul of Thebaide, Antony the Great, and Pachomius, appeared in the fourth century. In the Mediterranean basin, the ostrich has been known since the fifth century BC (Cazenave 1996, 61). Studied more carefully since the eighteenth century, the ostrich family was given the scientific name *Struthio camelus* in Linnaeus’ *Systema naturae* (1707–1778), *struthio* for 'ostrich' and *camelus* 'camel' in relation to its arid habitat (and perhaps the shape of its foot, which seemingly resembled a camel's hoof). In Arabic, the two words *naʿam*, 'herbivorous animals' (col.), i.e., sheep, camels, cows, and goats, and *naʿām*, 'ostriches' (col.), are part of the same word family, derived from the root *n–ʿ–m*. This terminological closeness may reflect the feeling of Arabic speakers that the ostrich is an animal related to a quadruped. There was also an Arabian species, *Struthio camelus syriacus*, now extinct, which lived in the Sinai Peninsula, in the territory of present-day Syria, and the Arabian Peninsula. *Struthio camelus camelus* is the name of the largest species of ostrich, which produces the largest bird egg in the world: c. 18 cm long and 15 cm wide, and weighing 1900 g, equivalent to 25 chicken eggs, it can support a weight of 250 kg without breaking.

A male ostrich mates with two to seven females in the same season, giving birth to a colony. After 10–14 days, the females begin to lay eggs in a circular nest, previously dug by the ostrich for the strongest female, which is the first to lay eggs and becomes the hatcher for the whole nest. Its eggs remain in the centre and the other females lay eggs around them. Thus, in the event of an attack by a predator (jackal, hyena, snake, bird of prey, mongoose), the less viable eggs are more exposed. The ostrich has always had a host of predators that have sought to steal its eggs, endangering the perpetuation of the species. Up to 60 eggs are laid in the nest, but only 15% will hatch. The female hatches during the day and the male at night, taking it in turns to guard the nest, which is never left unattended for about 40 days until hatching. Cooperation between family members and the organisation of nest guarding make the ostrich a special case in the world of wild birds.

The earliest mentions of the parable of the ostrich are present in the Old Testament: Leviticus 11.16; Deuteronomy 14.15; Job 30.29; 39.13; 39.16; Isaiah 13.21; 34.13; 43.20; Jeremiah 50.39; Lamentations 4.3; and Micah 1.8. Thomas J. Kraus (2019) compiled inventories of the creatures with symbolic value mentioned in Leviticus and Deuteronomy that are found in versions of the *Physiologus*, some of which discuss the ostrich. While some biblical passages only refer to the ostrich as one of the 'beasts of the wilderness' (alongside the jackal), others give details of its behaviour in the nest. In Job 39.14–16, it is said: "When she lays her eggs on the ground and lets them hatch in the hot sand, / She forgets that someone may trample them underfoot and some wild beast may crush them. / The ostrich is as fond of her young as if they were not her own and cares nothing for her vain toil."

Aristotle included the Libyan ostrich in Part IV of his *On the Parts of Animals*, stating that "it has hooves, like the quadrupeds." In his *Natural History* X.1, Pliny the Elder (d. 79 AD) adds that the ostrich can eat anything. Other ancient authors who mention the ostrich are Diodorus of Sicily; Claudius Aelianus; Saint Augustine (originally from Hippo, a settlement in North Africa); Saint Isidor, bishop of Seville; and Albertus Magnus (Green 2006, 34; Crețu 2020, 409–415). Those who wrote about ostriches in early times had a poor understanding of their behaviour. This led to ideas that lasted for centuries, such as: ostriches can eat iron, which they digest, having a very acidic gastric juice (Duchet-Suchaux and Pastoureau 2002, 30), and even red-hot coals; and the female ostrich hatches the egg only by staring at it for a long time, the egg being thus heated until it hatches, and the young mysteriously emerge (Cazenave 1996, 61–62). Green (2006, 34) notes that the former belief had a very long posterity, since Shakespeare has Jack Cade, a character in *Henry VI, Part 2* (act 4, scene 10, l. 29), threaten: "I shall make thee eat iron like an ostrich." The ostrich is shown in western bestiaries wearing a nail or a horseshoe in its beak, to distinguish it from other birds depicted in miniatures (Duchet-Suchaux and Pastoureau 2002, 31; Pastoureau 2011, 159).

The ostrich's life and behaviour were common knowledge for the Sketis desert residents and, among them, the first monks who established hermitic life in that uncomfortable environment. From the fourth century onwards, the ostrich appears as a character in the early monastic writings known as *Apophtegmata Patrum*, the spiritual teachings of the desert fathers and mothers. Along with the camel, pig, satyr, and centaur, it is one of the desert animals mentioned in the teachings of Saint Anthony the Great of Egypt (c. 251–356), the father of monasticism (Agaybi and Vivian 2022, 38, 57).

The ostrich is mentioned in the earliest versions of the Greek *Physiologus*, an anonymous writing composed in the late second or early third century in the Christian milieu of Alexandria, Egypt, which was among the most widely translated works both in the East (in Coptic, Geʿez, Syriac, Arabic, Armenian, and Georgian) and the West (in Latin and Slavic languages). As is well known, the name of this work means *The Naturalist*, and it refers to the anonymous author of this short treatise on the natural sciences, dedicated to c. 40 animals. The journey of the ostrich legend to Europe was due to the Latin versions of the Greek *Physiologus*, which gave rise to the bestiaries composed in the West from the fourth century onwards, in Romance and Germanic languages. Closest to the Latin *Physiologus* is the French bestiary composed by Pierre de Beauvais in the early thirteenth century (Bianciotto 1980, 19).

Based on two manuscripts in the Bibliothèque nationale de France, Émile Legrand (1873) published, in his work *Le Physiologus, poème sur la nature des animaux en grec vulgaire et en vers politiques*, a Greek edition of this work and its French translation. The chapter on the ostrich also appears in the 1936 critical edition by Francesco Sbordone, who consulted 77 manuscripts (Sbordone 1936). Here is the passage on the ostrich from the Legrand edition (Legrand 1873, 116). The English translation is mine.

> The ostrich is a big, beautiful bird, / his neck is long like a camel's,
> His head like a viper's, his back arched, / He has strong wings and flies a little.
> It eats iron, eats nails, / his stomach is warm and immediately devours them all, / the male goes along with the female / and they nest, lay two eggs, sit and heat them with their eyes.
> When the female stays, the male leaves, / grazes and eats until the time comes,
> then he returns, he stays, and the female leaves, / she grazes as well, until she again knows [it's time to return].
> So, they divide their days and nights; / And if they hear a noise or a sound and turn back

to see what this cry, sound or noise is, / or if they happen
to fall asleep while heating them, / they immediately let
out a cry, for they have lost their chicks....
Allegory.
Therefore, man, their eggs are suspended
High in the churches, for the remembrance of the Word.
And remember, don't slack off
And lose repentance, for you lose your prayer.
But listen to the angelic hymn they sing
and all the care of life and the world
remove and banish from your mind,
and put [your] desire in Christ, the King of all,
and do not let a soul be lost for lack of care.

2.2. The Natural and Supernatural Ostrich Egg

2.2.1. Circulation and High-Society Usage

Ostrich eggs have been a prized product in all Mediterranean lands since the pre-dynastic period of Pharaonic Egypt (Green 2006, 30). As a container for liquids, the ostrich egg was used as far back as 5,000 years ago in ancient Egypt, Mesopotamia, and Crete. The archaeologist Tamar Hodos, who conducted a study for the University of Bristol comparing ancient artefacts made from ostrich eggshells with contemporary ones, interpreted the inscription on a tablet from Nimrud (in present-day Iraq) from the ninth century BC, concluding that hunters followed ostriches to the nest to steal their eggs and take them to the royal court. Apparently, the hunt was very perilous, because the ostrich could kill the hunter with a blow of its beak. Archaeological excavations have revealed that in ancient times eggs were transported in a complex trade long distances from their climatic area of origin.

Most eggs came from Libya and Nubia. They appear in the figurative art of prehistoric North African caves, on painted ceramics and stones, in the mural painting of Tutankhamun's tomb (for the pharaohs had the privilege of hunting ostriches, chasing them with horse-drawn chariots), and in the mosaic of the scene of the great hunt in the Villa Romana del Casale (3 km from the town of Piazza Armerina in Sicily), which dates from the first quarter of the fourth century. An ostrich egg with animal paintings was found in the cave of Isis at Vulci in Italy; ostrich eggs decorated with silver and gold were placed in Etruscan hoards (Hodos et al. 2020, 1–20). The legend of Leda has a version recorded in Sparta that says that, after she conceived by Zeus in the form of a swan, Leda laid an ostrich egg, from which the Dioscuri hatched. Thus, a large silver egg in the shape of an ostrich egg was suspended in the Spartan temple dedicated to the famous Twins (Green 2006, 32; Shanawany and Dingle 1999, 1). Ostrich-egg cups from the Bronze and Iron Ages have been found in archaeological excavations in south-eastern Europe.

Mentions of ostrich eggs appear in western writings from the time of the Crusades, when these objects were among the goods frequently brought from the eastern Mediterranean, especially through Italian ports (Green 2006, 46), and they aroused the western aristocracy's curiosity. Along with the object itself, its story was also imported, which acquired spiritual values specific to the western world by taking on an allegorical garb.

In the Age of Enlightenment, ostrich eggs were beautifully chiselled into feasting cups. The silverware collection of Exeter College, Oxford, contains one such cup dated to 1610. A beautiful silver-gilt ostrich egg cup engraved with the arms of Christopher Báthory, Prince of Transylvania, dated about 1570, is displayed in the Wellby Gallery of the Ashmolean Museum in Oxford. The Pitt Rivers Museum in Oxford possesses several ostrich eggs, carved and painted with art elements specific to different world cultures. In the seventeenth century, princely courts added to their halls a Kunstkammer or Wunderkammer (art or curio cabinet) where feasting cups made of ostrich eggs were displayed. Such cups are exhibited in the splendid museum of the Duke of Gotha (Germany).

In the nineteenth century, a fashion emerged for decorating interiors with ostrich eggs as a result of the Orientalist movement in the visual arts and an increased ease of travel. In 1850, Archduke Ferdinand Maximilian of Austria brought back numerous eggs from his trip to the eastern Mediterranean for the oriental salons of his residences in Trieste, Villa Lazarovich, and Castello di Miramare (Prosdocimi 1864). Photographs of these oriental salons are displayed at the Weltmuseum in Vienna, Austria.

A special usage that was still common in the last century was that reported in 1958 in the Parisian magazine *L'Orient syrien* (Khouri-Sarkis 1958, 392): in some villages in Lebanon, where the craft of silkworm breeding is widespread, to protect the worm eggs from frost, damp, and pests over winter, until the next season, the peasants would take them in a sack to the parish priest, who would put them in hollow ostrich eggs hanging in the church.

2.2.2. Symbolism in Various Religions

In all cultures, the egg is considered the archetype of the oval, the symbol of life in gestation and perfect knowledge, the cosmos and the fecund principle that generated it, the 'alchemical egg' (Battistini 2008, 133), the germ from which gods, kings, and ancient heroes were born, etc. The ostrich egg has had symbolic value from West Asia to West Africa, being endowed with magical, ritualistic, and creative powers, linked to life, fertility, and protection. On account of being able to swallow stones and pieces of metal without suffering, the ostrich has become a symbol of Justice, which can resolve any contentious issue, no matter how complicated. Another argument along the same lines was that its wing and back feathers are equal, a rare phenomenon in birds (Soave 2017, 90–91; Cooper 1992).

The ostrich egg has been laden with symbolism in all Abrahamic religions, in different forms, and for different reasons. In his 2020 article *Ostrich Eggs as a Conceptual–Symbolic Accessory in Jewish Synagogues*, Abraham Ofir Shemesh presents a picture of the rabbinic sources and meanings ascribed in Jewish culture to eggs in general, and the ostrich egg in particular. He explains that, in ancient times, hanging in synagogues, particularly in Yemen, Safed, Meron, and Jerusalem, the egg was used as an exhortation to attentive prayer, based on the ostrich's supposed ability to hatch its eggs only by looking at them (Shemesh 2020, 8–10). The primary source of his study is the biblical exegesis of R. Mordechai ha-Cohen, one of the great Jewish scholars of Aleppo in the mid-seventeenth century. Shemesh also notes that the practice of hanging ostrich eggs in synagogues was common in countries under Islamic rule, not in Christian European countries. Shemesh's intention to compare the ostrich-egg customs of Judaism with those of Christianity and Islam is, however, not carried through: the description of the traditions of these two religions on pp. 4–8 is schematic, refers mainly to the symbolism of the egg in general, not that of the ostrich, and presents concrete instances of the presence of ostrich eggs in places of worship, not their significance in the two faiths.[2]

A comparison between the Christian view and the Jewish one, in which the ostrich was considered only a stupid and cruel bird that runs very fast, was also drawn by Robert Amadou, starting from the Old Testament texts of Job, Isaiah, Leviticus, and Micah (Amadou 1958, 484–87). The discussion had begun in the magazine's previous issue (Khouri-Sarkis 1958, 391–92), when a reader's question about the meaning of hanging ostrich eggs in church was addressed.

Building on archaeological discoveries of the last century that have demonstrated the wide geographical spread of ostrich eggs (Laufer 1926; Moorey 1994, etc.), Nile Green (2006, 1) explores in his article *Ostrich Eggs and Peacock Feathers: Sacred Objects as Cultural Exchange between Christianity and Islam* "the nature and limits of cultural heritage and cultural exchange between Christianity and Islam." He notes that Islamic civilisation adopted the ostrich egg primarily as a symbol of life after death,

---

[2] The author also confuses, on p. 9, Saint John Damascene with the Coptic author Ibn Sabāʿ, attributing to the former Ibn Sabāʿ's *Book of the Jewel in Ecclesiastical Sciences* (*Kitāb al-ǧawhara al-nafīsa fī ʻulūm al-kanīsa*), to which I shall return.

as can still be seen today in many a sultan's tomb in Istanbul (such as that of Suleiman the Magnificent, d. 1566). Green (2006, 35, 53–54) explains likewise the presence of ostrich eggs in the tombs of Indo-Muslim saints, the Sufi mystics.

Another significant contribution to the subject is that of George Galavaris (1978, 69–78), who discusses Christian and Muslim places of worship in which lamps and candles are suspended from chains with ostrich eggs on top. Galavaris wrote this article as a tribute to Sir Steven Runciman, whose authoritative history of the Crusades has informed much of our understanding of Islamic and Christian traditions. He states that a book remains to be written on types of illumination, the particular use of lights, and their complex symbolism in the eastern Church (Galavaris 1978, 70).

For western Christians, the ostrich's story has also created an allegory of the Synagogue: just as it abandons its eggs in the sand, the people into which Jesus was born abandoned Him and gave Him to the dead (Duchet-Suchaux and Pastoureau 2002, 30).

3.0. From Religious Symbolism to Ecclesiastic Art

3.1. A Quick Look at the Ethiopian Tradition

The Ethiopian tradition is different from what we know from other Christian cultures. Amazingly, in the ostrich's lands, the place of the egg is not inside the church but outside, on top of the roof of round churches—the most frequent shape of Ethiopian prayer halls—and they adorn the cross, attached to a circle that can hold from five to seven eggs. The explanation the local guides and priests gave to me was that they symbolise the eternal Afterlife and God's incessant protection of the faithful who come to pray in that church. In his recent book published in Addis Ababa, *Visiting Ethiopian Churches: Understanding the Paintings of Eight Frequently Visited Churches of Ethiopia*, Dawit Teferi Anbessie explains several symbolic interpretations of the ostrich egg. After he mentions two of the common ones I described above, he ends with the specific Ethiopian one (Teferi Anbessie 2019, 18–19):

> On the exterior, round churches resemble the round thatched huts that Ethiopians commonly live in. The main difference is the pinnacle cross that appears on the churches which is commonly decorated with ostrich eggs. Ostrich eggs are chosen for a symbolic reason.... The most plausible explanation is given by Priest Gedamu of Narga Sillasse. According to him, ostriches incubate their eggs nonstop. If they discontinue, the eggs do not hatch. It is the same for us; we have to be always with the church [God], if we go astray, we perish. We do not know when ostrich eggs began to appear. The earliest written account, which could be taken as circumstantial evidence to their application, is a eulogy of Emperor Iyasu I (ruled 1682–1706) composed during the second decade of the eighteenth century.

One of the best sources for images of ostrich eggs on church rooftops and for a general image of the churches of Ethiopia is the splendidly illustrated album *Ethiopia: The Living Churches of an Ancient Kingdom*, published by Mary Ann Fitzgerald and Philip Marsden in Cairo in 2017.

While visiting Ethiopia in March 2023, I noticed that on some church roofs, traditional eggs were replaced by metal ones.

This mostly occurs in urban communities, probably for an economic reason, as metal is more resistant to weather conditions but also more expensive. The most spectacular case is the seven-egg circle around the cross on the rooftop of the Saint George Cathedral in Addis Ababa.

3.2. Symbolism of the Ostrich Egg in Western European Arts

The depiction of ostrich eggs in western art forms is not the focus of the research presented here. In ancient times, artists and creators of cultic vessels understood the significance of the ostrich egg in a variety of ways: virginity, creation, death and resurrection, eternal life, and social status, on account of its rarity. By the thirteenth century, when the German theologian Guilielmus Durandus/Durantis (1237–1296) described them in his *Rationale divinorum officiorum*, a treatise on the symbolic meaning of church services, ostrich eggs were already a common feature in the decoration of cathedrals and western mortuary chapels, an object kept in abbey treasuries and cabinets of curiosities (Durandus 1906; Green 2006, 35–36; Davril and Thibodeau 1995; 1998).

Many art historians have addressed the representation of ostrich eggs in medieval and Renaissance art, in particular Piero della Francesca's painting for the chapel of the Montefeltro family in Urbino (Italy), in which such an object is associated with the Madonna—the ostrich being also one of the heraldic emblems of the Montefeltro family (Green 2006, 36, with other references to works by Mantegna and Benaglio, as well as other examples of

Italian art, especially church art). From 1952 to 1980, the subject enjoyed many commentaries, many published in *The Art Bulletin* (Clark 1951; Gilbert 1952; Meiss 1954a; Meiss 1954b; Marinescu 1958–1959; Meiss and Jones 1966; Ragusa 1971; Meiss 1975; Meiss 1976; Brisson 1980; Sullivan 1994).

The most comprehensive and up-to-date study is that authored by Sebastian Bock in 2002, *The "Egg" of the* Pala Montefeltro *by Piero della Francesca and Its Symbolic Meaning*. Bock comments extensively on the scene, starting from the aforementioned passage in Durandus' writing and addressing many other paintings. He concludes that, of all the suggested explanations for the depiction of ostrich eggs in western visual art in the Middle Ages and Renaissance, the most truthful is their function as a *warning or admonitory example for the pious*, but without a precise reference to prayer (Bock 2002, 15). The explanation must therefore be sought in its 'traditional sense', the hanging ostrich egg reflecting a call to always heed God (Bock 2002, 20).

On December 14, 2021, Krisztina Ilko gave an online talk for The Murray Seminars at Birkbeck, with the catchy title: 'Medieval Fabergé: African Ostrich Eggs, Global Currency'. The topic had less to do with the famous Fabergé eggs and more to do with the artistic items preserved in Western European museums that were manufactured from ostrich eggs by painting, carving, and mounting in precious metals, such as the seventh-century BC decorated ostrich egg excavated in Vulci (The British Museum), the double-headed chalice reliquary donated by Pope Leo IV to the old church of Saint Peter (Palazzo Pitti, Florence), two ostrich-egg reliquary pendants of the fourteenth to fifteenth centuries at

Saint Servatius (Maastricht), and a 43.5 cm tall reliquary (c. 1320) made of an ostrich egg covered in gilded silver, precious and semi-precious stones, rock crystal, and glass, preserved at the Cathedral of Saints Stephen and Sixtus in Domschatz, Germany. The speaker concluded that ornamented ostrich eggs were used in the fourteenth to sixteenth centuries as reliquaries, lighting devices, or symbols of celestial bodies, i.e., 'spiritual beacons'. Despite a brief mention of the *Book of the Precious Jewel in Ecclesiastical Sciences* of Ibn Sabāʿ (which I discuss below), this last idea was, unfortunately, not investigated further. The connection between vigilant prayer and the ostrich eggs hanging from narthex chandeliers was not even suggested.

To conclude, art historians have proposed various explanations for the frequent presence of ostrich eggs in Western European cathedrals, either as decorative objects or in paintings and frescoes. Millard Meiss (1954, 221) calls Wolfgang Lotz, another enthusiast of the subject, "a fellow oölogist." However, no source sheds light on the function of the ostrich egg as a symbolic item in the Christian Orthodox churches, where this exotic artefact reveals its highest spiritual significance linked to unceasing prayer.

3.3. Christian Arabic Manuscript Sources

3.3.1. The Arabic *Physiologus* and its Posterity

Arabic-speaking authors read the *Physiologus* in Coptic and Syriac translations and the original Greek. The first Arabic translation of the *Physiologus* is preserved in MS Sinai Arabic 481, dated 1091, at the Monastery of Saint Catherine on Mount Sinai. Two other early copies are known, dated to the twelfth century (MS

Sinai Arabic 453) and thirteenth century (MS Sinai Arabic 448). A description of these manuscripts and an extensive commentary on the *Arabic Physiologus* were included by Adrian Pirtea (2021) in his work 'The Arabic Tradition—Second Part: Phys. Arab. α'. A manuscript preserved in Leiden was edited by Jan Pieter Nicolaas Land in 1885, with an introduction, translation, and commentary in Latin. From this, ʿIsā Aliskandar Maʿlūf extracted fragments that he edited and commented on a century ago in the Syrian journal *Al-Niʿma* (Maʿlūf 1911; see Nasrallah 1983, 186). This version does not mention the *struthio*. However, it appears from the summary table that Land found a chapter on *Struthiocamelus* in eight of the 16 manuscripts he researched, which include Greek and Latin versions, as well as in an 18-folio Syriac manuscript in the Biblioteca Apostolica Vaticana (hereafter, the BAV).

Fragments extracted from the *Physiologus* were copied alongside other original texts or translations by Christian Arabic authors (the Melkites), often together with works by the great eleventh-century scholar 'Abdallah ibn al-Faḍl, who may have been the translator of the *Physiologus* from Greek into Arabic. Several dozen such manuscripts dating from the eleventh to nineteenth centuries are known today, held in collections in Beirut, Aleppo, Sinai, Baghdad, the Vatican, London, Paris, and St Petersburg (Graf 1944, 548–49; Nasrallah 1983, 186–87).

I have so far identified four Christian Arabic texts that contain a chapter on the spiritual interpretation of ostrich eggs.

3.3.2. Ibn Sabāʿ, *The Precious Jewel in Ecclesiastical Sciences*

Yuhannā ibn Abī Zakāriyā ibn Sabāʿ (active c. 1280) took up the contents and the moral of the ostrich's parable in his work *The Precious Jewel in Ecclesiastical Sciences* (*Al-Ǧawhara al-nafīsa fī ʿulūm al-kanīsa*), based on a Coptic text but only preserved in its Arabic version (Cândea 1993; Green 2006, 35). This is an encyclopaedia of dogmatic theology, liturgy, and orders of the Coptic Church. Jean Périer, professor at the Catholic Institute of Paris, published in 1922, in the collection *Patrologia Orientalis*, the Arabic text and a French translation of a late fourteenth-century copy preserved in MS Ar. 207 of the Bibliothèque nationale de France (111 r/v folios; cf. Ibn Sabâʿ 1922, 170). The Arabic text was established by collating BnF Ms. Ar. 207 with two others, BAV Mss Ar. 208 (dated 1638) and Ar. 130 (dated 1697). The work seems to have circulated widely, since the following editor, Victor Manṣūr Mistrīḥ, consulted 18 manuscripts. In 1966, Victor Manṣūr Mistrīḥ published another edition of the Arabic text, with a Latin translation (*Pretiosa margarita de scientiis ecclesiasticis*), in Cairo, at the Franciscan Centre for Oriental Christian Studies. The 18 Arabic manuscripts consulted included 11 from Egyptian collections and seven preserved in Lebanon, Paris (BnF), and Vatican City (BAV). In this edition, the text on candles and ostrich eggs, with identical content, is found in chapter 55, and the story of the ostrich appears on p. 163.

In the 1922 edition, the commentary on the ostrich is placed in chapter 52. The author describes the appearance that the 'earthly church' must have had, adorned as beautifully as possible, with lighted candles during services and the Holy Mass, for "it depicts the earthly heaven, with its stars shining." Indeed, according to another source, "Ornaments of this kind added majesty and splendour to the House of the Lord" (Galavaris 1978, 70).

Ibn Sabāʿ continues as follows:

> //110r//... Ostrich eggs are suspended between the candles because ostriches, female and male, have the habit, unlike //110v// other birds, of not hatching the eggs from which their young will come. The male or female is content to stare at them for a certain time until the chicks are ready to hatch. If the male gets hungry or thirsty while he is looking at them, he lets out a cry, and then the female, having an innate ability, understands and turns her eyes to the eggs, so that they stay not without the gaze of one of them for a moment. In the same way, when the female gets hungry, she begins to scream before going out for food, and then the male understands and turns his eyes to the eggs. If they are deprived for a moment of the gaze of one of them, the eggs spoil and no longer bear the expected fruit. The egg thus lost is taken and suspended in the church between the candles, not as an ornament, //111r// but to show anyone who sees it that he must be careful that his mind does not wander from prayer, lest his prayer be lost as the egg was lost because it was not guarded with the gaze.

3.3.3. The Anonymous Work on *The Priesthood Ordination*

The second writing is an anonymous Arabic translation with the title *The Priesthood Ordination* (*Tartīb al-kahanūt*), a 22-chapter manual for Coptic and Melkite altar servers, which was attributed to Severus ibn al-Muqaffaʿa, bishop of al-Ashmuneyn in the tenth century, during the Fatimid dynasty. This attribution has been convincingly invalidated by Yuhanna Nessim Youssef (2004; 2006), who has proposed a mid-fourteenth-century date, supported by solid historical arguments. A single manuscript copy of the Arabic translation, dated 1720, is preserved in the library of the Coptic Patriarchate in Cairo (and a photocopy at the BAV). It was edited by Jules Assfalg in 1955 in Cairo as *Die Ordnung des Priestertums: Ein altes liturgisches Handbuch der koptischen Kirche*. Chapter 8 refers to candles and ostrich eggs suspended together, this being, as far as we know, their earliest mention in a Christian Arabic text. The text is identical in content to Ibn Sabāʿ's writing, with some more elegant wording (Graf 1947, 313):

> ...The Church is an earthly heaven and a heavenly earth, since it is here that the angelic and spiritual services and prayers take place, and those who sit here are heavenly and angelic people on earth.... As for ostrich eggs, they are not placed in the church without reason, but the reason for placing them there is that the ostrich family is different from all the winged birds that lay eggs.... The people of the Church take [the barren eggs] and hang them between candles not for beauty but to show that they have become barren because they were abandoned by the parents' gaze. Thus, it is shown to anyone who prays that if his mind, which is the mother of the word, forsakes the attention to prayer, then his prayer becomes barren just as the ostrich's egg becomes barren and no young comes out of it anymore. Therefore, the ostrich egg is suspended in the church for prayer. There is here a good teaching and a correction for the wise souls, who will have enlightened minds if they grasp this profound meaning.

3.3.4. Macarius III ibn al-Zaʿīm, *Book on the Features of Certain Animals*

An Arabic-speaking author who also drew on the Greek version of the *Physiologus* is Macarius III ibn al-Zaʿīm, the Patriarch of the Church of Antioch (1647–1672), who travelled to Romania, the Cossacks' lands (present-day Ukraine), and Russia in 1653–1658. Together with his son, the Archdeacon Paul (called 'of Aleppo'), he compiled a translation of the *Physiologus* in his *Book on the Features of Certain Animals* (*Kitāb fī baʿḍ ġarāʾiz al-ḥayawānāt*), fragments of which are found in several of his miscellanies. The original of Macarius' Arabic *Physiologus* was the Greek version of Damaskinos Stouditis, which also circulated, in numerous manuscripts, in the Romanian Principalities, translated into Slavonic and then into Romanian. The work was printed in Venice in 1643 and was dedicated by the author to the great *spathari* Mihai Cantacuzino. Patriarch Macarius probably obtained this book in Wallachia or Moldavia. Mihai Cantacuzino (1640–1716) was one of the six sons of the great postelnic Constantin Cantacuzino, head of a noble Wallachian family of Greek origin. He held important offices at the court of Wallachia in the rule of Constantin Brâncoveanu.

After 1650, Patriarch Macarius III collected excerpts from ecclesiastic texts and translations from Greek into Arabic, adding commentaries to them, in a notebook which accompanied him on his trip to Georgia in 1664–1665, when he had the opportunity to enrich it. The original notebook is preserved at the Institute of Oriental Studies in St Petersburg in MS B 1227. Two manuscript copies are known, one in the BAV, MS Vat. Ar. 689, copied in 1757 by Leontius Salīm (Graf 1949, 101), and one in the Greek Catholic Diocese of Aleppo.[3]

In the St Petersburg manuscript (148 r/v ff.), most of the text is in the handwriting of Patriarch Macarius III. A few folios were written by Niʿma b. Fathallah al-Sahir, while on ff. 100r and 127 r/v there are two notes written by the Patriarch Cyril V ibn al-Zaʿīm, grandson of Patriarch Macarius. The text contains passages from the *Physiologus* devoted to *The Mermaid* (Ch. 36), *The Pelican* (Ch. 38), and *The Raven* (Ch. 39). As for the mermaid, the editor and translator, Nikolaj Serikoff (1999–2000, 529), does not identify the source of this passage beyond that it is "probably Greek." The siren appears in Ch. 14 (f. 42) in the manuscript of the Arabic *Physiologus* in Leiden, edited by Land (1885, 143–44). It is mentioned by the editor in the summary table as occurring in several Greek and Latin manuscripts (Land 1885, 136).

On ff. 115r–116r, Ch. 42 contains a *Brief Explanation of the Good Deed Done by Those who Bring Candles, Candle Oil and the Like to Church, of the Kind of Birds Called Ostriches* [Ar. *ṭuyūr al-naʿām*] *and the Reason why Their Eggs are Suspended in Churches* (in MS Vat. Ar. 689, Ch. 45, on the ostrich, is found on ff. 150r–151r). Bearing in mind that seventeenth-century manuscript copies of Ibn Sabāʿ's work have survived, it is possible that Patriarch Macarius also had this text at his disposal. Here is the passage in the St Petersburg manuscript.

> //115r (l. 10)// Know that the Holy Fathers commanded the faithful to light candles and [candle] oil in churches

[3] I am grateful to Carsten-Michael Walbiner for bringing this second copy to my attention.

> and hang mirrors and an ostrich egg inside... to teach us to act when we sit at prayer as ostriches act when the female lays eggs, for she immediately focuses her eyes on them with all her concentration, does not move away from them in any way, and does not turn away to the right or the left. The male goes to eat and drink, but when the female senses that the male has returned and sat down to guard her chick eggs, only then does she fly away and wander about to eat and drink her fill. The male stays put and guards the eggs with all care and attention, neither moving to the right nor the left. And only when he sees that the female has returned and has sat down beside him to guard the eggs with all care does he fly away, and he later returns to guard [the nest], according to custom. They do this for 40 days. Then the female hatches the eggs and out of them come chicks that start to fly. But if during these 40 days the female or the male does not do as shown, if they take their eyes off them while they are guarding them, or if any of the eggs are snatched away by hunters who seek them to steal and take them away, to sell them to some people who eat them, as they are in many places, or to eat them themselves, then at once those eggs are completely ruined and start leaking. In the same way, when they are in church and at the times when they are praying, Christians must be with all their heart and all their mind and all their thoughts towards God, neither turning to the right nor the left, nor speaking to one another during their prayer, so that God may fulfil their prayer and receive it. They should not turn and talk to one another while they pray, so their prayer may not be in vain, and their toil may not come to nothing. //115v (l. 19)//

Macarius then states the purpose of bringing to the church incense and five small buns, each with a special meaning explained in detail. He concludes by declaring that the purpose of all these ritual gestures is for God to receive the Christians' fervent prayers addressed to Him at church, in a suitable environment, carefully prepared, and in the presence of certain ritual elements.

3.3.5. Isṭīfān al-Duwayhī, *The Light of the Holy Mysteries*

Isṭīfān al-Duwayhī, a Patriarch of the Maronite Church and a great scholar of his time (1630–1704), whose works include texts on the history of the Maronite Church and religious poetry in Syriac, composed a text on the meaning and order of the Holy Mass, with the title *The Light of the Holy Mysteries* (*Manārat al-ʾaqdās*) or *The Ten Lights* (*Al-Manār al-ʿašar*), in which he states that in the churches of the Maronites and the Jacobites there are round mirrors and ostrich eggs, placed there as decorative objects (Graf 1949, 375). An Arabic manuscript preserved in the Monastery of the Mother of God in al-Luwayza (Mount Lebanon), written in *garšūni* and dated 1711, was edited and published by Fr Rašīd al-Šartūnī at the end of the nineteenth century (al-Šartūnī 1895–1896). The passage about ostrich eggs is placed in Chapter 9 of vol. 1 (126–27), which is entitled: *On the Pulpit, Crucifix, Bells, and those within the Nave.* After explaining the regulations concerning the pulpit and other architectural elements in the nave, the author comes to point 5:

> Fifth, mirrors and ostrich eggs are suspended in the [holy] house. It is said that these were also suspended in the Temple of Solomon.... As for the ostrich egg, it is placed there to show that prayer and piety are needed during the holy services of the Lord, for it is said of this bird that it does not sit on its egg and hatch it, but watches it from afar, and

> when the female tires, the male sits in its place to watch the eggs. And if it takes its eyes off the eggs, they turn barren and spoiled. In the same way, if we want our prayers to be received, we must be steadfast in lifting the eyes of our minds towards God. And if we still think of worldly things, then our prayers will be in vain, lost, and not fulfilled.

The commentary on ostrich eggs is followed by explanations of the bells, their spiritual meaning and their usage from the Old Testament times to 1700.

4.0. Conclusions

The fact that many of the Arabic works I discussed date from the sixteenth to seventeenth centuries reflects a similar situation throughout the Eastern European regions: the deeper meanings of certain rituals and cult objects were lost, so clergy and scholars felt it necessary to explain them by referring to ancient sources, unknown to the believers of later times.

In the Christian Orthodox world, ostrich eggs are common in the churches of princely foundations, monasteries or churches, always placed in the narthex, and sometimes on the choir side, which might suggest that their message is addressed to the monks who usually sit in this pew. We can say that the ostrich egg fulfils, in visual form, the function of the call "Upright!" by which the faithful are exhorted to listen to the reading of the Gospel pericope standing and in a state of vigil, not sitting idly. As Confucius famously said, "A picture is worth ten thousand words." Therefore, to the warning addressed to the ear is added a warning perceptible with another sense, that of sight, to reinforce the message, thus conveyed in two ways.

Here are just a few Orthodox churches in Romania and abroad where ostrich eggs hang in the narthex and other areas of the church.

1. In Romania:
   - Bucharest: at the Monastery of Radu Vodă (installed around 2007 by the Archimandrite Nectarie, the current hegumen) and the Darvari Skete.
   - Moldova: in Iași, at the Monastery of the Three Hierarchs and the Putna Monastery.
   - Muntenia: at the monasteries of Hurezi, Bistrița, and Surpatele, and at Saint Stephen's Church in Râmnicu-Vâlcea.
   - The Sinaia Monastery: the egg that hangs from the chandelier in the narthex was presented by Charles I, the king of Romania, in 1903, when the church was reconsecrated.
2. In Egypt, the church of the Monastery of Saint Anthony the Great (Sketis desert).
3. In Syria, the Church of Saints Sergius and Vah in Sadad (east of Homs), built in the eighteenth century.
4. At the Monastery of Saint Catherine on Mount Sinai, where there were in 1965 several dozen ostrich eggs as candle holders, or free-standing in the narthex and other areas of the church (the *paracclesion* of the Burning Bush, north and south galleries). One egg (natural or ceramic)

hung above the Saint's tomb, between the candles. Most of them are still there today. Photographs in which they appear were published in 1966 by George H. Forsyth, Kurt Weitzmann, Igor Ševčenko, and Fred Anderegg in the album *The Monastery of Saint Catherine at Mount Sinai: The Church and Fortress of Justinian—Plates*. They are also present in an engraving in Sir Charles Wilson's work *Picturesque Palestine: Egypt and Sinai* (1881, 1:233). It is worth noting the author's assessment in the description of the church: "The Church of the Transfiguration is an early Christian Basilica traditionally ascribed to Justinian, and the interior is a very imposing specimen of Greek ecclesiastic decoration" (Wilson 1881, 1:235).

5. On Mount Athos, there are numerous examples. Perhaps the most spectacular is the large chandelier in the narthex of the church of the Vatopedi Monastery, from which twelve old eggs are suspended. A documentary film is accessible online (CBS News 2011).
6. In the Holy Land there are countless occurrences, including at the Holy Sepulchre, the Tomb of the Mother of God, the monastery of Sts George and John Jacob in Hozeva (Wadi Qilt, Palestinian Authority), and in Bethlehem.
7. In Cyprus, in Nicosia and Larnaca. Bewildered by the large number of ostrich eggs in the church in Kykkos, Mihail Harbuzaru (formerly protos of the Sinaia Monastery, north of Bucharest), asked for an explanation and was told that it was a practical solution: the eggs prevent mice from getting to the oil in the candle.

Today, if the curious tourist asks about the meaning of ostrich eggs suspended in an eastern church, the answer will be practical: it repels flies or mice, or it is a decorative item, etc. The spiritual significance seems lost. We cannot know how many of the buyers of ostrich eggs in church shops are aware of their spiritual meaning when suspended in the narthex. Likewise, the connection between the significance of the lamp or candle and that of the ostrich egg as objects hanging from the same chain in eastern churches (a connection that Galavaris only suggested) deserves further investigation, since both are meant to draw the supplicant's eyes upwards and illuminate him, literally and figuratively. When researching the presence of ostrich eggs in places of worship or visual art forms, one should remember that it cannot be reduced to an artistic act with an exclusively aesthetic value.

In searching the Christian Arabic texts I mentioned, I intended to expand the range of sources on this topic, seeking confirmation that, of all faiths, Greek Orthodox Christianity drew spiritual teachings from the behaviour of the ostrich and preserved an enduring rule concerning the vigilance of the mind: the one who prays must be careful not to be overwhelmed by worldly thoughts and temptations when directing his voice, mind, and heart towards God.

References

al-Šartūnī, Rašīd. *Manārat al-ʾaqdās*. 1895–1896. 2 vols. Beirut. Republished 1980, Zgharta: Cultural Association 'Patriarch Isṭifān al-Duwayhī'.

Amadou, Robert. 1958. 'Encore les œufs d'autruche'. *L'Orient syrien* 3 (4): 484–87.

Agaiby, Lisa, and Tim Vivian. 2021. *Door of the Wilderness: The Greek, Coptic, and Copto-Arabic Sayings of St. Anthony of Egypt—An English Translation, with Introduction and Notes.* TSEC 23. Leiden: Brill.

Bianciotto, Gabriel, Pierre de Beauvais, Guillaume le Clerc, Richard de Fournival, Brunetto Latini, and Corbechon. 1980. *Bestiaires du Moyen Âge.* Paris: Éditions Stock.

Bock, Sebastian. 2002. *The "Egg" of the* Pala Montefeltro *by Piero della Francesca and its Symbolic Meaning.* Freiburg im Breisgau: Heidelberg. https://doi.org/10.11588/heidok.00003123.

Brisson, David W. 1980. 'Piero della Francesca's Egg Again'. *The Art Bulletin* 62 (2): 284–6.

Cândea, Virgil. 1993. 'Les œufs d'autruche et la vigilance'. *Revue des études sud-est européennes* 31 (3–4): 301–3.

Cazenave, Michel (coord. ed.). 1996. *Encyclopédie des symbols.* Paris: Librairie Générale Française.

CBS News. 2011. 'Mount Athos, part 2'. YouTube video, 26 December. https://www.youtube.com/watch?v=J1lvruy-j2c, accessed 15 August 2024.

Clark, Kenneth. 1951. *Piero della Francesca.* London: Phaidon Publishers.

Cooper, J. C. 1992. *An Illustrated Encyclopaedia of Traditional Symbols.* London: Thames & Hudson.

Crețu, Bogdan. 2020. *Inorogul la porțile Orientului: Bestiarul lui Dimitrie Cantemir.* 2nd ed. Chișinău: Cartier Publishing House.

Davril, A., and T. M. Thibodeau (with the help of B. Guyot). 1995. *Guillelmus Duranti: Rationale Divinorum Officiorum*. Vol. 1, *Books I–IV*. Corpus Christianorum, Continuatio Mediaevalis 140. Turnhout: Brepols.

———. 1998. *Guillelmus Duranti: Rationale Divinorum Officiorum*. Vol. 2, *Books V–VI*. Corpus Christianorum, Continuatio Mediaevalis 140A. Turnhout: Brepols.

Duchet-Suchaux, Gaston, and Michel Pastoureau. 2002. *Le Bestiaire médieval: Dictionnaire historique et bibliographique*. Paris: Le Leopard d'Or.

Durandus, William. 1906. *The Symbolism of Churches and Church Ornaments: A Translation of the First Book of the Rationale Divinorum Officiorum*. Trans. J. M. Neale and B. Webb. London: Gibbings.

Fitzgerald, Mary Ann, and Philip Marsden. 2017. *Ethiopia: The Living Churches of an Ancient Kingdom*. Cairo: The American University in Cairo Press.

Galavaris, George. 1978. 'Some Aspects of Symbolic Use of Lights in the Eastern Church Candles, Lamps, and Ostrich Eggs'. *Byzantine and Modern Greek Studies* 4 (1): 69–78.

Gilbert, Creighton. 1952. 'On Subject and Non-Subject in Italian Renaissance Pictures'. *The Art Bulletin* 34: 202–16.

Graf, Georg. 1944. *Geschichte der christlichen arabischen Literatur*. Vol. 1. Vatican City: Vatican Library.

———. 1947. *Geschichte der christlichen arabischen Literatur*. Vol. 2. Vatican City: Vatican Library.

———. 1949. *Geschichte der christlichen arabischen Literatur*. Vol. 3. Vatican City: Vatican Library.

Green, Nile. 2006. 'Ostrich Eggs and Peacock Feathers: Sacred Objects as Cultural Exchange between Christianity and Islam'. *Al-Masāq* 18 (1): 27–66.

Hodos, Tamar, Caroline R. Cartwright, Janet Montgomery, Geoff Nowell, Kayla Crowder, Alexandra C. Fletcher, and Yvonne Gönster. 2020. 'The Origins of Decorated Ostrich Eggs in the Ancient Mediterranean and Middle East'. *Antiquity* 94 (374): 381–400.

Ibn Sabâ'. 1922. *La Perle précieuse traitant des sciences ecclésiastiques (Chapitres I-LVI), par Jean, fils d'Abou Zakariyâ, surnommé Ibn Sabâʿ*. Edited and translated by Jean Périer. *Patrologia Orientalis* 16.4. Paris: Firmin-Didot.

Khouri-Sarkis, G. 1958. 'Miscellanea'. *L'Orient syrien* 3 (3): 387–94.

Kraus, Thomas J. 2019. 'Von Einhorn, Hirsch, Pelikan und anderem Getier Septuaginta, Physiologus und darüber hinaus'. In *Christus in Natura: Quellen, Hermeneutik und Rezeption des griechischen Physiologus*, edited by Zbynek Kindschi Garský and Rainer Hirsch-Luipold, 63–79. Berlin: De Gruyter.

Land, Jan Pieter Nicolaas. 1885. *Anecdota Syriaca*. Vol. IV. Leiden: E. J. Brill.

Laufer, Berthold. 1926. *Ostrich Egg-Shell Cups of Mesopotamia and the Ostrich in Ancient and Modern Times*. Chicago: Field Museum of Natural History.

Legrand, Émile. 1873. *Le Physiologus, poème sur la nature des animaux en grec vulgaire et en vers politiques d'après deux manuscrits de la Bibliothèque Nationale*. Paris: Maisonneuve et Cie.

Maʿlūf, ʿIsā Aliskandar. 1911. 'مطبعة رومانية الارثوذكسية العربية الانطاكيه'. *Al-Niʿma* 3: 44–56.

Marinescu, Constantin. 1958–1959. 'Échos byzantins dans l'oeuvre de Piero della Francesca'. *Bulletin de la Société Nationale des Antiquaires de France*: 192–203.

Meiss, Millard. 1954a. *Ovum Struthionis*. Princeton: Princeton University Press.

———. 1954b. 'Addendum Ovologicum'. *The Art Bulletin* 36 (3): 221–22.

———. 1975. 'Not an Ostrich Egg?'. *The Art Bulletin* 57 (1): 116.

———. 1976. *The Painter's Choice: Problems in the Interpretation of Renaissance Art*. New York: Harper & Row.

Meiss, Millard, and Theodore G. Jones. 1966. 'Once Again Piero della Francesca's Montefeltro Altarpiece'. *The Art Bulletin* 48 (2): 203–6.

Moorey, Peter Roger Stuart. 1994. *Ancient Mesopotamian Materials and Industries: The Archaeological Evidence*. Oxford: Clarendon Press.

Nasrallah, Joseph (with Rachid Haddad). 1979. *Histoire du mouvement littéraire dans l'Église melchite du Ve au XXe siècle: Contribution à l'étude de la littérature arabe chrétienne*. Vol. 4.1. Leuven; Paris: Peeters; Chez l'auteur.

Nasrallah, Joseph (with Rachid Haddad). 1983. *Histoire du mouvement littéraire dans l'Église melchite du Ve au XXe siècle: Contribution à l'étude de la littérature arabe chrétienne*. Vol. 3.1. Leuven; Paris: Peeters; Chez l'auteur.

Pastoureau, Michel. 2011. *Bestiaires du Moyen Âge*. Paris: Éditions du Seuil.

Pirtea, Adrian. 2021. 'The Arabic Tradition—Second Part: Phys. Arab. α'. In *The Multilingual Physiologus: Studies in the Oldest Greek Recension and Its Translations*, edited by Caroline Macé and Jost Gippert, 263–80. Turnhout: Brepols.

Prosdocimi, Germano. 1864. *Histoire des arts industriels au Moyen Âge et à l'époque de la Renaissance.* Vol. 2. Paris.

Ragusa, Isa. 1971. 'The Egg Reopened'. *The Art Bulletin* 53 (4): 435–44.

Sbordone, Francesco. 1936. *Physiologus.* Milan: Società Anonima Editrice 'Dante Alighieri'.

Serikoff, Nikolaj. 1999–2000. 'Understanding of the Scriptures: Patriarch Mākāriyūs b. az-Zaʿīm and his Arabic-Speaking Orthodox Flock (From Patriarch Mākāriyūs' "Note- book")'. *ARAM* 11–12: 523–31.

Shanawany, M. M., and John Dingle. 1999. *Ostrich Production Systems.* Rome: FAO.

Shemesh, Abraham Ofir. 2020. 'Ostrich Eggs as a Conceptual-Symbolic Accessory in Jewish Synagogues'. *European Journal of Jewish Studies* 15: 1–24.

Soave, Lorenzo. 2017. *Simboli nell'arte: Breve guida per scoprire i significati nascosti nelle opere.* Modena: Palombi Editori.

Sullivan, Ruth Wilkins. 1994. 'Cracking the Egg: Jacopo Bassano's "Supper at Emmaus"'. *Notes in the History of Art* 13 (3): 27–35.

Teferi Anbessie, Dawit. 2019. *Visiting Ethiopian Churches: Understanding the Paintings of Eight Frequently Visited Churches of Ethiopia.* Addis Ababa: Nightjar Tours.

Venturi, Lionello. 1954. *Piero della Francesca.* Geneva.

Waida, Manabu. 1987. 'Birds'. In *The Encyclopedia of Religion*, edited by Mircea Eliade, 2: 225–26. New York: Macmillan.

Wilson, Sir Charles. 1881. *Picturesque Palestine, Egypt and Sinai*. 2 vols. London: J. S. Virtue & Co.

Youssef, Youhanna Nessim. 2004. 'Notes on the Traditions concerning the Trisagion'. *Parole de l'Orient* 29: 147–59.

Youssef, Youhanna Nessim. 2006. 'The Book *Order of the Priesthood*, by Severus Ibn Al-Muqaffaʿ Bishop of Al-Ashmunein, revisited'. *Bulletin de la Société d'Archéologie Copte* 45: 135–45.

INDEX

adab literature, 318
adverb / adverbial, 135, 146, 158–59, 161, 167–68, 266 n. 2, 300–2, 311, 370
Akkadian (Akk.), 26, 140–41, 143–46, 167
Aleppo, 111–14, 124, 126, 262, 292, 390, 397, 401–2
allegorical tales, 318
al-Shidyāq, Fāris, **75–107**
allusions, 318
al-Wāsiṭah (*al-Wāsiṭah fī maʿrifat aḥwāl Māliṭah*), 75–76
Amateur Radio, 6
Antakya, 112–13, 128
Arabic (Arab. / Ar.), 1–5, 7–8, **13–27**, 33, 41 n. 3, 59 n. 16, 62–63, 65, **75–107**, **109–28**, **135–68**, **175–198**, **201–57**, 262–63, 265, 268, 279–95, **299–311**, **315–35**, **339–73**, 383, 385, 396–405, 408
    Andalusi Arabic, 62, 339–40, 346–47, 351, 370–71
    Arabic dialectology, 1, 3, 14 n. 2, 299, 359–60
    Arabic dialects, 15, 22, 27, 61–63, 98, 109, 113, 124, 135, 146, 164, 180 n. 4, 182, 340, 343, 352, 360, 370, 373
    Arabic proverbs, *see* proverbs
    Bukhara Arabic (BAD), **13–27**
    Classical Arabic (CA), 23–24, 77–78, 85, 116, 177–78, 180–81, 183, 187–88, 190, 192–93, 195, 318–19
    Damascus Arabic, 114, 122 n. 23, 162–63, 166, 168
    Egyptian Arabic, 90–94, 101 n. 50, 107, 159, 163, 166, 340–42, 373
    Greater Syrian dialects, 90, 107, 113, 116, 126–28
    Gulf Arabic, 343 n. 2, 345, 362
    Ḥassāniyya, 135–36, 146–47, 151–52, 156 n. 28, 157–60, 164, 166–68
    Jordanian Arabic, 342
    Judaeo-Arabic
        of Libya (JAL), **175–98**
        of Qāmišli, **109–28**
    Lebanese Arabic, 159, 360–61, 369
    Levantine Arabic, 86, 90, 93–94, 95 n. 38, 102, 104, 289, 339–42, 347, 352, 354–56, 360, 371–3
    literary Arabic, 13, 27, 136, 147, 156 n. 28, 166, 178, 195

Mardini Arabic, **299–311**
Moroccan Arabic, 167–68, 320, 342, 346 n. 4, 351, 353
Negev Arabic, 164–68
Omani Arabic, 340, 343–45, 351–52, 355–56, 361–63, 366–68
peripheral Arabic, 13, 61–63, 300
Qashqa-Darya Arabic (QAD), **13–27**
Qurʾānic Arabic, 140, 167–68
Qəltu dialect group, 113, 117–18, 126
Sicilian Arabic, 62, 372
southern peninsular Arabic, 339, 356, 369–70, 372
Syrian Arabic, 113, 119 n. 13, 126–27, 288, 326, 342
Tunisian Arabic, 8, 189, 192–93, 195, 197, 216, 332–33, 370–71

Aramaic (Aram.), 8, 140–41, 143, 167, 213, 263, 268–69, 276, 282, 284, 287, 294. *See also* Neo-Aramaic, Syriac *and* Ṭuroyo
Argentina, 127
Assyrian Christians, 110
auxiliary, 18, 135, 147, 154, 192, 269, 289
Baghdad, 114, 397
Beirut / Beiruti, 112, 128, 320, 360, 397
Brazil, 127
Bukhara region, 13–15, 17, 22, 27
Canaanite (CAN.), 140, 143, 145
Circolo Gioventù Cattolica, 1
classical literature, 318
code-switching, 15, 19, 20 n. 7, 292–93
consonants, 24, 26–27, 35, 63, 76, 96, 98–99, 102, 105, 114, 118, 144, 276–77, 280, 282, 309
contact phenomena, 261, 364
customs, 124, 316, 329, 334, 391
Damascus, 9, 112, 124, 126, 262. *See also* Damascus Arabic *under* Arabic
decoration, 394, 407
degrees
Bachelor of Divinity, 10–11
B.A. General in Arabic and Classics, 4
B.A. Honours in Arabic, 4
Master of Theology in Orthodox Studies, 11
Ph.D. in Arabic and Semitic Studies, 4
demonstrative, 144 n. 11, 164, 282, 344, 370
Dēr ilQamar, 128
distributive *ši*, 340, 352, 354, 371
Diyarbakır, 110

Eastern Christian Tradition, 10
Egypt / Egyptian, 3, 75, 82, 88, 97, 101, 166, 217, 237, 322, 330, 334, 341, 385, 387, 398, 406–7. *See also* Egyptian Arabic *under* Arabic
enclitic *-š(i)*, 340–45, 348, 360–66, 372–73
Ethiopia, 393
Ethiopic (ETH.), 85, 87, 89, 140, 143
evidentiality, 165
existential particle, 367–70
folk etymology, 205
folklore, 147, 316, 330, 335
French, 83, 126, 148, 320, 330, 359, 386, 398
French mandate in Syria, 110, 262–63
gender distinction, 274–77, 279
glossary, 119
Gozo, 64, 90, 203, 209–10, 212, 218–19, 221, 223–30, 232, 234–37, 239–43, 245–54, 332
grammaticalisation, 135–36, 143, 145–46, 151, 167–68, 267, 288
Greek Catholic Church of Our Lady of Damascus, 9
Haifa, 109, 115 n. 6, 128
Ḥāṣbayya, 128
Hebrew (Heb.), 8, 87, 90, 110–11, 114, 116, 123–24, 126–27, 136, 140–41, 143–46, 167, 175 n. 2, 176–77, 179, 181–82, 184, 190, 193–96, 212, 216, 219, 233, 238
ḫidme 'military service', 25
History of Mediterranean Civilisation Programme, 5
Holy Land, 128, 407
hospitality, 331
ibn Sabāʿ, Yuhannā ibn Abī Zakāriyā, 391 n. 2, 396, 398–400, 402
informants, 15, 16 n. 4, 18–20, 112–14, 124, 126
Institute of Linguistics, 4–5
internal language development, 22, 24
interrogative, 20–21, 94, 106, 118, 154–56, 162 n. 34, 189 n. 6, 348, 350. *See also* polar interrogative *šay/ši/-x*
intertextuality, 317
Iraq, 3, 110, 113, 126–27, 159, 232, 263, 387
Iskenderun, 112, 128
Israel, 111–12, 114–16, 123, 126–28, 145–46, 179, 235
Istanbul, 76, 81, 302, 392
Isṭīfān al-Duwayhī, 404
Italian (It.), 37, 78, 82–84, 87, 89, 94, 96, 180, 190, 193, 240, 245, 388, 395
Jazīra (Syria), 113
Jerusalem, 109 n. 1, 128, 390

Jespersen cycle, 359, 361–64
Jews / Jewish (Jew.), 25, 43, 49, **109–28**, **175–198**, 210, 224, 239, 243–44, 249, 390–91
Jewish community, 112–14, 126, 194
Kfar Yāsīf, 128
koineisation, 261, 264–65, 270, 279, 295
Krachkovsky, Ignaty, 14
Kurdish (language), 110, 115, 127, 262–63, 279–80, 288, 311
Kurdistan, 110, 126–27
Kurds / Kurdish, 110, 113, 262, 264
language contact, 16, 22, 145, 261, 264–65, 279, 294–95
Latin (Lat.), 4, 37, 78, 87, 136, 239, 319, 385–86, 397–98, 402
Lebanon / Lebanese, 100, 112–13, 128, 211, 231, 262–63, 318–20, 322, 324–27, 334, 360, 389, 398, 404. *See also* Lebanese Arabic *under* Arabic
Levant, 75, 86, 88, 101, 213, 324–25, 340, 372
levelling, 265–66, 277–79
lexical diffusion, 63–64
Libya / Libyan, 2, 3, 8, 175 n. 1, 176, 178–79, 182, 188–90, 197, 226, 332, 384, 388
locatives, **209–311**
  locative adverbs, 146, 300–2, 311
  locative prepositions, 300, 302–11
Macarius III ibn al-Zaʿīm, Patriarch of Antioch, 401–3
Malta / Maltese, 2–5, 8–10, 36, 39–40, 57, 75–76, 78, 81–82, 84, 87, 106–7, 203, 211–12, 229, 231, 235, 243, **315–35**, 340, 370–71
Maltese (language) (Mal.), 2, 5, 7–9, 11, 13, **33–65**, **75–107**, 121 n. 22, **201–57**, 315, 323, 332–33, 335, **339–73**
Mardin, 109–10, 123 n. 27, 299, 302, 306, 311
matter replication, 280
Mediterranean Institute, 4
Mehri, 357–59, 363 n. 11, 364, 366–67
mentors, 5, 8
Mexico, 127
military service, *see ḫidme*
Mill-pinna ta' Saydon: Ġabra ta' Proża tal-Monsinjur Professur P. P. Saydon, 2
modal, 162, 164–65, 168, 288, 294
Modern South Arabian languages, 357–58, 364–67, 369. *See also* Mehri
Montefeltro chapel, 394–95

morals, 316
morphology, 104, 117, 124, 126, 214, 218, 284
Mount Athos, 407
music
Middle Eastern music, 7
World Music, 7
Muslim, 83, 110, 177, 201, 212, 217, 226–28, 231, 238, 240–41, 248–50, 253, 255 n. 13, 330, 340, 392
mutual intelligibility, 332
negation, 151 n. 20, 192, 341, 344–47, 358–66, 372
with *-š(i)*, 341–48
Andalusi Arabic, 346–47
Jordanian Arabic, 342
Maltese, 342, 350–51
Omani Arabic, 343–45
with *-šī*, 358–59
Neo-Aramaic, 261, 263, 267–68, 276
nomenclature, 203, 206
non-Jews, 115, 118 n. 10, 122 n. 23, 124–26
Nuṣaybin, 109–10, 126
obstruents, **33–65**
devoiced obstruents, 39–40, 42, 45, 47–48, 53, 56–57, 60
obstruent clusters, 34, 41, 44–48, 50–51, 53–55, 57, 59–62, 65
coda clusters, 38, 41, 48, 52, 54
onset clusters, 38, 41, 48, 52, 54
word-medial clusters, 41, 48, 52, 54, 181
voiced obstruents, 34, 38–40, 43–44, 47, 51, 56, 64
word-final obstruent devoicing, 34, 36, 40, 49, 51, 57–65
oral tradition, 262, 316, 321, 335
ordination, 9, 399
deacon, 9
priest, 9–10, 53, 389, 393
sub-deacon, 9
organisational skills, 5–6
time management, 9
timetable, 6
Orthodox Christianity, 11, 261, 396, 405–6, 408
ostrich, 381–88, 390–95, 398–400, 402, 408
ostrich egg, 381, 387–91, 393–96, 400, 403–5, 408
Panama, 127
Papàs, 9–10
Papers in Maltese Linguistics, 2
paremiology, 315
partitive *ši*, 340, 352, 354, 369, 373
pattern replication, 280, 287–88, 294–95
pausal forms, 117

perceptions, 142, 325, 327, 332, 335, 369
Persian, 21, 25, 87, 92, 95
personal assistant to Prime Minister Dom Mintoff, 3–4
Phoenician (Ph.), 77–78, 85, 87, 141
phonology, 77, 114, 126, 280
Piero della Francesca, 394–95
piety, 244, 404
place-name, *see* toponym
poetry, 77, 93, 281, 317–18, 347, 404
polar interrogative *šay/ši/-x*, 340, 348–49, 351–52, 354, 357, 369, 371, 373
  Andalusi Arabic, 348
  Levantine Arabic, 352, 354
  Maltese, 348–51
  Omani Arabic, 351–52
possibility, 25 n. 9, 155, 164, 166, 168, 215, 225, 322, 370
prayer, 323, 329–30, 387, 390, 392, 395–96, 399–400, 403–4
presentative, 164
priest, *see under* ordination
probability, 166, 168, 214
prohibitive *-š/-x*, 340–43, 360–61, 373
pronoun, 17 n. 5, 23, 96, 98, 118, 145–46, 151, 154–64, 166–68, 185–86, 189, 268–69, 278, 290, 302–3, 305, 309, 345, 350, 352 n. 7
proverbs, **315–35**
  Classical Arabic, 319
  Lebanese, 318–19, 322, 324–27, 329, 334
  Moroccan, 320, 322, 331, 334
  Palestinian, 322, 324, 328, 334
  Syrian, 322, 325–26, 334
  Tunisian, 322, 333, 335
pseudo-verb, 151–52, 154–55, 159, 166
Qāmišli / Qamishli, **109–28**, **261–295**
Qashqa-Darya region, 13–15, 19, 27
quantifier *xi/šay/ši*, 340, 352–54, 357, 369
  Levantine Arabic, 354–55
  Maltese, 352–54
  Omani Arabic, 355–56
Qurʾānic lexicon, 143
Rabbi Yehuda Ben Batira, 109, 123
regressive voicing assimilation, 34–38, 40–42, 44, 46–50, 52, 54–55, 57–65
relative, 107, 140, 143–46, 167, 185–86, 189, 197
Romania, 401, 406
Sabbath, 116, 121–22, 127
Safed, 128, 390

Saydon, P. P., 2, 239
Semitic, 1, 4–5, 11, 26, 33, 65, 136, 139–43, 145, 167, 201, 218, 239, 250, 267, 276, 299, 356, 358–59, 365
East Semitic, 142, 167
North-West Semitic, 142–43, 167
South Semitic, 142, 167
Semitic lexicography, 1
Shfarʕām, 128
simplification, 265–66, 274, 279
Sketis desert, 385, 406
stereotypes, 316
synagogue, 40, 109, 111, 122–25, 127, 192, 392
syntax, 97, 118, 264, 354
Syria / Syrian, 3, 82, 109–16, 118–19, 121 n. 21, 124 n. 28, 126–28, 261–65, 280, 283, 288–89, 294–95, 322, 325, 334, 360, 371, 383, 397, 406. *See also* Greater Syrian dialects *and* Syrian Arabic *under* Arabic
Syriac (Syr.), 1, 7–8, 87, 90, 96, 140–41, 143, 213, 261–62, 264, 268–69, 274, 385, 396–97, 404
Syriac Chrestomathy, 8
Tajik, 16–17, 19–24
taxonymy, 202, 204
toponym, **201–57**
trace, **135–168**
track, 137, 141, 147–49, 161 n. 33, 166 n. 41
Tsereteli, George, 14–15, 25
Turkey / Turkish, 109–11, 112–13, 124, 126–27, 261, 263, 299, 327
Turkish (language), 110, 115, 117–18, 123, 127, 279, 311, 327
Ṭuroyo, **261–95**, 305
Urfa (Turkish: Şanlıurfa), 110, 128
Uzbek, 13, 16–24
Valletta, 1–2, 9–10, 90, 235
Vassalli, Mikiel Anton, 37, 58–59, 89, 348–49
verbal composites, 16
vigilance, 381, 408
Vinnikov, Isaac, 14–15
vowels, 16 n. 4, 18, 76, 83, 86, 93, 95–97, 105, 116–18, 163 n. 37, 181, 187, 211 n. 11, 220, 276–77, 280–81, 285, 346 n. 3
Wadi el Natrun, 381
wisdom, 316–18, 320

About the Team

Geoffrey Khan and Alessandra Tosi were the managing editors for this book.

Anne Burberry performed the copyediting of the book in Word. The fonts used in this volume are Charis SIL, Scheherezade New, SBL Hebrew and SBL Greek.

Cameron Craig created all of the editions—paperback, hardback, and PDF. Conversion was performed with open source software freely available on our GitHub page at https://github.com/OpenBookPublishers.

Jeevanjot Kaur Nagpal designed the cover of this book. The cover was produced in InDesign using Fontin and Calibri fonts.

www.ingramcontent.com/pod-product-compliance
Lightning Source LLC
Chambersburg PA
CBHW051534230426
43669CB00015B/2593